# *The Devil's Blade is Dull...*

## A prisoner's compilation

*Remember the prisoners as though in prison with them and those who are ill-treated, since you yourselves also are in the body.*

Hebrews 13:3 NASB

# The Devil's Blade is Dull

T. B. T. G.

# Guardian
**BOOKS**

Belleville, Ontario, Canada

# THE DEVIL'S BLADE IS DULL
## Copyright © 2008, Randy Tunney

ISBN: 978-1-55452-251-4

**For more information or
to order additional copies, please contact:**

www.free2live.org
P.O. Box 321
Athens, Ontario  K0E 1B0

*Guardian Books* is an imprint of *Essence Publishing,* a Christian Book Publisher dedicated to furthering the work of Christ through the written word. For more information, contact:
20 Hanna Court, Belleville, Ontario, Canada K8P 5J2
Phone: 1-800-238-6376 • Fax: (613) 962-3055
E-mail: info@essence-publishing.com
Web site: www.essence-publishing.com

# *Imagine Being Imprisoned*

*Imagine being imprisoned as a child through to adulthood*
*Never understanding and no one understood*
*Your mind it was a prison with countless little cells*
*Most held like a tiny prisoner to whom the thought of freedom*
*dwells*

*Now life inside any prison can be a calamitous affair*
*All this human tragedy most in total disrepair*
*As at Jericho the walls came tumbling down as time would have*
*it be*
*You walked anew in this world of ours thinking finally*
*I am free*

*Now the bars are real*
*I feel the coldness in my hands*
*Before in my imprisonment*
*At least I walked the lands*

*Sitting down alone quite tearfully*
*My face buried deep in my palms*
*Humming hymns of holiness*
*Reciting verse from Psalms*

*Wiping away tears of happiness*
*Each tear a memory of the past*
*I look up, smile and thank the Lord*
*I know I am free at last*

*Now the philosophy of this poet*
*As you can plainly see*
*There are no greater prisons*
*Than trapped in conflict with your personality*

From my prison cell—October 2-3, 1987
11 p.m. to 2 a.m.

# Contents

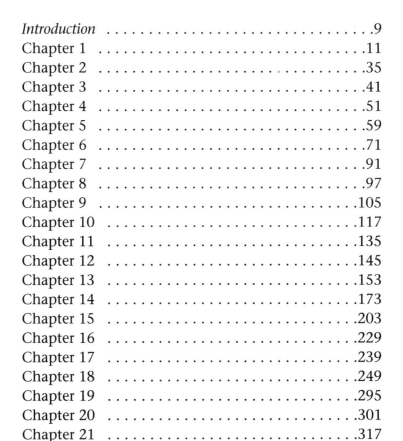

# Introduction

*From the author: Randy*

For the sake of the many persons who suffer from the unnecessary ills of this world, I present *The Devil's Blade Is Dull.*

This autobiography is a true account of my life prior to being a prisoner in a Canadian Penitentiary. As true as it is written it may not be as chronologically correct as I would have hoped. Certainly there are also omissions otherwise I would have had to write volumes.

There are also some quotes used that I know not the source. I apologize for this.

To the many persons I have met and subsequently had a less than positive effect on, I truly apologize to you all. Please forgive me.

*The Devil's Blade Is Dull* was written in the penitentiary and finished March 1988. The writing was to benefit those who have suffered from the worst of human nature. The cruel, harsh and honest writing in these pages can reach the depths of their tortured souls. Had I written not with such honesty it would have only been to be less ridiculed myself. I can assure you that in reality it was intensely worse.

Thank you for this time in your life.

Randy T. R. Tunney

# Annual North American Statistics

2,000 children die from child abuse
250,000 receive permanent physical scars
200,000 sexual abuse cases reported
56% of families hit their kids
one in four girls is sexually abused by the age of twenty
Tens of thousands of sexually explicit photos of children are transferred daily via the Internet.

# Chapter 1

The fifteenth day of January 1959 was much the same as other January days in Sudbury, with strong, bitter winds and near-Arctic conditions. Even amidst the cold, there was much warmth to be found that day as I entered the world, a new life of hope and promise.

I often wonder if my mother, Sonja, knew as she held me on that first day of my life that she was capable of the criminal injustices that she would inflict upon her family during the years to come. Being an unwed mother and having my birth father desert us both after my birth must have been a very traumatic experience for her. It shouldn't have been an experience that bred hatred towards me, but she started abusing me almost from birth.

Within three months of having me, my mother married a divorced gentleman named Harold. Harold brought to the marriage his adopted son, Doug. While I suspect the marriage was one of convenience, if it was one of love that love would soon be destroyed as the reality of Sonja's personality disorder surfaced. The story is told of how, when I was barely four months old, she threw me down a hill rather than carrying me down. Within a year of having me, she became pregnant again. Already with a family of four at the young age of nineteen, she started showing the violence and unhappiness of a very distraught young lady. Harold, Doug and I endured beatings and emotional torture that no one should ever have to live with. When her sister, Star, came to live with us, she stayed only a few years, terrified of my mother's wrath.

Much of those early years is stricken from my memory. I have been told I was beaten and whipped on numerous occasions, but I can't bring them to memory. However, one of my earliest memories involves an incident that occurred when I was approximately four years old. I had been grounded to my room and was supposed to stay in bed. A noise outside the window attracted my attention, so I snuck across the room and peered outside. The sun was shining, and the pleasant warmth of the rays streaming in the open window warmed me from the coldness of Mother's treatment.

As I was daydreaming, the closed bedroom door burst open. Catching me out of bed sent Mother into a rage, yelling, "What are you doing out of bed? I'll teach you!" She threw me across the room. My little body bounced off the wall and crumpled on the floor.

Mother dragged me to the window, which only a minute ago was a pleasant place. "Put your hands on the windowsill," she instructed. I did as I was told, body shaking and sweat beading on my skin for fear of an added beating. Instinctively, I knew what she was going to do. Placing her hands on the open window, she slammed it down onto my hands.

Pain seared through my body. Mother opened the window again and walked out of the room, leaving me writhing in pain, huddled on the floor. Getting back into the comfort of my bed, I pulled the covers up to my head, held my pillow against my chest and cried myself to sleep. Only four years old, I did not know this kind of punishment was wrong. Violence and hatred were being bred into my life. Rage was the only emotion that I was becoming accustomed to.

Starting school is a big step in life, learning about the world away from the home environment. My first day of school was an exciting occasion. I was dressed up in a new outfit and looking forward to not being around Mother. Being in kindergarten meant that I only went to school half a day, but it was a half a day I learned to enjoy.

Our family life was in turmoil. Dad was so scared of Mother that he wouldn't get involved in confrontations about her mental derangement and the physical abuse she inflicted.

My aunt Star had given up hope of her sister being cured and left our family. Doug, now sixteen, was fed up with the verbal, physical and emotional abuse and was at the point of leaving. Mother made his decision much easier one day that I will never forget.

The sun was streaming down from the near cloudless sky, and a warm summer breeze was blowing gently through the trees in our backyard. The sound of leaves rustling in the wind met our ears as we played in the afternoon light. We were running and enjoying the freedom of outdoors in a sportive way until Mother called out to Doug from the back porch.

We knew there was trouble from the way her voice rang out across the yard—even the flowers seemed to tremble. Doug was terrified as he approached the house. As I watched him walk up the steps to the porch, he reminded me of a condemned person going to the gallows. He reached the porch and entered the kitchen. Outside we stopped playing and sat down to wait. No sooner had we sat down than we heard the sounds of an argument and fighting. The sound of breaking dishes met our ears. Time seemed to have stopped.

The next instant, Doug was running from the house with Mother chasing him with a cast iron frying pan. She was hitting him over the head with it repeatedly. Doug seemed to jump down all the steps at once, then called to his friend, and they both bolted from the yard. I wouldn't see Doug again for eight years. I didn't understand why Doug left and never came back. Beatings were an everyday part of life that we had become accustomed to. I didn't know it was an abnormal part of our family's life. I thought every child received the same treatment.

Once Doug and Star were gone, I was the focus of Mother's rage. I would have thought no human being was capable of administering such abuse to another person and even more so on her own flesh and blood.

And so, I was looking forward to starting school. The thought of being away from Mother for five days a week were ones of happiness. I began attending Copper Cliff Public School. Mother drove me to school and kissed me goodbye. How I hated her lips against my face! I was glad to be away from her. I entered the schoolyard on the boys' side of the building, as the playgrounds were segregated. Seeing some friends, I ran over to where they were. We were all talking about who our teachers and classmates were going to be.

The school bell soon let out its loud ring, and we all lined up outside the entrance door. A teacher then let us in, and we went to our respective classrooms. I found my room and went in and took a desk near the back of the room. Everyone was talking, laughing and telling about the past summer's happenings. Silence came across the room as our teacher came in. She introduced herself and then had us introduce ourselves. We spent most of the first day just talking about our summer vacations. Of course, I could only tell about the good stuff, and even then I may have exaggerated.

Back at home I was sent to my room as usual. My room had polished hardwood floors, wallpapered walls, a set of bunk beds and a couple of dressers. I shared the room with Tom, my younger brother, while James, our youngest brother, had the other room. A window overlooking the street gave me a view of the surrounding neighbourhood. You could, if you wanted, open the window and crawl out onto the roof of the veranda. Directly across the street was my uncle's house.

Being confined to my room was becoming an everyday occurrence that I despised. I would go to school, come home, maybe get beaten, but always I had to go to that room. I was allowed down for supper and to do the dishes; then it was back to my room. On rare occasions I was allowed to watch television, but I came to hate even that because I always had to sit on the floor, Indian-style, with my legs crossed and hands clasped in front of me. My back had to be perfectly straight, my eyes directed at the TV. I had to sit perfectly still as if in a trance. If I so much as flinched, Mother would kick me square in the back.

Sitting as motionless as death itself, I would breathe through my nose and try not to show my fright. What I dreaded most about watching television was when my mother was ironing clothes behind me. I was always petrified by the possibility that if I moved, the iron might become her weapon of torture, for I had been threatened with it on many occasions.

Mom was pregnant again, which made me confused. Hadn't she had enough children? She couldn't, I reasoned, even be a proper mother to the children she already had. I already had two younger brothers, Tom and James, who weren't treated abusively like I was. I was beginning to loathe Tom—he had freedom, wasn't beaten and was shown affection.

Repeatedly, I'd try to sort it out. Was I so bad that I deserved the physical and emotional abuse that I was receiving? Sleeping had become a problem as I was having recurring nightmares, so I was given some kind of green liquid to help me sleep. I took this for a couple of years or so. At school I was becoming the class clown, looking for the attention that I inherently longed for. However, when Mother was told that I was misbehaving in school, I would get a beating at home. She seemed to love whipping me with the buckle end of a belt until I was black and blue.

I hated this woman with a passion. The beatings didn't change my ways at school; in fact, I became worse and even started stealing.

The first crime I committed was when I was six and

in grade one. The class was saving pennies for the Red Cross. We had a big jar, which was full of the small copper coins. My brothers were always receiving candy and things from Mother while I did without. Tired of being left out, I decided to steal the class's money.

We had been dismissed to go home for lunch one day, and after everyone left I came back and took the container, which seemed quite heavy for a little fellow like me. It seemed like a veritable gold mine, hundreds of shiny pennies.

I left the school and made my way home for lunch but stopped along the way to stash the cash. On my way back to school after lunch, I retrieved my treasure and stopped off at the local candy store. I put the money on the counter and browsed around. I picked out my favourite chocolate bars, candies, comic books and toys until all the money was spent. While walking back to afternoon class, I gorged myself.

Back in the schoolyard, I shared everything with the other children. By the time the school bell rang to end lunch, all I had left were some comic books. Sitting back in class, feeling guilty about my actions, I stared around the room. Our teacher walked into the room and looked over the class slowly. We were told about the missing money and were asked if we knew who the culprit was. Of course, everyone knew who had done it, because I was the only one handing out the fruit of my crime at lunch. The classmates who had indulged in my kindness looked at me in disbelief. I had no choice but to confess.

The teacher told me to go down to the principal's office. Walking solemnly along the cavernous hallways on my way to have my first encounter with the principal was a frightening experience. I had seen him in the hallways and had learned that his nickname was Big Red, because of his hair and skin tone. He was also an oversized man, about six-foot tall. After reaching the secretary's office, I was told to go in to see the principal.

Big Red was sitting hulkingly over his desk, and I was told to sit down. Then I received a lecture about the wrong I had done. My response was an apologetic "I am sorry, and it won't happen again." Big Red explained that punishment was in store and that I was to receive five strappings across each of my hands. Being used to getting beaten, I just sat there while Big Red opened his desk drawer and pulled out a black leather strap about a foot long. He held the strap in one hand while holding one of my outstretched palms with the other and then proceeded to inflict my punishment. Each time I was struck, stinging pain shot through me, but not as much as I had become accustomed to.

"This wasn't so bad," I thought. I knew I could endure much more pain than this. Mother had beaten me far worse and for lesser reasons—and most of the time for no reason at all. Big Red had not near the strength Mother possessed. It was only when the last stroke struck me that I became truly terrified. Would Mother find out what I had done? I hoped not, because I knew what the consequences of my actions would be.

Sure enough, the school had phoned home, and Mom was on her way to pick me up. While sitting in the office awaiting her arrival, my mind was crazily thinking over what would now happen to me. Up to this point in my life, I had been severely abused for usually no apparent reason. Now giving her just cause, I expected the worst beating imaginable. Seeing Mother entering the office sent shivers through my body, I cowered like a frightened puppy in my chair.

Mother spoke with the principal for a few minutes in a very nice way. She had a knack for making everyone else believe she was a nice person. When finished conversing, she turned to me and said, "Randy, dear, you must learn not to take what is not yours."

We left the school, and I was driven home. Mother was very controlled, but I knew it wouldn't last. Getting out of the car, I walked to the house. This was reminiscent of the day Doug left, how he must have felt while walking to the house not knowing what would happen once inside. My heart was palpitating faster with each step. I cringed in fear, my mind envisioning the scenes of what might soon happen. My thoughts, I would find, were too kind.

We entered through the back door, which led into our small kitchen. The house was empty; brothers Tom and James were at a neighbour's. As the door closed, the volcanic temper that Mother possessed erupted. She yelled and threw me against the wall. Next I was savagely kicked wherever her feet connected.

Mother grabbed me by the throat and proceeded to bash my skull against the kitchen table, one, two, ten, maybe twenty times. This enraged woman was crazy. Getting free, I ran through the dining room, down the hall and up the stairs. Mother was pregnant, so she couldn't catch me. She began screaming at the top of her lungs, but I wasn't going down.

I was in my room in dizzying pain. As was her nature, as abruptly as she had erupted she cooled down. Crying in my room was nothing new. This place that I slept in was becoming a prison cell. I would go to school, come home and go to my room. Even at this early age I was crawling into a shell and trying to forget my everyday experiences.

Mother's mood swings kept getting worse, and her violence within our home escalated. Dad was receiving a lot of abuse as well, both verbal and physical. He did not deserve any of this. He always worked hard to give us everything. We had a home, a cottage, a car and never went without life's necessities. As a family we attended church each Sunday, and Mother was always involved in social activities. She would even work as a waitress to earn extra money. To everyone who knew us, we were just another typical family in the community.

As the days and months went by, I was changing very quickly. I now had three younger brothers at home, Tom, James and newly born Robert. My feelings of animosity towards Tom's freedom kept growing. I was wondering why I was hated so much; was I really that bad? Nightmares occurred more frequently, and I was becoming afraid of the dark. Trepidation towards others was increasingly alarming. How I wished she loved me like the others.

At school, my behaviour was getting worse, and visits to Big Red's office were now a regular part of my day. With all this happening, Mother was becoming more abusive and started calling me "crazy" and "retarded." As the years went by, I started to believe it myself. I skipped grade three, not due to educational advantage but, I believe, because the teacher was elderly and the staff must have thought I would be the death of her. Subsequently, I failed grade four.

Summertime arrived the year I was to begin the fourth grade and with it two months off. This meant that most of the time was spent in Mother's presence, and I hated it. As in summers past, we would spend most of our holidays at our cottage. Father would come to camp only on weekends, except during his summer vacation.

Even with the abuse, I had many special moments there over the years, when I was allowed some freedom. I found happiness being outside, either fishing, swimming or learning to water-ski. Summer always brought me a little bit out of my private world of fear and loneliness. There at the cottage, I had a chance to be a little boy for a change. Because there weren't many people around, Mother wasn't as worried about me getting her into trouble. I was grounded only half as much at camp as at home.

Our summer home was very nice. Dad and his friends had worked very hard to build it. They had to carry every tool, nail and piece of wood by hand down a steep, rocky incline from the road—the same incline Mother had thrown me down when I had been just a wee babe in arms. Even by today's standards, it was a comfortable cottage. We were lucky to have a good father who provided us with everything we needed.

But Mother was destroying us all slowly. There was no chance for love to take root with her around. Although some of my most treasured moments growing up were at camp, so were some of the most painful.

When I was to get a beating, Mother would cut a fresh switch from a young tree or shrub. A switch is the best whip, and the excruciating pain it delivered was unbearable. After a beating, I would be black and blue and have blistering welts on my hind end. My most vivid recollection of one of these beatings goes as follows.

It was a beautiful summer's day. Lunch was over, and it was my turn to do the dishes. After piling them up on the dish rack, I dried my wrinkled hands and started to dry the plates. In my hurry to complete the chore and return to playing outside, I dropped and broke a plate.

Mother angrily immediately began to physically punish me. Though I struggled to get away and run outside; she was right behind me. She took hold of me, she also grabbed a branch from a small tree beside the cottage. I screamed for mercy, which fell on deaf ears. She beat me as if her life depended on my succumbing to her madness. A minute later she was dragging me into the cottage like a victorious hunter bringing home her quarry after a successful hunt. Needless to say, I was sent to my room and was grounded again.

The summer ended, but not before I was to endure numerous more beatings—not just damaging my body but a constant beating down of my spirit.

Returning to school in the fall, I was almost eight years old and beginning to develop crushes on girls. Over the next few years of school I would become friends with most of them. With our school recess areas being segregated, we would always meet at a hydro pole that was the border line between the boys' and girls' sides.

Grade four, which I completed twice, were bad years both at home and at school. My desk was usually outside the principal's office, beside the teacher's desk, which I didn't mind, or outside the classroom. I could always bring the students to riotous laughter, and they thought I was great. I craved the attention, which also meant my report cards and letters Mother received weighed heavily against me.

Being a prisoner in my own home became worse. I hated going home, and thoughts of running away or dying were becoming more frequent. Always pondering the question of why my mother hated me so much, I came to the conclusion that it was because I was a boy. So, I started fantasizing about being a girl so that Mother would love me. I didn't know at that time that I had been born of a previous relationship and that my existence was a constant reminder to my mother of her failure and pain.

I was grounded in my room almost constantly, and while in my room I couldn't make so much as a noise. I would sneak across the room to go to the bathroom, and since the hardwood floors made noises, I had to know every creak of the floor. On tippytoes I would enter the bathroom and pee in the sink so I wouldn't have to flush the toilet.

I was going stir crazy in that room. My nightmares were worse, and I would see and hear things at night. I believed I was possessed by the devil and started seeing the devil in the dark. I had begun hating myself with a passion, and this prison life was destroying me slowly.

In the solitude of my private world, suicide attempts were taking place unknown to anyone but me. I would usually take a belt and slip the loose end through the buckle, then place it around my neck and tighten it by hand. My feeble attempts brought only dizziness or unconsciousness, from which I would revive, unfortunately. Then I would have to face Mother again.

During my second term of grade four, I ran away for the first time. Report card time had arrived, and I was given mine. After reading it over I knew I would get killed this time for sure. *What should I do?* I thought. I figured that running away would solve it.

So this little kid of about nine years of age set out to conquer the world. Walking through the vast halls of the school for what I thought would be the last time had an eeriness about it. As I pushed open the double doors, a cold wind struck my face. I could not have picked a worse day to be outside. Once off the property of the red bricked school, I chucked my report card into the biting wind. The Big World consisted of this little town. Where would a young boy like me go? I walked around the neighbourhood until darkness fell. Copper Cliff is such a small town that I was only minutes away from home at all times.

I was becoming quite cold, as I was only dressed warm enough to be outside for a short while. Three hours had passed, and it was long past the time when I was supposed to be home. I had to find shelter from the biting wind and also had to get off the streets before I was found. Finding shelter was easy as I knew of a place close by. In the town's gravel pit was a galvanized steel cover of geometrical shape, big enough that two small kids could fit in it.

I had to climb through a small square opening after taking off my bulky parka. The cold wind was bone chilling. Once inside, I lay in near total darkness, but at least I was somewhat sheltered from the wind and the cold.

Hours went by, and I was shivering like a leaf in the wind. I feared that if I didn't get some more warmth, I would freeze to death. Peering out of my makeshift home into the night was frightening. The shadows from the row of garages in the distance took on human characteristics. Beyond the garages an apartment building containing a barber shop, a grocery store and a candy store rose a few storeys into the air. Behind me and above the rocky hill was Gribble Street. I knew that at one house on that street in the backyard was a child's playhouse. Maybe something to keep me warm throughout the night might be inside. I took off my parka and pushed it through the small opening and then climbed out myself.

The winter wind had increased, and as it blew against me, my skin seemed to freeze instantly. I slipped on a patch of ice while picking up my parka and then put it on as fast as possible. Becoming a human icicle was not what I had in mind when I left school. I climbed up the hill to the playhouse, which was in sight from my shelter.

Opening the door, I stepped inside and groped around in the dark. My hands felt something soft. Could I be so fortunate? Yes, I now had two wool blankets to help me make it through the night. I was proud of myself for being able to be on my own. My Boy Scout lessons on survival were paying off. I retraced my steps down the hill to my shelter. Back inside and bundled up, I stared outside, looking for anyone who might be looking for me. I was wishing I had a loving mother so I would not be living this dehumanizing life. On one hand, I had most everything a boy could want. I went to Boy Scouts and played goaltender for hockey, but I knew that I was only allowed to because my younger siblings did the same. On the other hand, emotional pain was eating me alive. I had so much sorrow and no answers to any of the questions that haunted me.

Having gone without food for ten hours, I was quite hungry. I needed to eat, so I set out for the grocery store. The store had a stockroom in the basement next to the superintendent's apartment. I was hoping I could break in. I walked to the building but stayed in the shadows so no one could see me. As I entered the building, I was met by a rush of warm air, which I drank in in great gulps as if to warm my chilling body. Standing in the lobby, I pressed my ear against the door leading to the basement and listened for footsteps. Hearing nothing, I proceeded down a flight of stairs and down the corridor to the super's suite.

As I made my way down the hall, I noticed my body was thawing out and my fingers and toes were starting to sting as the cold left me. As I got closer to the stockroom and the super's apartment, my heart palpitated. No sooner had I reached the room than my worries about hunger were over. Outside the door was a box of bananas that must have been dropped off after closing hours. *Somebody in this world must like me*, I thought, and I thanked God for His kindness. The bananas were quite green, but I didn't care as I peeled two of the hard fleshy fruit and hungrily ate them in a minute. Finishing, I grabbed a bunch in each hand and made my way outside by way of a different exit. Met by the wintry wind as I stepped outside, I wished I could have stayed inside. I knew, though, that this building would be the first place anyone would look for me.

Wanting to get out of this frigid wind, I ran back to my tin shelter as fast as I could. Back inside, I felt the cold chilling me, even though I was wrapped in blankets. Staring into the blackness, I tried to visualize a happier life. I thought back on earlier days, about all the tension that always reigned in our house. The mystery was always there. I kept wondering what was wrong with me, why was Mother always so terribly mean to me. When you're a child, you have only one source for your answers: your parents. I wanted to be loved like my brothers were and to understand. A child misses little!

These troubling thoughts continued until, eventually, I fell asleep, only to be awakened by the sound of voices in the distance. Peering outside into the depths of night, I noticed images in the darkness about 100 feet away. A search party was looking for this scared and mixed-up kid. I was sure to be found. I lay back down, shaking from both fear and the bone-chilling cold that had gripped my body.

Long minutes passed, and the voices soon became inaudible. Thank God I wasn't found or surely I would have gotten the beating of my life, as I had never run away before. This and the fact that I had thrown my report card away certainly sealed my fate.

My family attended church on Sundays, and I had learned to pray to God. There in my cold shelter, I started to pray for forgiveness for running away and for being so bad that Mother hated me. Tears came to me as I lay huddled and freezing in my little shelter. The tears froze to my face as if to keep me from forgetting the past. I was so desperately lonely, and that loneliness hurt more than any beating. Going in and out of a fitful sleep was awful. Once I saw through the darkness Mother's face, and I feared for my life.

As the hours dragged by, the feeling in both my hands and feet was disappearing. I couldn't stand the cold, but at the same time I knew I would rather freeze than face Mother, so I toughed it out. Hungry again, I reached in the darkness for the bananas, which long ago had frozen solid. I couldn't get the skin peeled, so I did without. As the night faded away, thoughts of warming up after the sun rose were pleasant.

Much to my dismay, a sun-filled morning didn't materialize but rather the opposite. I realized that I had only two choices: die from exposure or go home and face a deranged mother. I chose the latter—at least I would be warm, although Mother's coldness sure made the decision debatable. I crawled out of my shelter to greet this day of uncertainty. I picked up my coat, which I had shoved out ahead of me. Doing the zipper up was a task in itself as I had lost all feeling in my tiny fingers. After managing it, I started to walk. My feet! What had happened to them? I couldn't move my toes, and my feet felt like ice cubes. Walking had become a painful chore.

I took the route that would involve the least amount of human contact. I was terrified about facing

Mother, but I had to have warmth. As I reached home, a neighbour saw me, and I was helped into the house. This was a blessing in disguise, for I knew Mother wouldn't hit me in the presence of others.

I was hugged and kissed and told how much I had been missed. What a crock of bull. Dad and my brothers were there and didn't say much, because Mother was the boss. I'm sure I would have gotten beaten had it not been for the neighbour's presence. I received the loving mother routine that Mother put on while around outsiders. A warm bath was run while I got undressed. Now that I was warming up, pain like that of being pricked with hundreds of needles shot through my hands and feet.

My tiny body was still shaking from the past sixteen or more hours in the cold. My fingers and toes were white; Dad was worried about frostbite. Standing in the bathroom, I could feel the steam from the just-run bath. The warmth opened up the pores of my skin and permeated the depths of my tormented soul. As I stepped into the warm bath, my feet stung, so I recoiled momentarily, then lowered myself into the tub. Taking a bath was usually enjoyable, because this bathtub was one of those huge old cast-iron types with bear claw feet. You could fill it up and have a veritable swimming pool. This time I just lay there worrying about my inevitable punishment.

The punishment was delayed, as it was decided that I would go to the hospital to be checked for possible frostbite. I got out of the tub, dried off and changed into clean clothes. My hands and feet were still stinging. Dad brought me some hot chocolate and warm toast with jam. I ate like a starved animal. Then Dad and I drove to the hospital, which was only minutes away. I had been there on a few occasions, usually with injuries received during one of Mother's beatings.

The doctor looked at my hands and then removed my shoes and socks to examine my stinging feet. He said there would be no long-lasting effects and that I had been lucky. On the way home Dad stopped and bought me some treats. He was always as nice as he could be, considering the turmoil in our family.

I did not receive a beating for this incident. This confused me. Mother...who was she? When she wasn't being violent at home she could at times be quite pleasant, though still unapproachable. As a cook and housekeeper she excelled. The many dinners she prepared were nothing short of superb. To people outside our private world, she was an ideal mother and well respected.

I've known nobody that could bluff his or her way through life as she was doing. The fronts that were put up were unbelievable, right to the point where people must have thought she was a saint. Mother was hostess to ladies' auxiliary meetings, church socials and the like. Eventually she and Dad were the boys' cub and Boy Scouts' leaders. Growing up in a Northern Ontario town, we boys played ice hockey, and Mom was more often than not a spectator. With all these fronts built up, she had no fear of people believing her to be anything other than what they saw.

The dark side of her was so well masked that Satan himself could be the only one in control of her mind, for no real human soul could inflict these inhuman acts upon her family for this amount of time. To delve into the mind of this human being would be a psychiatrist's dream.

Mother was a lady of many moods, as close to having a clinical case of a split personality as anyone, I would think. Her changes in personality in most cases would only take seconds, but they were seconds when she would change from quite a nice person to a raving lunatic. At the time I did not know that I would later develop some of these same characteristics. Mother could be kind one minute and the next be chasing you around the house with a butcher's knife.

Dad worked hard and spent a lot of time working overtime, sometimes just so he wouldn't have to face his wife. He was also a volunteer fireman and spent countless nights sleeping at the fire hall, to be away from her. My brothers and I thought it was his job to be there in case of a fire, but the fire hall was on our street and only half a block away. We would visit him there if we hadn't seen him for a couple of days. Going to visit the fire hall is every young boy's fantasy, just as it was mine. Seeing the big red fire truck was always exciting. Being able to sit in it, let alone go for a ride in it, was always something I looked forward to.

There were not many fires in our town, so weeks would go by without the truck being used. So to make sure everything was running okay, the truck was usually taken for a spin. On Sundays after going to church, Dad would on occasion take us for a cruise around town. Those drives were always exhilarating. My brothers and I would sit either up front with Dad or in the seats behind the cab. Driving around in the bright red fire truck always brought stares, and we would wave to everyone and pretend we were going to a fire. Dad would sometimes give a blast of the siren; how we loved that sound! We hated when those rides came to an end.

After we pulled back into the fire hall, we would clean off any dirt that we had picked up, because firemen always kept their trucks spotless. Dad always took time to check the many gauges along both sides of the truck and explain to us what they were for. After everything was checked and found to be as it should, it was back to the prison life of home.

Something else we looked forward to was the once-a-week fire practice. All the firemen would get together and test equipment. The kids around town would gather and watch. One time that stands out in my mind was the day I got to put out an imaginary fire. I wasn't grounded, so I was allowed to watch Dad at fire practice. My brothers, Dad and I walked to the old brick fire hall. The men were in the process of testing hoses for leaks. The hoses were brought out to the red iron fire hydrant that was adjacent to the fire hall. After a hose was hooked up to the hydrant, the water was turned on and we watched for leaks. Testing fire hoses can be fun, especially the leaking ones, because everyone tends to get wet. We kids wanted to hold on to the hoses as they were being tested, and we each took turns.

I was getting excited while waiting in anticipation of my turn. I put on a pair of fireman's boots, which were so large I could have got lost in them, and then a helmet, which wobbled all over my head as I walked around. I sure looked like a comic character, a midget fireman. I was about to find out why a child cannot be a fireman.

Dad handed me the next hose that was to be tested. Getting a good grip on the end of it, I waited for the water to be turned on. As the water rushed through the hose I could feel myself being thrown off balance. This sure didn't feel like the backyard garden variety that I was accustomed to. I regained control and, being the boy that I was, I started to turn the nozzle so the water would flow through with greater force. I was thrown on my back, still gripping the hose, which was now shooting water forth like a veritable geyser up into the air.

Most everyone in sight was getting rained upon. I was soaking wet now and let go of the hose. As the nozzle hit the ground, it started writhing about like a mad snake. It was only a matter of seconds before the hydrant was shut off. The kids thought it was great to be sopping wet, and now everyone was laughing. I looked like a drowned rat.

The men called it quits and packed up their equipment, and we kids went home. I was worried about what Mom would say when she saw me soaking wet. She had company over, so I knew nothing would happen. I told them what had happened, and they both laughed. She hugged me and told me to go and change.

How I hated her touching me.

# Chapter 2

Christmastime in our household was usually the most joyous time of the year, and Mother was usually at her best. Our house was always beautifully decorated, and outside Christmas lights always glowed brightly. Inside, Christmas cards adorned our living and dining room areas. The pièce de résistance was always our Christmas tree, which up until later years was always real. Christmas dinners were always superbly prepared, as Mother was the best cook in town. Mother and Dad always played their Christmastime roles perfectly.

This particular Christmas Eve was as beautiful as any I'd known. The family was down in the living room. Reflections from the flickering Christmas bulbs that adorned the magnificent tree danced about the room in accordance with their twinkling. We were all making our last minute adjustments to the now beautifully decorated tree. Underneath the tree were presents we each had bought for one another. There was still lots of room for Santa's gifts as we had made sure of that. Beside the tree on the floor adjacent to the fake fireplace was a nativity scene, with all of the complementing figurines:

Jesus, Mary, Joseph, and the three Wise Men with their gifts. This is what Christmas is all about, the birth of Jesus Christ.

The fireplace was decorated as well, and a wire was strung across the front. Socks were clothespinned to the wire, and each of our names, including Mother's and Dad's, was pinned to a sock. The glow from the fake fireplace could take our thoughts away as we gazed into its depths. Christmas music was playing on the stereo across the room. With the finishing touches put to the tree, we sat back and admired the beautiful surroundings, laughing and joking all the while. Mother left to get us our traditional bedtime snack, consisting of Christmas cake, cookies and glasses of eggnog.

I sat and gazed about; everyone was happy, things were peaceful, everything was picture perfect. Now staring into the lighted fireplace, I prayed to Jesus and God and asked for it to always be like this. Mother returned with our treats and extra pieces for Santa and his helpers. We couldn't forget them; after all the work they did, they would surely be hungry. We ate and drank up our delicious goodies; then it was time for bed. We four boys went upstairs, all excited; I even felt an almost unknown tinge of happiness. Mother and Dad tucked us in and gave us each a kiss. I hated Mother's kisses because I knew they weren't given with love. Warmed by the Christmas spirit, I accepted her kiss with gratitude and even felt the tiniest bit of love toward her.

Christmas Eve was a night when I always wanted to get to sleep as fast as I could. I was the eldest and knew that Mother and Dad were Santa, but my brothers had yet to find out. I shared my bedroom with Tom, whom I was growing all the more jealous of. He slept underneath me on the bottom bunk. Not being able to fall asleep right away, I crawled out of bed and down the ladder and quietly went across to the window.

I peered out the window and up into the star-filled heavens. I visualized a little red-dressed man with flowing white hair and beard, guiding his sleigh with tiny reindeer across the horizon. Looking down from the night sky I watched the snow sparkle as the light from the lampposts illuminated the snow around. Everything always looked so peaceful, but no one knew of the great emotional war being constantly fought within my tormented soul. How could I appease the insatiable craving for love unknown? I was nodding off, so I climbed back into bed, pulling the covers to my head. I was soon fast asleep and dreaming of all the toys I might get.

I was awakened by my younger brothers in the next room. Their youthful exuberance was unlike my desolate solemnity. Sure, I was happy in the way I knew happiness, but I wasn't happy in the way a child of my age should be. We had to stay upstairs until Mother awakened and gave us permission to go downstairs. We knew Santa had come and gone because our stockings had been generously filled and placed at the end of each of our beds. The socks were full of candy, trinkets and, as always, a tangerine. This year there were colouring books, and mine was of Superman. I sat in bed eating my orange and leafing through the colouring book. I had always admired the feats and strength of Superman and wished I was like him so nobody could hurt me.

Soon my brothers ran out of patience and woke up Mother and Dad. I stayed in bed, because I didn't have the nerve to wake Mother up. Downstairs, they ran excitedly to see what Santa had left. I would wait until Mother went downstairs. As she came from her room, she saw me in bed and asked me what I had received. I smiled and held up the prized Superman colouring book. At that moment her expression changed; her eyes seemed to bug right out of their sockets.

She yelled, "You switched colouring books during the night!"

"Honest, Mom, I didn't."

Mother screamed, "You will never learn, will you?" as she reached out to grab me. Either she or Dad, in the darkness of the night, must have put the colouring book picked out for me on my brother's bed and vice versa. The only other explanation was that Tom had done it, knowing I would get the blame. Whatever the reason, I was going to pay the price for this really insignificant mix-up.

Mother was still trying to grab me while I cowered like a little terrified animal in the corner of my bed. I had the advantage because I was on the top bunk and out of reach. Mother was enraged and climbing the ladder of the bed. I was terrified. She caught hold of me and pulled me over the edge of the bed. The beating I received was swift and cruel. With each lashing I let out a scream so remorseful and fraught with anguish that it in itself was equally painful. Everyone in the house must have heard me. My mother by blood only relentlessly kept whipping me with an electrical cord until she had run out of breath.

While gasping for air she managed to say, "You're lucky that's all you get" before leaving me sprawled on the floor, in great physical and emotional pain. Red welts appeared on my flesh wherever the cord had struck. My head was throbbing; everything was going in circles. I tried to stand, but I ached everywhere. Managing to get back into bed I lay crying. As I heard my brothers laughing and opening their presents, I cried even more.

That had been the most emotionally upsetting experience in my life thus far. I sobbed most of the day and missed Christmas dinner and all the fun. Company had come over and was told I was sick in bed, which was true—I was becoming more emotionally disturbed with every passing day. For probably the first time in my life I wished Mother was dead.

Merry Christmas.

# Chapter 3

I had become a prisoner in the house that I had to call home, and it was quite unbearable, to say the least. I had seen movies in which criminals convicted of murder were treated better than I was. As time and ill-treatment continued, I was consumed by my fantasies of being a girl so Mother would love me. Mother was judge, jury and warden of this private jail, and my life was regulated like clockwork, literally. In fact, the town was regulated in somewhat a lesser degree by the same system.

Living in a company town, in company housing and with most people working or having had worked for the corporation meant we were all somewhat regulated by three daily shift changes. How we were regulated had become Mother's prison time clock. The company plants were located around town, with the main plant being a block away from our home. Within the main plant was a clock that at certain times would let out a shrill whistle as the timing device opened the valves to the pressure pipes, along the same idea as the whistle of an old steam locomotive except much louder. The high-pitched whistle could be heard throughout the plants and the town, and we knew the shifts were either starting or finishing. Since I was born I had been hearing the whistle nine times daily, every day of the year, except when the company was on strike—7:30 a.m., 8 a.m., noon, 12:30 p.m., 1 p.m., 4 p.m., 4:30 p.m., 5 p.m., and then finally at midnight, only to start again in the morning. As I became older these whistles and the times they sounded became hated memories.

Mother, the jailer, used those whistles to control me, and I became terrified to hear them at times. The noon and 4 p.m. whistles could spell doom for me. My life was a daily race against time, with the company's whistle being the timekeeper and Mom being the judge to punish me if I was so much as a minute late. Punishment meant being grounded in my private prison cell of a bedroom, a Mother-who-hates-her-son beating, or both, which was usually the norm. There could be no arguing over whose time was right. There was no doubt about who was or wasn't guilty, because that whistle was for all to hear.

I had to be up by the 7:30 sounding and have eaten and almost be ready for school by the 8 a.m. whistle. I would leave for school by 8:30, for which there was no whistle. Classes started as the 9 o'clock school bell rang. The mornings ended at 11:40 and the afternoons at 3:40. This meant that I had twenty minutes to get home before the noon and 4 p.m. whistles blew. There was just enough time to go to my locker to get either books or a coat or to put books away and then walk straight home. I did not have a watch, so I kept time as best I could. There were days when I had to run as fast as I could in order to get home on time, because I may have stopped to talk to people or had a detention after school. I will be the first to admit that for reasons unknown I was becoming quite a troublesome boy. They didn't realize at school that holding me for a detention meant there was another beating awaiting me upon my arrival at home.

One of those whistle-monitored days stands out as vividly in this instant as on the day it happened. It was a warm, glorious summer afternoon. I had spent the day at the Parks and Recreations' summer program located at the high school in town. When not at our cottage during summer vacation, my brothers and I (provided I wasn't grounded) were allowed to spend the weekdays participating in the activities that were set up. I always looked forward to being away from Mother whenever possible. I could for a few hours be a regular little boy, running, playing and being with the other kids.

This particular day, my brothers and others were still milling about. I knew I had to be home by the 4 o'clock whistle. After helping for a few minutes I asked one of the staff for the correct time and was told it was about five minutes to four. Getting home in five minutes would be next to impossible as it was about a mile's distance. I would have to be an Olympic athlete to get home in that time. After telling a staff member I had to leave right away, I broke out into a full sprint. You would have thought this was a race for my life. I was running as fast as my legs could carry me. Scared of being late gave me a supernatural strength as I made my way up the street. My body was fully energized and

I was gulping in great quantities of oxygen to replenish my weakening legs. I couldn't weaken now, I thought. I caught my second wind and my speed came back. My heart was pounding against my chest like someone inside of me trying furiously to get out. As I passed the halfway mark, I stopped dead in my tracks as the four o'clock whistle let out its screech. It was hopeless now, I thought, or was it? Maybe mother was at a neighbour's and wouldn't notice if I was a couple minutes late. With renewed vigor I started to run the rest of the way home as fast as possible. I may not have been an Olympic athlete that day, but I knew I must have Olympian strength in me. Just to go home every day not knowing what would happen to me when I faced mother took courage. That woman was so unpredictable and always full of tragic surprises. I was out of breath as I reached our yard and was gasping for air as I climbed the back steps. Climbing those steps day in and day out was something I dreaded, because mother was usually home and I hated her enough to kill her. Facing her every day of my life was a living hell and mother was satan in the flesh. Glancing in the window as I passed, I saw the she-devil making supper. I would have to face her the moment I stepped in the door. I was about three minutes late. My mind was racing. What mood was she in? How bad might I get beat? The world seemed to stop whenever I was about to face that woman and today was no exception.

I turned the doorknob and slowly pushed the door inward. As the door opened I saw mother furtively glance at me while she continued preparing supper. I stepped into the house and closed the door behind me.

Mother was now staring at me as I bent down to untie my shoelaces. At that moment everything went into slow motion. Mother stood erect and faced me, while holding a carving knife in one hand. She was running off at the mouth saying every conceivable foul word in the dictionary and then some. Her standing there, not more than five feet away from me holding an eight inch knife in her hand, was the most terrifying encounter thus far in life. I always had prophetic visions of her killing me one day and I guess today was the day. this harridan* raised the knife as if to throw it, I let out a horror-stricken scream as she released the knife. The bladed weapon sliced its way through the air towards me. Everything all of a sudden sped up, I don't know how it happened but the knife missed me and penetrated the door. I turned towards the door and gasped in terror at what she had just done. Mother wasn't human, she was demon possessed, she had just tried to kill me. I feared for my life as she lunged at me with her arms outstretched. I screamed, "No, no, no, please, please don't hurt me!" I pleaded. God only knows how many times I had gone through this routine before, for I had surely lost count. I should have known by now it was a losing situation. This enraged lunatic had no feelings for me. She grabbed me and hurled me against the wall, while screaming, "You son of a bitch, you'll never learn, you are nothing but a crazy retarded bastard." She was now in her usual state of psychotic madness as she bashed my head against the wall a number of times. mother reached for the

---

* Meaning a bad tempered old woman.

broom beside the door and started hitting me all over with it as if in a fencing match. One blow crashed down on the back of my neck and the broom handle broke. Mother was now more maddened and she screamed, "You broke my broom you bastard" and dropped the half she was holding. Now she was relentlessly kicking me in the stomach. God, I was so petrified, I couldn't take any more of her insanity. I wish I had the guts to grab that knife from the door and plunge it endlessly into her body. Once for every one of the hundreds of times she had bashed, whipped or verbally abused me over the years. But no, I was a brave little boy and took this punishment for some unknown reasons. all I had ever wanted was for her to love me. Still kicking me, this woman had now crossed the line of sanity and was now deep into her own misery. Why was she taking out her hatred on me? Satan's mistress stopped kicking me, just as I thought she had stopped, the harridan reached into the cupboard and retrieved an electrical extension cord. I was huddled in a corner, a broken child and in unbearable pain. I kept silent as she started whipping me, outside of the switches she made of tree branches at the cottage, extension cords hurt the most. Every lashing of the cord stung my tender flesh. Excruciating pain of the physical sense shot through me as did the equally punishing emotional accompaniment.

How she must have hated me for what I stood for in her life! I couldn't help that I was a boy. Why couldn't I have been a girl? She relentlessly whipped me. My cries of agony reverberated through the house. As always, no sooner had she started than it ended. I was left huddled in fear, crying my head off, so to speak. She had wreaked her fury on me, and I was ordered to my room. Gathering myself together, I removed my shoes and solemnly walked past Mother, who was back to preparing supper as if nothing had happened. If there had been a gun and bullets around, I wouldn't have thought twice before killing her. Ironically, unknown to me at the time, Dad did have two rifles and shells hidden in the pantry. Thank God I had no knowledge of them in my youth. As much as I wanted her love, I hated her.

I walked down the hall past the pantry. Climbing the stairs hurt, and I could feel the welts blistering my skin. Closing the door behind me, I was once again back in my jail cell. I sat down in a chair in the corner but was too sore to stay sitting, so I walked to the window, knelt down and stared out at the street. A steady stream of cars was going by, as it was shift change. Every day those people drove by our house; little did they know what a house of horrors was behind our closed doors. I was still crying from my punishment for being late as the 4:30 whistle blew. I shuddered as the sound echoed in my mind.

Back at the high school one day I didn't feel like participating, so I just sat outside daydreaming about life at home, how bad I was and how I didn't feel like I belonged in this world. As I sat there, a Parks and Recreation staff member came over and asked why I wasn't playing with the others. I said, "I don't feel like it." This young lady asked if anything was the matter. I thought deeply for a few seconds and then just started crying, first a trickle, then a flood. Tears were streaming down my face. The staff member sat beside me, and I told her I never wanted to go home again. I told her that Mother had tried to kill me with a knife and that I was always beaten up, mostly for unknown reasons, that I was going crazy living there. I kept sobbing while I showed her the marks, and she comforted me and said she would phone someone to help me.

She put her arms around me and squeezed gently. For the first time in my life I enjoyed being hugged. She went back to her job, and I spent the better part of the afternoon pretty much alone. As I was getting ready to go home, the girl who had been so nice to me told me that someone from the Children's Aid Society would come to my house and check my story. I walked home with a couple of my girlfriends and was home before that 4 o'clock whistle blew. Mother was still in a pleasant mood, and I was allowed to watch television until supper. I didn't care much for watching TV because of Mother's strictness. I was sitting in my mandatory position on the floor, Indian style—legs crossed, hands clasped in front of me, my back straight and my eyes directed at the TV.

My thoughts turned to what might happen when the people the girl had phoned came to check on my story. I hoped they would take me away. I hated Mom, and my brothers because of their freedom. I only loved Dad in my own way because I knew not the true way to love one's parents. *This is so confusing*, I thought.

Dad was home that night. Supper was served; some of us ate in the kitchen and some while watching TV. During the course of supper I was very quiet. At any moment I expected to hear someone coming to the door. I started having second thoughts about what I had started and had no idea what the consequences of my actions might be. I now wished I hadn't uttered a word to the young lady. I supposed I really was no good if I would try to get my own mother in trouble.

The rest of the time at supper was spent feeling guilty and full of shame. Although I did not know what the word *bastard* meant, I sat thinking *I must be the bastard Mom always calls me.* With supper finished and the dishes done, I was then sent to my room. At the window I sat, thinking in disgust of myself, *Only a bastard would get his mom in trouble. I should be dead.*

Some time went by, and then I heard a knock at the door. I tried to listen, but not a word met my ears. Minutes passed; then Mother's voice beckoned me. "Randy, dear, can you come down here, please," in an unusually friendly tone. Walking down the stairs, I faced what lay ahead. What would happen to me if they didn't take me with them and I was left in the hands of my mother?

Reaching the kitchen, I stood nervously in front of Mother, Dad, and a stranger or two. Mother introduced me to these people, who, I was told, were from the Children's Aid Society and checking on a suspected case of abuse.

I said, "Hello," and the social worker told me that someone had anonymously called and requested a check be made on our household. The worker then began asking questions, which I can't remember well. Had I been beaten excessively lately? Boy, was I terrified to talk now, especially in front of Mother! It was now or never, I thought, and then I replied, "No."

I was asked if I had ever told anyone stories of me being abused; again I answered, "No." Mother and Dad were asked questions, to which they lied. Dad didn't have a choice, because he was always yielding to the power and authority Mother held over his head. Mother would have gotten him back later anyhow.

The social workers finished up and left. Thank God I wasn't asked to let them look at my bruised body. I had saved Mother's neck, but she got quite a scare out of the visit. She even let me watch TV, but I was still in that stupid rigid statue position.

Mother was a good liar and had everybody terrified of her. Even had I told the social worker the truth, Mother could have proven I had lied before and they would have thought I just fabricated the whole thing.

I was just a kid not to be believed.

# Chapter 4

For a few weeks after the visit from the Children's Aid Society, something must have made Mother think twice about being physically violent, for she treated me with an unusual amount of kindness. I was allowed as much freedom as my brothers had. I wasn't grounded, and I actually started to let my guard down somewhat for the first time in my life. I seemed a little more relaxed, and Mother was letting me do most anything I asked. In my ten or so years I had never experienced so much enjoyment for such a long time. I was out playing, unbelievably, every day and wasn't stuck in my room. Watching TV even became more enjoyable as I wasn't kicked in the back once and even got to sit in a chair instead of as always on the floor. For the first time I was feeling better about life and Mother. I had never before seen her being so nice for such an extended time.

At the same time that I was experiencing this new-found freedom, I started taking advantage of it. I would stay away from home all day until 4. I would have lunch at friends' places instead of at home. I wanted to be respected by my friends, so I started to shoplift daily,

giving away most everything to my buddies and girlfriends. When Mother was occasionally working as a
waitress she would have what seemed like countless
amounts of change in her purse from tips she received.
I would steal a few dollars before she had a chance to
count it. Then I would buy my friends—especially my
girlfriend—little kindnesses. I was becoming quite a big
shot, and I was happy having everyone looking up to
me. But as I had learned, all good things soon come to
an end. Mother was returning to the old hag that she
was. She caught me stealing and beat me black and
blue with the buckle end of a belt. I never learned my
lessons from these beatings and just became more
rebellious.

I would have been beaten no matter if I had gotten
in trouble or not. The floggings were no more severe
than when I was an innocent victim. I didn't care any
more anyhow; I was building up an immunity against
physical pain. One day when I was to receive a whipping for some reason or other, Mother told me that my
father was going to give me the belt this time. I was
sent to my room to wait until Dad got home from
work. I sure was terrified while waiting. Dad had never
so much as laid a hand on any of us. I thought over
how much pain Mother usually inflicted upon me.
Surely Dad, being a man and much stronger, would
really be able to hurt me. Man, was I in a state of emotional distress! I suppose at the time Mother was
having second thoughts about what she was doing to
us; the visit from the C.A.S. must have made her think
that she now had to get Dad involved in the beating of
me, I guess so if anyone said anything she would be

able to say Dad was beating me, and Dad would never lie if confronted. I don't understand how minds work at times.

I sat dejected in my room, feeling hatred towards everyone, including myself. The thought of both Dad and Mother beating me now was so unbearable, I might as well be dead. Yes, dead. Thoughts of death came almost every day. I had tried a couple of times before but failed—I never could do anything right. Living in a world of endless fear was unbearable. I sat thinking of the whipping I was to soon receive. *I can't stand living another day in this abuse-filled life. Death is the easiest way out. Yes, I will die today!*

Every time I thought of killing myself, a rush of frenzied excitement overwhelmed my inner soul, for I knew I would be, at last, in peace. Going to heaven and living in perpetual happiness had always been a fantasy of mine. As in the past when I made futile attempts at suicide by self-strangulation, today I would once again try to strangle myself. Today, I was determined to succeed! Being confined to my room left me with the problem of what to use. Had there been rope around, I am sure I would have been dead by now, but I always used my belt. When I made these attempts I was always at the point of insanity, just as Mother was. *I just have to die,* I thought as I took the belt from around my waist. While holding the black leather belt with the shiny brass-coloured buckle in one hand, I would loop the loose end through the buckle with the other. At the same time I was feeling great hatred of Mother and myself. I should kill her too, for we were both terrible people, and we should not be allowed to live and should reside in hell. I was always scared to kill myself for only one reason, and that was, if I was as bad as Mother had always told me, then I would not got to heaven. It didn't really matter anyhow, for to me to live was death and to die might be gain. At least my chances in death were fifty-fifty.

I looped the belt around my neck and started to tighten it. You can't even begin to imagine the hatred I felt towards Mother, for her never-ending tormenting, and towards myself, for all the trouble I had caused, really in innocence. Anger filled my mind, my heart, my soul with the greatest intense feelings of hatred. I tightened the belt around my neck, slowly cutting off the life-giving oxygen from my body. Across the room I could see in the mirror an ever-changing contorted image of my face as I pulled the belt ever so tightly. Tighter, tighter, with both hands, my face reddening, my eyes seemingly ready to pop right out of their sockets. I was glad to be dying. The tighter I pulled, the redder I got. More feelings of hatred, so much hatred, hatred, hatred. I was starting to get dizzy. This was it. I was almost dead; everyone would be happy.

My face felt like it was going to blow up and spray showers of blood all over. I was losing consciousness, and I knew that this time, my misery would be over. With every muscle in my body working I made one last mighty pull on the belt. As I started to fall to the floor, I knew I was going to die, because I had never pulled so hard on the belt before. I fell dead to the world. I felt my soul leave my body happily. I was free, free at last. I don't know if it was seconds, minutes or longer, but— you guessed it! I regained consciousness. What a failure

I was! Gasping for air as my body started to revive itself, I lay on the floor, staring at the ceiling.

I now would be getting the beating from Dad soon. Sitting up I angrily took the belt off from around my neck and threw it against the wall, getting up slowly, I looked in the mirror, my face and neck still red. I climbed into bed and stared blankly at the ceiling while waiting for the 5 o'clock whistle to go.

Dad got home about five minutes before the whistle sounded, and I could hear them conversing but couldn't pick out any words. I envisioned her telling Dad he had to give me a beating. I was petrified of getting my first flogging from Dad; why was I still alive to receive it? The time was near. A couple of minutes passed, and then I heard the creaking of the old wooden stairs as someone started to ascend the staircase. I started to perspire as I counted each step.

Dad now stood in the doorway with a perplexed look on his face. For the first time in my life I was terrified of him. This was to be his debut as a child-beating father, who up to now had never raised a hand, let alone a belt, to anyone.

Dad walked into the room. He didn't look mean or angry; just the same, I was fraught with terror. Not knowing how to react to this strange but real situation, I just sat up in bed. Dad spoke, saying he was told to give the belt to me and that he didn't want to but didn't have a choice. He asked me to get out of bed and go into the bathroom with him. This was strange; Mother never cared which room I was beaten in. On the way to the bathroom I asked Dad not to hit me very hard. Although I could stand the pain, it didn't mean I liked it.

Dad closed the bathroom door. Was I scared now as I stood there awaiting my punishment! Mother often used my small belt on me, and it stung incredibly. Now Dad removed his belt from his pants. Holy cow, his belt was twice as long as mine! I stood there eyeing that piece of leather and thought that it must hurt twice as much as mine did. With Dad's man strength and his huge belt, I could already imagine the intense pain that I was momentarily going to feel. Sweating and shaking like a leaf, I pleaded with him to not whip me.

Dad told me to bend over and yell and scream as if I was being whipped. He placed a towel across the sink and started whipping it, while I let out yells from imaginary pain. What a guy! I never thought he would be like Mother, and I was glad it was true. With all my experience yelling and screaming in agony, it sure sounded as if I was getting the beating of my life. I didn't mind letting out blood-curdling screams with every lashing that towel received. I could just picture Mother downstairs while I was upstairs pulling the wool over her eyes. I felt great.

Dad stopped and told me not to say anything or he would be in trouble and I might really get beaten then. I told him I would never utter a word, and then I went back to bed. I wished all beatings were so painless. Minutes went by, and then I was called for supper. I had to keep up the facade so I put on my saddest face as I washed up for supper. Downstairs I was faking pain as I faced Mother in the kitchen; I wondered what she was thinking. Mom told me to sit down and eat, which I did. During the course of supper I fidgeted in my chair as if I had a sore bottom, all the while feeling gratified at making a fool of her.

The dishes were done and I was sent back to my room. I spent the rest of the evening transcending into my fantasy world of love and having a loving mother. As usual, I had thoughts of what it would be like to be a girl, as boys were always bad and I wanted to be good. I had even started wishing one of my brothers was a sister so that I mightn't get beaten and because I got along better with girls. All I wanted was to be loved.

Another abuse-filled summer had come and gone and now I would be starting grade five and was almost eleven years old. School had by now become routine, and I was one of the proverbial ten-most-troublesome students in our school. In fact, I was numero uno. I had formed somewhat of a gang, which included my brothers. We would steal anything, and I was the brains behind our organized thefts. My brother and I had the largest share of the loot. We could boast of having the largest comic book collection, the most marbles, large and small, or anything that was the novelty of the time. I always loved May when firecrackers were sold over the counter, until they were banned in Canada. Our gang would steal boxes of them and sell them at a discount, so we always had extra money at that time of the year. My brothers and I usually now had paper routes and delivered the *Sudbury Star*. Even at that young age I had a knack for making money.

Our gang's merchandise was quite diversified and changed with the season. In spring it could be marbles or yo-yos; in summer we had the market covered for golf balls, tennis balls, baseballs and even legitimate lemonade stands, to be able to account for any extra money we had. During winter and hockey season when all of us kids played in league teams, we sold pucks and hockey sticks. It was somewhat of a thrill to steal, an addiction of sorts, and I was a master of thievery. I had to keep proving it or else I would lose respect, and I certainly couldn't lose that, not when the members of my gang were the only ones who looked up to me. I was like a sponge and soaked up all the glory. Oh, what a feeling! I suppose it filled part of my emptiness.

My girlfriends filled another need, the longing to be fussed over. I loved being around females more than being with my gang. Kissing had become quite an interest of mine, and at times I could be caught kissing two at once. Up to now I had hated being kissed, because I despised Mother's kisses. She would only give me a kiss when in front of outsiders. Yes, home life was still the same. Mother never showed me any caring; the beatings continued. The more I looked for attention outside of the home, the more trouble I found myself in.

Another year had passed, and now on to another abuse-filled summer, the details which I need not go into.

# Chapter 5

In October 1970 when I was in grade six, my brothers and I found out that Mom was pregnant again and that the baby would be born in April the following spring. I told Mom I wanted a sister more than anything else in the whole world. Also about this time, Dad bought a house at the other end of town, and we would soon be moving. The house was not nearly as old as our turn-of-the-century clapboard house and was sure better. It was of average size, with three bedrooms, a living room, dining room, kitchen, and best of all a full basement; our current home had none. We couldn't wait to move in. Well, I couldn't leave that house and my bedroom prison cell soon enough.

We had always lived in Copper Cliff, and this was the second time we had moved. Shortly after we moved this time, the company home was torn down, just as had happened after we moved from the first house. I wondered in later years why, out of all the houses in Copper Cliff, ours were the only ones torn down.

After settling into our new house I found out things wouldn't change. I had a new prison cell; the only difference was the view. Mother's madness continued despite her pregnancy.

When I was allowed away from home I was becoming more of a juvenile delinquent. I was still stealing money from Mother and now her cigarettes. Yes, smoking was becoming the thing to do. I had an image to uphold, so I turned my gang on to smoking. We all thought we were so cool. Fall went by, and it was now hockey season, and as usual I played goaltender for a league team. I was actually quite good and had won a few trophies. Then it was Christmas and my twelfth birthday, January fifteenth. I was a whole twelve years old and terribly confused, to say the least. Soon I would hopefully have a baby sister, and nightly I prayed for it to be so. I did not want another brother, or else I would run away forever. I figured all these years that Mother wanted me to be a girl, so it only made sense that if she was to give birth to a daughter, I would be off the hook and Mother would be forever happy. Kids sure have a way of perceiving things, don't they?

Well, the time finally came, and Mother was taken to the hospital. It was the first week of April 1971, and Easter was coming on the weekend. I thought of no better gift than having a new baby sister. While Mother was hospitalized I prayed fervently. A lady friend of the family was looking after us while Mother was away, and I sure was happy to be free. We spent the days with this lady while Dad worked. Dad had given the lady money for our needs, and I figured she wouldn't miss a twenty, so I stole one from her purse. I rounded up our gang and we bought a couple of cartons of Rothman's cigarettes, then went to one of our hideaways, Elephant Caves.

They weren't really caves but a lot of little crawl spaces amongst some gigantic boulders. It was a place to hide and play and keep the fruits of our crimes from the weather. The afternoon was spent smoking our little lungs out and eating stolen junk. With Easter weekend ahead and Mother away, I would have lots of time for myself, so I planned our capers for the next few days.

It was getting close to suppertime and I didn't have to worry about those whistles for a change. We hid the cigarettes, and those who were brave enough took a few home. On my way home the 4 o'clock whistle went. I was startled, but I realized I wouldn't get in trouble, except maybe for skipping school that afternoon. Yes, I had just skipped my first class, but I doubted I would be found out.

Upon arrival at home we were greeted by the nice lady who was "babysitting" us. She looked at us suspiciously, especially me, because like everyone else in town she thought of me as a troublemaker. No one knew what went on behind closed doors—the beatings, whippings and tongue lashings. Neither they nor I at the time understood truly why I was driven to be a juvenile delinquent. Still staring at me, the lady asked who had taken $20. Of course we all denied having taken the money. The lady told us she would have to tell Mother about the missing money. "I did it," I blurted out. "Please don't tell Mother, please," I pleaded.

She asked if there was any money left, and I told her it had all been spent on food and junk. "You spent $20 on junk? You must have some left!" she questioned.

"No, I gave it to friends," I replied. There was no way I could tell her we had bought cigarettes or it would have been Armageddon when Mother found out and I would receive punishment accordingly. Little did this lady know how I would be beaten. Later, when the lady talked to Mom on the phone, she informed Mother of the theft. The babysitter relayed the message back to me that I would be taken care of when Mother got home. Well, I would just have to enjoy my freedom while it lasted, for I was sure to be grounded for a long time.

The next couple of days were great, and I spent a lot of time thinking hopefully about having a baby sister. The night of April 8, as I said my prayers, I asked for a baby sister. As the next day would be Good Friday, I also prayed to Jesus, who died so that the world might be saved through Him. I fell fast asleep and didn't wake until the cacophony of my brothers aroused me early Friday morning. For us kids it was just another day off from school.

The day was to be cloudy with intermittent showers. Dad was home from work, as he also had the day off. We didn't think of the day in a Christian sense. Later in the day Dad received a phone call from the hospital, and yes, God had answered my prayer. I now had a baby sister, but I wouldn't see her for a few days, until Mother came home. I was so happy, I jumped up and down and spent the rest of the day telling friends and neighbours the good news. Ironically, with my nightmares about the devil and thinking of Mother as Satan's helper, I thought it quite incredible later on in life that my sister, named Vickey-Mae, was born on this special day.

When Sunday came we got up and went on our traditional family Easter egg hunt. It was always fun looking for hidden treasures of milk chocolate and more fun eating them. We didn't go to church that Easter, because of my sister's birth. I couldn't wait to see Vickey! We spent the day gorging ourselves with sweet chocolate and playing. For some reason Easter Day seemed always to be cloudy and rainy. I had always wondered if it was symbolic of Christ's death on the cross. As the day ended I happily went to bed and dreamt about seeing my sister, Vickey.

I woke up cheerfully on Easter Monday morning, because it was the day of my sister's homecoming. We weren't much of a family, and I was sorry my sister would have to grow up amongst us, but I was elated just the same, for I finally had a sister. I truly believe that anyone who has neither a brother nor a sister longs to have at least one of each. All the beatings in the world couldn't have saddened me that day.

Dad left to pick up Mom and Sis, and we waited impatiently at home with a babysitter. Soon the trio pulled into the driveway, and we all crowded about. Mother emerged from the car like a queen with her little princess held proudly in her arms. All the feelings of hate seemingly disappeared for the moment as I realized Mother had brought us four boys a beautiful blue-eyed baby sister with as blonde hair as I had ever seen. Mother had finally done something right for a change.

Mother looked overjoyed as we all asked her to let us hold Vickey. I waited my turn impatiently, and when I was handed my sister to hold I felt the happiest that I had ever been. Vickey was the most beautiful baby in the world, and she was my sister. It was love at first sight. I knew from that moment that if Mother ever hurt my sister physically or emotionally I would kill her. I didn't think Vickey would ever be physically hurt, but I knew emotional strangulation was worse. I handed Vickey to a brother and stood back and thanked God for answering my prayers by bestowing upon our family this precious child. Friends and family fussed over Vickey all day, including yours truly.

That Easter Monday in 1971 was a great day in my life and one that saw our family together and happy, all conflicts put aside. I hoped Mother had forgotten about the $20. That night as I lay in bed, I prayed that Mother would be happy now that she had a beautiful daughter, and that our family might be closer and happier. I fell blissfully to sleep and was awakened later by the cries of my sister. I hoped she was okay. I fell back to sleep, only to be awakened later by Dad telling us to get up for school. I made my bed, washed and got dressed.

Downstairs I saw Mother with Vickey and went over to see my sister. Vickey looked so cute and cuddly and so very tiny, I found it hard to imagine that I was once so small. Mother glared at me with piercing eyes and told me to go and eat and that I would be dealt with later. Well, so much for visions of long-term happiness!

The morning at school was spent telling everyone about my little sister. As we were let out for lunch I realized nothing would change. I was back on that timetable and would have to get home by that stupid 12 o'clock whistle. On my way home I thought of running away again but reconsidered because of the cold and the want of my sister. Getting home before the noon whistle was no problem that day, and as usual I feared walking into the house. I knew I deserved a beating for stealing the money and walked into the house expecting to receive my usual punishment.

Mother had company over, and they were talking about my baby sister, so I knew I wouldn't be hurt at lunch. Mother was her usual two-faced self around visitors and catered to my every need. She fixed us a nice lunch while I went to see Vickey, who was in her crib. It had only been a day since she had come home, but already I felt a special bond between us that I had never experienced with anyone before. Mother called us for our lunch; my brothers and I ate and got ready for afternoon classes. Before leaving we each kissed our sister goodbye. I spent the afternoon in class thinking about the abuse I would receive sooner or later.

When school was let out for the day I contemplated running away again, but as usual, with all the courage I could muster from within my emotionally distraught mind, I went home to face the music. As on every other day I played beat the clock as I rushed home ahead of the 4 o'clock whistle. How many hundreds of times had I rushed home against that God-forsaken whistle? I couldn't stand it any more; I was going insane myself. That day I made it home again, luckily. The hell I was in, this was some ungodly punishment, this life of mine. I walked back into the arms of insanity every day.

Mom didn't greet me as I walked in the door, she was somewhere in the house; I could hear her making noise. After taking my shoes off I then went upstairs to my prison room with my books. Mother was in her room straightening things up, Vickey was asleep. Mother, noticing me, told me to go downstairs. In the kitchen I sat down at the table, moments later mother came downstairs, and by the crazed look on her face I could tell she was all worked up again. She yelled, "You stole money and bought cigarettes?" How the Hell did she know about the cigarettes? I suppose from one of my spoiled siblings. Mother screamed, "So you like to steal and smoke! I'll teach you sooner or later you good-for-nothing son." She then proceeded to inflict another beating on me.

When finished she told me to get the Hell upstairs and wait in the bathroom. What was she going to do next? Up the stairway of Hell, I heard her coming for me as I sat on the closed toilet.

Mother came into the bathroom with one of Dad's big White Owl cigars and told me I would have to smoke the whole thing. I promised her I wouldn't smoke any more, but I was just told to shut up. She put the cigar in my mouth and then lit it. She told me to inhale the smoke. I knew you weren't supposed to inhale cigar smoke, but I didn't have a choice. With every puff came a choking sensation. And I thought soap covered with pepper had been bad! The 4:30 whistle blew as I sat there sucking back on that stogie. Mother kept saying "deeper, deeper" as I filled my lungs with that sickening smoke. I told her I'd be sick, and Mother said, "Good; it will teach you a lesson." I kept smoking; all the while I could feel my stomach start to turn and my face start to sweat. "Keep going, you bastard," she told me.

*Why does she punish me so?* I thought. I knew I was a troublemaker, but somehow I couldn't change that. I now felt quite ill. Finally I couldn't stand it any more and fell off the toilet onto the floor. I was so dizzy that the room was spinning in circles. I made a desperate attempt to lift the toilet seat but was too dizzy. I felt ready to pass out when all of a sudden I threw up all over myself. I lay there until I started to regain my composure and had broken out in a sickly sweat. Again, feeling the aggression of nausea overwhelming me, I lifted the toilet seat and expelled what seemed to be my entire guts into the bowl. I knelt there trying to suck in air as I choked on my own sickness. Vomit was clinging to me. I sure must have looked pitiful and a sight that any real mother would have wanted to console, but no, my mother wasn't human. She told me to clean the mess and to wash my clothes in the tub.

*Someday, yes, someday I might kill her*, I thought. My face was still flushed and I was still sick as a dog, still throwing up, but it was now more of a gut-wrenching feeling as there was nothing left inside of me. Mother left me there choking while she went to tend to Vickey. I was still gasping for air as I started to fill the bathtub with water. I thought the greatest gift of life was the breath of life, which is our own. Yeah right, how many times previous to this had I tried to strangle myself, run away or wished I was dead? Why couldn't I just stop living? Why?

With the water running in the tub, I stood and looked in the mirror. My eyes were bloodshot from the past hour of physical and mental anguish; my hair was dishevelled; my mouth, chin, neck and clothes were covered with that had been the day's meals. I ran water in the sink and washed up while still in a sickening daze. There was now enough water in the bathtub, so I turned off the faucets and started to undress. The bathroom was getting steam filled, and I stripped down to my undershorts. The warmth of the vaporizing water seemed to have a calming effect on me as it permeated my skin. Throwing my clothes in the tub, I then left the bathroom to go downstairs to the basement and get some rags to clean up the mess. While walking down the two flights of stairs I realized I was in some kind of deep mental turmoil within myself, somewhat lost to the world, a space cadet of sorts.

Before I knew it I was washing the bathroom floor, with no conscious memory of coming back upstairs. As I cleaned I found that cigar behind the toilet. It had now burnt out. As I picked up the remains of that stogie, the most extreme form of hatred arose from within and tore at my inner soul. I insanely crushed that cigar in the palms of my hands as a symbolic gesture towards Mother. I threw the handful of tobacco against the wall, only to realize that I now had to clean up another mess. Not in control of my senses or emotions now, I blamed Mother for this mess, and with every bit of that cigar I picked up, the revulsion towards her was incalculable.

Another wave of nausea rushed throughout my tormented soul, and I managed to sustain the feeling. Dad was home now; I could hear him arguing with the she-devil downstairs. I started to hand wash my clothes while I transcended to the height of surrealism. I didn't even hear the 5 o'clock whistle blow. Scrubbing away at my clothes with such anger that my knuckles became red, I went farther into an unnatural mental state. I was half in and half out of this hateful world. As I wrung the water from my clothes, I fantasized that it was Mother's neck I was wringing. I wished I had the strength of a superhero and could crush her with a single blow. I stood up, hung my clothes on the shower curtain bar, drained and rinsed the tub and went to my room. Climbing into bed I lay there in some kind of psychotic mental state, just staring at nothing, but yet I saw everything. Soon I was back in control of reality once again. The taste of that stinking cigar could be sensed throughout my whole self, and I still felt quite ill.

Dad checked in to see if I was okay. I told him I would be fine soon and that I didn't want to eat supper. That was about the extent of our father-and-son relationship. Dad could never break away from the bonds Mother had him wrapped in psychologically; he was also a prisoner of this ungodly household. Dad and I had been prevented by this woman from developing anywhere near the maximum of our potential as individual personalities because of being physically abused or emotionally victimized, at times to the breaking point. Still staring about the room, I promised to seek revenge one day, months or even years away.

Every second I lay there with that sickening feeling in my stomach brought back thoughts of the past, present and even what the dreadful future might bring if I should be so unfortunate as to live that long. I was slowly deteriorating as a normal human being and succumbing mentally to the never-ending onslaught of emotional deprivation, somewhat like being starved to death in the longest and cruelest of ways. I heard my sweet sister crying in her room, and my heart wept for her. As much as I had wanted a sister in my selfish way, I hated knowing how she might grow up emotionally after seeing all around her nothing but hate. Being the eldest brother at home, I promised to watch out for her as best I could.

# Chapter 6

As time and years passed, Mother's treatment of me did not improve. By the time I was thirteen years old, I had become quite an emotionally disturbed young boy. I didn't understand why I thought and behaved so differently from other people. Always in a state of utter confusion inside myself, I struggled every day with my feelings of being effeminate, of maybe being retarded. I repressed all fear and anxieties and did my best to be like others, but I just had innate knowledge of the fact that I was different, and it bothered me every second of my life. I was getting abused as much as ever after having somewhat of a break during the summer. Brother Tom and I fought constantly, and my jealousy of his freedom was on the rise. My male friends had pretty much become distant acquaintances. Female friends were many, and I fit in as if I were one of them. The girls loved my naturally curly shoulder-length dirty-blond hair. I was still stealing and smoking daily.

The beatings continued on a regular basis. I hated school and wasn't doing well. Even in music class, which I enjoyed, I stopped playing percussion instruments and just sat in class, drawn within myself, daydreaming away. My music teacher asked me on a few occasions why I wasn't participating with the enthusiasm I once had. I said I just didn't feel like playing instruments any more. Well, after a couple more music classes with my nonparticipation, I went home one day and found out Mother had been informed and she was madder than hell at me. I was going to be beaten again.

She started her usual cursing and screaming, then the head banging, and finally the whipping with the belt. You know the routine by now. I just took the abuse in stride. She said that sooner or later I would learn and some sense would be knocked into me, but I knew if anything I was becoming more senseless. I was sent to my room again. *Oh well, this is life.* Needless to say I was participating in music class again, although as I beat the drum to the rhythm of the melodies, I was in fact playing them as an outward showing of hatred against life, and I hated it. From that day on all the pleasant feelings I used to have in music class were destroyed, and it was now just a way of expressing my anger and disillusionment with the world around me. Mother always had a way of taking the fun out of anything that I came to enjoy.

Daily the rage grew within me, a rage born of never knowing why I was treated the way I was, of not understanding why I was unloved, why I was abused. If I could have screamed as loud as I hurt, houses would have fallen, the sound barrier broken. I was old enough now to realize the effects of all this emotional trauma. It seemed to hurt more than any physical abuse and was leaving me to atrophy in a slow and painful death.

At night I lay in bed, sobbing and praying for help from God to save me from this hellish life on earth. I thought about how I never really meant to be a troublemaker; it was just that I craved much-needed attention, and I usually went about getting that attention in a troublesome way. I had, that year, learned that we had two rifles around the house, one a 20-gauge shotgun and the other a 22-gauge semi-automatic rifle, and the shells for each of them. I had urges to put about ten bullets in the semi-automatic and pump Mother full of lead. It always excited me to picture her begging for her life as I had done countless hundreds of times during the course of my life.

However, as angry and powerless as I felt, fate didn't have it in the cards for me to become a teenage murderer. Mother is lucky to be alive today, and from where I sit as I write this, I am glad that I never killed her, because with my understanding today I don't think I could have lived with myself. No doubt it would have been a murder-suicide anyhow.

Alone in my room I quietly submerged myself back into my world of fantasy. I knew I thought differently than others and that I had severe emotional problems, but what I didn't have was the knowledge of why I thought and behaved in such antisocial ways.

High school was a time of challenge for me in that regard. The first few days of school were great, but after that the novelty wore off. I was being called to the guidance counsellor's office and was always being pumped full of questions. The answers I gave were lies; I couldn't tell how life really was for me because I was frightened of breaking up our family.

On top of it all, I hated gym class. The class itself was okay, but afterwards in the change room I felt strange. I couldn't undress to shower because I noticed I hadn't developed sexually as the others had, and it freaked me out. So I spent a whole semester skipping showers. Because I wasn't developing like the other boys, I really thought I was half female. All these thoughts were eating me alive. What had started off as a fantasy to have Mother love me was now some kind of freakish reality. Physically I was a male, but psychologically I was becoming more feminine. I was sure that if anyone found out I would be sent to a mental institution.

That year was also the first time I actively fought back against Mother as she beat me. This was the first time anyone had retaliated against her, and I think it triggered her to be more violent than ever. And although she "won" and overpowered me, I knew something had changed in me. I had never flipped out before in all these almost fifteen years. Sure I had fought with Mom before, but this fight was different.

I wanted to die, and I wanted her to die as well. Mother wasn't deserving of the life God had given her. She was a sinner in the most horrible of ways. Everything God represented in life she destroyed. She was a antichrist, ruled by Satan. Her church meetings and community involvement was just a facade to hide the reality of her eroding personality. How I hated this two-faced excuse for a human being! She was supposed to be a mother showing me all the beauty I possessed inside, giving me a sense of pride, letting me learn to love myself and others. But nothing in my life was done right. I was an ugly person inside, I had no pride, and I hated myself almost as much as I hated Mother. Crossing back and forth along the fine line of sanity, I struggled to maintain a hold of myself. I was sinking deeper with each moment to the bottom of my soul, my spirit broken.

Minutes passed and I couldn't seem to grasp on to reality. I felt so different now. I had fought back and hit Mother. My emotions couldn't be held back any more. I had to defend myself. As I moved about I could feel the welts from the beating swelling and stinging, and it hurt intensely.

I was horrified that I had fought with her. I had become like her, a very violent and deranged person. I was a sick animal, in the image of my mother. How could I live with myself now, knowing how sick I was? Physically I was alive, but spiritually and emotionally I was in a state of atrophy. Part of me seemed to have died during the fight.

My temper and emotions flared easily, and I was becoming more hostile to the people around me. Hatred of Mother had grown more intense, and I knew I had to get away. Even looking at mirrored images of myself I saw visual changes in me. A look of emptiness showed on my face, a sullen, lost look that seemed to bare the pain of almost fifteen years of horror. Hating what I saw was becoming unbearable, and I wished I could die. Thoughts that I was crazy, retarded, a bastard—all the things Mother had called me all too many times—were now believable. I was now as insane as she was, and how I hated it.

As the days passed, I slipped farther. I tried to be as normal as possible and fit in with everyone else. I knew

I was screwed up, but I couldn't tell anyone or I'd be sent to the loony bin for sure. A week passed with no sign of my returning to reality. I started skipping classes at school. On one of those days I was riding around Copper Cliff on my shiny green supercycle ten-speed that Mother had bought me in the spring. I got the idea of riding into Sudbury and not coming back. Now riding our bikes into the city was forbidden by most parents. Riding into Sudbury meant riding along the highway for a couple of miles, then through all the city traffic. Today I didn't care, and as I started out I was only worried about someone spotting me and informing Mother.

I was just a lost soul in this world, trying to survive a life sentence in hell. Seeing people laughing and smiling made me even more depressed. It was near suppertime, and I wasn't going home now or ever. What would I do? I could go and bike to some faraway place like Ottawa, which I knew I liked. I decided to just hang around downtown for that night. I bought some fast food and ate hungrily. Then I walked around the city awhile in a trance-like daze.

Since that battle with Mother I couldn't seem to regain my usual composure. It was like something had permanently snapped, and I was now distant from my surroundings. Wishes that I were loved by a nice mother crossed my mind constantly, while thoughts of my sexual confusion drove me deeper into disillusionment with reality. Physically I was male, but my emotions were in constant flux between the two. Believing I was crazy only made everything worse.

Making my way back downtown I rode my bike back up to the parking garage that overlooked Elm

Street. I stared out into the ever-darkening skies and prayed for someone to save me from this life. I thought of home and what they would be thinking since I didn't come home for supper. Tears were rolling down my face at the thought of my beautiful little sister. How I loved her and wished she wouldn't be growing up in our crazy family!

It was dark now as I stared disheartened at the people and cars as they went by. Why did all this happen to me during this unusual life? Why? Why? Feeling sorry for myself, I started crying. As more time passed I started wondering where I could spend the night. It was fall and the weather was quite warm, so I knew if I stayed outside I wouldn't be too cold.

Time passed and the mall closed. The streets were empty as most everyone had gone home, and I wished that I had a nice, loving family to be with. I heard some footsteps in the dark and worried that it was the police or someone looking for me. I was a little paranoid. The footsteps came closer, and I made out a figure in the dark. An older man came over and said, "Hi." I returned the greeting.

He asked what I was doing, and I said I was watching cars. He told me his name was Pierre, and I told him mine. When he asked my age, I lied and told him I was sixteen, knowing that because I was almost fifteen I could get in trouble. Pierre told me that he liked cars and owned a racing car. My curiosity was piqued, and I told him that I tried to watch as many auto races on television as possible. I asked him what kind of car he owned and was told it was a stock car. Pierre said that he was from out of town and his car was on a train that would be arriving in the city soon. He asked if I would like to see it, and I excitedly agreed.

Pierre said that we would walk over to the train station to check the train schedule and to make sure the train with his car onboard would arrive on time. On the way to the station (which was only a five-minute walk) we talked about cars. At the train station he asked me to wait outside while he went in and checked the schedules. A couple of minutes later he returned and told me that the train would be delayed and that we would have to check back later. He decided that we could walk around awhile to pass time. He asked me what time I had to be home, and I replied that it didn't matter.

A while later we checked back at the train station, and again Pierre said the train wouldn't be in for still a couple of hours. He then asked if I would like to wait with him in his hotel room. I said that I would. We walked back to the parking garage, retrieved my bike, and then walked the block to his hotel. Pierre told the man at the desk that he was my uncle.

This place was a dump to say the least. We walked up a flight of stairs and then down a hall. Pierre unlocked the door and we went inside. I looked around the dingy room, filled with antiquated furnishings, a couple of beds, chairs and an old mirrored dressing table. A window covered with dirty curtains overlooked the street. I saw my shiny green ten-speed locked to a pole. He asked if I was thirsty, and I was. He asked if I like rum. Trying to act grown up, I said, "Yes." Really I had never drank before, outside of a few sips of beer. He mixed us each a drink of rum and Coke and handed me mine. I drank a couple of mouthfuls, and it wasn't too bad.

Feeling nervous being in a stranger's room, I stood fidgeting at the window. Pierre told me I was a nice boy, which relaxed me. I had never heard those words before, and they made me feel a bit better. It was tragic how good those words from a complete stranger made me feel. I drank up the rest of my drink hastily. I didn't know I wasn't supposed to drink so fast. Pierre mixed me another and handed it to me.

He talked about cars, and I listened with keen interest. I started feeling a little light-headed and more relaxed. "So this," I thought, "is what booze does to you?" As I drank more I became even more relaxed as I conversed with Pierre. During the past couple of weeks I had not mentally relaxed once, and it felt nice. I drank more and kept feeling better. "This stuff could cure a lot," I thought. Pierre told me he liked me, which made me feel good. No one in my family or any other adult had ever said they liked me. Mother had told me she loved me a few times in the presence of others, but I knew otherwise.

Still standing by the window staring into the night, I felt a hand on my shoulder and turned to look into this stranger's face. He gave me a hug and again told me that I was a nice boy. Taking my glass he refilled my drink and proffered it to me and asked if I wanted to smoke hash. I replied that I had never taken drugs before and I thought I shouldn't start.

Pierre then held me in his arms and kissed me and again told me I was a nice boy. Not knowing this was wrong, I let him keep kissing me. I had always dreamt of someone liking me enough to show and tell me I was okay. We sat down on the bed beside each other, and I finished my third drink.

It sure was nice to have someone like me. Pierre kissed me again, but this time I kissed him back. Pierre told me he wanted to make me feel good. He fixed me up another drink, sat down and began fondling me sexually. It felt good, so I let him continue. No one had ever told me about sex, and I had never had any sexual contact with anyone. I didn't even know it existed. He kept fondling and kissing me. He asked me to touch him too because I would make him feel good too. It felt like nothing before—here was a perfect stranger seemingly liking me and showing me affection for the first time in my life. The alcohol was having more of an effect on me than I understood.

I told Pierre I had never felt loved before and that I wanted to stay with him so I would never have to go home again. I told him I liked him, and he said he would take care of me. I shudder now at the thought of how many others have run away out of desperate loneliness and had their first ever experience of affection this way.

Time passed, and we passed out in each other's arms. I awoke the next morning to find him touching me again. It felt nice being loved. I didn't know at the time that I would over the next several years equate sex with love because of knowing nothing else.

Later Pierre said he would take me out for breakfast. I felt a little sick from the drinking I'd done the night before. During the course of breakfast I started feeling strange in the presence of this man. I sensed that something about the night before wasn't right, but I didn't know what. No one had ever explained the birds and the bees to me.

Finishing breakfast I told him I had to go home for a while and I would meet him later. Pierre gave me some money—less than $10. I then said goodbye. I didn't know what a prostitute was, but at the time, I had just got paid for last night's sexual encounter. Walking up the street, I felt humiliated and hatred for him.

"Are there no nice people in the world?" I wondered as I walked back to the hotel. I was now more confused than ever. I had already been in a confused state of mind and then this happens. Already I had begun to distrust everyone around me. At the hotel I unlocked my bike and rode back to the parking garage, descended the stairs and went into the mall. My head was aching from my first hangover, and my sense of perception was distorted.

Shame kicked in. I was confused about myself and hated what had happened to me the night before. How could I be so desperately lonely for affection to let what happened last evening happen? What would I do now? Where would I go? I felt so alone in this world among so many. All my life I had felt alone, and I craved attention.

Time passed, and I found myself walking up and down the streets of Sudbury, emotionally lost. As I walked, I passed Pierre and didn't even acknowledge his presence. I was horrified that in my drunk and lonely state of mind, I had told this man I wanted him to love me and take care of me forever. I knew I had been a fool.

I didn't know and had never even heard about homosexuality before, but instinctively I knew I had done something that was an abnormal part of human behaviour. What should I do? Where should I go? When I had run away before and returned home, Mother was always so nice to me, partially because everyone would be looking for me and she had to show motherly concern about missing me. I stayed downtown for a couple of hours and then decided to go home again. Small cities are not places you can run away from.

Cities like Toronto, on the other hand, are ideal for runaways, and teenagers from smaller cities usually descend upon larger cities only to find hundreds like themselves, which makes it easier to adapt. If I had known of such places I am sure I would have gone to Toronto myself. Why I was going home was something I never understood.

I walked back up to the parking garage, unlocked my bike and made my way down the ramp and onto the busy street. I carefully made my way out of the downtown core and along the streets that would take me to the highway that led to Copper Cliff and my "loving family."

Fifteen minutes later I was riding along the highway and only minutes away from home. I decided to pull off the highway and walk my bike through the fields along the roadway. I wanted to sneak a look at our house before I rode into town. Our house was one of the first houses you could see as you made your way off the highway. The banks of the tracks that supported a bridge made a natural fortress for me to spy from. From my viewing area I could see some of my family and neighbours conversing in the backyard. They were probably talking about me. Like a fugitive, I made my way back down the banks of the railway tracks and hid, lying down behind a sand hill so as to prevent anyone on the highway from seeing me. I was hungry but had no food. I had money, but the store was ten minutes away if I walked. Since everyone knew me, I would be seen, so that was out of the question. Lying on the hardened ground I looked up into the sky above and drifted off into fantasy land again.

As usual all kinds of horrific thoughts crossed my mind. I was a lonely boy and needed love. I was now confused more than ever about myself psychosexually. Day-to-day life was a struggle that I tried as best I could to hide from everyone. How I wished I could be normal, but I now knew that wouldn't be the case. How could anyone be normal after living through the things I had lived through?

As I lay there contemplating life, time passed. Soon the whistle resounded through the skies and I knew it was 4 o'clock. Deciding now was as good a time as any, I made my way down to my bike, picked it up and made my way to the highway. Gathering up some inner strength, I got on my bike and made my way home. Still not understanding why I always returned home, I rode up to our yard. My heart was beating against my chest with intensity.

One of my brothers yelled, "Randy's home!" and everyone came outside. Mother and Dad asked if I was okay. Mother made a fuss over me, which I could have killed her for. I wished I had the guts to tell her to get her sick hands off me. Mother fed me well, and then they talked with me. I told them I had spent the night in downtown Sudbury and had earned some money helping someone fix their car. I showed them the money I had earned. Mother said she was proud of me for earning money while I was away.

At that instant I became filled with intense anger and hatred. I wanted to reach out and strangle her but refrained from doing so. If only she knew what I had done to receive that money. Look what she had done to me, an innocent child! She had driven me away from home in a mentally ill frame of mind. After all the problems I had had within myself about wanting to be a girl to receive Mother's love, what could have been worse than having sex with some sexual deviate? This just filled me with more hatred towards Mother and myself.

What was worse was harbouring all those intense feelings of hatred within myself and suppressing all the horrific things that had happened to me. I knew I was as emotionally ill as my mother was, but I kept struggling secretly to keep a tight reign on my sanity. Seeing I had finished eating, Mother told me to go to my room because I had worried everyone. That room. How I loathed being in that room for so many hours on end! All that time spent alone only made matters worse for me because I had so much time to think.

The next few days were very emotional for me. At home and at school I had become totally antisocial, more so than ever before. Visions of violence were increasingly at the forefront of my mind.

School had ended for the day, and most of the students were outside in the park in front of the high school. There was a football game just starting against a rival school. I was sitting on the sidelines, my shiny green ten-speed beside me. The game was being videotaped by Joey, a visual arts student. As I watched the football game I realized it was almost 4 o'clock and that I would have to rush home momentarily.

I was becoming full of anger at the thought of not being like others. I couldn't play football; not only that—I couldn't even stay to watch the game. I rose to go home and picked up my bike, which was lying on the grass. Someone made a comment about me that I didn't like. That comment, coupled with how I felt, just let the anger boil over. I started yelling and cursing at everybody. All eyes turned to me; even the football game stopped. I was losing control in front of everyone, including some teachers. In a violent rage I turned to face my bike, which I was holding, and started kicking it apart. Mother had bought me this bike, and I was now destroying it in some kind of symbolic gesture. I picked the bike up and threw it to the ground, wishing it was her.

I had had enough of this world. Not even realizing what was happening, I was now lost in my private world of turmoil. I started jumping up and down on the wheels, breaking every spoke and bending the wheel rims. Yelling and swearing at the world, I continued in psychotic madness. Finally I stopped, picked up my bike, walked the short distance to a creek running parallel to the football field and threw it in.

Turning and facing everyone, I noticed the camera trained on my actions. Instantly I realized I had been videotaped, and now I knew I had to destroy the camera. Running while yelling and cursing insanely, I made my way across the field towards the camera, set on a tripod. When others saw what I was about to do, they made like a football team and rushed and tackled me, then held me on the ground. In my madness I hadn't been aware of my actions, but now as I lay there pinned down I started to realize what I had done. This was now the second time in almost as many weeks that I had flipped out.

Everyone was telling me to calm down and to go into the school. I started to relax a little; then I started crying my fool little head off. In the office I begged them not to call Mother but was told they had no choice in the matter.

Within minutes Mom was at the school. Being so very two-faced she listened and showed much concern about my behaviour. Mom told them what she had to put up with daily and could now truthfully substantiate her claims of my craziness.

During the course of supper Mother told Dad about how I had flipped out and destroyed my bike. I was then told I would learn my lesson by earning money to have my bike repaired. I thought that was fair enough, Mother had finally made a proper decision, and I wouldn't be receiving my usual beating, which surprised me. Finishing supper I helped with the dishes, which was expected of me. Then it was back to the solitary confinement of my room to spend the rest of the evening.

The thought of having to face all the teachers and students who had witnessed my behaviour made me cringe. What about that videotape? I had never witnessed anything, except for Mother, as bizarre as what I had done, and I was sure none of the witnesses had seen the like either. They had a first-hand look at a terribly lonely and emotionally disturbed young boy. How could I face them? How? I spent the evening in my usual mental misery.

Waking in the morning and getting ready for school was an emotional struggle, but as always I found courage from deep within to fight on through another day. Meeting some acquaintances on the way, I walked with them, but I didn't really fit in with anyone or any group any more. I was becoming quite the loner. I noticed that people were talking about me and looking at me funny, like I was some kind of weirdo. I went to my class and sat at my desk. The room was unusually quiet. Everyone must have heard about my rage.

As I made my way to my second class, someone said, "Here comes the movie star." People were telling me they had watched the video of me on television in the audiovisual room. I was being laughed at, which fuelled the anger in me. I refrained from letting the temper that I was developing explode. How could people be so cruel? They had no understanding of why I had exploded into rage. Even I didn't really understand fully why I was becoming as violent as Mother was.

As the day went by, all I heard about was my meteoric rise of fame, infamous at that. Everyone in school knew of my violent actions. I felt quite alienated and wished I didn't ever have to face these people again. The rest of the day was spent listening to the gossip about myself. I was very angry at the whole world and especially at the people I had thought to be my friends.

Rumour had it later that day that the principal had ordered the copy of the tape destroyed.

The harm had already been done though. As I left to go home I was filled with feelings about myself that I had never felt before. My imagination was running amok, and fears of becoming crazy and retarded were now fact as far as I was concerned.

Over the next couple of weeks my nightmares about the devil persisted. School was the pits, and I struggled more than ever with confusion about males. Since that emotional outburst I had become more of a loner, and some of my friends, including girls, wanted nothing to do with me. I mean, what kid in her right mind would want to associate with a crazy person? I rode around for a bit and then went home. Why? I'll never know.

Winter came, and I began to drink a lot. Ever since my first encounter with alcohol on that sickening night spent with Pierre in his hotel room, I had wanted to drink again. Drinking relaxed me a little around Mother, and I could sleep better if I took a couple of swigs before bed. Alcohol was helping me to cope with this sad life I lived.

When, after I got incredibly drunk at a school dance one evening, Mother did nothing to punish me, I was left more confused than ever. I didn't know whether she had stopped beating me out of fear of my retaliation or if she was holding back for some bigger punishment. In my own way, then, I began punishing myself.

As the next couple of weeks went by, my drinking sessions became more frequent and also more enjoyable. I was learning about my drinking capacity, and as I did, drinking began to take on a new dimension. I learned that if I drank a few quick drinks and then only a couple of mouthfuls every hour or so, I could stay under the influence indefinitely and in a state of relaxation.

Even at school my drinking went unnoticed. I was in the habit of stashing bootleg liquor along the way to school and then getting moderately drunk. As well, to support my ever-growing habit, I would supply people with deeply discounted stolen goods. With the money I would get a school bootlegger to buy me my alcoholic beverages. Alcohol was my one and only friend, and the love affair between us was wonderful. After fifteen years of loneliness, I had a true friend, a friend whom I could talk to openly and who would listen contentedly; a friend much like me, who just wanted, like me, to be loved. As the weeks passed I started to fall in love with my friend, who was always there when I needed it.

Mother, with all kinds of proof of my craziness, decided to send me for night group sessions at the Sudbury Algoma Sanatorium. How I hated her for this, as at the time I thought she should have been the one going. I surely couldn't admit to what had gone on during my life. What I did get out of it was a friend who introduced me to doing break and enters. Thanks, Mother!

My first B and E was very exciting. I loved the rush I got from always having to be on my guard in a very different way than anticipating Mother's beatings. I could now get money easily.

# Chapter 7

It was the spring of 1974, and things at home between Mother and Dad were becoming hostile. I couldn't believe the torment Dad had also endured over the years and had always wondered what kept him from divorcing Mother. Lately, he had been sleeping on the couch with the coffee table pulled against the couch while he slept. Dad was terrified that Mother might stab him during his sleep.

After a particularly bizarre fight in which Mother threw a video projector at him, Dad grabbed his things, yelled "You're crazy! You're crazy!" and left. I went up to my room and bawled my eyes out. The whole world around me was being blown to pieces, and I wished I could just jump off. When would this craziness end? I was so emotionally distraught from all this abuse. I'm sure the rest of the family was suffering as well, although luckily to a lesser extent. They had never been beaten, but I knew emotional abuse was far worse than any physical abuse. I even felt badly for Mother. Why she kept perpetuating her own misery was beyond anything I could reason at the time.

During the next couple of days, we missed Dad, and I hated having to live at home with Mother. After about a week of not seeing Dad, it started to become apparent that he might not be coming back. Dad had given Mother money to buy us groceries and necessities. He had never taken out his anger on us.

His work was only a five-minute walk from home. We waited impatiently at the edge of the plant's entrance for him. My heart sped up somewhat, and when Dad saw us his face lit up in happiness. We greeted him and told him we missed him and that we hoped he would come home soon. At that statement his smile left his face. He told us that he wasn't coming home. Dad said for now he was going to stay at our grandmother's.

Nana was the nicest lady you would ever want to meet. She was always making things for us and sending us little presents. She was now sharing a house with one of my girlfriends' grandfather, who was just as nice. If nothing else, I knew at least Dad would be in the company of two very nice people. He gave us a bit of money so that we could buy ourselves something and then said we should get back home before Mother started wondering where we might have gone. We gave Dad a hug and then tearfully went home.

As I walked home I felt a great urge to kill Mother so that we could live without her. I knew that if she were dead our family would be happier together. She was what caused us to be unhappy and afraid. Something would have to be done about her, something so drastic that we would be rid of her for life. I couldn't tell anyone about her because she now had enough on me to have everyone think I was making up stories.

A few heartbroken weeks passed, and school ended for the summer. During the past year I had flunked grade nine English and math but was going to have a chance to do math during July. Also I had been told I couldn't return to this school in the fall, so I would in September be attending Sudbury Secondary School in downtown Sudbury. I did manage to pass my math though.

At the same time, I was introduced to smoking marijuana, and I loved the feeling of being high as much if not more than drinking. Our family wouldn't be going to the cottage this summer because of the marital breakup. I spent the summer becoming a break-and-enter artist, breaking into many homes in Copper Cliff and Sudbury. I usually took all the booze and money that was about. My new drug habit was an added expense that I couldn't afford otherwise.

With Dad gone, Mother had been out more often, waitressing and out with her friends, which meant I was babysitting for her a lot. For the first time in my life, I enjoyed some freedom while at home. I could actually watch TV and not sit in that Indian position. I could raid the fridge, and best of all I could drink without getting caught. I started spending a lot of time with Vickey, who was now three. I loved her very much and loved taking care of her and giving her the love and understanding that she needed.

I had more time alone, especially after the rest of my siblings were asleep. During this time I would drink to forget who I was. I used this time to fantasize about being a girl and would go into Mother's room and play out my female role. I was always worried about being caught, but the urge to cross-dress was becoming an obsession and I was willing to take the chance. Once dressed up and made up, I would look into the mirror and see a person Mother would love.

More than that, I didn't have to be the person who did nothing but cause trouble all his life. I believed I was the one to blame for Mom and Dad's breakup, and I hated myself. I would walk around Mother's room for a few minutes, and I thought I looked pretty good as a girl. These stolen moments as a female seemed very fulfilling to me. I knew, though, that it was abnormal to harbour and bring to life my fantasies. After about seven years of feeling the way I did, I was really psychologically living two separate lives, one as an emotionally disturbed male and the other as a happy young female. The real problem was that the female personality of mine was at peace with herself because she did not have to face life's tragedies. I hated when I undressed and saw that girl disappear before me, as she was such a nice person, unlike myself. How I wished I were her.

I would leave Mother's room and close the door behind me. I didn't like leaving me behind. Being so confused was very difficult, and living this dual life was also creating problems with how I thought of people. There was no way I could tell anyone about my true feelings because I would be sent to an asylum. Look what Mother had already done back in the spring when she had me attending sessions at the sanatorium! How I wish now that I had told them everything then instead of perpetuating my inherited misery. But what would have become of Mother?

# Chapter 8

Summer passed, and then I started grade ten at Sudbury Secondary School. I was just a face in the crowd as there were about 2,000 students in attendance. I met a lot of new people, and a lot of them were into drugs and booze as well, so I fit right in. School was a bore as I was always preoccupied with my thoughts. I still had no real conception as to how abnormal my behaviour really was. My drinking was becoming worse. I would do almost anything to get money to support my habits, which meant stealing, lying and cheating people.

As far as stealing went, I was shoplifting on a professional basis. My steal-to-order business was booming. I was becoming a very proficient thief, until I got caught shoplifting at the City Centre Mall, in the Bonimart department store. A female store detective caught me lifting a travel alarm clock. I was taken to an office, and the police were informed. I had never been in trouble with the law before and didn't know what to expect. I was still fifteen, so I knew I wouldn't be going to jail. I was more worried about Mother finding out. The police came, the information was taken, and then

Mother was called. Since she couldn't pick me up I was driven home by the cops.

My first ride in a cop car was frightening and sure made me think. I stared out the window and wondered how severely I would be beaten for my crime. I should have asked them to lock me up. I was frightened to say the least as we pulled into our driveway. The police officer got out and opened the back to let me out. Sure enough, Mother was waiting right at the door for us, and when I walked through the doorway ahead of the police officer, she told me to sit down and wait until the officer left. They spoke for a few moments, and then the policeman left. As he did I became utterly terrified of being left alone with Mother.

Trembling throughout and with Mother standing by my side, I waited nervously for what was to come next. Mother said, "Go to your room and I will deal with you later." As with the video episode, she did not beat me.

Something was always strange about how Mother handled my punishment whenever I got in real trouble. It seemed that whatever trouble I got myself into in front of other people, I was not reprimanded in any way. In fact, in the past year I had not been beaten any more, but that wasn't to say I was suffering any less.

Regarding the shoplifting, I went to juvenile court some weeks later and was given a lecture and told not to go back into the Bonimart department store. That time faded into the first Christmas without Dad around. It was depressing, and the only joy I had was from my sister, Vickey.

By the time I turned sixteen, I was so caught up in the world of drinking, stealing and smoking up that I was constantly in a daze. One day while skipping school, I was caught in Bonimart, the same store where I'd previously been caught shoplifting. Because I had been banned from the store, I was told I was going to be charged with trespassing. Again the police came, and since I was now sixteen, I was taken for pictures and prints and then given a summons to appear in provincial court as an adult. As I left the police station I pitched the summons into the wind.

I was going crazy inside and hated everyone and everything, including myself. I didn't know what kind of demons I was fighting against, but I was continually losing. I walked up the street and into another store and was again shoplifting without a care in the world of being caught. I didn't know what was happening to me, but I would steal anything, as if I were trying to get back at someone—namely, Mother.

She never found out about the charges. Dad got me a lawyer. I made my court appearance and was put on probation for a period of time. I was taken to sign some papers and than released and told to keep the peace and be of good behaviour.

I felt a surge of hatred towards the whole world as I left the courthouse. I vowed revenge upon everyone as I walked the few blocks down Elm Street to the City Centre Mall. Outside the mall I met up with a couple of acquaintances who lived in a boys' home on Bancroft Drive. I told them how mad I was and that something had to be done about this. We talked a bit and then I decided that I would phone the cop shop and tell them that there was a bomb in the mall.

First, though, we would create a diversion. I had

learned to make match bombs that would explode into flames. The three of us walked into the mall, and we bought hundreds of matches and some aluminum foil. We then went up to the parking garage to make the first bomb. Back in the mall, I dropped the fist-sized match bomb into a lidded garbage can, placed paper on top and then lit the paper on fire. Soon a flash fire would ignite and create a commotion. I was mad as hell as I walked away to find a phone.

Outside, I went to a pay phone outside a pool hall. I looked up the phone number, dropped a dime in the slot and dialled. I thought that the person who answered the phone would surely get an earful. I said I had planted a bomb in the City Centre by Food City in a garbage can. I was insanely mad as I continued talking and then hung up. My heart was thumping and the adrenaline pumping, and I was extremely excited. What a rush! I couldn't believe I had done it, and I just had to go back into the mall to watch what would happen.

My two acquaintances rejoined me, and I told them what I had done. We hurried through the mall and climbed the stairs up to a walkway that went around the second floor, which contained offices. From this vantage point I could see everything. We could already see people going through the garbage containers throughout the mall. There were police, mall security and plainclothes people checking everywhere. Looking into the storefront of the grocery store, I could see that my match bomb had caught fire, as whiffs of smoke were rising out of the garbage container.

What was amusing was that two elderly gentlemen were standing beside the can and didn't even notice that there was a fire inside.

I was really getting bothered that nobody was taking notice of my fire. I decided to phone the police back and tell them where to find what they were looking for. Back at the same phone as before I redialed the number and told them that they were looking in the wrong place. After hanging up I walked back to my vantage point. My acquaintances had left and as I peered about cops were everywhere.

A couple of minutes went by, and then I noticed a couple of men walking towards me. My sixth sense informed me they were most likely plainclothes cops. I started to run, but it was no use. They caught me before I had a chance to get very far. I was informed that my two acquaintances had told them that I was the one who phoned in the bomb threats. I was questioned, charged and had my picture and prints taken. Again I was given a summons and released. When I showed up in court sometime later I was given a suspended sentence for a period of some time. Provided I stayed out of trouble during that time, the charges would be dismissed.

Life with Mother was growing all the more unbearable. Added to that, my own behaviour further complicated everything. I had to leave. In a minute I was at Dad's. He told me I would have to sleep in his room and offered to share his bed with me. As he said that I became very self-conscious at the thought of being in bed with another man, which brought me back in time. "Dad, I'll sleep on the floor, okay?"

Silently I lay there so as to not wake up Dad. Finally I slumbered off into a not so tranquil sleep and spent the night tossing and turning. Awakening to the light and hopefully a new life, I sat up. Dad had slipped out quietly that morning as his bed was empty. Unlike after some of my drinking sessions, the mornings after smoking dope didn't leave me with a hangover. Now that was very much appreciated. Lying back down, I thought of what I might do today, the first day of the rest of my life. I vowed to myself that I would make something of myself someday, somewhere, somehow! Yes! Yes, I would.

Donning my clothes, coat and shoes, I then combed my hair, opened the bedroom door and peeked out to see if the elderly lady was up. Dad was not at his mother's anymore. Not hearing anything, I made my way downstairs. Outside in the cool morning air I did up my coat and put my hands into my pockets to get a joint. I needed an early morning high. I loved the aroma of marijuana, and in minutes I was high again. Now my thirst and craving for my friend was becoming insatiable. I thumbed my way into Sudbury and smoked a joint in the mall parking garage.

The morning had worn thin, and it was near noon. Leaving the garage and walking to the street, I made my way through the crowds of shoppers, just wandering about. I walked through an open door and walked down a flight of rickety stairs and into the local pool hall, where all of us No Goods hung out. Being still quite new to the downtown scene, I found myself watching unknown people playing pool and eating junk food. Some faces were familiar, and I knew them as drug pushers.

I stopped at the liquor store and, although I was only sixteen, was able to buy some booze. Sitting in the stairwell on the cold concrete steps, I could have a real drink, one that my innards were craving for. Taking a drink of this potent liquid and swallowing hard took away some of the craving. How good this tasted as I took drink after drink.

I was only one of thousands. Feeling mildly drunk, I put the top back on my bottle and stuffed it in the waistband of my pants and decided I was hungry and needed some junk. Down the stairs I walked and then into the mall and through the small crowds of milling shoppers, browsers and people like myself—"stoners." I felt good and proud walking through the main walkway with booze and drugs on me. Stopping at a newsstand I lifted a couple of chocolate bars. It was still early afternoon, so I decided to go back to the pool hall.

Later that day, after getting stoned with a new friend, I headed out to find Dad. He had phoned Doug, my older stepbrother, and was told I could stay there for a while. Dad said we would stop by Mother's so I could pick up my clothes and things. I sat back as Dad got into the car and we drove to the other end of town.

The five o'clock whistle blew. Thank God I wouldn't have to put up with those whistles any more! I would just have to face Mother today for the last time. The booze and pot had filled me with false courage. I thought that if she gave me a hard time about leaving today I would beat her up.

I was still a little nervous as Dad parked in the driveway. "Just get what you need for now," he told me. Getting out of the car I walked up to the door and knocked. Now talk about bizarre, here I was at my own home knocking. I felt like I should ask if one of my brothers could come out to play. When one of my brothers answered the door, I told him I was just here to pick up my clothes. He looked shocked. I walked past Mother and a couple of my brothers. As I solemnly walked to the stairs I saw my beautiful young sister, Vickey. That little gem of a girl was the nicest thing that had ever happened to me.

Upstairs in my room, I packed some clothes while thoughts of not seeing Vickey bothered me. Tears came to my eyes. Hurriedly I threw my clothes and a few personal items together. Downstairs at the door I gave Vickey a loving hug and told her I loved her and would miss her. She was only four years old, and I knew she didn't understand what was really going on as the family around her was falling apart. First Dad and then me. But I knew I couldn't stay there any more, so I left, in tears.

Dad was waiting with the car running. Tossing my stuff in the back seat, I got in the front. We backed out of the driveway and were on our way. *I sure could use a drink*, I thought. I wondered what everyone at home might be thinking. I figured surely Mother would be thankful to be rid of the cause of all our family's destruction. My only concern was that she might start with one of the others. I was now rid of all that physical and mental cruelty that I had endured for as long as I could remember. In fact I knew of nothing else. Now I was as free as a bird! All I was sure of now was that a great and fulfilling life was ahead of me, free of being Mother's slave and punching bag. Nothing now could be as hard as what happened in the past.

# Chapter 9

I was glad to see Doug and his wife, Marg. Marg was expecting in the next month or so and thus was pleasantly rounded. They had been married about three years now and made a nice couple. In some ways, it was awkward. I didn't know him very well but always felt comfortable around him because he knew what I had put up with, as he had endured much of the same. As well, they were allowing me to stay with them awhile and that was very loving of them.

Dad stayed for a while. Doug showed me my room. Wow! For the first time I had my own room and went about tidying up things to my liking. *I could sure use a drink*, I thought again, as the booze had by now worn off. I had also come down from my high. Dad said he was leaving and gave me a small amount of money. I walked out of the car with him. He told me to take care of myself and to go to school. I replied that I would. At that Dad got in the big Dodge station wagon and left.

Later that night, flicking off the lamp beside me, I lay staring into the darkness, thinking about finally being free of Mother's wrath and insanity. I could now live as I was supposed to. After what seemed like hours

I dosed off and dreamed about the great things that would happen now, since I could finally be me.

I spent my first day "free" scoring dope and messing around town doing drug deals and stealing things. What a day I'd had, and I had nothing to worry about for the first time in my life! It was the beginning of a new era in my life. No school or curfew, and now that I was away from Copper Cliff, no more of those haunting whistles that went off like clockwork. Best of all, no more Mother. Life was finally taking a turn for the better. How many nights of lost sleep had I had over the years, dreaming of being old enough to leave home and be free? Now those dreams would be realized.

Over the next few days, I started to live it up. I didn't go to school except to sell drugs. All of a sudden, like never before, I had lots of "friends." Being young, I was blind to the fact that to them I was nothing but a source of dope. I felt important, so I didn't care. I was becoming quite a salesperson and was selling the stuff as fast as I could get it. Being downtown every day was teaching me the way of the streets. I was learning about all the different drugs and was now experimenting. Uppers to get you flying, downers to bring you down.

One day I tried something called chocolate mescaline, which cost about five bucks a "hit." I believe you could snort it, but I just swallowed the hit. Mescaline is a chocolate-coloured powder. Later I couldn't believe how high I was flying on this stuff. Man, was I "rushing." Along with the booze I drank and the pot I smoked, I stayed high for hours. If I was coming down, I would just smoke a joint of grass.

Man! This was the life. After all those depressing years at home, being high all the time and free to be me and to do as I pleased was ecstasy. Even though this was the most harmful way of inducing happiness, I couldn't understand how wrong it was, as I was now becoming an addict. With this dealing drugs, having money, and being happy, I started dreaming of getting more involved in this scene and becoming a big-time drug pusher.

Doug and Marg were under the impression that I was going to school and behaving. Little did they know. There was going to be a rock concert the following weekend, and as luck would have it, my stepbrother and his wife were going away on the weekend to visit relatives. I couldn't wait until next weekend! I would be on my own with my "own" place. I had never been allowed to attend a rock concert before, and I was excited.

One day at Doug's, I was wanting to get high, and I had noticed Marg was taking these red capsules for some reason. I surmised it was for her pregnancy. Out of curiosity, I cut one of the non-prescription capsules, and lo and behold, the stuff inside looked the same as the mescaline that was going around downtown.

Ding, ding, ding, bells were ringing in my head. I would pull off a drug rip-off at the concert. Although I had never been to one, I assumed everyone at the concert would be high on something, and if they dropped a hit of this stuff, they wouldn't know if it was bad or good. Well, the next week went by slowly. I was impatiently waiting to be able to earn some big money so I could finance my growing drug business. I had written the name of the stuff Marg was taking, and on the Friday before the concert I went into a drugstore to purchase the capsules. Since it wasn't a prescription, I asked the pharmacist on which shelf would I find these capsules. The aisle was pointed out to me. Finding what I wanted, I purchased two bottles. As I paid about $10 or $15 for them, I was thinking of the money I would have on this weekend if everything went well. At five bucks a hit, I could have upwards of $500 for a night's work. My only concern was that if I was found out to be selling junk, I could get my head smashed in—or even worse. I figured I would take the chance.

Saturday morning came, and Doug and Marg left. Moments after their departure, I began my task, taking care of important matters first, which meant grabbing a cold brewsky and doing a bit of devil's weed. Now that I had normalized my body and brain, I could get to work.

From my bedroom I took the capsules, from the kitchen a roll of aluminum foil, and finally, from the bathroom, a razor blade. What I had to do was cut a square of foil along with one of the red capsules. Then pouring the contents of the pill onto the aluminum foil, I would then have to fold the foil into as neat a square as possible.

First I cut about 100 uniform squares of foil. Finishing just that took over an hour. Music from the radio kept me company.

Now I was hungry and was craving my friend. Getting up from the kitchen table, I went through the cupboards looking for liquor, as beer was like water to me. As my stepbrother and his wife weren't the biggest of drinkers, there wasn't any alcohol to be found. Man, I was gasping for some real booze, not some lousy beer. The cogs of my mind were turning, maybe somewhat out of sync but turning just the same. Yes, the guy who lived downstairs—his car wasn't in the driveway this morning. He lived alone and must be gone for the weekend. I would just pull a break and enter.

Donning my shoes and coat, I went outside and cased the place by walking around it to make sure I wouldn't get caught. Figuring the coast was clear, I got a screwdriver from the house. It was easier than I thought to jimmy the door. Opening it slowly, I peered inside. As on other B and Es that I was involved in, my heart was beating fast and I was perspiring. In all, it was quite thrilling doing these criminal activities. Just the thought that you could get caught was a rush. The fact that I was still high from toking earlier only heightened the stimulation.

This was a smaller place than upstairs, and the guy who lived here needed the assistance of a maid service, as everything was in disarray. Into the kitchen I went, and after opening a cupboard or two, I found my friend in a twenty-six-ounce bottle. I took a cup and poured a few ounces of liquor into it. After thirstily taking a couple of swallows, straight up from the bottle, I refilled the bottle with water to the level at which it was in the first place. Placing it back in its spot, I closed the cupboard.

Out of curiosity, I decided to rummage through the place and see if there was anything I could steal that would not be missed. No one was to know anyone had broken in. Finding a couple of small items, I pocketed them. Back in the kitchen, I took the cup of booze and left as stealthily as I had come. Back in my place, I took some pop from the fridge and mixed up a stiff drink. Oh what a feeling, as I swallowed a mouthful of this spirit from a bottle. This stuff was medicine to my sick and sorrowful soul.

Now came the longest part of the day, passing the next couple of hours or so until it was time to head downtown to the Sudbury arena. It did start me to wishing that this place was truly my own place. Even though I was enjoying my liberty, Mother was still hauntingly on my mind. All I had to do was think of her and she in all her madness would be forefront on my mind. I knew I was screwed-up in the head, but it wasn't all my fault, was it? I just wanted to forget every-thing, and as I pushed horrific memories into the recesses of my mind, I would have to cover them up. So I had started abusing drugs and alcohol to blot out these thoughts. When I was high on most occasions, at least my mind would be on a better track.

I showered and picked out and ironed the clothes I would wear to the concert. I wanted to look my coolest, like a big-shot drug dealer. Once dressed, I put all the drugs in various parts of my clothing: some in my socks, more in the lining of my coat, which I had pulled apart purposely for this occasion. In a few min-utes, I was picked up and was now on my way to my first rock concert and to making big bucks.

Hundreds of people were already gathered and waiting to be let inside. I wasn't going to chance selling drugs outside as I heard there were narcotics officers milling about. Seeing people and familiar faces in the crowd, I let out the word that I would be selling some dynamite weed and some mind-bending mescaline. The word spread through the gathering crowd, and by the time the doors opened, I had verbal orders for about half my supply. In dollars, that meant about $300. This was totally awesome, and I guess you can see now why I was soon to be caught up in the drug business—the business of helping people destroy themselves.

Once inside, I was getting somewhat paranoid, because of the brisk business I was doing. Customer after customer! My pockets were filling up with cash, after I had served the multitude of teenagers and drug addicts who were just looking for a quick high so to be able to trip out. I went for a walk with a trusted acquaintance and asked him to hold my cash for me in case I got busted. I surely didn't want to get caught and lose everything. I wanted to sell all this phony dope and grass as soon as possible. I wanted to get high and enjoy the concert as much as anyone.

As the lights went out, the cheer went up in antici-pation of the warm-up band coming onstage. I was excited at being able to watch a live rock concert. Back to business. I went through the crowds and soon was sold out of joints except for a couple dozen I kept for myself and my acquaintances. I surely hadn't expected to sell all this so easily. I still had a quantity of "phony mescaline" left, but that didn't matter as I already had a few hundred dollars. I figured I might as well get high myself and join the party as the first band was already playing. Taking a joint out, I lit up and took a toke. This stuff was heaven to me.

I was standing down on the covered ice surface amongst the hundreds of concert goers. Looking around, I saw that the arena was almost filled to capacity. Everyone seemed to be in the party spirit. I hoped they were getting real high from the "mescaline" I had sold them. Ha ha. At least the marijuana was good. My only worry, outside of the cops, was of someone realizing they had been burned by buying the foil-wrapped powder. Visually, no one could tell the difference. As I sucked back on the joint, I got pretty high and started tripping out to the music and accompanying light show.

I now went looking for my money. That's all that mattered for the time being. Along the way, I sold some more of the garbage dope. Going to where my acquaintance was to be sitting, I got my money and sat down to enjoy the concert. I now had over $400. Not a bad return on a less than $100 investment. Talk about mega bucks for no mega work!

Enjoying the music and lights, we and a group of about ten smoked joint after joint. I could now be generous and a spendthrift. After a while, I walked around and sold a few more $5 hits and decided that with now almost $500, I'd call it a night as a drug dealer. I felt rich, really rich. Never before had I so much money. I loved money. Do you know what it's like carrying around hundreds of dollars in ones, twos, and fives? My pockets were full. Another drug pusher asked if I wanted to buy some beans— "uppers." I said I'd take a couple and pulled out a fist full of money and paid the guy ten bucks. I would soon be flying in the stratosphere.

After a while, someone walked up to me and asked if I had any more of that "mescaline." I said sure! He asked me to come with him. I hesitantly followed him to where some others were standing. I noticed one of them was this huge guy whom I had sold some of the fake mescaline to earlier. Now I was really paranoid. I hoped I wasn't going to have to take a walk with them, not with my pockets full of money. When he asked how much I had left, I replied that I had a couple dozen hits left. I also started to wonder if these guys were narcs. Here I was with about $500, a few joints, and a bag of phony dope. This dude asked if I wanted to make a deal for the stuff. I said sure.

I couldn't believe this. I was just going to throw this stuff out anyhow when I got home. Now I had a chance to get some money for this worthless dope. I said, "You can have the rest for three bucks a hit." He agreed on the spot and took out his wallet. He paid me, and I gave him his change along with the so-called mescaline.

I left and went back to my acquaintances. They thought I was something else, all the cash and dope I had. I was a big shot now and relished all the glory. They had no idea I had been selling fake drugs, for that was my secret alone. Even some of them had taken a hit of it. With all the joints we had smoked and pills we had dropped, no one would ever know the difference.

"Do you want to go and get something to eat?" I asked.

"Sure," was the reply. Our group had by now dwindled to five. We went downtown to a Chinese restaurant to pig out. I treated them to the meal, and they thanked me. Leaving the restaurant, we decided to call it a night and we went our separate ways. I was looking for a taxi to drive by to pick me up. Walking down Elm

Street stoned out of my mind was a blast. Everything around seemed out of proportion. It was like I was walking into some sort of satanic dream. I was hallucinating and constantly seeing visions. Cars were staring at me through the darkness. Their eyes, piercing and bright, were singling me out. Being alone, I was becoming paranoid. I just had to get home as soon as possible. One doesn't realize how high one is when in a crowd, but get by yourself and you could start to flip out. A taxi was coming, and I hailed it to a stop. Back at Doug's I was freaking out and making promises to myself to change. I passed out.

Waking up Sunday morning, I saw money lying around the place. The remembrance of the night before came back to me. It was mid-morning and I was totally spaced out. Reaching to the coffee table, I took one of the few joints I had left. I needed something to pull me out of this depressive state of mind. I lit up and toked back a great quantity of smoke, last night's promises already being discarded by the wayside. Oh well, I'd take my chances. Getting up off the couch, I picked up the money lying about. I took the money from my pockets and placed everything on the wooden coffee table. Counting the money while smoking up, I started dreaming of all the things I would buy, most notably drugs and booze. Now with all this cash flow, I could become more involved in drug dealing. During the rest of the day, I sat around smoking the last of my joints and ate pizza and Chinese food I had delivered.

Doug and Marg came home around 10 in the evening, and as I heard them pull into the driveway, I went to my room and feigned sleep. I was still quite stoned as I lay staring at the ceiling. I hadn't had anything to drink today. My body was craving the medicinal effects that booze had on me. Tomorrow I would make up for it anyhow. My cash flow would ensure that I would be able to sustain a high for quite some time to come.

Waking up Monday morning after a solid night of sleep, I was ready to greet the awaiting day. Stepbrother and sister-in-law were up. I asked them how their weekend went and they did likewise. I said I had enjoyed the weekend immensely, the rock concert was great, and that it was nice to be on my own for a change. Doug soon left for work, and I left shortly afterwards for "school."

It was well after 10 when I stepped into the house that evening. Doug and Marg were still up. Doug said he wanted to talk to me and to sit down. In a chair with a stoned look on my face, I listened. He had been told by the guy downstairs that some things were missing from his place. Doug had checked my room and found the missing merchandise. I replied to the accusation with the truth, that I only went down there to have a couple of drinks and on the spur of the moment took what I had thought were insignificant items. Because of this I was told that I might have to find somewhere else to live. I told him I was sorry and went solemnly to my room.

Throwing myself on the bed, I stared hypnotically at the ceiling and thought of the worst, as usual. I would have to go home to Mother. It was a good thing I was still high and tripping out or I might not have been able to cope with these thoughts. I felt rejected and unwanted again. The searing pain of loneliness burned at my inner soul. All I wanted was to be loved and accepted into a family—any family, as long as I had a sense of belonging. Disheartened again as usual, I crawled into bed under the covers. Sleep that night was elusive and my mind took many paths before it was found.

During the next couple of days I stayed high, sold drugs, and flashed money around. I was getting a lot of respect from the dudes that hung out downtown because of my drugs and cash. At least I was accepted somewhere!

# Chapter 10

It didn't bothered me about maybe having to move until one afternoon during the week in May that I went back to Doug's and saw Dad's car in the driveway. It was too early for him to be off work, so I knew something was up. I went into the house and stood at the doorway. Dad started talking and finally came out with the statement that I was going to have to live at a boys' home on Bancroft Drive. He said Marg's baby was due soon and there wouldn't be enough room here. I knew there were other reasons, such as my stealing. We had words for a few minutes, and then I had no choice, so I went to pack. I hid my dope amongst my things and shoved my wad of money into my pocket. In a few minutes I had thrown my things into the car and we were on our way. The Bancroft Drive boys' home was only five minutes away from Doug's. It wasn't going to be bad, I guessed, because I knew two guys there, the two who were with me when I made the bomb threats to the City Centre Mall. Still, I was a little apprehensive about living there.

Dad parked the car. I just sat looking at the drab concrete split-level building. I then reached into the back seat and grabbed some of my belongings while Dad got out and opened the back door and helped with the rest of it. His big Dodge station wagon seemed kind of big for one person and used to be fine for all of our family as we travelled around. Now there was no family, and it was getting smaller all the time. Today would be the first day of my life when I would have no family member to go home to. I was being discarded like a piece of trash that had no usefulness left.

We walked into the building and to the administrative offices. A blonde middle-aged lady greeted us and told us to have a seat in her office. I glanced furtively around as I sat and waited for her to speak. She introduced herself, and we talked for several minutes about me. The lady must have phoned my school before my arrival because she knew I had not been attending. I was told if I was living here and not going to school, I would have to find a job. I agreed to her terms. Dad soon said he'd be on his way and shook the lady's hand and thanked her and then left.

I was now on my own—no family, no love, no nothing. I felt betrayed, and now I had more reason to hate the world. When the lady finished signing me in, she then introduced me to the other staff, and one of them said he would show me to my room. As we went through the hall to the stairs, I noticed a large TV room and dining area. I also saw my so-called friends that I knew; the rest of the faces were unfamiliar. I was given a key to my room and told that the staff had a duplicate. Two guys shared each room.

Opening the door and stepping inside, I was somewhat surprised at the sight of a rather pleasant room. It was quite large, with a bed on either side, and was partitioned off in the middle with a particle-board-type wall, which would give each of us privacy. We each had our own clothes closet, desk, chair, and table lamp. The room was as nice as any room in our home, which made me feel comfortable. I was left alone to unpack, and then I would come downstairs for supper. My roommate wasn't there, and I tried to make this place feel like my home. With my things put away, I had to stash my drugs and did so. My money I kept with me. I then went downstairs to wait for supper.

Downstairs in the living area, I talked to the guys I knew. Looking around the room, I saw that it was quite large and airy. There were lots of windows that let the sunlight in the room. The furniture was like white pine and of a modern style of construction. The built-in cushioned backs were brightly coloured. The floor was carpeted, and the lighting was fluorescent. End tables matched the couches and chairs. In one corner was a colour TV, which was on, and the tinny sound from the small speaker wreaked havoc on my eardrums. I guess some of the guys were deaf. The living area was adjacent to the dining area in an open concept. Three or four tables were lined up, forming what looked like a boardroom table. Numerous chairs surrounded the table. There were a few windows with a southern exposure. I couldn't see into the kitchen as the counter, which was a pass-through self-serve type, had its stainless-steel hinged window closed.

Since I was a new person here, I was looked at suspiciously. Someone asked if I was given my masturbation papers in the office when I signed in. Did this guy think I was born yesterday? I told him to forget it as I already knew of this prank. I told him I had sent a number of new students at school down to the offices to ask for their papers. We all laughed, and it seemed they thought I was okay.

The stainless-steel window opened and supper was called. We all lined up and were served and then took seats. I had the munchies as I was still moderately high from the afternoon. I sat beside Mike. I don't know why, because he was the one who had told the cops about the bomb threats. I was introduced to some of the guys that were about. A dozen or so guys lived under this roof.

There was Charlie, a big guy for his age, about eighteen and about six foot three. I was told he had an electric guitar and amplifier in his room. There was Charlie's friend Gary, who also had a brother living here. Gary was a mean-looking dude; I certainly didn't want to have to mess with him. I was told that the weirdest guy in this place was Phrenic Freddie, a schizoid who, I was told, always attempted suicide. But obviously, like myself, he had failed. He was also the least attractive guy there, a little wimp of a boy about five four and a hundred pounds. Also there was a mean-looking punk by the nickname of Chief. I guessed that he had picked up the name because of his Indian ancestry. I was told that Chief was somewhat bizarre and had taken a shotgun and blown the cherry off a cop car. I don't know whether this was fact or not. I seemed to be the only one not sent there because of police run-ins.

Supper was good, and I was surprised. Finally finished, I went outside with a couple of guys to smoke a couple of joints. I kept secret about my stash because I couldn't trust any one of these guys. High as a kite, we went inside and I was shown downstairs. There was a pool table and a boxing ring. I got in the ring and donned a pair of gloves and challenged anyone to a sparring match. One of the guys donned a pair of gloves and climbed into the ring with me. I took a couple of swings and missed my target. What was returned to me was a flurry of quick punches in rapid succession. I was knocked to the mat, like a Bozo-the-clown punching bag. Unlike Bozo, I didn't just pop back up to take some more punishment.

I told him I wasn't a fighter but a lover, and they all laughed. I didn't laugh inside, as I knew I had never been a lover, only a hater of everything. Drugs and alcohol were what was keeping me from going insane in this lonely and hateful world. Getting to my feet, I took off the gloves and hung them up. That was the end of my boxing career. I had bigger and better things in store for me in life anyway, like being a big-time drug dealer or pulling off the biggest bank job Sudbury had ever experienced. These were my aspirations.

I spent the rest of the evening there feeling out of place, studying the staff and the other guys. We watched some television and then it was time for bed. As I lay in bed that evening, I was filled with hatred. Now I had no brothers around, no mother, no father. Most of all I missed my dear sweet sister, Vickey. I hoped she wouldn't end up like me. I tossed and turned but couldn't go to sleep. I took out my stash and dropped a yellow jacket (upper). Soon I was high again and drifting melodiously through the heavens. What a nice life, to be free, away from all the horror.

Drugs have these effects on you. Your personality can change at the flick of a switch as they alter the chemical makeup of the brain. One minute good and then the next bad. Maybe Christlike, and then the gates of hell open and you could rise as a bond slave to Satan. These personality transformations were not uncommon to me as I had been having them since I was about eight, my male-female or my instantaneous love-to-hatred conflicts. Drugs only heightened or lowered these experiences. The realism of these changes could make me dangerous to myself and others. I always fought to keep things in check.

The upper was taking me higher as the time passed. It must have been about midnight as I flew through one dream to another, my imagination wrecking havoc inside my head. As I was getting more into popping pills and such, hallucinatory images, as lifelike as if you were next to me in the flesh, would appear. I was finding out that when you started hallucinating, bad times were ahead of you on your particular drug trip. My thoughts transcended from one extreme to another as I lay there in mental turmoil fighting the unseen, the unknown, fearing that someday my dark thoughts and inclinations would come to a boiling point and overflow.

Picture a volcano lying dormant near a populous area. One day the seeds of destruction start boiling and multiplying. There has to be a release of sorts at some point. How much devastation results, if any, depends on how soon the pressure is released. The longer it is held in, the more power of destruction it has upon release. Finally the eruption occurs, spewing forth maybe a small river of lava, like a tear on a face, or of an intensity that doesn't hurt people directly but only their surroundings, like a burglar to a house. What is lost can be replaced. But if that volcanic eruption is of such magnitude as if the gates of hell have been thrown open upon the earth, I would hate to think of the human lives that could be taken in that one single moment of monumental madness. With the top blown off the mountain, all that is boiling inside will spew forth until the pressure recedes to a much more controllable level. In the meantime, irreplaceable lives have been taken, like a murderer's victim. Thoughts like these occurred often to me as I struggled daily to keep a lid on my increasingly violent emotions. Thankfully, the mind eruptions had not physically hurt anyone.

As I lay there tripping out, I thought of the future. Daily I was being transformed into something that deep down inside I knew I didn't want to be. I was getting to the point where I couldn't even trust my own actions at any one time. These sociopathic tendencies were grasping me tighter and deeper into their hold. Knowing this was happening scared me to an almost virtual death. I couldn't tell anyone, or else I would be sent to an asylum to basket weave my days away in total disillusionment with the world and its ungodly offerings.

I tripped in and out of reality for a while and finally I fell asleep, alone, so terribly alone, without family. I awoke a couple of times to the laughter of Satan, who had me in his grasp. A boy with such heart, only lacking in love and guidance. I awoke drowsily at the call for breakfast and was still in bed at last call. Begrudgingly I got up and haphazardly got dressed. I rinsed the sleep from my eyes and under a drug-induced grogginess went down to the dining area. There were only three or four of us at the table, excluding a couple of staff I had yet to meet. I was introduced and went on with my breakfast. Outside of my grade eight school trip to Ottawa, I had never eaten breakfast in a group-like setting. I felt as if I were being watched by the staff, almost like an animal in a cage. I'm sure they were wondering what kind of punk hoodlum I was. I mean, I now had been discarded by my family. They don't throw away good kids, or do they? I could go to Mother's if I wanted, but I would have to be crazy to go back to where I had just left after sixteen years of bitter hell.

After breakfast, I chatted in the living area for a bit and then was called to the office by the lady who had checked me in. Sitting across from her, I listened to her speech. She asked if I was going to attend school. I replied that I would in the fall. Well, in the meantime, I was to start looking for a job, she said. I told her I would try my best and that I didn't have a social insurance number. Coincidentally she had the forms to fill out, so I was given one. I was told that today I could make myself at home, but tomorrow I had to start job hunting. Leaving her office, I went to my room and filled out the form for a SIN.

The rest of that week and into the next I stayed high and mildly intoxicated from alcohol. Marg gave birth to a baby boy, and I was glad for my stepbrother and sister-in-law. I talked to Dad on the phone for a few minutes, but we never spoke about anything other than Mother's madness. Aside from that, I had no family contact whatsoever.

I was very lonesome and was becoming quite rebellious. As far as job hunting was concerned, I wasn't much of a hunter. But I had blown most of my hard-earned money, and I wasn't selling much dope. Even my own drug supply was getting low, mostly because of my generosity to others. Job hunting to me was just making a daily appearance at the local student employment centre that had just been set up in the basement of the main post office. Every weekday morning I checked in as early as possible so as to be one of the first ones in. At the office, I usually saw the same worker, and she became aware that I was truly interested in working. Seeing my enthusiasm, she told me one day that I didn't have to come in any more and that if something came up she would phone the boys' home and leave a message.

It was only a couple of days after that when I received a message that Kmart was looking for someone to work during the summer, covering for salespeople on holidays. I thought it would be okay, as it was only one bus ride and about fifteen minutes away. I phoned and made an appointment with the personnel manager for the following day. I even went and got my hair shortened to a more reasonable length. I didn't smoke up or drink that night, in order to be clear-headed in the morning. I had never had a job interview before, and I didn't know what to expect. I didn't like being straight and not under some kind of influence. I made sure my best clothes were neat. It didn't matter what time I was at Kmart as long as it was before noon. In bed that night, I had a hard time falling asleep as I craved some drugs or booze.

The next morning, I ate and got ready for my interview. The store opened at 9:30, so I figured I would show up about 10. Later I caught a transit bus and was soon walking across the parking lot into Kmart. As I walked through the aisles, my thoughts turned to my past. Imagine me, who always went into department stores for only one purpose—to permanently borrow merchandise—now having the chance to work in a store. I was directed to the personnel manager's office at the back of the store and up a flight of stairs.

I met a Mrs. P., the manager, who seemed very nice as we carried on an introductory conversation. Well, the meeting went well, and I was hired on the spot, with all my "sales experience" unknown to her, of course. I knew I could do the job well. I had been selling stolen retail items for years. I would start the following Monday, filling in for a vacationing menswear salesman. I would be paid the minimum wage. I filled out some forms and was on my way.

Outside I figured it was time to celebrate and lit up a hot one. I decided to go downtown and wait for the bars to open. It was now June 1975, and I now had a job. I was proud of myself for being able to take care of myself. I had a few days left before I started working, and I was certainly going to make the best of it. I'd buy some clothes with the rest of my drug money and party until I dropped. I finished up the joint, walked to a bus stop, caught a bus, and was soon downtown. The next few days I did as I planned.

It was now Monday and my first day of work. Getting out of bed was difficult, as I hadn't recovered from the weekend of teenage delinquency and drugs. After dressing and eating, I was asked into the office at the boys' home and told that since I was now going to be earning money, I would have to pay $20 a week for room and board. I agreed and we chatted a bit longer, then I was off to work.

That first week of work was okay. I found out I could sell quite well, and I learned to use the cash register at the back of the store by the automotive department. I didn't use it much, as most of my sales were rung up by the girls working at the checkouts. Oh, the girls! They were older than me; in fact, I'm sure I was the youngest employee in the store. I figured I had better keep my fantasies to myself. One that stood out amongst the rest was a cute blonde about eighteen who drove a gold 340 Duster with Monster Boot tires. I never did get introduced, and at the time I didn't know I would run into her some eleven years later, at which time I wouldn't know it was her when I stuck up for her on a bus trip after some guys were being offensive. I then sat with her, and we soon found out we had once worked in the same store. Chivalry reigns again!

My only sexual experience had been a couple of years earlier, and you know about that. That episode often painfully reran in my mind. Anyway, lately I hadn't thought about sex much anyway. I was too involved with my growing dependency on drugs and booze, although I did have some passing fantasies, since after I started working I cut back on my alcohol and drug use somewhat, at least to the point of only being moderately high. I abstained completely during working hours, unlike at school when I had been attending.

After two weeks of work I received my first pay-cheque, which amounted to only a couple of hundred dollars. I had been given my cheque despite the fact I still hadn't received my SIN yet. I felt good earning my own money legally, although I could have made that amount in a couple of days selling drugs. I opened up a bank account, cashed my cheque, and paid $40 to the boys' home for my room and board. At Kmart I bought some stereo equipment, a tape deck and speakers, and used my store discount. I didn't like the idea of paying room and board very much.

During the evenings at the boys' home, only two staff members worked, and we could get away with quite a bit. What we boys didn't like was that the kitchen was always locked after supper. Secretly I was planning to somehow snatch a set of keys when the opportunity arose. As of yet it had not. Things were pretty routine now, and I wasn't hanging out down-town very much now that I was working.

With money from my paycheque, I went out on the weekend and got wasted. These habits of mine weren't so awe-inspiring any more. Whereas before I used to always get on a good high and feel wonderful, my trips now were more downers than anything. Sure, I was stoned, but the euphoria was not there so often any more. As my addictions became more apparent, I seemed to be regressing back into the unhappiness of my past. I guess subconsciously I had less power over my actions than I thought. My drug dealing had pretty well stopped because of my work, except among friends. My dealings now usually just covered what I used personally. In other words, I could drink and do drugs at no cost. At today's prices I would be spending a few hundred dollars a week. Prices then were about a quarter of that.

I finally managed to lift a set of keys for the kitchen. A couple of other guys and I then started our nightly raids upon the refrigerators. I had been there less than two months and was already a hero. I had always tried to be the best at whatever I did, whether in a positive or negative sense. I had money, clothes, dope, and now the keys to the place.

I had now received another paycheque and had to pay another $40 for room and board. Now I didn't like the idea of paying rent, so I devised a plan to change the situation. I figured that if I waited until after 5 p.m. to pay for my room and board, the offices would be locked, and no one that worked in the evening had keys, not even myself. Maybe if I gave the night staff the money, they would slide it under the door and I could retrieve it later. With this in mind I approached one of the workers and gave them forty bucks for room and board. I was promptly given a receipt. I sat in the living room area pretending to watch TV. Sure enough, the money was put in an envelope and slipped under the locked office door. Later that evening, I walked by the office, which was almost out of sight of everybody. Kneeling down, I peered under the door. The outside lights illuminated the office quite a bit. I sighed to myself. Perfect! Now all I had to do was open up a wire coat hanger, roll up a small bit of tape, sticky side out, and then shove it onto the end of the wire, and—presto. I waited a while, and then with the stealth and precision of a burglar, I tried out my plan. Within a minute, I had retrieved the forty bucks. I also had the receipt. I thoughtfully patted myself on the back. Man, I was so smart, quite a genius. With this money I could buy more dope for myself. There was never enough money to support my habits. Well the past several weeks had gone by with hardly a thought towards my family. The exception was my beautiful sister Vickey who I missed greatly. I had not called home once to hear how she was. I could not give in to mother. I just forced myself to stay away and have no contact with them whatso-ever. Had I been closer to any of them I would probably have gone back by now. This was my choice now and I would show them. I wasn't a piece of trash.

However, I was so damn alone and lonely.

I was soon found out, about the keys for the boys homes kitchen and reprimanded.

I was also having some of the most dangerous drug trips to date and after one particular rock concert I did not come down off my high by Monday. I absolutely could not go to work and quit.

After some days, I half-heartedly looked for a job. I was high daily and started selling drugs again.

Also constant thoughts that I might be gay were driving me deeper into my misery. I liked girls and everything, but had yet to experience them sexually. Now with the way my personality had developed after all the emotional and physical abuse during my childhood, it stood to reason that I might turn out gay; one of life's manufactured homosexuals. I hated the thoughts of the possibility. All those years of wishing I was a girl so Mother would love me had altered me in very disturbing ways that I could not comprehend.

Prior to leaving Mother's, I had I had been cross-dressing *just to be free of myself*. Now that I was on my own, I wanted to be a man more than anything. A total man with no thoughts of femininity whatsoever. The feminine thoughts would just not disappear and I was left on a psychological swing that never stopped. Back and forth, back and forth. Even away from so called home I was being punished in far greater ways than any brutal beating I had endured in the past.

The scars unseen to others seemed to be getting worse as the never-ending emotionally disturbing onslaught continued. Drugs and booze had been the only escape. Now my addictions were taking control of me. I was, it seemed, punishing myself for being a mental case. I knew I wasn't normal like others, but I couldn't ask for help and I didn't think there was enough help for me anyhow.

Okay, out of my sorrow and back to finding a job.

Soon I was employed making pizzas at Golden Pizza on Regent Street South. I worked from about 6 p.m. to 2 a.m. five nights a week. The owners always gave me a ride back to the boys' home afterwards. I didn't mind the hours as I was a drug addict and enjoyed the night life. The pizza place was a hangout for all the local punks. I was meeting a lot of party people like myself and my drug business was good on the side. At the boys' home, I was paying room and board and stealing it back as before until finally I had been found out. Again I was reprimanded and lectured.

The Grand Prix Hotel behind my workplace became my favourite watering hole. After two weeks of pizza making, I decided to quit. The staff at the boys' home didn't like my attitude, and I told them I would be going back to school in a couple of weeks when school started after the Labour Day weekend. I just wanted to party as if I would soon party no more.

A couple of days after quitting, I bused it out to the area in the morning and met an acquaintance at the pizza place. At precisely noon, we were at the Grand Prix Hotel for first call. It was lunchtime, and lo and behold, my stepbrother Doug came in with a couple of co-workers for lunch and a brew. Doug's head office was only minutes away. I hadn't seen him since I moved into the boys' home, and he was kind of shocked to meet up with me there. After he and his friends had lunch, I suggested that we meet there after he got off work and then we could get down to some serious drinking. I had never been out drinking with him, as I was only sweet sixteen. I stayed at the bar most of the afternoon, leaving only a couple of times to smoke up and check out the pizzeria.

As the supper hour arrived, Doug showed up with a friend of his. My own drinking buddy had left to go home for supper. Doug phoned his wife and said that he had met up with me and that we were going to hang out together for a while. I felt good drinking with my stepbrother, and I was acting like a big shot. I was buying the rounds, since I was loaded with the fruits of my illegal criminal activities.

After about three hours of this socializing, I decided to go and check out the Golden Pizza. I wanted to see if any of the girls I knew were about. I had been drinking since noon and it was now about 8 p.m., so I was quite drunk, to say the least.

Well, in the next hour or so, we managed to get barred from two more bars, each one worse than the previous. Finally we were at the Brockdan Hotel, where Doug used to sling beer part-time. Doug knew most of the staff, so we didn't have to worry about getting the boot, and the party continued. There was a live band, and I was having a riotous time. I was also drunk beyond the beyond, but still able to hold my own. I don't know if Doug was impressed or not. He is ten years older than me, but I could outdrink him, as he was finding out. Pitifully, as it ended up, I was proud of myself. It ended up we closed the place down. I had opened one bar and closed another and was still standing. Thirteen hours of non-stop drinking and about $100 spent having the time of my life.

We decided that we would go back to Doug's friend's place to continue our drinking. After a crazy night, I had to return to the boys' home, where I was lectured once again about continuing to disobey the rules. I was told that any further problem would mean I would have to leave. After this verbal tongue lashing, I went to my room and crashed in order to catch some sleep.

Over the next couple of days I became increasingly disturbed emotionally. My thoughts were driving me crazier. All the drugs and booze were taking their toll on me. My personality was changing for the worse. More hatred than ever filled my lonely soul.

My time at the boys' home was drawing to an end. I knew I wouldn't go back to school, and I couldn't hold a job. I phoned Dad and told him I had to leave there. Dad told me the only place I could stay was at Mother's. I had sworn never to go back there. After more conversation, he said he would check with Mother and for me to think things over. I hung up and went to my room and cried buckets. My thoughts turned to my sister; how I missed her! Vickey was four years old and a bundle of joy. I still feared for her, because I knew that growing up with only one parent could be detrimental to her. What about all the things she would hear about her family and her mother? How would all these things affect her? Maybe Mother would be nicer to me now that I had been away a few months.

Dad got back to me later, and he that Mother would have me back if I wanted to go back. I said I'd give it a try, and Dad said he would pick me up the next day. He made the arrangements for me to leave. I meanwhile packed up my belongings and passed the evening at the home partying with the guys and having a high time. The night dragged by, and I didn't sleep well. I wondered if I had made the right choice to return home.

# Chapter 11

The next day Dad picked me up and we went out for lunch. As usual, we didn't say much. When we did, it most always pertained to the latest stunts Mother was trying. For instance, she was always trying to get more court-appointed payments out of Dad. He told me that since I was going back, Mother would get more money. That statement just made me feel miserable. Mother might just as well put me to work on a street corner. *Well, at least I am finally worth something*, I thought.

We finished our meal, and Dad drove me to Mother's. As we drove to Copper Cliff, which I hadn't seen since I left, thousands of segments of my life in this town flashed through my memory bank. Each different scene seemed to send a small electric shock through me.

I could see the house as we exited the highway. At first glance, the house stood hauntingly in front of me and I became very nervous about returning home. I could imagine some of the things Mother might have said to my younger siblings about me coming home. None of it very good, I'm sure.

Once parked, Dad helped me with my things. A brother and Vickey came out to greet me. Vickey was overjoyed to see me and vice versa. I held her in my arms and gave her a big hug and kiss. My eyes were watery. There was only one thing I loved in this world, and that was my beautiful blonde, blue-eyed little sister. I put her down and grabbed some of my belongings and went into the house. Mother said hi and so did I. She said it was nice that I came back and to take my things up to my old room. It felt so strange there; it wasn't my home. Not one good feeling towards Mom prevailed. Only my sister mattered.

I ran into my brother Tom, and I felt the same intense hatred arise from deep within as I had before leaving. Since I had left, I had hardly given a thought to my family, except Vickey. I had wanted to wipe them from my mind, and I had done a good job up to now. Drugs and alcohol had helped me suppress all the feelings I had and bury them deep within my psyche. I knew then that I wouldn't be there for long.

Over the next few days I was pretty quiet, like a visitor amongst my own family. Sure, Mother seemed nice and all, but I saw through her phoniness. I was just money in the bank to her. We seemed to be testing each other, and trust, what was that? We were like two strange cats put in the same house together, always searching out the other. I had freedom and got high daily with some acquaintances that I hadn't seen during my stay in the city. At so-called home, life was most unbearable. The memories were haunting, the sight of Mother disturbing. School would be starting in a week, and Mother was bugging me about going back. I hated her immensely and couldn't stand the sight of her.

It was time for me to leave and be out on my own. I decided that I had to get away from this city, and since I knew a few families in Ohio, that was where I was going. Not even a week had gone by since I came home. One night I snuck around the house gathering the things I might need. I could only take one knapsack full of things, so I had to be very choosy. A sleeping bag, eating utensils, a bit of food, clothes, and grooming aids. I had about $100 and a bit of dope.

The next morning I didn't get away as early as I had wanted. By the time I had bused it to the four corners and Highway 69, it was after 10. I had left home without saying goodbye to Vickey. As far as I knew, I wouldn't be seeing her for a few years.

It wasn't long before I got picked up and was on my way to seek my fortune and happiness. Now I was on to my way to Ohio, USA, and my first destination was to be Toronto, then Niagara Falls, USA, and on to Ohio. All I knew was that it was a fifteen-hour non-stop trip, and I figured it would take me two days. Well, it took me about four rides and seven hours to make the four-and-a-half-hour trip to Toronto. I had never been to Toronto, and all I knew was that Yonge Street was the main street. So that was where I asked to be dropped off by the last driver who picked me up, who just happened to be a very nice young lady. She told me that if I wanted to get to the highway that would take me to Niagara Falls, I would have to first go to the end of Yonge Street and then ask for directions.

It was after 5 when I started down Yonge Street, and I figured if I got to the highway soon I would be in Niagara Falls before nightfall. I was going to find out soon how wrong I was. I walked and walked and walked some more. My knapsack now seemed to weigh a hundred pounds. Was there no end to this street? Unknown to me was the fact that Yonge Street is the longest street in the world and goes on for endless miles. I don't know where I had been let off, but it took over three hours to get to Yonge and Bloor. If only I had asked someone how far it was I would have saved some energy and taken the subway, which I didn't know ran underneath Yonge Street until I was almost downtown.

I couldn't believe the size of the buildings or all the people and cars, zillions of cars. It was kind of frightening in a way. Downtown I asked for directions to Niagara Falls and was told I would have to get to the Queen Elizabeth Way, and hitchhiking wasn't allowed on the expressways. It was getting late, so I followed the given instructions as best as possible. I walked and walked. Running away is a tough job. I had eaten some supper, so I now wasn't hungry. Toronto was too big, and I just wanted to get out of the city. I passed skyscrapers and I saw my first streetcars. I passed some kind of midway, which I didn't know was the Canadian National Exhibition. Finally I saw an off-ramp and a sign saying Gardiner Expressway and QEW. I passed a brew factory and wished I could have a brew.

It was a good thing I got to the ramp, because it was almost dark. With my thumb again stuck in the wind, I was soon picked up by a guy in a van. I told him where I was headed, and he said he'd be able to drop me off at the QEW but first he had to make a few deliveries as he was working. Since it was late, I said okay. Since I wasn't from Toronto, I was kind of scared being driven around by a stranger. I could have very easily been dropped off in the middle of nowhere or worse. He made his deliveries, and at the last place he asked me if I wanted to go in with him. He was going to give me a tour of a huge factory. I followed him on his round through the factory and was quite interested.

Now my mind seemed to be putting the pieces of this puzzle together. Here was a man who picks up a sixteen-year-old runaway, if you can could me a runaway at sixteen. Actually I was a "run to," to freedom and happiness. This guy's doing deliveries and tells me he will drop me off at the QEW after he's finished. Now with my past experiences with men and what I had heard about hitchhikers disappearing, murdered, I figured this guy for a queer at best or a sicko at worst. Now I was worried that my life might be endangered as I tagged along with him through the factory.

He made his parcel delivery and we left and returned to his van. I didn't know what to do. It was night, and I was 250 miles from home, in the middle of nowhere as far as I was concerned. In his van I asked him how far it was to the QEW. He replied that it was about ten minutes away. We started out, and he was talking to me about this and that and also it was not safe to hitchhike on the QEW. He added that if I was going to do that I should at least do it in the daytime. As we kept driving, I was deeply frightened that he might be a sicko.

In a couple of minutes, he dropped me off at an entrance ramp with a huge overhead sign reading QEW, Queen Elizabeth Way, in huge light-reflecting letters. What a relief as I grabbed my knapsack and bid thanks to him! I don't know if I was any better than him, I did know that I was a sexually messed-up kid. I walked down the ramp and along the expressway with my thumb out. Cars were whizzing by at the speed limit or well above.

After I walked about a mile or so with no luck in getting a ride, an OPP cruiser pulled up behind me. The officer got out and spoke with me, telling me I wasn't allowed to hitchhike along the freeway. He stated that I wouldn't get a ride out there, because the cars were going too fast and wouldn't be bothered to stop. The officer asked me for ID and asked me where I was going and where I was from. I told him vaguely the details. I believe he ran my name with HQ. He showed some concern about my lack of knowledge about these super-highways and offered to drive me to a busy collector lane, where I was legally allowed to hitchhike. I took him up on his offer and got into the back of the cruiser. In a couple of minutes he dropped me off and told me to be careful and good luck; then he was off. Thank God I wasn't searched, as I had a bit of grass with me.

Well, it wasn't long before I received a ride that ended up with me near Hamilton. Next I was picked up by a guy in a Chevy van. He was a guy about twenty who was going to Niagara Falls. We got along okay, drank some beer and smoked a joint, which made the rest of the trip a breeze. I was dropped off at Lundy's Lane, which he told me was the main street and would take me to the falls. It was about two in the morning, and the streets were almost deserted except for the basic city night life. Hot rods and bikers were cruising the streets. The bikers seemed to be everywhere, and I was scared as I passed them. I didn't want them to know I was a stranger, but my knapsack was advertising that fact.

In about fifteen minutes I heard the roaring of the falls. The last time I was here it was a family affair several years back. I walked past the motels, shops, and museums, all their lights flashing and lighting up the street as if it were high noon. I walked down the main drag to the park that ran parallel with the Niagara gorge. What a beautiful sight was bestowed upon me as I stood mesmerized by the view of the cascading water flowing endlessly over the top of the falls and into the gorge below!

I figured I wouldn't cross the bridge to the USA at night because I would get lost on the other side. I just parked my buns on a bench to pass the night away. I gazed at the falls for hours and contemplated life. What a lonely night it was. Tomorrow I would be in Ohio to start a new life.

As dawn approached, I felt the chilling cold from the dampness of the falls and the rising mist. The sun was rising above the eastern horizon, and I knew that today would be a glorious day as far as the weather was concerned. I thought as I sat on the dew-covered bench about the loneliness that I was constantly filled with. All I ever wanted was to be part of a loving family.

I grabbed my knapsack, which contained everything I had brought to embark on a new life. I was hungry, so I went looking for a restaurant that might be open this early. It was about 6 a.m. as I walked along the main drag, the flashing neon lights still seemingly beckoning me to come in and have a look. I walked silently along the deserted streets. Inwardly a violent struggle to keep my sanity was going on. If people could have heard the screaming of the battle inside of me, I would have woken up this sleeping city. The roar of the falls would have seemed like a babbling brook thereafter.

I found a motel restaurant that was open, and I had a hearty breakfast. Here I was 400 miles away from home, hoping to change all the misery of the past by literally leaving the country. I must have been brain-washed by television to think that life in new lands could make me happy. I knew I would be happy once I got settled. For now, I would just have to carry the past upon my shoulders, much like Atlas carrying the world.

I expected to be in Ohio by that evening. Since I thought Ohio was only about six hours away, I decided to stay in town for the morning to check out the museums and such. After breakfast, I strolled back down to the falls. Once the shops opened, I checked out most of them. After having my fill of all the museums and stores, I headed for the bridge and a new land on the other side. I figured all I had to do was go across the bridge and at the U.S. side tell them I was on my way to friends in Ohio. I had my ID ready and my friends' addresses.

Halfway across, I stood on the boundary between Canada and the United States of America and looked to the falls. I pitched the last of my grass into the gorge, as I could get searched by the border guards. A border guard asked me what I was going to the U.S. for, and I stated my plan to visit friends. I was asked how much money I had with me and replied that I had about $70. After a few more questions, he escorted me to an office. He made a phone call and then we chatted. Within minutes, there was a knock on the door, and then two Canadian cops walked in. I was told I was to be taken to the Niagara Regional Police station so that a check could be run on me. I gathered my things, and since I hadn't done anything against the law, I figured I would be able to resume my journey shortly.

Back in Canada, I waited at the cop shop and was asked some questions. I was told that if the police check came back clean I could leave, but not to the U.S. Apparently you had to have a minimum of $200 on you if you were hitchhiking from Canada into the U.S. This was supposed to cut down on any crimes you might commit while crossing the states. Well, my check came back clean, and I was told to get back to Sudbury. So much for a new life!

Out on the streets of Niagara again, I wondered what I should do next. I figured I had no choice but to go back to Sudbury. All this hitchhiking and risking my life for nothing. I made my way to the QEW, got a ride to Toronto, and then a few rides later I was back in Sudbury. It was night when I arrived, and I wandered the streets. What a trip! In the past day and a half I managed an 800-mile round trip to Niagara Falls and didn't even bring back a souvenir. I slept that night between a couple of buildings, like a street person.

In the morning I gave in and caught a bus to Copper Cliff. Back at Mother's, I knocked at the door and was let in by a brother. He called for Mother, who came and asked where I had gone. I told her what happened, and she seemed amused by it all. I was told I could stay if I wanted. I didn't have any alternative at the moment, and I knew nothing about the welfare system. Inside I knew I would have to make my stay here as short as possible. My sister was glad to see me, and I felt the same towards her. Back in my room, I unpacked my things, had something to eat, and then went to bed to catch up on some sleep. I slept until lunchtime, when my brothers awoke me.

Later in the afternoon, I phoned Dad at work and told him about my hitchhiking ordeal and told him I couldn't stay here any longer as I felt as if I didn't belong. Dad told me to hang tough for a couple of days and he would work out something. Dad and I kept in touch, and I stayed high. After a couple of days, Dad phoned and said I could move up to his apartment, which he had recently rented. I said that was great. That day he went out and bought me a new captain's bed that had drawers in it. I moved in that evening.

# Chapter 12

M y new home was still in Copper Cliff but up in Little Italy, known to me as Wopville. The apartment was actually the second story of a house owned by an Italian family whose kids I had gone to school with. As a matter of fact, one of the daughters was the same age as I was, and we had spent most of our school years in the same classrooms. The place was small in comparison to our house. There were two bedrooms; the smallest was to be mine, and there was just enough room for my bed and a dresser. I didn't care; at least it was my own. The bathroom was small and contained the basics. The kitchen, like the bathroom, contained the necessities. I noticed the living room was furnished in what I called early camp style, as most of the furniture was the antiquated hand-me-down pieces Dad had kept after he had to sell our cottage in order to appease his ex-wife's insatiable appetite for money. She had run up some quite large bills prior to their divorce.

In all, the place was cozy, and I figured I would soon feel comfortable there. After a few days, sure enough, I was quite at home and was finding out I pretty well had the run of the place. Dad worked every weekday, came home for supper, changed, and went out to his girl-friend's. Even on the weekends, I was going to find out, Dad was hardly ever there.

I started having acquaintances over in the daytime to party, and party we did. I was doing acid often, but only one hit at a time, unlike the first time. Most trips into the beyond were rather pleasant, so I kept up the acid tripping. I smoked up every day, as had been my habit for months on end now. As far as booze went, I had mickeys of my favourite beverages lined up against the wall behind my bed. I usually started the day now with a drink of something or other straight up. Yes, living pretty much on your own as a sixteen-year-old is great. I started up a drugstore in the apartment and had a couple of punks selling drugs for me. My initial financing came from break and enters in the city. The money was rolling in, and I wanted more.

After about two months of living with Dad, things even got better. Mother was taking off to Toronto with a couple of my brothers and my sister and some alco-holic guy named Jack. What luck was coming my way! Dad was now going to be living down at the other end of town in his house. Now virtually I had my own place to call my home. What else could a sixteen-year-old ask for? Now more than ever I had parties, parties that went on like a never-ending trip into the outer galaxies of our solar system.

Personally that is where I seemed to be also, but mine was a trip into a deep, dark psychological void within the infinite perimeters of my mind and soul. It was amazing how far I could travel within myself. I could go anywhere I wanted, be anyone or anything I wanted to be. I could be the proverbial "boy next door" or, like Dr. Jekyll and Mr. Hyde, change instantly into a raving lunatic. A monster of the human kind, spewing forth words of hatred upon the people close to my heart, however distant they seemed. Wreaking havoc upon the innocents who I thought were trying to gang up against me. Yes, a paranoid existence is a part of the drug scene, along with the personality conflicts. The dramatic mood swings that could pick you up like a breeze picking up a kite and taking it to the limit of the string attached. The danger that went with these highs came when the string broke and you were carried along on a trip out of control, at the mercy of the winds of sort. From these highs you could, on most occasions, fall back to the earth undamaged, able to fly high again. But if the trips were bad, like a kite blown from the skies into a hydro line, the damage could affect the multitudes, from a mere electrical shock to a catastrophic nightmare.

By myself now, the world seemed so eerie and strange. Far worse than that, my deep, dark secrets about the things I had done or thought about might be uncovered as well. I knew I was a desperate mental case of sorts, but that was well masked to others, I thought. No one could ever find out about my personality disorder. I would somehow conquer my problems someday.

I resorted to phoning Doug. It must have been after 2 a.m. when I picked up the phone and dialled the number. One ring, two rings; I could picture Doug cursing whoever was phoning at this hour. "Hello" was what I heard.

"Doug, it's me. I'm stoned on acid and junk and ready to OD. I gotta talk until I come down a bit." He was used to this, being woken up in the middle of the night by his drug-crazed stepbrother, and tried to console me in my time of self-perpetuated misery.

At this point in my life, I didn't even know what perpetuating anything meant and always blamed Mother for my madness, which in most cases was true. I didn't have the guidance to know enough to start taking control of my life now that I was on my own and away from the woman of the majority of my nightmares. Talking to Doug kept me on the good side of the tracks, as far as my sanity was concerned. I rambled on incoherently about this and that. Doug was just listening on the other end, but it was comforting to know he was taking me through another bad trip. I was seeing things, hearing things, and just on the verge of crossing over the fine line of sanity. I'm sure I had crossed back and forth a few times already that evening, but I wasn't going to admit it. After a couple of hours of this rambling on, I knew that I had made it through another bad trip, and before I hung up I promised Doug, as in the past, that this was the last time that I would do drugs.

In the morning I felt suicidal again and took a rifle and contemplated putting a bullet through my tormented mind. Instead I settled on a drug-and-alcohol overdose. A few pills, some acid, alcohol, and a couple joints later, I found myself with the stereo turned up to muffle the sounds of the rifle as I took potshots at the smokestack of the smelter I could see from the back window. This smokestack was one of four and the tallest in the world. Tonight the smokestack was a figure in effigy of Mother, and I shot her until she died. I could just picture her screaming and begging for her life as I had done in the past on hundreds of occasions. She was now paying for her insanity with the inheritance I had so ungraciously been bestowed with. I was mad, mad, mad, ha, ha, ha. I put the rifle away and drowned my misery with a mickey of hard liquor straight up.

The music was now playing as loud as one could have it in an apartment. I was going to die—punishing myself for being me. Or was it to get revenge? I knew it wasn't all my fault; I just couldn't stand the thoughts of living any more. I was turning into everything Mother had told me I was from when I was young until I was on my own. I certainly was proving her correct again. Mother had some brains? I was now a drug addict as well as an alcoholic. Every day I was committing a crime of one sort or another. I didn't know if I was straight or gay. I didn't know what love was. All this, and I was only sixteen. Nothing to live for as I delved deep into my distraught psyche.

I smoked another joint, then another, took my second hit of acid, more pills and booze. Yes, I was going out first class. This flight was definitely going to crash. I was flying beyond the limits of earth. The flight was one of great turbulence, like flying into a hurricane. At any time I would crash. The turbulence was increasing as time passed. More booze, more drugs; this hurricane was going to take a life. I started to nod off into a drowsy state of consciousness, but thoughts kept jolting me back to life. Finally I was falling from the skies, unable to maintain control. I knew I was going to another world, hopefully one more peaceful. I was jolted back to life a few more times. I don't know how much time may have passed before I fell into a state of unconsciousness.

I didn't come out of it until the phone rang Sunday afternoon. Groggily I reached for the phone, as it was right beside me. I turned down the stereo. "Hello?" It was Dad checking up on me. He said he was going to drop by later and pick up some things. "Sure, Dad," I said, and then we said so long. I hadn't gone to bed, and not very enthusiastically I got to my feet and started to pick up the mess I had made. A half bottle of piss warm beer, an empty mickey and an ashtray full of spent joints.

The thought didn't even strike me that I was alive, and I was still stoned out of my mind. Again Satan hadn't taken me into the depths of hell beyond hell on earth. Like usual, something or someone was keeping me alive. The night before I had taken enough drugs to put an elephant down. I sure must have one hell of a strong ticker. With everything straightened up, I lay down on my bed and passed out into a deep slumber. I was awakened for the few minutes Dad dropped by and carried on our usual couple-dozen-word conversation, and then he left.

I again dozed off and awoke after dark. It was about midnight, and I had missed out on a whole day of partying. I'm sure people must have phoned, but I certainly hadn't heard the phone ring. I watched some TV until the stations went off the air. I hadn't eaten for twenty-four hours and had no desire to do so. I soon fell asleep again on the couch. The weekend had ended, and over the past three days I had drank about a two-four of beer, a couple of mickeys, dropped three hits of acid, a couple dozen pills, and smoked about the same number of joints. Tomorrow I would start the process over again.

For the next couple of weeks, the parties continued and were becoming the best in town. To us the best were judged by how much alcohol and dope were consumed. They were also becoming quite rowdy. One particular night the landlord made an appearance, and the next day Dad was informed that we had been evicted. We just packed up, and since I had nowhere to stay I moved back down to the other end of town on Balsam Street.

# Chapter 13

Back at "home" amongst my brothers, I felt strange. Vickey was still with Mother, who had now moved back to Sudbury from Toronto. I settled in and started to party as before. Dad would be at work until 4:30 each weekday. The whistles by now had no meaning to me except to tell time. We would party until then. Everyone would leave at 4 until after supper, when Dad almost nightly went to his girlfriend's. On the weekends, Dad was almost never around. So it was as if my younger brothers and I lived alone in our three-bedroom house. What else could we ask for?

Some days were spent downtown at Master John's, a shoe store, dealing dope. Our business was still flourishing, and we were getting somewhat worried about being busted. We now kept minimal amounts in the store and more often than not had guys dealing on the street. We were still creating quite a stir amongst the bigger dealers in town. The only thing that I think kept us from not getting involved in some kind of "war" was the fact that the competition probably thought our operation was headed by the Master John's operations in Toronto. I'm sure they thought we had some big connections and were not to be fooled with. Really, we were just three budding entrepreneurs with "high" aspirations.

I was now starting to head up a break-and-enter gang, and a very successful one at that. I cannot go into details as, out of the hundred or more over the ensuing years that I was personally involved in, I have only been charged with one. I was caught because of a drug bust, which I will go into in detail later. There were also car thefts and arson, but I was never caught. With our successes, my gang thought pretty highly of me, which is what I wanted. We were a low-profile gang, and I was the only one in charge of getting rid of the loot. That was so property wouldn't end up where it might be found out as stolen. Also, if one of the gang was caught, he wouldn't have a clue as to where to send the cops to look for it without implicating me, and they certainly wouldn't want that, because they also thought I had connections. All the gang received was cold cash and dope as their earnings. At the time I thought I was a smooth operator.

Christmas 1975 came and went, and for me, it wasn't too exciting. I had given up on Christmas after the time I had been beaten over a colouring book. New Year's Eve was what I was looking forward to. I had planned the biggest party yet. There would be about thirty people coming, and we knew Dad would spend the night at his girlfriend's. I had bought about ten two-fours of brew and numerous bottles of liquor. For food I bought junk food and pop for mix. The gang chipped in about half a pound of marijuana, the best available, not near as potent as grass today. The devil's weed was rolled into a couple hundred joints. We had a couple dozen hits of acid and a bowl full of uppers. The party was a success, and let me tell you, there wasn't much left over as far as booze and drugs were concerned, not to mention the few million brain cells we each must have killed off. What a way to end one year and begin another.

Things downtown at Master John's were becoming increasingly risky. The narcs had the place under surveillance around the clock. The over-the-counter business was wrapped up, and we had to become very discreet. Chris, Louis and I never held dope on our persons any more, as we would be the first to get busted. Also, our homes now were not safe either. The three of us were becoming more of a management team, delegating the work to our subordinates. The narcs were around day in and day out, and we now had nothing to worry about. We started putting to memory the faces of the narcotics officers and put the word out that things had to be kept as quiet as possible.

The cops must have thought we weren't on to them, because they were getting braver in their investigation and sent narcs in to try and buy dope. Louis was handling things beautifully, and we never gave them a chance to bust us. We had now gotten into the habit of not talking to anyone about new business. Our big parties were put on hold, and by the end of January we were getting a little bored.

I decided to have another "New Year's Eve" party at our house the following weekend. I figured our place would be safe for a party. I had brought home some grass and rolled it up to over one hundred joints and had it stashed in the attic underneath some insulation.

One weeknight, Dad was out as per usual. Tom, who was a year younger, and I had another one of our sibling rivalry fights and ended up threatening to kill each other. One thing led to another, and eventually he called the cops on me and told them I had drugs there. It didn't bother me, as I thought only a couple of cops would show up and I knew they wouldn't be able to search the place without a warrant. Besides, no one would find where I stashed it.

Within a few minutes I heard sirens screaming, and what seemed like the whole police force was converging on the place. In another minute, the place was surrounded by cops. They must have thought their investigation had come to an end prematurely and they were going to make the bust of the decade.

Tom, who had just turned sixteen and thus had the authority to do so, said that they could search the place. After years of battles between us, he was finally going to win. He led the cops upstairs and even to the attic and within minutes handed over my party stash. I'm sure the cops were disappointed and had expected a major bust. Small potatoes to them. For me, I was now being busted for possession for the purpose of trafficking. I was handcuffed and led away to the cop car. Yelling back at Tom "You will die for this! I guarantee you will die; mark my words," I was tossed into the back of the cruiser like a piece of garbage.

I sat looking out the window. Cops were everywhere. The neighbours were around and about in a nosy sort of way. I'm sure they had expected this sooner or later. It wasn't the first time the cops had been to our house because of a family dispute. I figured I'd be out on bail in a few days and then put on probation, as this was my first drug offence.

I was whisked downtown to regional police headquarters. I kept quiet all the way with thoughts of how I would eventually get back at my brother. Now I hated Tom as much as I hated Mother and wished they would both go to hell. I was hounded with questions during the ride into the city. I ignored them and sat solemnly in the back of the cruiser. I had the feeling this was going to be one hell of a long and unforgettable evening. After pulling into the parking lot, we waited for the garage door to open. The cruiser was driven in, and the electric motor started and the door closed behind me. I asked myself if this was really happening to me, and if I hadn't had the cuffs on, I would have pinched myself.

I was let out of the cruiser and escorted down a hall and up a flight of stairs and into a room with a conference-type table with a few chairs about. I defensively put on a tough guy act. The room was well lit but not as one would expect after being bombarded over the years with cop show after cop show on the television. There was no retina-burning spotlight. My handcuffs were taken off, and the arresting officer put them back in the leather pouch attached to his belt. His police-issued 38 hung by his side. He asked me to write out a statement after reading me my rights from a piece of paper tucked inside the lining of his officer's cap.

With all formalities taken care of, he started at me with the questions. "We know who you work for. Are you going to tell us?" By now the other pig who arrested me had joined us. It was quite unlikely the three of us were going to smoke the joints laid out on the table in front of us. I didn't answer their questions. "How about break and enters, car thefts?"

I replied, "You don't have anything on me. Even the dope wasn't for sale; it was for a weekend party."

"We know you are dealing dope, along with your other activities." They were trying to bluff me and didn't get anywhere with their questioning, much to their chagrin. Questions were asked about Master John's, and I said not a word.

I was told I was being charged with possession for the purpose of trafficking. They hauled me out of the chair and took me downstairs for a photo session and fingerprints taken for posterity's sake. I was then escorted ever so kindly to a private suite. The cold steel door was slammed shut and a metal key was inserted into the lock. With a twist of the wrist, the cop turned the key, the mechanism clicked unforgettably, and the key was removed.

I was now not only a prisoner of my mind but a prisoner of the law. Let me tell you, the two don't mix harmoniously. "Get lost, you pigs," I screamed as I stood against the cold steel bars. This was worse than imagined from TV. I grabbed and tried to shake the bars apart like a caged gorilla in a zoo. From glancing about, I realized I was alone in here; the other cells were empty. I was like an enraged lunatic in that cell, yelling, screaming, and then threatening suicide. I was threatening death upon Mother and Tom, and, in general, the whole world could go to hell. If I had ever thought

I was mad before, as when I fought back with Mother or the time I destroyed my bike in front of half of the school population, I would now be correctly labelled insane by anyone.

For at least half an hour I kept this up until I finally collapsed on the cold steel frame of a bed, welded to the cold steel wall. I sobbed like a little baby and never felt so sorry for myself. Why me, why me? I had never asked to grow up like this. I certainly didn't do these things on purpose. To others, it would seem that way. It was survival. I needed the attention, to be the big shot with money, drugs, booze, girls, and the list goes on. What had started out in innocence had now become a way of life because of my addictions.

The steel bed was uncomfortable—no mattress, pillow or blanket. Streams of tears flowed down my face. My shirtsleeves were wet from wiping away the tears of this emotional breakdown.

I felt as if the bottom had fallen out of the world and I was going to hell. The hatred and anger were welling up inside of me like the smoke from an out-of-control forest fire. I found myself yelling again like an animal gone mad. Vengeance upon mine enemies was all I could think of. Mother, that pathological liar, would someday pay for her madness. Tom had the same coming to him. Him being Mother's pet and all had always been too much to handle.

I went on and on until I finally was exhausted. I sat on the cold steel bed with my tear-stained face buried deep into my palms. I must have been in some kind of emotional shock, because as I sat there I felt totally removed from the world and was floating around in space in a cage.

Only when an officer came around to check on me did I start screaming again. Curse words must have been the specialty of the day, and I used them like never before. I stayed up all night. I craved a drink, a joint, pills, anything. By the time morning arrived, I was pretty well burnt. Mentally I was very distraught and felt as bad as with any drug trip that had turned on me. My mind was in a psychological void. I couldn't hold a thought for any length of time and needed drugs.

About 9:30, I was taken from the cell, handcuffed, and tossed again into the back of a cruiser. I loathed those tough-guy cops. The electric motor started behind me and the garage door rose. We backed out, and now I was on my way to court. It was a dull day in more ways than one. The sky was overcast, and the wind was blowing the snow around in great swirling clouds of turmoil, much like what was going on inside my head. We drove the few city blocks to the court-house and pulled into the rear of the building and parked. The cops got out into the cold February air. The back door was opened for me, and I stepped out, only to be met by an arctic blast, and here I was in a summer leather jacket. I was led inside and the cuffs were removed, and then I was ushered into the prisoner's box at the front of the courtroom. I sat amongst a few others who had apparently come over from the adjacent city jail to face their own charges.

It wasn't very often that I didn't like to be the centre of attention, but now I felt ashamed to be sitting in the prisoner's box in front of a nearly filled courtroom. Someone was going to pay for my being so humiliated. As expected, when my name was called, the case was remanded until a later date and a bail hearing would be held at 2 p.m. that afternoon. In the meantime, I would be held in custody at the district jail.

After a few more cases, court was dismissed, and we who had already been dealt with were being ushered out of the courtroom. I had never made this trip before to the "DJ" and thought we would have to go outside in order to get to the jail next door. This wasn't the case—we were taken to the basement of the courthouse and walked through a tunnel that had locked steel doors at each end. It was eerie, and I felt like I was walking through a metal cavern buried deep in the bowels of the earth on our way to hell. The walls were a puke green colour and cold to the touch. At the end of the tunnel, we waited until guards came to take us into the jail. As we passed through, the second metal door closed behind. Up some stairs, through another tunnel, until yet another steel door clanged closed behind us.

At first glance, I knew I had reached hell. I felt like an animal who had just been captured and herded through a maze of tunnels that led into a bullpen, which is exactly what this cage I was now in was called. Then you wait to get branded, pictures and prints. I had my pictures and prints taken as well as information pertaining to my background and next of kin, in case of an emergency. The only emergencies I had ever heard of happening in jail were either suicides or murders.

Since I was going back to court that afternoon for a bail hearing, I was locked back up in the bullpen to pass

161

the time. I couldn't wait to get a hold of Tom and wring his neck. All I had to do was get in touch with Dad and I would be on the streets pronto. After the bail hearing I was taken back to the district jail. I was informed that I would be put in with the rest of the jail population, which meant I had to change into a set of prison blues. I was mad as hell, and this was a waste of time, and I told them so. I was told to strip and put my clothes in a bag, which was given to me. Then I was told to take a shower and was handed a towel and some de-licing junk. More and more I was feeling as if Mother was ordering me around. For the past year, I had so much freedom from not being around Mother that this discipline was bringing out all the suppressed anger.

I showered and was then asked my sizes for clothes. I was issued a standard set of blues and then got dressed. After dressing, I suddenly felt like I had been stripped of my rights and felt truly like a prisoner. Next I was issued a blanket, sheets, pillowcase, towel, comb, toothbrush and paste, cup, plate, and bowl and then escorted upstairs, down a hall, and into a cellblock. I was told which cell was mine. I threw my things on the bed after the bar was pulled unlocking the door.

Immediately I told a guard I needed to make a phone call in order to have someone sign the bail bond. Dad was phoned, then Doug, by the prison staff, and to my dismay, they wouldn't sign for my release. I was fraught with hate towards them and the rest of the world. Just like I always had thought, nobody gave a care about me. I was now imprisoned, and my court date wasn't until the next week. *Man, someone is going to pay for this*, I thought, as I paced up and down the approximately seven- by twenty-five-foot caged corridor. I wished I could have gone into my cell, but they weren't open until after supper. Caged in with me were another half-dozen or so other guys of various assortment, none of whom I knew. I was cursing under my breath all the while.

At suppertime, a couple of guards came and unlocked the corridor door and we filed down the hall to a pass-through at the kitchen. We were each given a tray of food, and upon re-entering the corridor, which was now going to be my home for at least a week, were handed spoons. No forks or knives at the Crowbar Hotel. I took a seat at one of the two picnic-type tables of wood and steel bolted to the concrete floor. I didn't feel much like eating and was really craving some dope and a nice stiff drink. It now had been twenty-four hours without anything to appease my addictions. Just thinking of going a week without anything was making me very uneasy. I needed a drink in a bad way! That day and the previous night had wound me up, and I needed to unwind.

I got to talking to some of the guys and found out I was the youngest guy on the block. I had heard stories about what happened to us young fish in jails amongst the habitual criminals and gay men. I would have to put on my tough-guy act to cover up my insecurities. I talked big and acted big. I mouthed off to a couple of guards as they passed. The other guys immediately took a liking to me. I figured if I was a prisoner, I'd be the toughest.

Soon the cells were opened and a black-and-white TV was wheeled into the corridor. We would be allowed to watch the tube until 10 and then would be locked up for the night. I didn't have a choice but to try and relax somewhat. How could I relax with all the guilt and hate I was carrying around? Plus, I needed drugs. I holed up in my cell most of that first evening after making my bed on the top bunk. No one was double-bunked with me, but I was used to sleeping on the top. There was a bunk bed, toilet and sink in this jail cell. Laying in bed, I broke down and silently wept. The tears were just rolling down my face. I had never felt so alone, so rejected and unloved in all of my life. At the same time, I had never felt such a boiling of anger from within. As if I hadn't suffered enough over the past seventeen years! Drying my puffy eyes, I then lay staring at the ceiling, just like I used to when confined to my room during the years of my childhood. At least I didn't have to sneak across the room to go to the bathroom—the toilet was beside the bed!

I would be able to watch TV when I wanted during TV hours. I did watch a bit of TV that night, as I would on following nights. At 10 the TV was shut off and wheeled out of the corridor. The radio was then switched on. The speaker in the hallway filled the cell-block with music from a local radio station. We were told to lock up and we all went to our cells. Each door was individually locked after an overhead locking system was activated manually. We would be awakened at 7 a.m. for breakfast.

The music would play until 11 p.m. The time spent listening to music really got to me. I was constantly reminded of the parties, the drugs, the booze. How I wished I could be with my friends rum and Pepsi, marijuana and beer. Yes, I wish I could drink in my friend's sweet liquid flesh. Maybe share a joint with her. The anger and hate could be forgotten most times when I was with my friends. I needed the friendship so badly right then. There was no way in the world I could be with her tonight or even the next nights to follow. Even after the music ceased to play, I couldn't sleep and lay tossing and turning. The guards came by like clockwork and punched their portable time pieces as scheduled.

Laying there in the quietness was having paranoid effects on me. My mind was playing tricks on me. I could hear the strangest of noises, the odd scream, in another part of the jail. I just stared at the ceiling into the depths of the nightlight that shone dimly in the semi-darkness.

Well, I caught a few hours sleep that first night in the district jail. During the subsequent days, I learned about the routines of jail life. The radio would play all day long during the weekdays from 7 a.m. until after supper when the TV would be brought in. Breakfast about 7:30, lunch about 11:30, and supper around 3:30, 4 o'clock. On the weekend, the TV would be brought in after lunch. We were locked out of our cells by 9 a.m. on the weekdays. On the weekends our cells were open all day.

When locked out of our cells we spent the long hours in the caged cellblock pacing back and forth, playing cards or reading books or magazines. I spent the days craving addictive substances. We showered two or three times a week, down in the basement of the jail where the shower room was located. We received a change of clothing twice a week and bedding once. I personally got used to this routine quickly as it wasn't as bad as I had known in the past, living under the roof of my Gestapo Mother over the majority of my childhood. In comparison, I now had more freedom in most cases, and I guess that's why I adjusted to this institutional setting. For example, at home for years on end I had to sneak across my room to go to the bathroom. If I made one noise I could get beaten, so I pissed in the sink so that I wouldn't have to flush the toilet. Here I could take a piss whenever nature called. In fact I could announce it to the whole world.

Unlike those endless hours spent "grounded" to my room, while locked in my cell I could read, which was unheard of at home, or talk. Everything ran like clockwork in here and regulated my life much in the same way those whistles had in the past, except I wouldn't be beaten for being late. How could I be late? I was in jail. I wasn't going anywhere. Even the simplest thing like watching television was better in this prison environment than in my childhood one. I didn't have to sit Indian style with my back as straight as a wall. Yes, the comparisons were many, and had I known that being in jail was better than living at home, I as a child would have rather been in this physical prison than the emotional prison of home. The benefits in jail were many. I suppose that is why many of these repeat offenders didn't find it so bad there. Compared to their home life, if they had one at all, jail was the best home they had ever known.

The day of my court appearance had arrived. After 9 in the morning I was taken down to the bullpen. I was let out to change into my civilian clothes, "civvies." At least I felt better about the apparel. Back in the bullpen to wait with the others. About 9:45, we were led through the underground tunnel to the courthouse. This was becoming a habit I didn't like. Back in the prisoner's box again, how humiliating. My Legal Aid lawyer was there, and we chatted about the charges. There was the trafficking charge and also a trespassing and public mischief charge. I had received a suspended sentence for the latter two the previous year, and now that I was in trouble again, I would be sentenced for them. Now they would all be tried together. By the time the court recessed, my charges had been put over for another week.

We were then taken back to the jail. I figured I could make it through another week of this. I knew I would get off on these charges because another guy had just recently been sentenced to sixty days for trafficking and he had been caught with over fifty pounds of marijuana. Since I was busted with only over 100 joints, and he got about one day in jail for each pound, theoretically I should get less than a day in jail. Since I had already been in here doing dead time, which should go in my favour, I would be free the next week, wouldn't I?

The long days went by, and the day I would be set free arrived. All I had to do was go to court and be sentenced to maybe a probation order of some sort; then I'd be on the streets by noon. The first thing I'd do upon release is get some much-needed dope and alcohol, as I was gasping. The last two weeks or so had been hard on me, especially those first few days. It was a good thing I wasn't a speed or heroin addict, or I would have totally gone over the edge, with the withdrawal symptoms and all. Just the same, I had developed quite a psychological dependence on the drugs I used. Alcohol, on the other hand, had helped me through the past couple of years.

I was dressed in my civvies and taken to court. In the prisoner's box for the last time, I waited impatiently for my name to be called. Finally I was called and stood up in the judge's presence. The judge read the charges and the crown stated their case, which my lawyer defended me against. After all was said and done, His Honour spoke. "Mr. Tunney, is there anything you would like to say before I pass sentence?" I replied with some sob story in order to try and get his sympathy and laid it on real thick. His Honour pondered momentarily and then spoke again. I was shocked at the verdict. In total I received about six months or so in jail, which would be spent at an out-of-town prison. I couldn't believe it and was set ablaze within. I kept my cool, but I wanted to yell and scream at the judge. I was thinking of how crazy I would go in prison.

At court recess I was taken back to the jail. In the connecting tunnel, I started flipping out and was fighting with the guards, screaming, "No! No! No! You can't do this to me!" I was carrying on like a mad man and fighting just the same. They locked me in the tunnel, and I didn't stop screaming. Tears were streaming down my face. When the tunnel opened again, about six guards jumped me, cuffed me hand and foot, and carried me into the jail. I was carried up two flights of stairs by the officers and thrown into a solitary confinement cell, the "hole." The cuffs and leg irons were taken off me, and I was told to strip and was then searched. I was then handed a security gown that wouldn't tear and a matching blanket, as I was threatening to kill myself. I was locked in and left alone, oh, so alone.

I immediately crossed the line and started banging at the solid steel door like an enraged gorilla. I was totally flipped out and wanted to die like never before. That was impossible in this solitary cell. The furnishings consisted of a toilet and a bed. The bed was a concrete slab about five inches thick, placed on a metal base. There were no bars, and the walls were of concrete and steel. Even the door with its solid steel construction only had a five-inch-square window of inch-thick glass. I had a view of a steel wall. A slot in the door was locked and only opened for meals. Now this was as bad as those countless hours "grounded" in my room except I could freely use the toilet. I found out I couldn't have any reading material except the Bible, and I certainly didn't want to read that. I felt as if I were imprisoned alive in a large steel tomb of immense proportions, designed on a scale to hold some Palaeolithic giant of times gone past.

I was mad at the whole world and everyone in it who had conspired to have me locked away. Words cannot describe what I felt. To say that I was fraught with insane madness might be too mild of a conclusion. I yelled, kicked and threatened to kill myself. "I want to die, I want to die!" I screamed. This was Mother's fault. Someday, somewhere, somehow she would pay her debt to me. She had raised me to be in her likeness, and she had done a great job. "Like mother, like son." I was as insane as she was now, and my mind was messed up real bad. If I lived through this

169

jail sentence, she would die in her own ice-cold blood for destroying my mind.

My verbal outbursts subsided somewhat, and I suffered silently twenty-four hours a day. Over the next few days and nights spent in the hole, my mind was taxed to the limit. I didn't eat the bean junk they served me. My nightmares were recurring nightly, and I would awake as I had as a child, in a cold sweat. I would scream in the middle of the night, and then a guard would come and check on me. Thoughts of being possessed by the devil were again in the forefront of my tormented mind. Those thoughts had been in a suppressed state somewhat for the past few years. It was unreal what was coming to my mind constantly.

I did quiet down somewhat, and it was decided that I would be put in population with some other cons on a cellblock. Once given my issue of clothes and such, I was escorted to a cellblock, where I wasn't double-bunked. This would be my home until I got transferred out of there. I had seen a doctor a couple of times, and after he took note of my addictions, I was told that if I hadn't come to jail, I would have most likely died within the next few months as my addictions grew. I told him I didn't care and wished I would drop dead now.

I had found out that I was going out with the next "chain gang" on a bus called the Goose to a jail up north near Timmins, in a little town called Monteith. Back in the jail routine again, I waited for the day to come when I would be transferred. In the interim, I had no visitors and I dwelled on what was ahead of me. To me six months was a hell of a long time to be sitting around doing nothing when I could be partying. Others who had been in prison for years would laugh at such a short term of imprisonment.

Really though, this was just a continuation except Mother wasn't the jailer.

# Chapter 14

The day arrived that a group of other convicts and I were being shipped out to other reformatories or penitentiaries around Ontario via the Goose. I was taken from my cell and down to the now full bullpen. We were all changed into our civvies for the trip. One by one we were then handcuffed and shackled with leg irons. If I ever felt like a criminal, this moment in time was it. We were lined up against a wall until each had on his restraints.

I was filled with animosity towards these guards for making me feel like the scum of the earth. Alex Hailey wrote in one of his novels, "Only with experience will you know the true depths of animal despair and degradation to which the prison system can reduce a human being." We each had to grab a red canvas sack that contained our personal effects. Then, as I had seen on TV many times, we were marched in single file down the tunnel and out to the awaiting bus. The walk was reminiscent of the old movies where the prisoners were cuffed, shackled and had to drag around an attached steel ball so they couldn't run. I suppose we were lucky that we weren't dragging a steel ball around. Walking like this was bad enough. You had to walk like a tiny infant taking his first steps. Just little half steps, or else the shackles would bite into your ankles. By the time I got to the bus I was cursing because of my sore ankles.

So this was the Goose? I stepped up carefully into the blue converted school bus. The windows had been tinted and metal screens had been screwed over so no one could escape. A steel screened partition was in place across the width of the bus behind the first row of seats. I walked through the opened partition and took a seat near the back. When we were all aboard, the door of the screened partition was shut and locked. The driver and his escorts loaded up our belongings, and we headed out in this mobile prison cell. It was early afternoon when we started out. We would stop in North Bay for the evening and then the next day we would be so kindly driven to our destination at the Monteith Correctional Facilities.

We drove down Elm Street, the main drag, and I saw a few familiar faces. In about ten minutes we were leaving the city via Highway 17 East. I gazed sullenly through the screened window at the passing scenery. I was really taken back by the sights. The highway to North Bay was a route I had memorized as it was the route our family took to our cottage on Lake Nipissing back when we were all together. Hundreds of times I had driven on this route. Today it took on a whole different appearance. As we drove, I envisioned driving down here with my family. Now the family had fallen apart and never again would all be together at one gathering. The sights along the road brought back the thoughts of freedom as I knew it once to be. Now I would have to put freedom on a mental hold, for fear that dwelling upon such thoughts might surely drive me mad. I had always been a prisoner of sorts, but unlike now I at least walked the land. I tried not to think about things, but with every bump, hill, turn, tree and house along the way I couldn't forget.

Just over an hour later, we drove up to the front of the district jail in North Bay. We got off the bus and were escorted through the barred doors. I guess all the jails are the same, the bars, the locks, the uniformed guards. We were taken to a cellblock, issued bedding and given cells. We would be locked in all evening with no TV or radio. Supper was later served to us in our cells, and the rest of the evening was spent in solitude. I must have gone over hundreds of events in my life that night. I cried and cursed the night away silently until I was finally overcome with sleep.

Awakened at 6 a.m., we ate breakfast and shortly afterwards were put through the routine of being cuffed, shackled and herded back on the Goose for the rest of the trip to Monteith.

We travelled deep into the snow-covered Northern Ontario countryside. It was quite a scenic excursion that under other circumstances I might have enjoyed. The ride was long and uncomfortable. School buses are not the most satisfying modes of transportation to be using on extended trips. It seemed we were travelling to some far-off uninhabitable land.

When we were finally out of the bush, looming ominously ahead was a huge building complex, the prison of Monteith. We drove through the town of scattered houses. If you blinked you would have missed it. Some guy on the bus who had obviously been there before stated that prison personnel were the only people who lived there. As we got closer I noticed that other buildings surrounding the main prison. The Goose pulled up to the front of the main building. We were taken inside and escorted downstairs to the basement to Admitting and Discharge.

We went through the process of being finger-printed, having our pictures taken, and being issued clothes, bedding and grooming aids. The clothes were the same as those in Sudbury except they were brown, more tan than anything. I noticed a couple of guys being issued blue clothing and wondered why.

We were given a rundown of the place. The jail was divided into two sections, the brown and the blue. The blue side was usually for older convicts and repeat offenders. There was no contact between the blues and browns. That was to keep the older and more experienced cons from coming on to us young and mostly first-timers.

We would sleep in dormitories, situated on an upper floor. Since this was a minimum security prison, the bars were kept to a minimum also. For our meals we would come downstairs to where we were now and go down a hall to a common dining room. Once we were settled in we would be expected to get involved in programs that were available. We would have canteen once a week as well as library privileges. Canteen, I learned, was a sum of money that we actually never saw but could order such things as tobacco, chips, magazines, etc., with. It consisted of only a few bucks a week.

We were taken upstairs and shown to our respective beds, which would be home during our stay there. My time would amount to about four months with good time taken into consideration. It was almost March now, so I would be free about the end of June. Beside each of our beds was a footlocker to keep our belongings in. The brown side of this prison consisted of two dormitories, and in each were about three dozen or so beds, most of which were occupied. A walled hallway divided the two rooms. An office was situated at one end where the guards could watch over us. At the other was a door leading downstairs to the basement. We were shown how to make our beds properly, "hospital style." Every morning we would have to make our beds in this manner or else we could be disciplined. As I made my bed I looked furtively around out of the corners of my eyes. I guess I was sizing the place up. I didn't like the idea of sleeping in a room full of guys because of my past experiences with men and my increasing disgust with them. Also, I didn't feel like being jumped at night, as I heard happens in these places every once in a while. I would have preferred to do my time in my own little cell.

The first night I hardly slept and tossed and turned. When I did fall asleep, I had a nightmare. Over the past almost month in jail, my recurring visions of devils constantly bothered me, and like in my childhood, I thought I was possessed by the powers of Satan.

During the first couple of days at Monteith I just got acquainted with my new surroundings. The routine would pretty much be like at the Sudbury jail except that we could be involved in workshops or schooling during the days. I had been interviewed and had decided on taking two shop classes, bricklaying and woodworking. Now Monday through to Friday I would at least be busy. Both shops happened to be in the same building, which looked more like a converted barn. We had to go outside to get to the shops. We weren't escorted, and since there were no fences, we could have taken off at any time. A couple of nights a week we were allowed to go to the gym and work out with weights or play team sports.

The first couple of weeks went by without incident. I took up smoking a corncob pipe, as that was the thing to do around there. My brand of tobacco was Borkum Riff. I guess it helped pacify my urges to smoke dope. Chewing tobacco was in too, so I did that as well, taking a pinch of snuff and pressing it against my gums, then constantly spitting brown-gravy gobs into a Styrofoam cup. I didn't see the point to it all but had to be like the others.

At the shops I was learning about bricklaying and mortar mixing, which wasn't too exciting. Woodshop on the other hand was okay as I had in grade nine learned to use a wood lathe. I went right to work fashioning pipes that I traded with the cons for canteen supplies. Once a businessman, always a businessman. The pipes were used for smoking tobacco or contraband dope that had been smuggled in. One thing I never did in jail was do drugs. I was too scared of going on a bad trip. I'm sure I would have crossed the line permanently. I had plenty of opportunity to trade my pipes for dope, but I was just too frightened.

Sleeping was a dreadful experience. My nightmares

were becoming more vivid and real. I guess some kind of schizophrenic paranoia was taking control of me. More than ever I felt possessed by the devil. The turmoil inside was getting so bad that secretly I wished I could sell my soul to Satan in order to be set free from jail and from myself. I would wake up in the night in a cold clammy sweat and gaze about in the semi-darkness for hours. I would see visions of the devil that I had seen as a kid.

In the daytime during leisure hours I started getting into transcendental meditation of a sort. I would sit in a trance, staring at the painted concrete block wall. I would focus on a particular block and just stare at it, focusing all my psychic energy upon the block. I had remembered reading about strange things, power of the mind and such. I figured that if I could create enough psychic energy I could make the concrete block fly loose from the wall and smash into my head with such force that my brainless head would be splattered all over the place. I just had to get out of here.

A fellow named Brodie, who I had casually gotten to know, approached my bed. Brodie stood about five foot six and had a protuberant stomach that was shirt-button popping. He had jet black hair that lay straight upon his head, style somewhat outdated, like the Beatles. Brodie had deep brown eyes that blended well with his olive-skinned complexion. He always seemed mild-mannered and was very soft-spoken.

We said our hellos, and then he opened up the conversation. "Randy, I understand that you would like to sell your soul to the devil in order to get out of jail." That statement stung like a whip across my backside.

How did he know I had been thinking of that? He went on, "If you want to give your soul to the devil, all you have to do is tear up a Bible, then flush it down the drain. If you do so, upon your leaving jail you will gain all the riches you desire, money, cars, a wife, and then you will die and your soul will be the devil's."

I sat and listened intently to him telling me these prophetic visions of what could be mine. Just what I wanted, I told myself. Still more to come as Brodie told me the details of some of my nightmares. Again I was shocked. He left me alone by my bedside. I asked myself over and over, how did he know of my dreams and wishes? I looked across the dorm and gazed at Brodie's profile while he sat on his own bed. As I stared at him, it dawned on me that maybe he was Satan's helper. His skin, his hair, his eyes, his meek manners.

I shuddered at the thought of this being real and became instantly paranoid. I had probably been talking in my sleep and was overheard. Brodie's bed was only a dozen feet away. I had to get out of here; I was going insane. "Mother, you are going to pay for this," I yelled in total madness. I started throwing things about the dormitory. Everyone became instantly silent and motionless and stood out of range as I threw things about. A guard came, and I threw a metal-framed chair at him. He retreated and went hurriedly to the office. I didn't know what was happening; I was out of control. I was a reproduction of Mother brought to life.

Four officers appeared in the doorway. I yelled at them and called them dirty names. Seconds later they rushed me like a pack of wild dogs, the sound of their military-style boots pounding the floor as they ran towards me. "I'll kill every one of you," I screamed hysterically. They jumped me, and we struggled in a pile of arms, legs and bodies. I kept yelling insanely at them. One guy grabbed a leg, as did another, then my arms.

They carried me across the room and down the stairs. I was in a blind rage. I finally was going to spend time behind the steel door in solitary confinement. Inside I was ordered to strip, which I did against my will. There was something I didn't like about standing naked in front of these men. I felt like at any moment I would be sexually abused by them. I was given a security gown and blanket, identical to the ones in the Sudbury jail. A cell was opened for me, and I was thrown bodily in. The cell door clanged shut and was locked. The big entrance steel door was slammed shut and locked as well. I stood with the blankets and gown against my chest. I threw them to the floor and started yelling and screaming insanely, oblivious of my surroundings.

When I did settle down long enough to notice my surroundings, I saw a solid steel frame, the dimensions of a bed, welded to the wall. I surmised that was what I was to sleep on. Also in this cell was a hole in the floor where the toilet normally would have been. The lighting was minimal, and I was in semi-darkness. What a hole, a living hell to say the least. I grabbed the bars that were the front wall and screamed, "Let me out of here, let me out of here! I will go insane if I stay in here!" The place reeked of dried urine and feces. A few bugs were scurrying about in their search for sustenance.

I donned the heavy tear-proof gown over my nakedness in order to not feel so much like an animal.

It didn't help! I was now broken down and in tears. Here I was, a seventeen-year-old victim of a tormented upbringing and being tormented more by my perpetuating misery. Mother was hundreds of miles away, yet her presence was still deeply embedded into my battered psyche. Her spiritual presence was every bit as real as if she were physically there. Such can be the results of years of abuse. The physical scars heal; the unseen emotional scars may never. I wished I could have dug my nails deep into my skull and scraped out every painful memory of her. That sure would have left a vacancy inside of me.

I sat on the cold steel bed tearfully, my face buried deep into my palms. This was like being two prisoners at once, one within myself, another physically by horizontal and vertical bars. God, how I wanted to be set free from both prisons! I was, however, finding out one thing of consequence: there is no greater prison than being trapped in conflict with your personality.

I stood up and grabbed the bars and felt their coldness in my hands. I started screaming, "I want to be free! I want to be free! Please! *Please!*" I then paced around my cage like a captive animal. Lunch came later and was passed through the slot in the barred door. I cursed the guard as he left. The big steel door clanged shut, echoing through to the farthest reaches of my mind and beyond.

"I'm not eating this junk," I yelled as I gazed upon the paper plate. I had heard about the meals down here in the hole. You ate the same thing for each meal. I couldn't believe this was real. My lunch consisted of a cup of jailhouse tea, dishwater variety, two slices of nearly dry white bread, and, for the main course, bean cake. Now this bean cake junk was a mixture of various beans mashed together and fried up in a ton of grease. It was served up like a piece of cake. I took a taste of it using the accompanying plastic spoon. Man, it tasted worse than it looked! I threw the meal on the floor outside the cell, along with the so-called tea. I don't think the bugs would have eaten it either.

Mother must have been happy when she found out I had gone to prison. I'm sure in some sick way she was gloating over my failure. To her, my imprisonment would only substantiate her claims that I had deserved all the punishment over the years. The law had just proven that. She had the mentality of a billy goat. I had inherited many of her traits. I knew and admitted it to myself that I was crazy. Surely she must have known it of herself, even though she never admitted it. I mean, who would want to? I knew it of myself, and I certainly wasn't going to admit to someone that I was greatly emotionally disturbed. No, it was just a secret battle for survival. Man against madness.

It wasn't long before a couple of officers came and got me from my cell. The head of the psychiatry department wanted to see me. He introduced himself and started rambling off a series of pre-programmed questions.

"What's wrong?"

"Nothin'."

"Is there anything that's bothering you?"

"Yeah, talking to you!"

"Have you ever had any homosexual relationships?"

"*No!*"

And the list went on. I certainly wasn't going to say anything to some educated quack who prowled around like a burglar in other people's minds. He saw no point in carrying on this one-sided interview and told the guards to return me to my cell. I left, thinking I had made a fool of him.

Back in the hole, I sat on the steel bed and stared at nothing. I mean, there was nothing to look at anyhow. Supper came, the same as what was for lunch. I wasn't going to eat that junk and didn't. The time dragged by, and I was constantly thinking of how to wreak revenge upon my enemies, once released from jail, if I lived. Every hour I was checked on, and I just cursed at them. I tried to sleep that night but just dozed off for a while and then would be awakened in the middle of a satanic nightmare or because of being uncomfortable. How could one sleep on a piece of steel? I had placed one blanket across the metal to keep the cold off me. That blanket was my mattress. The second blanket I used to cover myself while I lay in fetal position. Hunger was gnawing at my innards, as I hadn't eaten since breakfast.

For the next couple of days I neither ate nor drank a thing. Every hour when a guard came to check on me, I would blow up in a visual and verbal outburst. When the other cons from the brown side came down for their meals they would have to pass by the closed steel vault-like outer door. I always made it a point to yell and scream as they went by. I could hear them making comments about me in their passing. Always on my mind was what Brodie had told me about selling my soul to the devil so I could be free. I knew that if I asked for a Bible it would be given to me, as that was all we were allowed to read while in solitary confinement.

By the morning of the fourth day, I was physically and mentally burnt out. I had hardly slept and was as hungry as a bear. When breakfast arrived, I decided to eat it. I drank the warm tea, ate the two slices of bread, and spoon-fed myself the strange-tasting fried bean cake. Let me tell you, if ever I was to see bean cake listed on a menu in a restaurant, I would leave. At least now it curbed my appetite, although my taste buds would be messed up for life. Later the same meal for lunch, then supper, and repeatedly over the next days.

I was now pleading to be put back into prison population, to no avail. I was going crazy and was succumbing to the animal despair and degradation the prison system can reduce a human being to. If ever I felt like a good-for-nothing person before, I now felt twice as bad. Subliminally, being in prison was uttering the same words Mother had told me over the years. This time was incredibly dehumanizing—sleeping on a metal bed, no mattress, no pillow; the hole in the floor; the bugs; the serving of that bean cake, tea and bread meal, morning, noon and night. I was no better than the cockroaches.

By the tenth day, I even started to like the food. The repeated nightmares of various beginnings but parallel endings were tormenting me. This was a living hell! Some of the days I sat for hours in a hypnotic trance, staring at the bars. I would focus all my psychic energies on the bars and try to bend them so I could escape from this hell. Those mind-bending experiences didn't work, but they sure passed the time.

I was finally told I was being let out of the hole. Apparently they could only keep you in segregation up to fourteen days and then you had to be released. I was given a lecture by the Big Brass. I sat in front of him, answering his barrage of questions and orders on how to behave in a sociable manner in accordance to the rules and regulations of this particular institution. "Yes sir...yes sir...yes sir," I answered. I would have shone his shoes there and then if it meant getting back to the dorm any faster.

When I got back upstairs with the others I found out I was an instant celebrity amongst the other cons. I mean, I had fought with four guards at once and had stuck it out in the hole for two weeks. I had become a tough guy and now fit in with most of them. This is the mentality we had as prisoners. I was offered smokes, tobacco, candy, etc. Well, the first thing this hero did was take a shower and have a shave. My body odour was quite offensive as I had only showered two or three times and hadn't shaved at all. After refreshing myself, I felt like a new person and couldn't wait to have a meal down in the dining hall.

I noticed Brodie hanging around and wanted nothing more to do with the strange dude, devil or no devil. Downstairs, having my first real food in two weeks, I was ribbed by the guys about the diet I had "bean" on. I stuffed myself to the maximum. That night I slept peacefully, as I hadn't been sleeping well. Even though these beds were uncomfortable, I felt like I was sleeping on a brand new mattress in comparison to the steel bed in the hole.

Over the next week or so I got back into my routine, going to shop, to the gym and involved in all other aspects of regulated jail life. At the gym I usually watched the guys work out. Some of them were quite huge in comparison to my skinny, underweight body. I started wishing I could be more muscular and healthy instead of an alcoholic and drug addict. Watching them reminded me of when I was a kid, wishing I was Superman so Mother couldn't hurt me.

Twenty-four hours a day I was on guard against other men. Because of my acquired sexual hang-ups, I was always in a state of confusion. I had noticed that a couple guys in particular were always trying to catch my eye. These guys were the older ones amongst us, not that they were old men or anything. It was just that I was one of the youngest in there. I never took these non-verbal insinuations to heart and tried to ignore them. If I had not been so worried about myself psychosexually, I probably wouldn't have even noticed. Always in my subconscious was the possibility that I might be gay. It was just another aspect of my personality that was driving me insane, if I was not already. The sexual crisis that had been perpetuated since I was about the age of eight was probably the foremost damaging aspect of my personality.

What had started out as a wish to be a girl so to be loved by Mother was now having devastating effects on me psychologically. I now wanted to be a girl just to be free of me. This problem in itself was what was probably fuelling the vindictive attitude of mine towards Mother, myself and society in general. Yes, the feelings of hate I had towards myself were as many as those against Mother. Between the two of us we could win a world war with our combined madness.

The days went by, and I had been out of the hole for about two weeks or so. One day I was in the shower area alone and standing under the shower head. A steady stream of tepid water was cleansing my body. Showers always seemed to revive me somewhat from this arduous life. One of the guys who had been eyeing me sexually came into the shower area and took the one next to me. There were no partitions between us. Instantly I became uncomfortable in his presence and stepped out of the shower. I started to towel myself dry. When I turned around, three other cons were standing, fully clothed, in front of me. I was told not to make a sound or I would end up getting killed. One of the three was the guy in the shower's friend, who had also been eyeing me insidiously. They grabbed me and I was stricken with terror. "Okay, pretty boy, we are going to have some fun."

The guy in the shower had by now advanced towards me. I struggled silently as others would hear and I didn't want them to know what was happening to me. I was sexually molested and forced to perform sex acts in return. At that moment I wanted to kill them and then myself. In a minute, as if nothing had happened, the clothed guys walked away. The naked man next to me was smiling with a grin of satanic wickedness. He stated that if a word was said I would be shanked (knifed). I just glared at him with a look that could kill and put on my pants and went to my bed.

I collapsed on the bed and buried my head into the pillow and wept as silently as possible. I had never felt so much disgust or hate ever before. I felt as if I had been killed and wanted to destroy the whole world.

Mother was going to pay for this. It was her fault I was here; it was her fault I was so messed up; it was all her fault. She had to pay, she had to, had to, had to. A silent volcano was erupting inside; how could I keep it in?

I had to get away from these guys. I wanted to crawl into a hole and die! A hole, yes, that's it! I got up from the bed and grabbed a chair. I walked carrying the chair out of the dorm and down the hall towards the guards' office. I raised the chair and hurled it at the door. The glass window shattered. The guards inside jumped in fright and rushed me. Again I fought and again I was carried bodily to the hole. Again I was stripped and given security blankets and a gown. Again I stood cursing and swearing at them as they left me alone in that bug-crawling cell. I screamed at them, telling them I was going to starve myself to death. Yes, that was what I was going to do.

I donned the gown and kept screaming. I had to let out the anger and madness. Nothing in my life was normal. I was living my life in hell on earth. First fourteen years of physical and mental cruelty that left seemingly incurable scars. The messed-up sexual identity. Then the drug and alcohol addictions; the homosexuality; the rebellion against Mother, myself, and society. The crime, the jail, and now the homosexual molestation. Man, when was it going to end? Satan was doing this to me! He wanted my soul, and he was going to get it. I had to die! I had to! Again I broke down in the cell and bawled my messed-up head off. The desperate loneliness was unbearable.

The first three days passed down in the hole more or less the same as my last visit. The yelling, the nightmares, the refusal to eat. The difference this time was that as my anger grew I didn't give in to that bean cake. I didn't know at the time that a human can only go about seven days without drink and forty without food. I had lost all will to live after that dehumanizing sexual assault. Throughout my life, I had endured life's tragedies and had lived a life no one should even know existed. The fact is that I was only one amongst the multitude!

Everything that had happened to me previously in comparison to this sexual assault was now kids' stuff. If someone had approached me and given me the choice between being beaten and whipped 100 times, which would have left countless welts and bruises on my person, or being raped and forced into a sexual act, which would leave unseen emotional scars, I would now without hesitation have chosen the first. I now knew more than ever that emotional abuse far out-weighs physical abuse. I didn't even have a mark on me, yet I hurt more than after any one of the hundreds of physical beatings I had endured over the years at the hands of Mother. In fact, Mother was a saint compared to those men upstairs.

By the end of the fourth day without liquids or solids my stomach was sending out signals to my brain that it was in desperate need of food. The guards had been checking on me every hour, as was their duty. During the fifth day the prison doctor came and talked to me. I was told that they had places for people like me. I had always had a tenacious mind, and here was the ultimate test. If there had been any way of killing myself that would have been faster I would have been dead by then. I didn't know who I was or what I was and was in a state of utter mental confusion.

I started to imagine the scents of certain foods, pizza, steak, spaghetti—all my favourites. Even the scent of rank urine that hung constantly in the air took on a different odour. I was so thirsty that at times I was tempted to drink urine. I had lost several pounds through dehydration and was becoming more of a bone rack. My hair seemed to be drying out, and as I ran my fingers through it, dead hair would fall away from my scalp.

Every time the meal of bean cake, bread and tea came, it looked more appetizing. I sure as hell hadn't expected to start craving that bean cake. There it was every meal, sitting there, inviting me to partake. I'm sure even the tea would have tasted great, as they say it always does in commercials. The cups of tea seemed to be beckoning me with words: "I taste great, I taste great." I bet it did and watched as wisps of steam rose from the cup. I wished the steam was rising from Aladdin's lamp and would turn into a genie from Arabian folklore. Then I could have a wish. The wish would be to be free from me and this prison—and to have a turkey dinner, of course. No such luck, as each wisp of steam dissipated into thin air, only to be followed by another and another. No genie, no freedom, no turkey dinner.

The guards came and took away the meal, and again I was alone in this solitary cell. Alone, except for the company of my bug friends. Breakfast would come in about fifteen hours. I don't know why I thought of breakfast, as I wasn't going to eat anyhow. I tried to push aside the thoughts of food, but my stomach kept reminding me of its deprivation. I had never been so hungry before in all my life—for food, that is. I always had the insatiable and unfulfilled appetite to be loved. At the same time, I had never felt so much emotional pain nor like less of a human being.

I lay on the steel bed, a blanket for a mattress. I was totally isolated from the rest of the world and was going to die this way, in a hell hole, as was expected of me. The pains in my stomach were becoming more agonizing as the time passed. I figured it was after midnight, which meant I was in the sixth day of my starvation death wish. I had defied death on numerous other occasions, but now more than ever I wanted to die. I was lying on my back staring at the ceiling about ten feet above me, my hands clasped across my stomach. I was pressing my stomach in hopes of relieving the gnawing hunger pains. I started imagining death and being in hell. The thoughts of such an existence beyond the realm of mortal life terrorized my already disturbed psyche. I felt the approaching death before me. The ever-increasing visions of Satan coming to retrieve my soul were bringing me again to the limits of my sanity, if I had any left. I could have sworn I was about to die. I had never felt so terrified. It was happening to me. I was slowly dying; the gut-wrenching pain was excruciating.

All of a sudden I didn't want to die. I was up from the bed and grasping the bars and with frantic screams was hollering for someone to bring me food. "Bring me food, bring me food!" I yelled repeatedly. Still screaming, "I don't want to die, I don't want to die.

Please bring me some food! No, I don't want to die!" There were hours until breakfast, and here I was in the basement of a prison in solitary confinement, dying. How was I going to make it? The hunger pains were ever increasing as I flipped out in the cell. I figured I was going to die any minute, and I didn't want to. I was too scared to go to hell. I could sense the presence of Satan waiting greedily to pluck my soul from me at the point of death. The scent of death hung like a dense fog in the closeness of this cell.

I had gone insane and was banging on the steel walls and calling out for food. I don't know how long this went on; all I knew was that it was near the end. I was hearing voices calling out my name, "Randy, Randeeey, Randeeeeey." I was as paranoid as ever I had been.

"No! No! No! You are not having my soul. I'm not going to die!" I screamed.

"Randy, Randy," another voice boomed somewhere in this death chamber. "Do you want to live?" I heard it say.

"Yes, yes, I want to live; don't let me die."

"If you want to live, you will have to read the Bible from cover to cover," the voice said.

"I'll do it, I'll do it," I screamed. "Guard, guard," I screamed over and over.

Finally a guard on his rounds came to the door. "What do you want?" he asked.

"Can you bring me a Bible, please?" I asked in between gasping for air. I knew he wouldn't refuse me, because the Bible was all we could read while in the hole. He said he would try to find one and left after locking the outside vault-like door. He must have thought I had cracked as he went looking for a Bible in the middle of the night. The pangs of death were gnawing at my innards. I felt like a veritable basket case that held not the bread of life but the fruit of death, which was now all-consuming. It must have been 2 or 3 in the morning, and here I was, seventeen years old, on the verge of death by self-starvation. On top of that I wanted a Bible. That voice had told me that if I wanted to live I had to read it from cover to cover.

The guard returned and handed me a Bible and left. Now in my hands I held this book that had *Good News* written all over it. Little did I know at the time that I now held the bread of life and the food within would someday be my sustenance. I was in a very distraught emotional state and utterly confused. A voice told me that if I wanted to live I had to read it through page by page. I lay down on the steel bed, tears still wet on my face, and opened up the Bible. The first section was called Genesis, and as I read about the earth's creation, the pain started to leave my body. Soon I knew I would make it through the night.

Upon this realization, I started weeping uncontrollably. I started talking to God and asked for His forgiveness of my sins. I just cried and cried and let out all the pain inside. I rambled on in private conversation with God. I promised God that when I got out of jail I would go to church every Sunday, stop drinking and doing drugs. Also I would start helping others who had the misfortune of growing up under circumstances similar to mine. I would get healthy and strong like some of the guys in here whom I saw working out. I repeated these promises over and over. I told God that nobody deserved to grow up not knowing love. *Please God, let someone love me; all I want is to be part of a loving family.* The tears were streaming down my face.

I spent the rest of the night reading and praying. Finally breakfast came. I ate the bean cake and bread hungrily, like a starved wolf. The tea went down like fine wine. I had survived the night. God had saved me. The devil's blade was dull. For the next several days I lay in bed, if you could call it that, and peacefully read the Bible. By the time my days were up in the hole, I had read the Bible from cover to cover and had started reading some of the interesting sections again. I especially liked the New Testament, Psalms and Proverbs.

I was going to be put back in general population and didn't very much like the thoughts of facing those perverts who had partaken in my sexual molestation. How could I face them when I felt like killing them? Reluctantly I went back upstairs to the dorms. As my eyes came across a couple of those perverts, I felt like tearing them apart then and there. I went to my bed and lay down after making it up.

Later I saw Brodie. The strange-looking dude gave me the creeps. How was I going to be able to stay up here with these guys? I found out my place in the shop classes had been filled by a new prisoner. That meant I had nothing to do during the days except hang around the dormitory. What a drag, and I still had some time to do until my sentence ended. I was sure glad when it was mealtime so I could enjoy some almost-real food, as prison food goes.

After a couple of days hanging around the dorm and catching up on some meals, I decided that I couldn't stand it any longer. I was ready to go and do another fourteen days in the hole. I started mouthing off to a guard, and by now they didn't trust me the slightest. So I was again taken to the hole, this time with no resistance. This habit of being in and out of the hole continued for the rest of my jail term.

Finally my day of release came, and I, as well as the staff there, was only too happy to see me leave. I still wonder if anyone ever has caused as much trouble as I did. I sure hope not. There were a couple of other guys from various places leaving as well that day. It was the month of June, and I couldn't wait to be free and out enjoying the glorious summer weather. It sure wasn't summer up there in the north. During the last week of May it had snowed, and the trees had only just begun to bud. I was dressed in my street clothes again, and I sure felt good.

It was about 9 o'clock in the morning, and I was now waiting for my ride into Timmins, where I would catch a bus to Sudbury. I was put back in the hole to wait for whoever was to drive me into Timmins. The other guys had left, and I wondered why I was still left behind. I figured they had family who had come to pick them up. I waited and waited. My thoughts wandered to being home. What would it be like? What would people think of me? I had sent out only a few letters, one to Dad and the others to a girl in Ohio whom I would be seeing in July at West Arm Lodge, near where our cottage had been. Dad and the girl had been my only contacts in the outside world.

As time went by I started to question the guards as to why I was still there. They said they didn't know and just to be patient. Noon came, and I had lunch. This was the first time in the hole that I had not been served bean cake. I ate my last prison meal; thank God I would now be able to eat what I chose! Soon a guard came and told me I was leaving. "It's about time!" I exclaimed. A rush of excitement came over me as I walked down the hall for the last time. I wouldn't miss this hellish prison on earth.

We approached the administrative offices inside the entrance. On the other side of the door was freedom. I stood by an office and couldn't wait to kiss this place goodbye. The thoughts of being free and home partying that night were thrilling. I hadn't even left the prison and already I had forgotten my promises to God. All I thought of was getting stoned and drunk again.

In one of the offices I saw an OPP officer and thought nothing of it. He and a man dressed in civvies approached the office door. I moved out of the way to let them pass. They didn't pass; instead the guy in plainclothes asked me if I was Randy Tunney. I stated, "Yes." He introduced himself as a Sudbury regional police officer and told me he had a warrant for my arrest, pertaining to a break and enter charge. My jaw dropped from my face as I was handcuffed. I was told I was being flown back to Sudbury on a chartered plane. I said, "I am not going on any plane, as I haven't flown before and am scared of heights." I didn't have a choice in the matter and was escorted out to an OPP cruiser.

I couldn't believe this was happening to me. Then again, what had ever gone right in my life? I was informed by the cop from Sudbury that he had flown up there to an airstrip nearby. The OPP had picked him up and had driven him to the jail to arrest me. I just sat in the back of the black and white staring blankly out the window. In a short while we pulled off the highway and in a few minutes drove up to an awaiting plane on a deserted airstrip carved out of the bush. This wasn't an airport, just a path cleared for small aircraft. It was like a scene out of a movie. "Wanted criminal released from prison today, only to be arrested. Driven to private airfield where an awaiting chartered plane would fly him under arrest to the city where the charges were laid." This was something I thought they did for big-time criminals, not some punk like me. I thought, why hadn't they just let me take the bus to Sudbury and then arrest me upon arrival?

I was let out of the cruiser. The pilot stepped down from the small single-engine Cessna. I stood beside the plane and gave it the once-over. The plane looked like it couldn't stay together on the ground, let alone in the air. I told the pilot so. This was a three-seater aircraft, and I was told to get into the back seat. I asked if I could have the cuffs off. I was told no. What did they think I would do, try to hijack the plane to a tropical paradise? Sitting nervously in the back, I waited to be on our way and hoped we would make it.

The pilot and cop got in. The engine was started, and then we started moving along the hardened earth runway. The ride was like driving down a bumpy road in a beat-up car that had lost its tailpipe. The speed increased, and we were soon airborne and climbing above the treeline and into the near-cloudless sky.

Once we were up I realized it wasn't so bad and looked out the windows to the ground below. I had never dreamed that my first airplane flight would be as a wanted criminal being flown from one jail to another. The flight was a couple of hundred miles or so as the crow flies. The most interesting thing was watching the vegetation below. When we left the north country outside of Timmins, the trees were pretty well barren and the air was cold. As we flew south to Sudbury, things got greener, until finally we landed at the Sudbury airport.

The weather was gorgeous, hot; the trees were green; the flowers were in full bloom. In comparison, I was now in a tropical paradise. In the airport, people looked at me strangely as I walked through the terminal in handcuffs. The cop and I had to wait a few minutes until another cop in a cruiser came to pick us up and take us to police HQ on Larch Street. It would be about half an hour's drive from the airport to the cop shop.

The two officers, knowing I had just come from jail, decided to buy me a Big Mac, fries and a shake at McDonald's. We stopped at McDonald's on the Kingsway, and one of them went in to purchase the food. I thanked them for their generosity. I devoured the meal as if there were no tomorrow.

When we arrived at HQ, the cuffs were taken off. I had pictures and prints taken and was brought up to date on the charge against me. I was charged with a break and enter that had taken place the previous winter at the Copper Cliff Club. Apparently, after I was arrested in February, Dad's house had been searched from top to bottom and some evidence one of my brothers had was found. The evidence was some club tickets that were bought with cash and used as cash at the club. All the serial numbers had been removed from the books of tickets. In that case, they only had circumstantial evidence.

I was locked up in a cell again. I figured I'd get off on the charge and be free in a few days. I decided to stay cool and wait for my court appearance the next day. The following morning I was taken to provincial court, and, as expected, the case was remanded for a week. That afternoon I had a bail hearing, which was a waste of time. Now I was to spend another week in the district jail, which I thought I'd never see again. I hated being in prison and vowed that once released, I'd never be brought back to jail, or I would die. I hated being around men now more than ever. But after spending a few months in prison, and most of that in solitary confinement, I could surely stand another week.

My day in court came, and I was defended by my lawyer. I figured the judge would take into consideration the time I had already served. That was not to be, and I was slapped with another sixty days, plus eighteen months of probation afterwards.

I was escorted back through the tunnel again to begin my sentence. I was cursing and swearing as I was taken back into the bowels of hell. I couldn't spend any more time around men or I would go mad. With a sixty-day bit I would get a third off for good behaviour. This meant I had to spend forty more days and nights in this hell. Unknown to me, these were going to be the longest forty yet. Like Noah in his ark, I would have to ride out the storms that lay ahead.

The great biblical man himself had to put up with the longest forty.

"When is this nightmare going to end?" I screamed as I was led to a cellblock. The steel-barred door clanged shut behind me as I entered the cage. The other cons in the corridor took notice of my madness as I started pacing up and down the corridor after putting my bedding and such in my cell. I didn't care about any of these goofs, as I didn't trust them. Ever since that sexual attack, I had become paranoid. Well, I certainly wasn't going to take any bull from anybody any more, ever. I settled down after a while and sat in a corner trying to figure things out. How could I have been fooled by the Bible? I wished I had died!

I watched the other guys. They were a strange bunch of characters coming from different walks of life but most heading to the same ultimate destination—nowhere! I had been told that 80 percent of the guys in prison are repeat offenders. This was their way of life. Like everyone else, I vowed never to return. My reasons were more psychological than anything else. I just couldn't stand being in close confinement with men. I would just have to learn to become more secure with myself and learn to live alone, be alone.

# Chapter 15

My forty days were the pits. I was in and out of the hole until finally the day of my release. The past six months had been quite an experience, although compared to my childhood it had been kids' stuff. I left the district jail and had to only walk a block in order to catch a bus to Copper Cliff. I sure felt strange as I stood waiting for a bus. It was like everyone was staring at me and knew I had just gotten out of jail.

The July weather was wonderfully pleasant. The hot summer sun melted away some of the cold thoughts of the past several months. I wondered how everyone would react, my so-called family, the neighbours and townspeople. The bus came and I grabbed my belongings and boarded, paying my fare. As usual there was a familiar face. I took a seat and started chatting. I was brought up to date on the latest scoops.

As we approached the town and I saw our house, I became nervous. I got off the bus at the first stop, which bordered our property. I walked across the yard and up the stairs. I unlocked the door and entered. Dad and my brothers were at the West Arm Lodge camping.

Tomorrow I would hitchhike there so I could see Diana, the girl from Ohio I had been writing to in jail. She and her family were on vacation and only had a few more days left of their holiday. Thankfully I would be able to see Diana for a couple of days.

I put my things down and then raided the near-empty refrigerator. I sure felt strange being there, and it didn't feel very much like home. That first night I checked out the town, got high and drunk. So much for jailhouse promises. Those first tokes of devil's weed and drinks of alcohol were the sweetest things to my senses.

I did hitchhike to the lodge the next day and spent several days there relaxing and visiting with Diana. Over the next few months between August and December, I picked up where I had left off—the drugs, booze, break and enters and crime in general. The parties were as big as ever. My drug dealings were on a much smaller scale now as the Master John's operation had broken up because of police hassles. My friend Chris had been deported to his homeland, Greece.

My fights with Tom were still quite prevalent, and on numerous occasions we threatened each other. During one fight I told him he would be dead within a year. I never really meant the threats that were thrown about during these battles. Vickey was staying at Mother's somewhere in the city, and I had no contact with her. By the time I threw my second annual New Year's Eve bash, I was as burnt-out as ever. I turned eighteen on January 15th, 1977. Tom turned seventeen four days later. In April, Vickey turned six. Brother James was a teenager, and Bob was still a preteen.

Tom had become a religious fanatic and was attending church a couple of times a week or more. I was as jealous as ever of him but now because he was allowed to borrow the family car and I wasn't. Tom had his usual girlfriends, whom I usually ended up having. Over the past several months I had dated a few girls who had met Tom first. I guess it was my way of taking revenge upon him. Just now, this spring, I was seeing a young lady named Pauline, who went to church with Tom. Tom was seeing another girl, who lived out of the city some ways.

Now that it was May I also started flirting with an ex-girlfriend of Tom's who only lived half a dozen houses away. This young lady, J.D., was beautiful, tall and friendly and one of the most sought-after girls in town. J.D. was an only child and lived an extremely sheltered life, which was why she wasn't seeing Tom any more. She was hardly allowed away from home. J.D.'s father was an executive and her mother a stereo-typical housewife. Her parents liked Tom but despised me because of my background. To them, Tom and I were like night and day.

One night during the last week of May, Tom and I were arguing about him having the privilege of driving the car while all I got to drive was a ten-speed. He was getting ready to go to one of his religious meetings, which tonight was about fifty miles away and only several miles from where our cottage had been on Lake Nipissing. As he was leaving, I told him I hoped he died and went to hell. Tom left, and that was the last time I saw him alive.

Around midnight that night on the way home from church, Tom died in a head-on automobile accident.

He met his death while clutching a Bible, God rest his soul. I'm glad he wasn't going to hell.

The driver of the other car died as well, leaving a young wife and child. A young girl riding with Tom was thrown from the car and received a cut lip and a sore back. There was no alcohol or drugs involved nor any highway infraction. For some unknown reason, Tom's car just veered in front of the other automobile. When I look back now, I think that God took him at that point in his life because he was just too good for us. He was a Christian, and all his family around him were living lives of sin. I was the worst of all, and Mother came a close second.

I was in shock for days and didn't shed a tear. As I sat in the funeral home, I just stared at my brother. I had never been to a funeral before. It wasn't until the casket was closed and Sam Laderoute, head of the Copper Cliff Highlanders, for which Tom had been the main drummer, started playing "Amazing Grace" on the bagpipes that the flood of tears came forth. I knew then how much I really loved him and that nothing I could do could take back those last words I spoke to him. Hate had been the blinded love. Do you see, I never really hated, I just didn't know *love*. I wept uncontrollably and wished I could change places with him. I was the one who deserved to die. I was the black sheep of the family.

As the days passed after Tom's death, I grew to truly hate myself and drowned my sorrows with drugs and booze as never before. Tom had had his room in the basement, so I just sort of inherited it, I suppose. I went right to work redesigning the basement to suit me and my lifestyle. My plan was to turn it into the ultimate party room. With the money I was making from selling drugs and the bit of casual labour I was doing in order to keep my probation officer happy, I went on a spending spree. I bought carpeting, a rocker recliner, a coffee table, paint, pictures, lighting, etc. There was already a stereo, couch, and bed down there. By the time I was finished, which took most of a week, I had designed the most decent party room. The room was about eight feet wide and fourteen feet long. This floor space covered half the basement area. Stairs went up to the kitchen.

I covered the floor with a rust-orange shag carpet. I used an inexpensive way to cover the bare concrete walls. Two end walls were painted midnight black, and the one other was covered with aluminum foil that had been crinkled up, then stretched out. I did the same thing to the rafters of the basement ceiling. On each of the painted black walls I put three black-light posters with far-out freaky pictures or a kaleidoscope of colours. I framed each poster with a half-inch aluminum-foil trim. What a contrast on the pitch black walls! In the middle of the tin-foiled ceiling, I hung a revolving crystal-type light reflector. You know, the type you see at rock concerts and in ballrooms that, when lights are shone on it, reflects streams of light back on the walls and such. I clamped to the ceiling rafters an array of black lights and coloured bulbs that flashed on and off. I had lights that would flash to the beat of the music. For the final touch I made an aluminum foil sign that read "Tunney's Disco." The sign was above a set of black-light posters on one of the black walls. I covered the windows in dark green plastic to keep out the light. I wanted perpetual darkness, and let me tell you, without any lights on, you would swear you were blind.

By the time everything was hooked up I had lost count of how many extension cords I had used. The wiring had to be well hidden, because Dad had been a volunteer fireman and would have had me take it all down. Now, to test everything out and see how bizarre the final product looked. As usual, I was already stoned. I turned on the Akai-Sansui stereo system that had been Tom's. I then flicked on one by one the dozen or so lights, including the rotating light in the centre of the ceiling. The room lit up like any disco I had ever seen, and I stared in amazement at what I had accomplished. I now had the ultimate room for tripping out on drugs in. I would be the envy of all my druggie friends. Never had I seen such a room in any house outside of movies or TV. I could now get stoned and just sit there for hours, staring at the lights and colours reflecting off the aluminum foil or look at the freaky posters. I couldn't wait to have my first party down there. The room was simply marvellous. Tunney's Disco!

My first party was a runaway success and was just like the opening of a new bar. My friends and acquaintances couldn't believe their eyes. J.D., my girlfriend now, thought it was out of this world. Dad didn't think much of it and wasn't impressed. Oh well, who cared what he thought?

By the time summer ended, Vickey was living with us, as Mother had taken off to Toronto again, I guess in her search for sustenance. I was very glad to see Vickey, and I spent a lot of time with her. Since I wasn't working, I was to be like a substitute father to my younger siblings. Can you imagine me, as burnt out as I was, taking care of my two younger brothers and sister? Dad's routine hadn't changed much over the past couple of years. He went to work as a machinist at Inco five days a week. Most nights he would be at his lady friend's. On the weekends we hardly saw him. I took over the household duties, cooking, cleaning, doing laundry, a regular little house husband of sorts.

Vickey was in grade one and came home every day for lunch. Bob and James did too on occasion. They did as they pleased and had more freedom than any of their friends had. My brothers also lived an absolute discipline-free life. Vickey usually brought home a friend with her, so I always made extra. Vickey and I during this time became very close. I was, I guess, like a father to her since Dad was hardly about. I'd help her with her schooling, read to her, and spent a lot of time outside with her.

My relationship with J.D. was blossoming now that summer was over. During the summer I hardly saw her because of her restricted lifestyle. Now I was walking J.D. to school and home again, as this was the only time we could see each other. On occasion she would skip afternoon classes at high school so we could be together. We were in love with each other, and J.D. risked her parents finding out. She neither drank nor did drugs and remained sexually pure. She was the most beautiful and intelligent girl I had ever dated.

When I wasn't with J.D. I was partying at home. Acquaintances would drop by in the daytime, and we'd party down in my disco until 4:30, at which time they would leave because Dad would be home shortly. Then Dad would leave for the evening, which was usually three out of five weeknights and every weekend. I couldn't have asked for better circumstances to continue my lifestyle.

With my brothers and me having so much freedom, we started our own crime wave, which was 99.9 percent successful to this date. I wasn't the greatest influence as a brother and taught them all their skills. They became so proficient that they started teaching me a few things. We had no one to watch over us. It was as if the four of us, at eighteen, fourteen, twelve and six, lived on our own in a modest three-bedroom house in a middle-class neighbourhood. I honestly did my best to keep the house up, the lawn cut, the meals cooked, etc. The problem was that my addictions were controlling me. Had Dad spent time at home, I would have left, as we always argued. My drug addiction was getting worse, but I couldn't stop. I was into everything except heroin and speed.

I spent most of my time at home selling drugs and partying. I didn't go into the city much, as I was like the live-in help. My sister needed someone always around as she was only a child. I was becoming quite the loner, despite the wild parties. I had stopped frequenting bars. Although I hardly saw J.D., I was faithful to her despite the opportunities with some of the girls from the neighbourhood.

By the time Christmas had arrived, I had been out of jail about eighteen months and was quite the cross-addict. Most of my feminine traits seemed to have disappeared. I wasn't cross dressing and felt quite normal for a change. Still, in the back of my mind was the seed that was planted in jail about getting healthy and strong, like some of the guys I had seen. So for Christmas that year I talked my brothers into asking Dad for some weights so we could become supermen. Sure enough, on Christmas morning, there was a set of weights for us, a total weight of 140 pounds. We spent the day trying out the different routines that were shown in an accompanying booklet. The next day, my unseen muscles were aching, and I didn't particularly like the feeling. So much for weightlifting.

Dad was always out New Year's Eve, so this year I had what had become an annual affair, Tunney's third annual New Year's Eve drug and alcohol bash. This year the champagne was on the house. I expected about forty people on and off during the night. I purchased about twenty magnums of President's champagne, the cost of which would be recovered as I sold drugs to the partygoers. The evening would be a break-even affair for everyone attending. For most of them it was their first drug-and-champagne party, and let me tell you, drugs and champagne make for a volatile mix. We were all as wild as a bunch of Indians on the warpath. By the time midnight arrived we were out in the backyard yelling Happy New Year like a bunch of lunatics.

That also put an end to another year in my life, thank God. What did 1978 have in store for me? On January 15th I turned nineteen and could legally drink. What a joke. Four and a half years had passed since my first drink at the hotel. Tom would have turned eighteen on the nineteenth. I was haunted by thoughts of him and all of our fights. I wished I could have changed the past.

Vickey got used to all the noise of the parties. I would send her to bed about 9, and that was the last I would hear from her. For someone who had pretty well become a father to my younger siblings, I sure wasn't setting very good standards for them to follow. I was only a teenager myself and had no control of my own life. How could I help anyone else?

By the time spring arrived, J.D. had broken up with me and had started seeing some guy in a band. I was devastated and took a drug overdose. The only thing that kept me alive that night was a girl friend whom I had known for years who slapped me for hours to keep me from going comatose. J.D. was the first girl I had truly loved, and her rejection of me was too much to handle. My life was full of rejection.

For a couple of weeks to come I stayed in a drug-induced state of depression, although I would have been as upset without the dope. I was also into 222s with codeine and Dad's prescription drugs. It was getting so bad that I would sniff gas and glue. I was having trouble looking after Vickey and keeping up the house.

When I did come out of my depression somewhat, I started to lift the weights Dad had bought us for Christmas. I even went so far as to buy a bench press so that I could try and build up some chest muscles. When I brought home the bench press, I put it together and then tried it out. I only had 140 pounds of weights. I was six feet tall and didn't weigh much more myself. I found out I could barely bench-press the 140 pounds.

The weights were set up in my room in the basement, and I got in the habit of lifting the weights a short while every day. Within a few weeks I noticed that muscles were actually growing in spite of the fact I was still partying daily. Even my appetite was increasing.

When I had first started I could only bench 140 pounds. Now I was doing sets of ten and more. I was doing arm curls, shoulder presses, squats and sit-ups. I was even enjoying the feeling of working my muscles. I had given up on team sports because of my identity crisis. I still thought I might be gay. With everything I thought of myself and other men, lifting weights was perfect for me. I could do it on my own, which was great. Secondly, I could do it at home.

By the time summer arrived I was out in the backyard lifting weights a couple of hours a day. My druggie friends were complimenting me on my changing physique, especially the girls. That inspiration kept me motivated. I was putting on solid body weight, which I desperately needed. Most of all, I felt like I was accomplishing something for a change. I could see the results of the work I was doing. By August I was buying muscle magazines and reading books on health. I read about muscle and how important it is to eat properly. I was fascinated with how food is metabolized and restructured into muscle cells.

All this was positive for me, with the exception that I had heard that only homosexuals were so-called muscle men. This always played over in my mind. It bothered me constantly, but I liked the results I was getting and wasn't about to stop. So onward I went. I started eating raw eggs with milk and some of the other meals I read about. Sure enough, the food was like a magician in my body, and my physical appearance was constantly changing.

By September, I had outgrown the weights at home. Just four months before I could only bench 140. Now I was doing sets of up to twenty repetitions. I started thinking about joining a gym. Without even realizing it I had cut back on my drug and alcohol consumption. I was still partying and drug dealing but found myself spending more time pumping iron and reading about health. Vickey was now living with Mother, whom I hadn't seen since Tom's funeral. This meant all the time was my own.

On September 23, 1978, I went out to a gym called Vic Tanny's in the basement of the Ambassador Hotel. After a tour of the place, I signed up for five years at a cost of $275, and then $50 a year thereafter. Little did I know at the time that this money would be the second best investment I would ever make, the first being the money I would later raise or give to help the less fortunate.

I started going to Vic Tanny's three times a week, on Tuesdays, Thursdays and Saturdays. The club wasn't co-ed, so we had to alternate the days with the females. There were saunas, a whirlpool and a swimming pool. The gym had a minimum of equipment but sufficient for working out. One of the instructors showed me how to use the equipment properly. Now this guy, Ron, was a giant in comparison to the guys I had seen in jail. Apparently he was the reigning Mr. Sudbury. Ron and I got to talking, and I told him I would like to get into top shape. He offered his help in instructing me. I was told all I had to do was ask.

As I got to know the regulars, I realized most of the top body builders in Sudbury worked out there. The people there were very different than what I was accustomed to. Instead of always talking about the quantities of drugs and alcohol they could consume, they talked about vitamins, protein, proper nutrition and routines. All I had ever known was how to chemically destroy myself. These people cared about themselves. The more I saw and heard, the more I wanted to be like them.

Within weeks, instead of spending all my money on drugs and booze, I was spending my money on vitamins, protein supplements, yogurt and more magazines. I was learning to enjoy the food I ate as I learned what each food group did for optimum health. As much as I was looking better visually, my insides were repairing themselves after the almost five years of abuse. By Christmastime I was only a weekend addict and even started prophesying that I was going to compete in the Mr. Sudbury contest the following June. All my acquaintances laughed at me. "Come and see me then," they mocked.

New Year's 1978 I had my fourth annual bash. There were only half as many in attendance. I guess my acquaintances noticed the changes I was going through. Over the previous few months I had practically deserted them except for business purposes. My new friends at the gym were taking up more of my time. I was getting so involved with bodybuilding that I had all but forgotten my problems. I noticed that it wasn't true that all bodybuilders were gay. All the guys in competition who were around Vic Tanny's had girlfriends. In fact, I had started seeing a young lady named Diane. She lived next door to my stepbrother, who had by now moved into a new house in Val Caron.

My friendships at the gym were not too personal anyhow. It was like going to school. I went, did my workout and left. The only thing I didn't like about working out was being stared at by guys who might be lusting for me. I was always on guard and conscious of my actions when the supposedly gay guys were around.

Over the next several months Ron was true to his word and helped me as much as possible. On occasion we did our workouts together. Like a sponge I absorbed everything he taught me. Ron saw how determined I was and kept motivating me to improve. And improve I did. Muscles were growing everywhere, and by March, I had decided to train to enter the Mr. Sudbury contest at the end of June. I knew that if I wanted to look my best I would have to completely stop doing drugs and drinking alcohol. I was learning to like myself for the first time in my life. Fitness was saving my life, and I was becoming the Superman I had always dreamt of being as a kid. No one at the gym knew what I had been fighting to become who I was becoming. They just saw some determined twenty-year-old spending time at a gym. I was actually succeeding at something. My relationship with Diane was fine. We spent most weekends together, and I phoned her daily.

It was the middle of March, and I had gone a week without drugs or booze. This was the longest I had forgone satisfying my addictions since age fifteen, outside of my term of imprisonment. I was now living up to some of the promises I had made while in solitary confinement on that night I had screamed out for a Bible.

Since I was still dealing drugs in small quantities, I had to keep an eye out for cops. I swore I wouldn't go back to jail alive. One morning while doing the dishes I just happened to catch sight of some dude up a telephone pole across the street. He seemed to be working on the line. I would not have thought anything of it except that he was working out of a navy blue van that wasn't one of Ma Bell's. I started wondering if he might be working for the cops and putting a trace on our line. I was sure the cops would like to bust me. I was running things on the QT, and even my break and enters were done solo to avoid anyone ratting on me.

I let the sighting pass until a few days later. I noticed the same guy up the pole again. Now I figured this for a telephone tap, and there was only one way to find out. I decided to set up a phony drug deal over the phone in collaboration with some acquaintances.

I phoned up a drug partner and placed an order for a few pounds of marijuana to be delivered on the evening of April 1. The pickup was to take place by the R. G. Dow pool situated behind Lola's Confectionary on Balsam Street. We were to meet at 7:30 on the footbridge crossing the local creek. We discussed the price and came to an agreement, and then we hung up. The cops were now baited if our phone was tapped. This could turn out to be the best April Fool's joke I had ever played.

During the days now when people called for drugs I told them I was out of drugs and would have some on April 2. This would really whet the cops' appetite if they were listening. April 1 couldn't come soon enough, and I was excited at the prospect of pulling a fast one on the cops. If our phone was in fact tapped, the cops would be watching me and my acquaintances like a hawk that day.

Everything had been preset. My drug partner was to fill a gym bag full of newspapers and put it in the trunk of one of his cars and go about his business as usual. Then late in the day he was to take the bag and put it in the trunk of his second car, which he would use for the drop. Another guy and I would have an envelope full of Canadian Tire money to use as the cash. Now all we had to do was wait until the evening.

We couldn't wait for the day to go by. The worst that could happen to us was to get a lecture if we got busted. During the day others were informed of the possible April Fool's joke. They were told if they wanted to see the bust go down to stand unassumingly at the confectionary store and mind their own business.

As 7 o'clock in the evening approached, I took the ten-minute walk from our house to the confectionary store. The envelope full of Canadian Tire money was in my coat pocket. At Lola's I met up with my accomplice. I knew the bust was going to go down as planned. The first telltale sign was a white Trans Am parked in the confectionary's parking lot. A male and female were making out as if in Lover's Lane. My excitement grew; nobody went parking in this parking lot. I found it quite amusing. The Trans Am was parked only about fifty feet from the bridge where the deal was to take place. I glanced stealthily about and picked out two unmarked cop cars some distance away in different places. I also noticed a lime green AMC Pacer cruise by and during the course of the day had noticed the cop inside of it casing our house.

Well, I knew I was going to have the last laugh. Several people were waiting for this bust to go down. My accomplice and I walked across the bridge to the pool and back. All we had to do was wait for my drug partner to arrive with a gym bag full of newspapers. As scheduled, he arrived and parked in the pool's parking lot. I was on the bridge with my accomplice. My heart was racing from the excitement. My partner in crime took the gym bag from his car and walked to the bridge. We spoke momentarily and exchanged Canadian Tire money for the gym bag after I had opened it and read the headlines. A car horn honked, and all of a sudden unmarked cop cars were converging on us from every direction. I had the gym bag and started running as if I were really carrying dope. A couple of cops and a cruiser were behind me. With my new physical prowess I had them outdistanced. Well, after a short run with 38s trained on me, I stopped. An unmarked cruiser pulled up beside me. The cops in pursuit holstered their pieces and grabbed the gym bag. I was tossed into the back seat of the cruiser. The gym bag was searched, and to their dismay they got to read old news.

I told them they shouldn't tap telephone lines. One of them said I watched too much television. He stated they would throw the book at me if ever the chance arose. I was then told to get the hell out of there. I knew there wasn't a thing they could have done. And all on April 1.

I rejoined everyone at Lola's. I was an instant celebrity. A half-dozen or so cop cars filed out. Now they would have to answer to their superiors. I knew that this was one night I was never going to forget. I had made a complete farce out of Sudbury's finest. If ever they wanted me behind bars, tonight surely secured me a spot. I would have to be on my guard.

A group of us now went to a private party and celebrated. Mind you, I stayed drug- and alcohol-free. As April passed, I stayed clean, not a thing. The money I was making from drugs was all going towards my new way of life. I started preaching to my druggie friends about what fitness could do for you. I even started feeling guilty about selling them drugs, if you can believe that, so much in fact that by May I closed up business and vowed never to sell or do drugs again. It was during this time that I started thinking of helping the less fortunate, such as addicts.

The Mr. Sudbury contest was less than two months away, and I was now training seven days a week. When I wasn't at the gym I was working out at home and had started to take up jogging. I was becoming an addict of a different sort and was loving every minute of it. I was also becoming more secure about myself and was building self-confidence and esteem. I was still dating Diane and saw her almost every weekend. We fought often, though, over stupid things.

I decided to buy a ten-speed bike so that I could build more muscularity into my quadriceps and hamstrings and calf muscles. I purchased a $100 job from Canadian Tire with some of the money I had left from my past criminal activities. The bike was a nice silver-coloured Medalist ten-speed. I started putting at least twenty miles a day on the odometer I bought.

Now, riding a bike is somewhat of a bore. With my creative mind I decided to design the ultimate touring bike. With the rest of my crime funds I purchased a forty-channel CB radio, an eight-track car stereo, an AM-FM portable radio, a pair of small car speakers, six volt batteries, wiring, a headlight, signal lights, a stick antenna and other odds and ends. I mounted the citizens' band radio to the handlebars along with the microphone. To the front wheel assembly I hooked up the generator headlight. Behind the seat I attached your standard book-carrying rack. Atop the rack was a small red Sears Craftsman toolbox large enough for two six-volt lantern batteries. To the flip-top of the tool box I attached the eight-track player and AM-FM radio, which I plastic-cemented to the lid. On each side of the tool box I screwed on a car speaker. I screwed onto the rack a CB antenna and bike signal lights. What Johnny Cash did to a car, I did to a ten-speed. By the time everything was wired up and working, I had created a streamlined, aesthetically appealing work of cycling elegance. I had invested over $500 in my touring city cycle.

When I took it out for a test run, I was the envy of all the kids in town. I could picture them all running home and begging their parents for CBs, radios and such for their own bikes. I could cycle around and talk on my CB radio, or don headphones and listen to music. My handle on the CB was C. C. Rider, "Copper Cliff Rider." When I conversed on the CB and told people I was driving a ten-speed, they couldn't believe it. They would drive to my 10-20 (location) and check it out. I could listen to music on the headphones or have the tunes blaring behind me from the car speakers.

I traversed the town and city on this musical cycling machine. With all the added weight from the accessories, my legs and lungs were getting in better shape than ever. I would cycle to the beach on Lake Ramsey and park my bike beside me. The music would be entertaining the multitudes. The only drawback was that I couldn't leave my bike unattended for fear of theft. I rode that bike morning to night and doubled my mileage. Some days I put over fifty miles on the odometer. I was C. C. Rider, and the bike was dubbed the Silver Streak.

I did have one accident though. I was racing down the street one night in front of the City Centre Mall on Elm Street. I was coming to a red light, and my back brake cable snapped. I ran the red light and into a car making a right turn. I flew over the hood of the car like an Olympian hurdler. I was okay, just a few cuts and bruises. My bike, however, was all over the place. I ended up piling everything into a taxi for the trip home. In a couple of days I had rebuilt it to better than the original.

Well, I was certainly getting into shape as the date for the contest approached. I was eating like a true professional. Dad was complaining about me eating most of the food he bought. Every morning over the past couple of months I had started off the day with several hundred sit-ups before breakfast. For breakfast daily I ate a high protein and carbohydrate concoction—a dozen raw eggs, a quart of milk, a banana and a chocolate breakfast drink. I put all these ingredients into a bowl and mixed it with an electric beater. I would drink this over a period of an hour or so. Delicious! Mmm,

mmm good, right to the last drop. Even tasted better than booze. I was eating steak, fish or chicken once a day, a couple of quarts of milk, salads, fresh fruit, yogurt, and fifty Weider protein-90 pills a day. Over the past years I had put on over 40 pounds, and you couldn't pinch an inch. I now was six feet and about 190 pounds.

When I look back now, I can see that I was over-dosing on protein. My diet is still much the same, minus 50 percent of the protein, with increased carbo-hydrates. My friends were in awe of the change, not to say what I thought. Health is where it is at, and I rec-ommend all-around health to everyone. My philos-ophy now is this: "Health is a three-way proposition: spiritual, mental and physical." Note the order of the three. In 1977, the three went: "physical, physical, physical." From 1980 through to 1986, the three were "physical, physical, mental," mental health in the non-medical sense of being able to achieve whatever you wanted providing you kept a positive attitude.

One month before the contest, I cut back on my carbohydrate intake in order to bring my body fat down to about 5 percent. Ron was teaching me how to pose, and I was suntanning in order to have the right bronzed look. I was eating, thinking, sleeping, and working out like a professional athlete. I was learning self-discipline, which I so needed. Everything was done as perfect as could be with the knowledge I had, which was increasing daily.

I was competing for the experience and didn't expect to do very well. I was, however, determined to do my very best. Over the previous months I had even been training with some of the other competitors. I hadn't earned their respect yet as a bodybuilder. With my posing routine worked out to an accompanying piece of music, my body weight down to about 180, and a beautiful suntan, I was as ready as ever I would be.

Prejudging was in the morning of that Saturday in June. The show itself was in the evening. I took the stage in front of a few hundred spectators, television cameras, Dad, Doug, Diane, and the judges. Man, was I nervous. When it was all over, I, Randy R. Tunney, had won third place in the heavyweight. Two of my sometimes training buddies had won first and second. I couldn't believe it; I had actually made a dream come true. I wasn't Mr. Sudbury, but who cared? I was as proud as I ever had been. It was the first time in my life I had set out to accomplish something for myself and had succeeded. Only a year before I had been a burnt-out drug addict, alcoholic and criminal, as bad as anyone and worse than most. Now, a year later, I was drug-, alcohol- and crime-free, and on top of that, I was one of Sudbury's top athletes. Simply incredible!

My picture was in the newspaper, and the contest was later shown on local television. My friends didn't laugh at me any more. Now I was a confirmed believer that only the true believer will succeed in bringing his life's journey to a happy end. My confidence had built up, and I had a whole new attitude towards life. I now wanted to be Mr. Sudbury in 1980, and nothing could stop me.

With my training cut back, I was now spending more time with my girlfriend. I guess I didn't have what it took to have personal relationships. We fought one time too many, and she professed adamantly that she didn't want to see me any more. As before with the rejection from J.D., I was devastated. I just couldn't stand being always rejected, especially when I always meant well. I blamed not being able to keep a girl on my mind and strange personality. Although it was suppressed somewhat, I was always haunted.

So again I started drinking for a couple of days and slipped into the depths of despair. One day I found out where Diane was babysitting and took a bus out to that part of the city. I had been drinking and had an almost-finished bottle of Canadian Club concealed on my person. By the time I arrived to where Diane was, I was pissed drunk, just like the old days. I knocked on the townhouse door and was let in. Immediately we started arguing. I was told to leave or the cops would be phoned. I told her to go right ahead. Diane dialled the number and requested that I be removed from the premises. All the while the alcohol was having a profound effect on me as I had not so much as touched a drop for a few months. I was professing my love for her and telling her I couldn't live without her. I again felt so alone and lost. My pleas were rejected, and I was told to get out.

The doorbell rang, and as I had expected, a couple of uniformed police officers were there. Diane spoke with them, and then I was asked to leave or else I would be charged. I started cursing at them as I had at times before. I was in a drunken stupor, and the cops started towards me. I made a beeline for the open patio door. The sound of shattering glass was heard. The door hadn't been open. I had cuts here and there, none too serious. Now the cops had reason to arrest me and did just that. Once again I was driven to the cop shop, and I was booked for mischief.

I was again filled with intense hatred. Every time I had a falling out with girls, my suppressed emotions and feelings came to the surface, most notably the feelings of homosexuality. I hated thinking like that, but just couldn't help it because of my background. At the time I didn't know if it was so much the homosexuality or a deep hatred of women. All I knew was that I was being torn apart inside. The shock of being behind bars again sobered me up somewhat and enraged me to no end. Just like the first night I had ever spent in one of these cells, I flipped out. I was going insane, just like old times. Everything erupted again, full force. I was carrying on like never before. This performance went on for some time. I started banging my head against the bars in order to shake loose all the madness inside.

I guess when the cops noticed me smashing my head apart they decided to put me into safer surroundings. Five of them came to get me and take me to the padded cell. I told them I wasn't going and would tear them apart if they tried. I tore off my shirt, exposing a mass of muscle, and took a fighting stance. I knew I was stronger than any one of them. I was in peak physical shape and was ready for a showdown.

My cell door was opened, and they all lunged at me. I fought back and was handling myself quite well. Still, I was no match for five men. I struggled frantically as they each grabbed an arm and a leg. No one was going to put me in a padded cell—that was for crazy people. Finally one of the coppers put a choke hold on me, and I passed out.

When I came to, I was lying on a rubberized floor in my birthday suit. The room was dimly lit and reeked of rank urine. Around me were walls covered with imitation leather, vinyl. I stood up drunkenly and punched the walls. Sure enough, they were padded. There was a hole in the floor where a toilet would have gone. I could bang my head all I wanted now. I was mad. Those cops would pay for this. There was nothing to do but sit and try to sober up.

An idea struck me. I was always full of bright ideas. I checked out the toilet hole. The grated covering was a little loose and was bolted on with a couple of six-inch bolts. Now I figured that all the urine going down the drain over the years would have rusted and weakened the metal. There was enough room to wedge my fingers between the grated slats. I pulled with one hand, but it was of no use.

Now at the gym I had learned to concentrate all my energy on the muscle group I was working. I concentrated all my energy into that arm and pulled again with all my might. Sure enough, it broke loose. In my hand now I held the grate, and out of it stuck the two rusted bolts. Perfect, I thought, and went to work tearing at the vinyl. Now I was getting back at the pigs. I ripped all the vinyl to shreds and pulled out all the underlying foam, thus exposing the plywood walls underneath. I was having a grand old time and couldn't wait until they came and checked on me. I heaped up all the thick foam in the centre of the windowless cell. This would be the second time this year that I had pulled a number on them. By the time I was finished I had a three-foot pile of foam on the cell floor.

I had fun bouncing around on top. I replaced the grille and thought maybe they wouldn't figure out how I had managed to destroy their cell.

When an officer came to check on me, he stood dumbfounded at the sight. I was lying naked atop a pile of foam. The officers who came to check this out cursed at me. I was dragged back into a barred cell, still in my birthday suit. Shortly afterwards, an officer who lived in Copper Cliff approached me and asked if I wanted to get out of there. The catch was I would have to go up to the sanatorium. This was a hospital for nutbars. I agreed only on the basis that I didn't want to go back to jail. I was given back my clothes and driven up to the Sudbury Algoma Hospital. I spent a couple of days there drying out and then went back home.

I had been charged with two counts of mischief. By the time I appeared for sentencing, the damages for both incidents had been paid, so I was let off. Thank God I wouldn't be going to jail. I had to do some community work, though, and ended up doing some of the hours at a Sudbury nursing home for the aged.

# Chapter 16

I put Diane out of my mind and decided to forget about girls. I concentrated my energies on my time at the gym. I was now quite a loner, and when I wasn't at the gym, I was riding my customized bike. I always seemed distant and sort of out of touch with reality. I was desperately lonely and longed to be loved. At the gym I was steadily improving, which gave me incentive to keep training harder. Now that I had a title behind me, more people were asking me about nutrition and training. I always obliged them and was still constantly learning myself. I loved being healthy. Over the past several months I had only drank once and hadn't touched drugs at all. I was totally against drug and alcohol abuse and had visions of helping others someday if I ever could be in total control of my life. When I was out jogging I had visions of running across the continent extolling the virtues of a healthy life.

Living a crime-free life meant I had no money, and jobs were scarce. Dad was on my back, always asking for money, and he was getting to be a pain in the neck. I was getting maybe $20 a week, which was a far cry from the hundreds I used to have. I didn't care, as nothing would make me go back to crime. I also had a growing reputation to uphold. I had made up my mind to be Mr. Sudbury, and nothing was going to stop me.

One day in the fall I was snooping through some of Dad's personal effects and came across his divorce certificate. I read it, and by the time I was finished I was crying. I couldn't believe what I had figured out—or what I thought I had figured out. Mom and Dad weren't even married when I was born. The certificate of divorce stated they had been married a few months after I had been born! Now I was worried that after all these years I might be the bastard Mother had called me over and over. There was only one way to find out.

Drying my eyes, I put away the certificate. I waited impatiently for Dad to arrive home after work. When he arrived, he started nagging me as usual. As always I talked back to him. After a few volleys of verbal warfare, I blurted out, "You aren't even my father!"

Dad replied, "I didn't even know your mother when you were born." My world that I was trying to put back together had just fallen apart again. I ran from the house and hopped on the Silver Streak and frantically pedalled down the street while trying to hold back the tears. I rode to the public park, which was a few blocks away. By now tears were streaming down my face. I parked my bike adjacent to a tree while I sat in the shade cast by the overhead branches.

What little family I had thought I was part of was no more. All the pieces of my abusive childhood were falling into place. Mother was nothing but a common whore. No wonder she had beaten me so relentlessly. Dad wasn't even my father by blood. My brothers and sister were only stepsiblings. Somewhere I had others. I sat there weeping uncontrollably. I didn't belong anywhere, and that was what I needed the most, a sense of belonging. No wonder Tom was Dad's and Mom's favourite. I had always wondered why! I had known Doug was adopted from Dad's first marriage. Never once had I had the thought I had been adopted.

As I wept and thought about Mother, my hatred arose again. She had taken out all her hatred on me because I was a bastard. All those years I had thought she hated me because I was a boy. Mother had despised me because I existed unwanted. I was messed up now because of my wishing to be a girl in order to win her love. Those times I had cross-dressed, wore her wigs, and put on her makeup. The thousands of fantasies of someday being female. Look what she had done to me! Not only me, but the rest of the family. She had destroyed everything that could have been nice, all because of me! Because I was a bastard child! I was livid. If she hadn't wanted me, why the hell didn't she give me up for adoption? At least I might have grown up as a mentally healthy boy instead of what I had become.

Every day of my life had been a struggle for survival. Even now that I had my physical health, I knew I was still messed up in the head, and now this. My fitness was, however, helping to keep things in more of a balance than before. Fitness was a physical and mental release that had positive effects on my life. Just the same, it was an addiction, a socially acceptable one. The great interior suffering still existed and only wore a different mask.

I sat under the tree sobbing. I thought I had been lonely before during childhood and in the solitary cell of a prison. Nothing before felt as now. I was so desperately alone within.

How could I live at home now in my stepfather's house? He probably didn't even want me there. No wonder I had been put in the boys' home. He probably hated me as well. The exception was that he was too nice of a person to openly admit it. I mean, he hadn't ever told me I was adopted. All I ever wanted was to be loved, that's all. Just loved, please!

What was I to do now? I had no family, no nothing. I didn't want to start selling drugs or go back to crime any more. Jobs were scarce. How could I live? I had something to live for now. I liked being healthy too much. On and on I went. I was still in a prison, a mental prison, and my clothes and my body were my cage. The story was unfolding now, revealing the truth and not lies.

I brought a hand up to my face to wipe the dampness from my eyes. I sat there gasping at all the horrific details. This kind of world I hated to see. I would show them I could be a somebody someday. My thoughts went to all the other suffering people, the abused kids and adults, the addicts, alcoholics—how I could relate to their reaching hands. All they needed was someone to grasp their hands and show them the compassion that can be the utmost of human strengths. Yes, someday maybe I could help these special people. We are all special.

I went back home, but I knew I had overstayed my welcome. Over the next couple of days I phoned a few of Mother's old friends and asked if they knew my real father. I hit pay dirt on one of the calls. The lady told me that my father was an Italian named Tony and in the restaurant business. She said that was all she would tell me and that I would have to ask Mother for the rest of the information.

I hadn't spoken to Mother for over three years. The last time I saw her was in the town post office months before. We were both mailing letters and were standing beside each other, about three feet apart. We glanced at each other as would two perfect strangers, and that was it. Words did not need to be spoken, as we both knew how we felt towards each other.

The only thing I found somewhat amusing about being half Italian was that I had grown up fighting them and was part of the gang wars at times that threatened them. Now, ironically, I was myself one of them.

I phoned Doug to see if he had known I was adopted. Sure enough, he had been old enough at the time to know. Everyone knew except me and my younger stepsiblings. Why couldn't someone have been honest with me? I now felt so alienated from everyone. I would just have to show them all I could be someone.

My stepdad and I weren't on speaking terms any more. As the days went by I spent more time at the gym working out my aggressions creatively. This was the first time that I had been so upset and didn't run out and get drunk. Fitness really was saving my life in more ways than one.

Now I was looking for a way to get away, to get away from everyone. I went to the welfare agency and made an inquiry. I was told I needed an address so that a worker could come and make an initial visit. I went and checked out some rooms around the downtown Sudbury core. I settled on a room on Pine Street. The place was a dump, to say the least. The room was half the size of my basement disco bedroom. It had an anti-quated bed, small closet, wooden table and one chair. The bathroom was communal. Oh well, it was a start. If it hadn't been for my stand against drug abuse, I would have started up my drug business again and rented a gorgeous apartment. There was no way I would, though, as I considered myself totally rehabilitated in the criminal sense.

I now thought of Dad as my stepfather and my sib-lings as stepbrothers and stepsister. Dad was nice enough to help me bring my clothes and a few personal belongings downtown. He gave me a few dishes and pieces of cutlery. I didn't need any pots and pans as I had no stove. My real worry now was if I would be able to eat properly. My nutritional needs had to be met in order for me to keep making significant gains at the gym. Since it was October and the weather was cool at nights, I used the only window in the room as a refrig-erator. Each night I would buy a litre of milk and a dozen eggs with some of the about $60 I was receiving a week, $22 of which went for rent. This money was barely enough to exist on, absolutely no extras.

Since I was now living only a couple of blocks away from the City Centre Mall where I used to always hang out, I ran into a lot of old acquaintances. They knew of my new lifestyle, and we now had nothing in common. The more I saw of them, the more I was glad I had changed. I had even started thinking of going to school to study physical education after taking some upgrading courses. I knew I didn't want to be a bum on the street. All the guys at the gym either worked or went to school. I knew I could do as well as any of them. I had in just over a year gone from being a cross-addict to being one of Sudbury's top bodybuilders. I had surpassed guys who had been training for years. My quick advances could be directly attributed to my past sufferings. I was determined to succeed so as to never suffer again. I didn't at this time check into going to school.

I had a key to the house in Copper Cliff, so some days I would bus it out there, and while my step-brothers were at school and my stepfather was at work, I would catch up on some cooked meals. Everything was still in the disco bedroom, including the Silver Streak. If winter wasn't around the corner, I would have gone for a spin. Since spring, when I had built it, I had put about 2,000 miles on it. I also had the thighs to prove it.

I hated spending time in my downtown room as I had no radio or TV and had to forego all comforts. As Christmas approached, I decided I didn't want to be living in this place. Also, I hadn't been eating as well as I should have been in order to keep making gains at the gym. I asked my stepfather if I could move back home. I was told I could. This meant, however, that I wouldn't be collecting any welfare benefits. To me the sacrifice was worth it because I would be eating better. As a competitive athlete, food was as important, if not more so, than the actual working out. The more I read about nutrition, the more I learned about the harmful effects of my past life as a cross-addict. Bodybuilding for me was becoming an art form and my nutritional needs for optimum performance a science. I was a sculptor working in flesh, and food was the clay. Actually, it is quite amazing what one can do to oneself. Outside of my struggles within, I had transformed myself into a totally new being. Whereas I once despised everything, I was now finding life to be quite a challenge.

I spent Christmas at home with my two brothers and Dad. Vickey came to visit. How she was growing! Vickey was now eight, and I had seldom seen her over the past year, which had helped fuel my perpetual loneliness. How I loved my sister! I never really thought of my siblings or Dad any differently now that I knew I didn't truly belong. It was only Mother that I hated more.

Also, this Christmas was about the fifth year I had not bought Mother a present. My gifts this year weren't much as I was only on a small allowance from Dad. I also didn't know at the time that this Christmas would be the last I would spend with any of my family, including Vickey, for a number of years.

With Christmas Day over, I put out the word that I was going to have another New Year's Eve bash. This would be the fifth annual. As I didn't drink or do drugs, I told them it would be a BYOB and BYOD party and I would buy a quantity of beer. I figured I could drink on New Year's Eve since it was a special occasion. Well, the evening arrived and I was all ready for a big bash. Dad and my brothers had gone their separate ways for the evening. The last few bashes had been ultimate drug- and alcohol-enhanced parties, and the house was usually overcrowded.

This year not one of my past acquaintances showed up. I figured it was because I had changed so drastically over the past year and a half—winning an award at the Mr. Sudbury contest, not selling drugs any more, maybe even the fact that I had been on television and in the newspaper. I guessed they thought I was too good for them now. Oh well, I didn't fit in with them any more either. All this just revealed I had a new life now. I was left with the beer and got absolutely drunk at home and was fast asleep by midnight.

Over the next few days I decided I wanted to take upgrading courses at Cambrian College to improve my education level. I knew that Canada Manpower would pay a student providing he or she qualified. I went through the procedures of registering only to find out later I didn't qualify because Dad was earning too much money. I told Dad I wanted to attend the courses, which would be starting in a couple of weeks. After some arguing about the costs, Dad agreed. I knew he didn't owe me anything, but I wanted to improve myself. Dad also agreed to increase my allowance somewhat.

I then registered and was once again a student. Who would have thought? I would be attending classes five nights a week. I had turned twenty-one on the fifteenth of January. So another promise I had made while in a solitary jail cell had been fulfilled. The only one not on my mind was my promise to attend church every Sunday.

Things were happening, although it was taking some time. One of my subjects was English and speed-reading. English had been my worst subject in high school. In fact, I had failed grade nine English twice, which meant I only had a grade-eight English level. I was an instant hit with the females, and I had a few one-night stands over the first couple of months. I didn't want any long-term relationships for fear of rejection.

I was weight training six days a week, Tuesdays, Thursdays and Saturdays at Vic Tanny's and Mondays, Wednesdays and Fridays at Connie Lou's Fitness Centre, which was now run by Cambrian College. My physical appearance was still improving, and I knew I had as much of a chance to win as anyone did. My grades at school were okay, and I was averaging over 70 percent. When you consider that I just barely passed while in grade nine, I was doing quite well. One problem was that I had a short attention span.

All this while, Dad was on my case about not working and how much everything was costing him. I don't think he realized how much I really wanted to improve myself. We had our usual arguments about everything, which I ignored.

# Chapter 17

One night in early April I was busing it home from night school as usual. I had transferred to the Copper Cliff bus and was about halfway home. The bus made one of its regular stops and, lo and behold, J.D., my first love, got on the bus. I hadn't seen her for a couple of years and had heard she had gone to Toronto. J.D. took a seat beside me, and we carried on a conversation. I had always been attracted to her as she was quite beautiful. Since we only lived several houses apart, we both got off at the same bus stop, which was bordering my yard. I nervously asked J.D. in for a coffee and didn't expect her to say yes. She accepted, and we went in the house. I made coffee for her and mixed myself a health drink as I didn't drink caffeine. We then went downstairs to my disco bedroom and sat on the couch together.

We chatted and caught up on what had been happening in each of our lives. J.D. was impressed with the complete turnaround in my life, the bodybuilding, school, and my new attitude towards life. I had turned on some of the coloured lights and put some quiet music on the stereo. Barry White was playing. That particular record had been our favourite when we were dating. We had a dance and called it a night. I felt as if J.D. had never left my life. I was in love already and was impressed with what she had been doing in Toronto. I asked if I could see her again, and she said yes. We made a date for the next afternoon, before I would have to go to school.

After our first date, hardly a day went by that J.D. and I didn't see each other. Also, that April I stripped the Silver Streak and sold some of the parts to have some money. J.D.'s parents, who still didn't like me, didn't want their daughter to have anything to do with me. Now that J.D. was older and had been on her own for some time, there was nothing they could really do. I was determined however to win her parents over. Her family always went to church, and she herself sometimes played the piano, and her father was a church elder. Since I now believed in working for something you wanted in this world, I decided to attend J.D.'s church.

The Baptist church they attended was all the way across the city, and for me to get there was a task in itself. Since the bus schedules were cut back on Sundays, I would hitchhike downtown and then catch a bus, after which I would have to hitchhike or walk the final couple miles. Coming home would be the same thing in reverse. I had gone three times and sat by myself before J.D.'s parents acknowledged my presence and then offered me a ride home.

It was strange being in church again. I found though that I felt very comfortable in God's house. I especially liked watching J.D. play the piano. Now I had a weekly ride to church. There weren't many words spoken between us, but at least it was a start. I'm sure her parents were shocked by my tenacity. Another quest accomplished. J.D.'s father is a man whom to this date I still have a lot of respect for.

I was sure making progress with my life. It was now the first week of May, and a job was available as an instructor. Ron put in a word for me, and I was given the position. I did have to work some nights and every second Sunday and ended up dropping my night classes. Ron himself now only worked part-time at the gym in sales, as he was now a member of the Sudbury fire department. I would be working with another instructor named Paul. Paul and I also happened to be training partners.

I figured Paul to be my only real competition in the Mr. Sudbury contest, which was about seven weeks away. The contest was slated to be the best this year as bodybuilding was becoming very popular. In fact, Ron had organized two contests for the same date. One, the Mr. Sudbury, for city residents, and the second a Mr. Northern Ontario contest, which was open to anyone.

One of the first things I organized at the gym was the second Vic Tanny's strength and fitness contest. Ron had organized the first one the previous year. The contest was designed in a way that it wasn't necessarily the strongest person who would win. It ended up that Ron and I were the two most fit people at the gym. This was another accomplishment to help me build self-esteem. Ironically, Ron and I were both recovered addicts, which goes to show that people who have experienced such tragedies, when determined, can change their lives.

The one problem I was having was getting to work on the Sundays I was scheduled to work. There were no buses early in the morning. Dad had been driving me, which meant he had to come home Saturday nights, which upset him. He said he would co-sign for a car loan. I couldn't believe he would do that for me. I picked out my dream car. As a kid I had once a Hot Wheels '68 Firebird, and that's what I wanted. I took one for a test drive and fell in love with it. When the time came to pay for it, I started having second thoughts about buying a twelve-year-old car. I ended up purchasing for $3,400 a burgundy-on-burgundy five-year-old Pontiac Grand Prix LJ. This mint-condition luxury sports coupe was loaded with all the amenities, including the largest engine available. A 455 four-barrel was underneath the hood. I had never thought I would own such a car.

Now I figured I had everything a man could want. All the desperate loneliness now was quite suppressed. I was attending church with the girl I loved. I was being slowly accepted by her parents. I had a job, my health, money, and I seemed quite happy. I also had a chance to be Mr. Sudbury, to top things off.

The contest was only a few weeks away, and I was on a very strict diet so that I would look my best in the contest. I had hurt my right shoulder and was training with the injury. To relieve the pain, I was popping several 222s (aspirin with codeine, a cocaine derivative) before each workout. The tension between some of the guys I would be competing against was tight. We always tried to psyche each other out. I was determined to beat a guy named Lincoln, who had placed second to my third in our division the previous year. Also, my friend Robert, who was the reigning Mr. Sudbury, wouldn't be competing this year. My toughest competition, I figured, would be my training and working partner, Paul. Paul would be in the lightweight division while I would be in the middleweight. We both figured we would each win our divisions and then would have to pose off together along with the heavyweight winner for the overall title. Paul and I were not getting along so good at work and had stopped training together because we each didn't want the other to know what we looked like.

The tension between us got so bad at work that I quit my job and went into seclusion to train at another gym for the last couple of weeks. This was to really psyche Paul out. I knew I had Lincoln beat as far as muscle development went. The problem was that 50 percent of your score was for posing properly. It was one thing to have a muscular physique and another to show it to the judges. I knew my weakness was in posing. I was a shy, introverted guy and after last year's competition realized I had stage fright. I felt very uncomfortable standing in nothing but posing trunks on stage in front of hundreds of spectators and the television cameras.

As the last days passed, I increased the quantity of 222s I was taking before a workout. My shoulder was in constant pain, and I couldn't have trained if the codeine wasn't relieving it. I was taking about thirty every day. At home Dad was on my case for quitting my job, and I told him I would get another as soon as the contest was over. Dad couldn't understand why it was so important for me to succeed at something. Previously the only things I succeeded at were my illegal business activities.

The day of the contest finally arrived. This Saturday in late June was the day I had trained for, and I felt great. J.D. came over, and we left for Sudbury Secondary School, where the contest was being held. It would be a long day. The contestants had to be weighed in and prejudged in the morning and then return for the evening show and awards ceremony.

There were two contests being held that day, Mr. Sudbury and Mr. Northern Ontario. The Mr. Sudbury contest was judged first. All contestants had to be current members of the OABBA (Ontario Amateur Body Building Association). Once the weigh-ins were taken care of, the prejudging began. The prejudging was more important to the contestants because that is when 90 percent of the judging and scoring takes place. The evening show is really for the benefit of the audience. I was to be in the middleweight division this year, as opposed to the previous year when I had been a heavyweight. My muscle density and definition had improved, and my body fat was down to 4 percent. In other words, I was "ripped," extremely muscular.

The lightweights were judged first, and as expected, Paul was the best as far as I was concerned. Next was my division. J.D. wished me luck before I went on stage. I had pumped up and had a thin coating of oil applied to my perfectly tanned physique. As I stood amongst the other contestants, I figured myself as the winner as long as I didn't screw up my posing routine. My only real competition in the division was Lincoln, as expected. I knew he could be the better poser, but I definitely was more muscular.

We all went through our compulsory poses. I had no problem. Then we were all off stage and would now return individually in numerical order to do our individual posing routines. Lincoln was ahead of me, and I watched intently as he went flawlessly and gracefully through his routine. I knew that to beat him I would have to do my routine perfectly. Fifty percent of my points depended on my posing. I had always been a show-off in front of people I knew, so it would seem natural that I could go before a crowd without hesitation. No so! In front of strangers I was quite the opposite.

I was a nervous wreck as I took the stage. I knew a first-place finish was at stake here. I started my routine and halfway through messed up by getting my poses out of sync, which threw my thinking off. As I finished up, I knew I might have blown a whole year's training in that one minute. I was silently mad as hell.

I wiped the oil off myself, got dressed, and told J.D. we were leaving. I knew in my heart that if Lincoln was first at the evening's show it would not be because he had a better build. J.D. and I got into my luxury sports coupe. I started up the 455-cubic-inch engine, revved it up and laid a patch of rubber as I pulled out of the parking lot. We headed for Copper Cliff.

I was quite agitated and felt very aggressive. I seemed to have a heavier foot than usual and was speeding somewhat. Just my luck, a cop car pulled up behind me with the lights flashing. I pulled to the curb. The cop came and asked, "What's the hurry?" I told him there was no hurry and I was just a little upset. I went on to state that I had just come from the Mr. Sudbury contest and had just blown my stage routine.

He responded by saying that if I let the lady drive I wouldn't be given a ticket. The guy was all heart, considering he knew of me. J.D. and I exchanged seats, and she drove us to Copper Cliff. The episode with the cop cooled me down a bit, and I came to my senses. I had done my best that morning and would just have to do my best that night. I spent the day just lazing about, deepening my already bronzed body. I caught a couple hours' sleep late in the afternoon.

The show was to begin at 8 p.m. By 7:30 J.D. and I were at the school and waiting in the now half-filled auditorium. Tonight was the night. I knew at worst I would place second in my division, which was a pleasing thought of sorts. The previous year I had a third-place finish, so second place would be an improvement. I was still determined to go for first place and beat Lincoln. If that would happen, I would end up hopefully placing second overall for the Mr. Sudbury title. Paul was in great shape, and I knew I couldn't beat him. Although I was more muscular, I lacked some symmetry to my physique.

The show was about to start. Ron was the emcee and the organizer of the contests. The auditorium was now filled to capacity. As a competitor I was excited and extremely nervous. During the prejudging, no music was allowed, but since the night show was mostly for the benefit of the audience, the competitors did their posing routines to their own musical selections.

The lightweight contestants for Mr. Sudbury were first, and after all was said and done Paul won first place as expected. Now it was the middleweight class, which meant that when my number was called, I would be on stage. I was waiting in the wings. Lincoln was ahead of me and had the crowd going crazy, which was psyching me out. When my turn arrived, I went on stage and went through my own routine, this time quite well. The crowd wasn't in a frenzy or anything. After all the middleweights had gone through their routines, it was time for our awards. I figured I would come second, and that's what happened. Lincoln with his superb posing routine had scored higher with the judges.

We received our trophies. I was a little disappointed because I knew I had the better physique. Well, there was always next year. While we three middleweight winners were on stage, Ron announced that two more trophies were being awarded and the recipients of the trophies were now on stage. The first trophy was for the best poser of the competition and went to Lincoln. The second was for the most muscular man in the contest, and that went to me. I couldn't believe it—me, Randy R. Tunney, reformed criminal, drug addict and alcoholic, was now the most muscular man in Sudbury. Who would have ever thought? I stood on the stage with my two trophies, beaming with pride. I knew J.D. would be proud of me.

Well, after the contest was over, Paul had been awarded the Mr. Sudbury title. I sat with J.D. and watched the rest of the evening's proceedings. I was in total happiness. To me, winning the most muscular trophy was as good as winning the Mr. Sudbury title. I had always trained for muscularity and muscle quality instead of muscle quantity. To me that was the essence of fitness, to be "lean and mean." Being the most muscular meant I had adhered to a better diet than the others had.

Wow, what a night! Two years before I had been a burnt-out drug addict. I was still an addict, but of the health kind. There is no better high than a natural high. To celebrate, J.D. and I went to the President Hotel, where a hall had been rented for a post-contest celebration. I allowed myself a couple of beer as this was a special occasion. I had now restricted my drinking to Christmas, New Year's and maybe a couple of nights like that night.

I was proud of my accomplishment and had deserved to win. Life had always been a struggle, and now I was conquering my shortcomings.

By the time J.D. and I called it a night, it was about 2 a.m. When I got home, I showed my brothers my trophies and told them they would be able to see me on TV when it was broadcast. I placed my two new trophies in my room beside the one I had won the previous year. I fell dreamily asleep thinking about next year. I knew I would be the best by then. Yes, I would be Mr. Sudbury in 1981!

# Chapter 18

Now ahead of me was to find a job. Sudbury isn't a good place to job hunt. I certainly didn't want to spend the rest of my days shovelling rock in a mine somewhere. Always being a businessman of sorts, I had aspirations of running a small business someday. Some of the members of the gym were self-employed and seemed to have the trappings of success.

For days I looked around for a job, including at the mines. J.D. and I started talking about my job hunting, and she suggested we go to Toronto. In other words, she wanted us to live together. She mentioned that she had several thousand dollars in the bank, which would be enough for us to start out with. I couldn't believe her offer. After all the years of suffering, something incredibly wonderful was happening to me. I didn't even have to think over the proposition. I would be living with the girl of my dreams.

J.D. had already spent time living in Toronto and said we could stay at another couple's apartment until we found one of our own. Was I ever excited! I had nothing to keep me in Sudbury, and getting away from the memories of my past seemed like a great idea. I started dreaming of a great future like never before. I figured I'd take whatever job I could get at first and then work my way up the corporate ladder. With my growing self-esteem, I knew I could do anything I set my heart on.

We decided to leave within the next couple of days. It would be more like an elopement, as I don't know if J.D. told her parents what we were up to. Her parents still weren't too pleased with their daughter and only child seeing me, although I was tolerated.

It was the first week of July when we took off. I had my Grand Prix LJ loaded up with clothes, personal effects, my trophies, and Tom's stereo, which I figured I inherited after his death. I had the last of my money, which was only a couple of hundred dollars. J.D. had some of her things also. We planned to get jobs first; then with her money we could rent an apartment, buy some furniture and essentials. She said she would make my car payments for the first few months.

I told Dad of my plans, and he seemed pleased. Now it was time to embark on a new life, in a new city. I figured the change would do me good now that I was what I considered straightened out and normal. We departed, and I hadn't even seen my sister to say goodbye. In fact, I don't think I had seen her since Christmas. There was no way I would go to Mother's house to see her. How I would miss her! Someday Vickey would be sixteen and would be able to do as she pleased.

As we drove to Toronto J.D. and I talked about our plans. The drive was okay, and I just put on the cruise control. Once in Toronto, J.D. gave me the directions, as she knew her way around. The couple we would be staying with lived in Scarborough on Sheppard Avenue East at Kennedy, one block north of the 401. I had only been to Toronto on two other occasions, once when I had hitchhiked to Niagara Falls and tried to cross into the States. I had briefly walked down Yonge Street. The second time was when a girlfriend and I drove to Toronto to visit the Ontario Science Centre for the day. I couldn't believe I was actually going to live in this large city.

Arriving, we drove up to the front of the apartment building where J.D.'s friends lived on the first floor. Her closest cousin lived in the same building, and I had met her once in Copper Cliff, while she was visiting J.D. But I would not be seeing J.D.'s cousin while we stayed there, because J.D.'s aunt had heard about my past criminal lifestyle. I wouldn't be too welcome, to say the least. Even though I had changed, the past was always there haunting me.

I met J.D.'s friends Connie and Darcy, and they seemed like a nice couple. They lived common law, as J.D. and I would now be doing. Yes, it was sort of like J.D. and I were on our honeymoon, as it would be the first night we would spend the whole night together. The apartment had two bedrooms, and we would have our own room to stay in while here. We unloaded the car, and I set up the stereo in the living room. The first night together was like magic, and I thought of the wonderful future that lay ahead.

The following morning I got a couple of newspapers and started looking through the want ads. I couldn't believe the quantity of jobs listed in the papers. J.D. and I were alone as her friends had left for work. Since J.D. had lived in this area herself, we decided we would live in the same area of Scarborough. I decided I could start by working in a gym or a warehouse. As there weren't any fitness jobs listed in the area, I would look for warehouse work.

J.D.'s friends both worked about fifteen minutes away. In fact, J.D. had worked there a short while as a receptionist. She said she would apply for a position there. There were a number of jobs listed in the paper in the Markham area. J.D. said Markham was two major streets north at Steeles Ave. I phoned the numbers listed and set up a series of interviews for that day and the next. I wanted to get a job ASAP. J.D. would also that day go to a branch of her bank and have her money transferred from Sudbury. She told me it would take a couple of days. I had some money, so there would be no problem.

I drove up to Markham and went to an interview. I couldn't believe the number of companies in Markham. I figured I would have a job in no time. Between interviews I went from building to building, applying for any position that might be available. The next couple of days passed with no success. J.D. also said her money hadn't been transferred yet for some reason. I knew nothing about electronic banking and did not give it a second thought.

The only company that seemed interested in hiring me was an electronics company in Markham called Paco Electronics. I had applied for a warehouse assistant's position. After a couple of more days, I phoned

Paco Electronics and spoke with the warehouse manager, Neil. He said he had not decided who he would hire yet. I told him I would phone back in a few days. J.D. again told me her money was not transferred yet.

Unbeknownst to me, J.D. didn't have a cent in the bank. I kept looking for a job, and it wasn't until a couple of days later that I questioned J.D. about her money. She insisted that the money would be available any day. I had no reason to not believe her, as she came from a family that certainly had no money problems and a few thousand dollars could actually be available.

I started feeling as if I was being conned by the girl I loved, and I started arguing with her. I accused her of lying, but she still claimed to have the money. Even Connie and Darcy started in on us. I just went along with what J.D. was saying. My money was getting low, and I was getting worried about running out. I had car payments to make, which J.D. had said she would pay. We were eating our hosts' food and weren't buying our own now.

I started drinking and had gotten drunk one day. I was getting depressed and was mad as hell at J.D. I just knew that J.D. had lied to me. For all I knew, she had lied to me from the day I started seeing her again. I was just about ready to give up on females. They were nothing but trouble. One night I got mad and decided to go for a drive. The key broke off in the ignition, and I didn't get anywhere. I had the car towed across the street to Williams' Shell Station. That cost me the rest of my money. Man, I was mad. How the hell was I going to pay for a new ignition? I was mad and was drinking beer and slipping into the darkness of my mind.

J.D. and I were hardly speaking to each other. I told her that if she still wanted me she had better get a job soon, as this Toronto idea had been hers. I loved her very much, but then and there I felt hatred towards her. If it had been anyone else, I would have walked right out on her. Where the hell would I have gone? I didn't have anywhere or anyone else to go to. No family, no love, nothing at all. Here I was 250 miles away from what little home I did have.

I was so mad at J.D. I had put all my trust in her, and here she was messing me around. I couldn't handle it any more. I got pissed drunk that night and slept on the far side of the bed. For two people who were supposed to live happily ever after, we were sure off to a bad start. I didn't understand why J.D. was lying to me.

The following morning Connie and Darcy left for work as usual. I awoke in a state of total depression and started off the day with a beer. I hadn't done that in over two years. By noon I was pissed drunk again and had made a bed on the living room floor. I lay with my head between the two stereo speakers as if I had on a giant set of headphones. The music was cranked up quite loud. I just lay there drinking beer in a state of near total despair and in great interior suffering. I was thinking of women and their useless role in this world. J.D. had gone out looking for a job, or so she said. She also had said she would check with her bank. Who the hell did she think she was fooling? That girl, didn't she realize you couldn't con an ex-con?

When J.D. got back, again she said the money wasn't there. Again I called her a liar. We fought like cats and dogs. It wasn't much of a fight, as I was drunk. I didn't care about anything and just wanted to crawl into a hole and die.

That evening as the four of us sat around boozing it up, we started arguing about all of this. Me, the innocent one of this total mess-up, was accused of being as much as liar as J. D was.

Well, that did it. I couldn't handle any more of this and in the drunken state that I was in went into the kitchen and grabbed the sharpest knife available. I told J.D. that I was going to slash my wrists and leave this messed-up world. Well, all hell broke loose and tempers were flaring. I ran to the balcony and jumped over the partition. Remember, J.D.'s friends lived on the first floor. I was standing in the parking lot of the apartment building screaming my again-tormented head off. I was threatening to kill myself. I guess everyone in the building heard, and someone phoned the cops or an ambulance to take me away, because I soon heard sirens approaching. I made a feeble attempt to slash my wrists. Again I tried, and this time I drew blood, and it was dripping onto the pavement.

In a minute a cop cruiser showed up and then an ambulance. At the sight of the cops I threw away the knife. I was highly unstable as the ambulance attendants looked after my cut wrist. I was told I did a lousy job.

Now they were talking to the cops about taking me to a psychiatric hospital. I pleaded with them not to take me as my wrist was being bandaged. They asked J.D.'s friends if they would take responsibility for me and if I threatened to harm myself again to call them.

They said they would, and that was the end of that.

I had left Sudbury to get away from all this bull. I went back into the apartment and spent the rest of the evening in the bedroom alone. The next morning when I got up I ate a small breakfast. Then I phoned the Shell station across the street and found out my car was ready and had a bill of around $80. Again I phoned Paco Electronics to see if I had gotten the job as warehouse assistant. Again the manager said that a decision hadn't been made. I told him that I was probably going back to Sudbury and would phone him in a few days.

Now I had a problem. How the hell was I going to pay for the car repair, as neither J.D. or I had any money? I walked across the street to speak to the owner, Mr. Williams, who just happened to be in. I explained to him my situation, that I was from Sudbury and had run out of money. He lent a sympathetic ear. I ended up bartering with him and we came to an agreement. The only thing I had of any value was my deceased brother's stereo. I would give him the Sansui amplifier in exchange for the bill I owed and a tank of gas when I was ready to leave for Sudbury. The amplifier was worth about $300. The bill I owed along with a tank of gas would amount to just over $100. I hated to do this but had no alternative. I walked across the street and retrieved the amplifier and then gave it to Mr. Williams. I drove the car from the Shell station to the apartment building.

I told J.D. I was going back to Sudbury. I asked her if she was coming with me. J.D. said yes. We talked about coming back someday. She suggested we look for an apartment. I asked how the hell we were going to pay for one. J.D. said she would send them the money from Sudbury, that once she got to Sudbury she would be able to get her money no problem. She would then send a cheque or money order to the apartment management. I didn't know whether to believe her or not. Anyway, I decided to go along with her idea. I was just a love-starved young man, and I loved J.D. in spite of the fact I was certain she had been lying. I would give her another chance.

I asked her if she knew of any places she would like to live. She got a newspaper and turned to the apartments-to-rent section. We would have to rent a furnished apartment at first until we bought some furniture. This narrowed the choices down somewhat. I told her we only had about half a tank of gas to use for driving around. After that I would be able to fill up for free across the street at the Shell station. I hoped that the tank of gas would get us home. When we had driven to Toronto, I had used well over a tank of gas, but I had been speeding quite a bit. My '75 Grand Prix was a gas guzzler. By my calculations, if I nursed the car back to Sudbury, we would have barely enough gas.

We checked out a few apartment buildings, and I couldn't believe the prices to rent a place. We ended up deciding on an apartment on the first floor of a twenty-storey apartment building on Thorncliffe Park Drive, in Don Mills. This apparently was one of the nicest apartment complexes in Toronto. The apartment we chose was a one bedroom and was luxuriously furnished. I knew I could certainly get used to living here. The rent was $750 a month. J.D. said she would take care of everything. She told the lady who was showing the place that we would take it for the beginning of August and would send them either a certified check or a money order in the mail. The lady said she couldn't hold the apartment without a deposit, but should someone else rent the place before the money was received, she would find us suitable accommodations in the complex. First and last months' rent would be needed on the open monthly lease. The total J.D. would have to send was $1,500. That was a lot of money, and I didn't know there were less expensive places around.

As we left the place, I already felt like a resident and even introduced myself to the doorman. In the parking lot I noticed a Rolls Royce Silver Shadow. I checked it out, as I had never seen a Rolls before except in magazines. I couldn't believe we would be living here amongst the wealthy. We drove back to Connie and Darcy's, packed our things and left behind a note and the rest of the stereo system. The note said we would pick up the stereo pieces when we came back to move into our apartment on August 1. We drove across to the Shell station and had the car filled up with gas at no charge. I thanked Mr. Williams, and then we were on our way. I kept at the speed limit or below in order to conserve gasoline. This was a challenge for me, as I loved driving fast. We had not more than a dollar between us.

By the time we got to Sudbury, the gas gauge was on empty. I nursed it through the city and towards Copper Cliff. We made it, and probably just. I had averaged about thirteen miles to the gallon and had a twenty-one gallon gas tank. This was the most MPG I had ever gotten from this gas hog. J.D. took her suitcase and walked down the street to her house. I went into Dad's house and spoke with one of my brothers. I borrowed $5 so I could put some gas in the car. I was hesitant to drive the one mile to the gas station, as I didn't think I could make it. Fortunately, I did. If home had been any farther, J.D. and I wouldn't have made the distance.

Since it was now about the middle of July, J.D. and I had a couple of weeks to spend in Sudbury and Copper Cliff to straighten out our affairs. I had previously made my July car payment, and the next was due in the middle of August. I trusted J.D. to take care of our rent in Toronto. I had to come up with some money of my own. J.D.'s parents now were aware that we were serious about being together. I could drop by the house on occasion, which I couldn't do just a few months before.

Over the next couple of weeks I earned some money working as a casual labourer for a moving company. I worked maybe three times a week. I was counting on J.D. to pay our bills as promised. She had told me the money had been sent to Toronto. I took her word for it, as I was quite trustful of people until crossed. I was certain she wouldn't lie to me again. I couldn't even prove she had initially lied to me. If I couldn't trust J.D., who could I trust?

I spent time working out at Vic Tanny's with some buddies, as I figured I wouldn't be back in Sudbury until Christmas. I also saw myself on television when the Mr. Sudbury and Mr. Northern Ontario contests aired. I had become somewhat of a celebrity around Copper Cliff and had gained a lot of respect from people who had once snubbed me as the criminal I had once been. I also saw my sweet sister, Vickey, a couple of times when she visited the house. As usual, I hardly saw Dad. I loved spending time with Vickey, as she was a jewel in my life.

One day J.D., Vickey, my brothers and a friend of ours decided to go horseback riding. I wasn't too thrilled about riding horses, as I had only done so on one other occasion and that had been disastrous. When I was about ten years old, my brother Tom and I went to a farm just a few minutes away from our cottage. We asked to ride the horse that they had. The brown mare was saddled up and ready. Being the eldest, I went first. I climbed into the saddle for my first time and felt in every way a cowboy. I was to ride the firmly muscled mare to the end of a gravel drive and back. Since I had never been on a horse before I was to just ride while the horse walked. Everything was just going fine, and I was enjoying my first horseback ride. All of a sudden, the horse, Flicker, decided to run full out. As we bolted down the drive, I heard someone scream, "Drop the reins, drop the reins!" They were actually screaming, "Pull the reins!" but I did as I heard. While the horse was still hell-bent on running, I was now bouncing around in the saddle and holding on to the saddle horn. Well, I was no rodeo star and fell off as fast as one could blink an eye. I gathered myself up, uninjured except for my pride. Someone ran to the horse, who by now had stopped running. I told myself I would never ride a horse again.

Now here I was over ten years older and a lot wiser. I was willing to give a horse another chance. We were going to Wagon Wheel Ranch, which was only about twenty miles from where our cottage had been. The place was a group home for teenage boys. Since I had never been there before, we got a little lost.

Once we had driven off the main road onto a gravel road I let Vickey drive. I sat in the passenger seat. Vickey could barely reach the gas and brake pedals. This was a road servicing the few farms in the area, so I figured it would be okay to let Vickey have a little fun. When we realized that we weren't going in the right direction, she drove up a laneway to a farm. The farmer came over to the car, and Vickey asked him for directions. He asked who the driver was, and Vickey blurted out, "I am the driver." The farmer looked puzzled as he began giving directions to my nine-year-old sister. We were all holding back our laughter as he spoke. Vickey thanked the farmer, turned the car around, and we drove off, leaving the farmer in a cloud of dust. We all burst out laughing and chuckled all the way to the ranch.

We paid our fees, and a couple of teenage boys saddled up enough horses. We would be taken on a trail through some bush and across some open fields. We each picked the horse we would ride. We then set out along the trails. We were all enjoying ourselves, and any apprehension I had previously to mounting the horse had now gone.

The trail led through the dense bush and thicket. When we emerged out onto an open field we were told we could let the horses run full out across the field. We all wanted to be the first across and soon were racing as fast as the horses would go. Halfway across, my horse's saddle started slipping towards the right side of the horse. Did the dumb horse have enough sense to stop? No, this stupid mare kept right on racing.

By now I was desperately trying to stay on this frantic horse while riding in the 3 o'clock position. I hadn't a hope in hell. I fell off as the saddle went underneath the horse's belly. I was nearly trampled by the hind legs. I was then stamped on by a couple of the other rampaging horses. Now I knew I would never ride a horse again.

The horse I had been riding was running straight back to the barn. Everyone was laughing at me as I stood there slapping dirt off my clothes. I ended up riding double back to the barn with J.D. So much for being a cowboy. I was teased all the way back to Copper Cliff.

A couple more days were spent around town, and on August 1 J.D. and I departed again for Toronto, to move into our lavishly furnished apartment. J.D. had a couple of thousand dollars, and our rent had been paid for. I drove speedily along Highway 69 and onto the 400. I had filled up with gas prior to leaving Sudbury. Between my lead foot and the gas guzzling 455-cubic-inch engine, the gas just seemed to evaporate, almost instantly. Every time I checked the fuel level indicator, it had moved.

By the time we reached Barrie we had to stop for gas and decided to eat as well. I exited the 400 and drove to the nearest station and topped up with petrol. I asked J.D. to pay for the gas as I had limited funds. She had said she would pay for things until I got a job. She now looked at me and told me she didn't have enough money. I called her a liar and more. Not wanting to create a scene there, I paid for the gas and then drove off, leaving a black patch of burnt rubber on the pavement. I drove to a parking lot and parked the car. J.D. and I proceeded to have an all-out verbal war. I called her every foul word in the book. She had lied to me again! Man, if I knew what was going on in her head, but it seemed she didn't know what the meaning of being truthful was. I was mad. I had again put my trust in her, as a person who loves another should. She was letting both of us down. How the hell did she think we could survive in Toronto with no money?

I questioned her about the apartment in Toronto. She swore that it was paid for. I said, "Sure, sure it is. We'll see." I told her to get lost, and I got out of the car. I wasn't spending another minute in the presence of this lying woman. It was either her or me, and I couldn't tell her to get out, as I felt responsible for her. I told her I would hitchhike to Toronto and start my life over by myself. I told her she could do whatever in the hell she pleased. Then I walked away, leaving her crying in the passenger seat of my car, which would now soon be repossessed.

I was mad as I walked purposely in the opposite direction of where J.D. would be going. I made my way to the highway and sat and watched for J.D. to head out for Toronto. I didn't know if she might head back to Sudbury, so I waited until I saw her heading south to Toronto. Now I had to hitchhike the sixty miles to the Big Smoke. What a damn life. Would nothing ever go right for me? Good-for-nothing-but-sex women! I didn't deserve this bull. J.D. knew that I knew of only two addresses in TO, one, her friends; the second, where we were supposed to live, which I now knew would be bull. Was I stupid or what?

I got a ride to Toronto, then took the subway and a bus to where we were to move. Guess what? Yes, you are right. By now I had cooled off but was in tears as I sat outside the building. I figured J.D. would show up sooner or later, as she had my car. What the hell was I to do now? Where was J.D.? I swore I would have nothing to do with her any more. How I loved her, though.

I thought and thought. J.D. wasn't near as bad as I had been, and she was willing to be with me. All she had ever done was lie and lie some more. As I sat there, I figured I would stay with her no matter what. I had changed in time and believed anybody could change if they wanted to. So I waited for J.D. to show up.

While doing so, I went to a payphone and called Paco Electronics. This was one of the places that had shown an interest in hiring me as a warehouse person. I spoke with the manager, Neil. I was told he had still not hired anyone. I told him I would get back to him another time. I didn't know why they were being so fussy over such a menial job, shipping and receiving.

As expected, J.D. showed up, and we had a little spat but nothing too serious as we both had had time to cool down. She had gone to her friends' place expecting me to show up there. I asked her why she was always lying. She answered that it was because of her parents' expectations of her. Since she was an only child and her father was an Inco executive, her parents had wanted her to go to university and become a doctor or a lawyer. She had just wanted to be herself and live as her own person. After she had originally moved to Toronto, she had started lying to them about what she had been doing, so as to please them. As the lies went on, they became more involved and complex. In fact, J.D. hadn't been living such a desirable life.

By the time she had come back to Copper Cliff, she was in way over her head and had no choice but to continue her lying. At that time, J.D. and I started seeing each other again, and she kept up her facade with me. Almost everything she had told me was BS, except for the fact that she loved me. She told me that she thought her Dad was disappointed in her for more than just not continuing school. She had always felt that her father would have preferred her to be a boy. So she had grown up alone and dissatisfied at times because she was a girl.

By now we were both in tears. I felt closer to her than ever. I told her I could relate to her because I had always thought my mother wanted me to be a girl. All these facts shocked me, to say the least. Here we were, two young adults growing up with opposite upbringings, J.D. with a sheltered, non-abusive childhood, while mine was non-sheltered and abusive. Yet we both felt similar about ourselves. We both felt we weren't good enough, in our eyes and in the eyes of our parents. Both of us at times had seriously wished we were of the opposite sex. Later in our relationship we would become aware of each other's past homosexual and lesbian experiences. For now nothing was mentioned, although the thoughts crossed my mind, as I'm sure they did J.D.'s.

Now can you imagine the magnitude of these identity crises on a national scale? J.D. and I had opposite upbringings and lived a half-dozen houses from each other. Considering this, one would surmise that these problems can explain the high percentage of bisexual and homosexual people. This would represent a problem of such magnitude that I shudder at the thought of all this human tragedy.

As I sat with J.D. in the car, I actually was now sympathizing with her, and the anger I had towards her had disappeared. We had acknowledged our weaknesses and failings to each other, the great interior sufferings. We professed our love for each other and vowed to love each other in spite of limitations. We would show them all.

But we had a problem. What would we do now? We had little money, maybe over $100. J.D. decided we should go to her friends' and stay for a couple of days and try to find jobs and take it from there. We didn't want to be in Sudbury or Copper Cliff any more. We ended up staying for a couple of days and were unable to land jobs. We had no choice but to go back to Copper Cliff until such time as we could afford to leave for good. We left her friends' place with all our belongings, including the rest of the stereo system, which I had previously left behind.

Back in Sudbury again, I now had the problem of making my next car payment, which was due in just over a week. I was sure I wouldn't be able to come up with the money, and I certainly wasn't going to resort to crime. My freedom was worth more than a car. I noticed that my two brothers seemed to be flashing around a lot of money. I asked them how they came to have it. They told me they would tell me providing we could use my car as transportation. I said yes, as long as I wasn't going to get into trouble with the law. I was told there was a bit of risk but nothing serious. I coaxed them into explaining to me how they got money.

Apparently they and numerous other people in town had stumbled across a veritable gold mine, except the gold was copper. Since Copper Cliff and surrounding towns were involved in mining, there happened to be several abandoned mines and out-posts about on the vast amounts of private property owned by Inco. What my brothers and others had been doing, including Inco personnel, was stripping the places of the copper wiring. They had been salvaging wire along with other saleable metal and then selling it to a scrap dealer.

Since Inco was involved in the smelting processes as well, their tailings had at one time been dumped back of Copper Cliff. These tailings lines ran for miles. When all this had once been going on, a catwalk had been built that ran from the smelter and out and along these now-abandoned tailings lines. When it had been in use by workers walking the line to check the tailings, it had been lighted and telephones had been placed at various distances so the workers could phone in. This meant there was mile after mile of copper telephone wire and electrical wire. This was what my brothers wanted to take, and at about seventy cents a pound it would add up to hundreds of dollars.

After I heard all this, I figured I would help them. After all, it had been abandoned for years and no one would miss it. The risk of getting caught was minimal. The real risk was to ourselves, as the aged wooden catwalk was falling apart and in places was high above the ground and rocks. We had walked it as kids and used to be scared. We would also have to climb up on the railings and reach up to cut the wires.

Well, now I would be able to earn some money in order to make my car payment and for J.D. and I to go to Toronto. My brothers knew of a place where we could park the car out of sight. The place was centrally located along the tailings line, just off the main highway, about a mile west of Copper Cliff. The tools we needed were hacksaws and extra blades. I wish I knew about bolt cutters then.

We had to walk across a marshy area and climb the steep embankments of the hills along the catwalk. Then we would have to get on the catwalk itself and cut the strands of wire. While standing on the catwalk we would be vulnerable to being spotted by someone driving across the property. We therefore had a lookout at all times. J.D. was usually that person. She was the most unlikely person to be involved in any kind of criminal activity, even one as mickey mouse as this. She found it exciting doing all this.

The first couple of days we cut and rolled up enough wire to fill the trunk of the car a few times and then made the trip to the scrapyard. What easy money we were making, although we worked hard cutting, rolling and hauling the wire down to the car.

Now by taking the wire to the scrap dealer with the rubber covering still on we weren't making as much money as we would have if we burnt off the rubber.

Also, making trips with only a trunkful of wire when we could be bringing it in by the truckload was not as profitable. Being the enterprising entrepreneur that I was, I started thinking of a way to make more money with less work. In other words, I had to increase productivity.

After some serious thought I came up with the perfect solution. We had an old tent trailer, which had pretty much met its end. The trailer was really just a metal box on wheels. A canvas tent could be put up once the sliding framework was in place. The canvas was now torn and tattered, much like the social fabric of our family. I had a trailer hitch on the car and figured if we stripped off the tent and underlying framework we could have a fair-sized trailer to carry the wire in. With the trailer stripped and loaded we would just then have to cover the open trailer with the original trailer cover. Since it was summer, we would blend in with all the other tourists on the road. No one would suspect that we had a trailer containing hundreds of pounds of copper wire. Then all we would have to do is find a place where we could burn the rubber off the wire. We would then have a trailer full of pure copper.

My brothers and J.D. were impressed with my brilliance. One of my brothers knew of a perfect place where we could burn the rubber off the wire, about a dozen miles away, out in the bush along a deserted gravel side road. The road had once led to a bridge that crossed a rapidly flowing river. The bridge was no more, which meant the road ended at the water's edge. Perfect! We could build a bonfire, throw the wire onto the burning flames, melt off the rubber and then toss the hot coils into the water to cool. I decided that we should work all day cutting, coiling and carrying the wire down to where the car would be parked off the main road. Then after supper, before dusk, we would take the trailer to where the wire was, load it and drive to the riverside. We would get to the river just before nightfall in order to collect the wood for a fire. Once under the cover of darkness we would light a fire and set to work. This burning had to be done at night because of the billowing black smoke the burning rubber would be giving off. We would have to bring some insect repellent to ward off the black flies of the north bushland. We would also commission the help of another for our expanded operation.

The next day we worked about eight hours cutting, coiling and carrying the wire down the hills, across the fields, to where our base of operations was located. Let me tell you, this wasn't an easy job, and the money would be well earned. I could see why no one salvaged the wire before, as it wasn't economically feasible. For us, though, it was fine. In the bad old days I could have made as much money in a fraction of the time and with next to no effort. I could've just as easily gotten some dope on consignment from past acquaintances and made a small fortune. Now in my healthy life, I was against drugs and crime.

After supper we hooked up the trailer and drove to our base of operations. The wire that we had cut, coiled and carried down earlier in the day was covered with dead brushwood. We loaded the trailer with about fifty coils of wire. There was a few hundred pounds in all. The canvas cover was tied onto the trailer as we waited, listening to the car radio. Then we took the short-minute drive to where we would be burning the rubber off the wire. Once off the main thoroughfare we had to drive along a gravel road that was in need of repair. The upkeep of the road had probably been cut off after the bridge crossing the river had been torn down.

We reached the river as the bright sun was about to set beyond the endless horizon. Once out of the car we noticed the bugs were bad and sprayed ourselves with insect repellent. We then set about collecting wood to build a bonfire. With the wood gathered we lit a small fire and waited for the darkness to be upon us. The trailer was unloaded and the wire stacked in a pile adjacent to the fire. Now under the cover of darkness we began tossing the coils onto the fire, about half a dozen at a time. The burning rubber sent billowing black smoke skyward. The underlying copper heated up and glowed brightly, and the colours kept changing. Once the rubber was melted off we would don some of Dad's fireman's mitts and with a strong branch lift each coil out of the fire and toss it into the cold running water of the river. As each hot coil hit the cold surface a blast of steam would rise in the air, as if the wire was expressing the shock of hot meeting cold. Once they cooled we would fork them out and put them into the trailer. This was repeated until all the coils of wire had been derubberized. We doused the fire, covered the treasure and drove home. In all the five of us had put in about a fourteen-hour workday, and it certainly had been work.

The next morning I drove to the scrap dealer and sold the copper wire. I received about $300 cash, which had to be split four ways. I kept J.D.'s share plus a little extra for the use of my car. I ended up with about $150 for fourteen hours of work. You can see why the company hadn't bother to salvage the wire themselves, as their employees were paid at least $10 an hour.

Over the next couple of days we kept busy "working." By the fourth or fifth morning my suspicions were aroused when I drove to the scrapyard. A guy was there who I was sure was a cop I had known. He was in plain clothes, and he was carrying a Dayco Steel brochure. I had a built in sensor for cops. Anyway, I sold the scrap as in the past. I was asked if I would mind taking a cheque instead of cash. I said it was okay. I left without any hassles, still suspicious of the cops maybe being on to me I kept my guard up. I figured if the guy who was waiting around was a cop, a stop-payment would be put on the cheque.

I immediately drove to my credit union and went to a wicket where a cousin of mine was working. I knew she would cash the cheque without question. Now I had our money and wasn't worried. I went home and divided the take. I told my brothers that we were taking a day off and that I was going to find out where the next closest scrap dealer was. I figured we would change dealers, because I was sure the dealer was suspicious of where we were getting our hundreds of pounds of copper wire on a daily basis. I then went to work vacuuming the trunk of my car and the trailer to remove any pieces of rubber and such that might be evidence of our work.

I went about my business that day, and late in the afternoon I was washing and waxing my car for a night of cruising about the town with J.D. I noticed about a block away an unmarked cop car but didn't worry, because all the evidence was gone. I went about the chore of cleaning the car. After some time the cops drove over and questioned me about the theft of copper. There must have been thirty or more people stealing abandoned copper wiring from Inco property, including some employees. I couldn't believe my luck.

Well, I was arrested and taken downtown to be booked for theft over $200. I spent the night silently at the cop shop and was taken the next day to court. The case was remanded a week, and later in the afternoon bail was set and I was booked into the district jail. The last time I had been there was four years before. Nothing had changed. I contacted Dad, and he said he would sign the bail bond. I was released on bail the following afternoon and was sure I had just spent my last might in jail forever.

After a couple of days Dad changed his mind about me being out on bail. I guess he was worried I would take off to Toronto. Man, was I mad at him! I was again arrested and would now have to spend a few days in custody until my court case. I had been in contact with my lawyer, and we figured I would get off because the copper from our last day of work had been recovered and the credit union had been paid for the money I had received from the cancelled cheque. Also, we would implicate some Inco employees who had been moonlighting as copper salvagers. Dad at this point in time got an court order stating that I wasn't allowed near his house. This meant if and when I got out of jail I had nowhere to stay. What would I do? I knew I wouldn't go back to crime, even a crime as stupid as stealing abandoned copper.

As we had figured, on my day in court I received a jail sentence of one day, which meant all I had to do was go back to the jail and sign out formally. J.D. was in court, and she waited for me to be released. It was good to be free again. J.D. had been using my car and had it parked close by. We went for a drive and then to lunch. I told her I had nowhere to stay and would have to sleep in my car. She said she would stay with me. Between us we decided that we would camp out in the car and stay where we had had our base of operations during our copper salvaging operation. I figured the credit union would repossess my car in a couple of weeks as I couldn't afford the payments and had one due now.

Neither of us had much money, so we would have to get food somehow. She could always drop in at her house and sneak out some food. I figured that during the day while my stepfather, who wanted nothing to do with me, was at work I could drop by the house. My brothers would let me in, or I could break in if no one was home.

We managed to get some food that day from our homes. We set up a little camp of sorts. To keep the perishables from spoiling in the hot August air, I dug a hole in the ground and lined it with a plastic bag. We could then put our food in it and cover it. The car wasn't the most comfortable place I had ever slept, but at the same time it wasn't the worst. I remembered those days in years gone past when I had slept on the metal beds in the solitary confinement cells of prison.

I slept sprawled uncomfortably across the front bucket seats while J.D. slept on the back bench seat.

Since it was summer, we kind of enjoyed this little campout. In the daytime we would stop by Dad's house. I usually had to crawl in the kitchen window and then unlock the door. J.D. and I would shower and such and catch up on some meals, etc. Also, we had to look for jobs. On a couple of days we went and pumped iron at the gym. I needed a job ASAP or I would be on the streets again. I didn't feel like collecting welfare as my pride would be hurt.

Now I had only a minimal amount of gas in the car and no money. We left the car at our makeshift campsite and walked the mile into Copper Cliff and back when needed. My brothers told me the credit union wanted to repossess the car. Time was running out. I desperately needed a job.

One day I drove the car around Sudbury a bit with J.D. By the time we were returning to our secluded hideaway, the gas gauge read empty. About a quarter of a mile away from our camp we ran out of gas. I pushed the car to the side of the road and knew I would never be driving it again. Now we didn't even have a car to sleep in. J.D. was talked into sleeping at home that night. I would sleep outside at our outpost. We decided to go again to Toronto and try to get a new life started. We would head out first thing in the morning.

Sleeping outside that night was quite pleasant but extremely lonely. I had a sleeping bag taken from the house and was quite comfortable. I lay for hours under the starry heavens thinking over life. I was twenty-one, with no parents, and the only security I had was myself and J.D. I was now more than determined to keep striving to better myself. I would show my mother, stepfather, and stepsiblings that I, Randy R. Tunney, could be something. I finally succumbed to sleep on the hardened ground.

The following morning I gathered my personal effects and walked back into town. I passed my abandoned car along the way. It broke my heart to know that soon someone else would be driving my dream machine.

Back at Dad's house, where I was forbidden by court order to be, I took a packsack and filled it with food and essential clothing, which included a set of dressy clothes so I could go job hunting. I told my brothers to tell Dad where the car was parked. He could then tell the credit union. Soon J.D. walked the block from her house. She had some of her things and about $30. At least we would have a few dollars in case of an emergency. Our plan was to spend at least a couple of days trying to find jobs. If we were successful, we were sure we could arrange to get money from welfare to start out. If not, we'd come back to Sudbury. This was our last hope to move to Toronto for the time being. We said our goodbyes and left. We waited for a bus, which then took us into Sudbury, and then we transferred to another bus. We were let off at Paris and Regent streets, at the four corners. We were now at the beginning of Highway 69 South.

We started to hitchhike, and it was some time before we received a ride. I'm sure the last thing J.D. had ever thought was that someday she might be hitchhiking. We loved each other, and nothing could separate us. Love sure can do funny things to people. Believe it or not, our first ride was offered by an elderly man driving an almost equally aged pickup truck. He said he was going almost to Parry Sound, which was about an hour and a half away. If we wanted a ride we would have to sit in the open truck bed. We accepted gratefully and started on our trek—a very bumpy trek at that. We found it quite fun riding along in the back of the pickup. At times kids in cars behind us would wave and we would wave back.

We had left Sudbury about noon, and it was after the supper hour when we arrived in Toronto. In all it had taken us a few rides. We would pass the night and then job hunt the next day. We wandered around downtown, taking in the fast-paced life of this populous city. We cruised the Yonge Street strip like a couple of transient tourists. We gazed at the strangeness of some of the people, the hookers, gays, punkers, and preppies. I was amazed at the number of expensive cars that cruised by, the Porsches, Mercedes, Lincoln Town Cars, and BMWs. Up to now these cars had just been pictures in magazines or on television.

After night fell we decided to leave the downtown core, as we didn't want to sleep downtown. We took a couple of buses to the northeast section of the city. We ended up spending the night sharing an open sleeping bag underneath a new off-ramp that was being built to connect to some main artery of a highway. We didn't sleep well and awoke as the sun was rising above the eastern horizon. J.D. and I packed up and left before any construction workers came to the site. While walking we ate a meagre breakfast of food we had with us.

Since I was a member of Vic Tanny's in Sudbury, I was allowed to use the Vic Tanny's clubs in Toronto, which were now Super Fitness Clubs. We would find out where the closest one was to our location and wait for it to open. We then could shower and change into some half-decent clothes for our day of job hunting.

About 9 o'clock I again phoned Paco Electronics in Markham to bug them about the job I had applied for. This time the warehouse manager, Neil, told me he had hired someone already. He also stated that he wasn't sure if the guy would work out. I told Neil I needed a job ASAP and that if the guy didn't work out to give me a call. Since I didn't have a phone or a place to stay, I gave him the number of Vic Tanny's in Sudbury and asked him to leave a message. Neil said he would, and at that I thanked him and hung up. This company had been my only real hope of a job, and I had to be persistent in my inquires. Now that had disappeared—oh well. J.D. and I looked up a Super Fitness club, phoned and received directions. We bused to the Don Mills Shepherd area.

Once we arrived, a problem arose. The club wasn't co-ed, and it was men's day. So I was the only one who got to shower and change. J.D. changed in a ladies' washroom in a mall. We spent the day in the Markham area, looking for jobs. As the business day came to an end the search had been fruitless. We decided to head downtown for the evening to check out the night life.

After eating a bit of fast food for supper, we again cruised the Yonge Street strip. We walked and talked about how things would be once we both were working. The early evening passed, and by 1 a.m. we were walking north on Yonge Street. The only people we both knew in Toronto were J.D.'s friends. We decided to go there and see if we could spend a couple of days with them. I wasn't so keen on the idea because of the past experiences with them.

We caught an all-night bus north on Yonge to Sheppard Ave. At Sheppard we had to walk east to Kennedy, as it was after 2 a.m. and the buses didn't travel to Sheppard at that hour. We walked and walked. At times we detoured down side streets and raided gardens for some vegetables to eat. We could have taken a taxi with the little money we had but had to watch every cent. Let me tell you, after walking all day this final trek across the city was exhausting. Once at Sheppard and Kennedy we still had a couple of hours to pass before morning. We certainly couldn't wake J.D.'s friends up at that hour. We went out back of the apartment building and lay down on the grass near a fence and fell asleep.

Well, we were awakened after daylight by two men who turned out to be plainclothes detectives. Someone had turned in a call that there were two bodies lying out back of their apartment building. J.D. and I explained the reason we were sleeping out there. This satisfied the cops, and they left. I seemed to draw the attention of cops everywhere I went.

J.D. and I figured that her friends would be up now and getting ready for work. We went to the building lobby and buzzed their first-floor apartment. They let us in, and after we explained our circumstances they told us we could spend the day in the apartment but not the night. We thanked them, and soon they were off to work.

After talking J.D. and I decided we had no choice but to go back to Sudbury, as we would have nowhere to stay that evening. What a life! I had nowhere to stay even in Sudbury and had no reason other than J.D. for going back. We would have to hitchhike back as we had not the money for even one bus ticket. Had we, I would have had J.D. take the bus. We would catch a few hours sleep and then late in the afternoon bus it to the 400 and then thumb it to Sudbury. We would be in Sudbury shortly after dark.

The day did pass, and we found ourselves at the on-ramp to Highway 400 at Finch Avenue. Getting a ride was easy, and we make it to Barrie at about 6:30 p.m. It took about another hour before we were offered a ride. Normally we would have taken Highway 400 to Highway 69 North. The guy who stopped was going north on Highway 11 to North Bay. Since rides were scarce, we accepted his offer and were on our way. This was an unexpected detour. From North Bay we would have to hitchhike west on Highway 17.

Night had fallen by the time we got to North Bay. We were now about an hour and a half away from Sudbury. Again it was quite a time before we received a ride. A white Trans Am stopped, and a young couple about our own ages offered us a ride as far as Verner, which was about halfway to Sudbury. We hopped in and again were on our way. It was quite apparent that the two of them were intoxicated and high on drugs. The guy, who was driving, sped out of North Bay at about eighty miles an hour while his female friend was laughing. The farther we got out of town, the faster this maniac drove. Soon we were speeding along at over 100 miles an hour. That in itself wasn't so bad, but this guy was under the influence. I wished we could have gotten out of his car. I had visions of us ending up dead.

Somewhere between North Bay and Sturgeon Falls we did almost do just that. We were approaching somewhat of a blind curve, and this dude was now entering the curve on the wrong side of the road, still well above the speed limit. J.D. and I were holding hands, more out of fear than anything else. All of a sudden oncoming headlights appeared, coming head on to us. The driver of the oncoming car must have felt as frightened as J.D. and I did. We were grasping each other's hands in a deathly grip and told each other we loved each other. We expected to die.

I felt my body stiffen in anticipation of death and now couldn't speak. Everything was in slow motion. The oncoming car veered towards the ditch. We just barely missed sideswiping him. I looked out the back window and saw that the other car had stopped. By some miracle we were still alive. My heart was beating faster than the car was going. The driver was laughing his head off.

At Sturgeon Falls we stopped, and the driver went looking for some dope at, I guess, one of his hangouts. J.D. and I weren't going any farther with these inebriated fools and got out of the car. I felt relieved as I stepped from the car and onto terra firma. J.D. got out of the car at my heels. We grabbed our belongings and started walking towards the highway. This trip was taking much longer than expected. We swore that we would never hitchhike again.

We walked west on Highway 17 and stopped at an OPP station to get some water from an outside tap. The place was deserted and no cops were about. It was well after midnight before we finally got picked up. The guy driving was a travelling salesman and was headed for Sault St. Marie. We were getting a ride not only to Sudbury but right through to Copper Cliff. After our long trek, this was quite a break.

We were dropped off at the Balsam Street entrance to Copper Cliff and thanked the driver. J.D. walked the block to her parents' house while I went to Dad's house, where I wasn't supposed to be. I slept in his empty garage. I was awakened in the morning as I heard Dad leaving for work.

After the coast was clear, I pounded on the door of the house in order to wake up one of my brothers. We talked, and I ate a hearty breakfast, as I was famished. Then I showered and shaved. Now I had to figure out where I would live and how I was going to get money.

Since I hadn't worked out for a while I decided to drop in to the Vic Tanny's for a few hours. While there I mentioned to the manageress that I had left a prospective employer their phone number to call if a position became available. I had a gruelling workout, and my body and mind came back to life. No matter how bad I might be feeling, always after a workout I felt renewed and invigorated. Now I was ready to face the problems at hand.

First, my living arrangements. I figured I would again have to get a dingy room and collect welfare until I found a job. In the meantime I knew I could stay at the Salvation Army. I hated the idea but had no alternatives.

Downtown on Larch Street I signed in for a few nights and was given my meal tickets. What a place. Here I was, a recovered alcoholic and drug addict who was now one of the top athletes in the city, spending the nights amongst some of city's most down and out souls. Seeing them from this perspective made me realize how lucky I was to now have control over myself. I could see where I would have ended up had I not stopped doing drugs and alcohol. I wished that some day I could help these people. Even though I was staying there I knew there were greater things ahead of me. The Salvation Army is a Christian ministry, and I spoke with some of the people doing God's work. They prayed with me about getting a job and such. I felt uncomfortable praying with someone, to say the least. I had checked out some rooms and hoped I wouldn't have to take what was available. I needed one with a fridge and a stove. Laying in bed on the second night in this dorm full of misfits—myself included—I just knew I would get a job. I would work hard and never again be on the streets and wandering.

Believe it or not, when I went to the gym on the third day I had a phone message from Paco Electronics in Toronto stating that I had a job if I wanted and to phone them collect. Talk about being saved in the nick of time! I phoned immediately and told them I would be there in two days and start ASAP. I was overjoyed; my persistence, as with my health and J.D.'s parents, had paid off. More than ever I knew that if I wanted something bad enough I could get it.

I phoned J.D. and told her the good news. We could move away from Sudbury and start our lives anew. I told her I would see her later. I was almost too excited to work out. After my invigorating workout I was ready to face the next problem. I had to get some money or else. I had less than $5 left of the money J.D. had given me. I didn't know at the time that welfare would give me some money. We would have to stay in some cheap motel until we found an apartment. I really only had one alternative. I phoned Dad at work and told him I had a job in Toronto. I didn't expect any help as he didn't want me around the house. He agreed to lend me a few hundred dollars, which would just be enough until my first cheque. I told him I didn't know if and when I could pay him back. I thanked him, and we set up a time and a place to meet. I figured Dad would be glad that I would now be gone from the area.

I got together with J.D. to plan what we would do. She told me that she had been keeping something from me. I couldn't believe what she told me next—she was pregnant.

Just when I thought things were getting better! When would something go right in my life? I was surprised how calm I was when I heard the news. I certainly wasn't overjoyed. I told J.D. we would just have to make the best of the situation. How, I didn't know, as I would only be making $5 an hour. I certainly would have to get a better paying job once settled in Toronto. Now we had to tell J.D.'s parents about her pregnancy.

That evening we told them, and they seemed to take it in stride, but I could sense a great deal of disappointment. One thing that wasn't mentioned was marriage.

J.D. and I had not ever talked about being married to each other, just living together.

The next day J.D. and I took the bus to Toronto. I was glad I wouldn't be spending another night at the Salvation Army. Once in Toronto we took the transit to Kingston Road, the southernmost street in Scarborough, running parallel to Lake Ontario. The motels there were some of the least expensive in the city. The problem with the location was that I would be working just north of the most northern street in Toronto, Steeles Ave. This meant I had to travel by bus from one end of the city to the other. Let me tell you, it's not like crossing the street. I would have to leave for work at 6:30 a.m. in order to arrive for 8. I wouldn't get back to the motel room until about 7 p.m.

My first day at work went fine. Paco Electronics was a small, private, family-run business. They were the Canadian distributor of Fuji audio and video cassettes, Concord car stereos and a few miscellaneous lines or products. One in particular was a line of chemical sprays called Chemtronics. This was somewhat of a separate entity in itself and was run by the owner's son, Donald, who was younger than me and fresh out of university. I didn't know it at the time, but Donald would end up being a great inspiration to me during the years to come. My job at Paco Electronics would consist of shipping and receiving duties along with the related paper work. I would also have to keep the warehouse neat and maintained in an orderly fashion.

J.D. was to look for an apartment while I was at work. After the first few days in Toronto, she became ill. I'm sure it had something to do with her pregnancy. After my first week of work, we went back to Sudbury for the weekend. We would both stay at her parents. I felt strange being allowed to sleep at her house and more so that a second single bed was put in J.D.'s room. Talk about how life can change! Her parents were very nice to me.

J.D. was still feeling ill. When Sunday arrived and we had to leave for Toronto, we decided that it would be best for J.D. to remain in Copper Cliff. This would be until she was feeling better or I found us an apartment. I didn't want her to be staying in a motel, feeling ill, while I was at work. I went back to Toronto alone. I sure felt alone, as I knew next to no one except the people at work. It was almost impossible to work all day and then look for an apartment afterwards. I wouldn't get home until about 11 p.m. and then had to be up at 5:30 a.m. and start all over again. I was looking for an inexpensive furnished apartment, hopefully in the general area of work.

One afternoon during my second week of work I received a phone call from J.D.'s mother. She said that J.D. had had a miscarriage. I was upset, which was quite a shock to me as I hadn't wanted ever to be a father because of my past. Although quite well masked, my sexual hang-ups wouldn't be conducive to good parenting. I still thought of myself as somewhat of a mental case. I told J.D.'s mom that I would come back to Sudbury that evening and visit J.D. in the hospital. I figured that J.D. herself might be quite upset. I spoke with the company boss, Perry, and asked him if I could leave early that day in order to get to Sudbury. I told him I would be back in the morning. I was given permission.

This would be a difficult thing to accomplish. I

would have to catch the 5 p.m. bus to Sudbury, arriving around 10 p.m. Visiting hours would be over, but they would just have to make an exception. Then I would have to catch the 1:00 a.m. bus back to Toronto and arrive about 6 a.m. I would then have just enough time to get back to work. This all seemed sort of stupid, but I just felt that J.D. might need to talk to me, even if it was just for a short while.

I made it to Sudbury, had my visit and returned to Toronto. I caught some sleep on my trip back south and made it to work with ten minutes to spare.

J.D. ended up staying in Sudbury until the following weekend, which was about the third in September. Her parents offered to drive her to Toronto and help us look for an apartment. I couldn't believe the change in attitude her parents were showing towards us. Although I didn't say so, I was overjoyed with their help. It meant everything to me to have them accepting me.

The first day looking for an apartment with the help of her parents, we found a suitable one. It was a sparsely furnished one-bedroom basement apartment in a house. The rent was $260 a month, and J.D.'s parents helped with the first and last months' rent. The furniture was second-generation hand-me-downs. There was one small bedroom and a living area. The kitchen was the largest room in the place, which suited me and my insatiable appetite. At least it was a beginning, and we would be together as a couple. That was all that really mattered. Again I had conquered another obstacle in life by persistence and not giving up. J.D. and I had gone through a lot of trouble and finally accomplished what we had set out to do, to be living and working in Toronto. All that was left now was for J.D. to get a job so that we could save money and move into a nicer and more permanent residence.

Over the next few weeks we settled into our routine. We were residing off of Bathurst, just north of Sheppard Ave. I had to take three buses in order to get to work. J.D. still didn't have a job, and I accused her of not trying very hard, as there were numerous jobs listed in the newspapers. My job was okay. My superior, Neil, was a jerk.

I had now also started working out again at Vic Tanny's, which as mentioned before was Super Fitness in Toronto. The club so happened to be the same one I had showered at once when J.D. and I had hitch-hiked to Toronto. The club was located between work and home. Tuesdays and Thursdays I would work out after work. This meant I would eat a brown bag supper before leaving work and then go directly to the gym. I would arrive by 6 p.m. and work out until 9:30, then shower and such. I would end up getting home around 11. I would also work out first thing Saturday mornings. On the off days I would do my running workout.

It was now October, and J.D. and I even attended People's Church on Sheppard Avenue a couple of times. We stopped because I felt that all they did during the service was ask for money. I thought if this was what church was about I didn't want to belong or have so-called religion. I now know that money is needed and realize I was wrong.

J.D. finally got a job. Now we wouldn't have to

worry about finances. Between us we were earning $20,000 per annum and were debt-free.

It was at this time that the subject of bisexuality arose. J.D. told me some young lady at her workplace had been coming on to her. We then went on to tell each other of previous experiences. I was shocked to hear of some of J.D.'s past sexcapades.

Soon J.D. was working late, and on occasion when I phoned she wasn't there. Well, we started arguing and always ended up making up. I was still mixed up about my own identity but seemed to have it under control. I was twenty-one and had only had two homosexual experiences, one five years previously and the other longer ago. J.D. didn't know about my rape in jail, as I couldn't tell her. Sometimes I thought that was the only reason I hadn't turned gay. With J.D. and I always fighting, I wondered if I really liked women at all for anything other than sexual partners. None of my relationships had been built around anything but sex. To me sex was love, as I knew of nothing else. J.D. was soon to quit.

Again I was the only one working, and I argued with J.D. about her being lazy. She finally got another job, which was located on the same street in Markham as my workplace. She was the receptionist for a fledging fitness equipment manufacturing company. Now we went to and from work together and had lunches together.

Fall passed, and Christmas 1980 arrived and was a solemn affair. We spent a few days at her parents' house. Although my stepfather and stepbrothers lived a half-dozen houses away, I had no contact with them.

Since Dad had gotten a court order for me to stay away from his house, I knew that I was now on my own, having nothing to do with them. The only one I truly missed was Vickey, my beautiful sister. Since she was living with our mother, seeing her was impossible. I bought no presents for any of them. This was a period of great interior suffering, which I spoke to no one about. J.D.'s family must have thought my behaviour was strange but asked no questions. I felt like an outcast from my family because of my background and the fact that I was really only a half a brother to them anyways. I had decided they would be better off without me being a part of their lives. I now had J.D.'s family, and as small as it was it was all I had. I respected her father very much in spite of the fact the words between us were few. Her mother was nice but a little too set in her ways, and understandably so.

I turned twenty-two on January 15, 1981, and things seemed to be going quite well. J.D. and I were both working, and occasionally we both did extra work on Saturdays at my workplace. I was keeping up my fitness and running programs and was still improving and considered myself an athlete in every sense.

I would compete again that year for the Mr. Sudbury title and was considering entering the Mr. Northern Ontario competition. My running ability seemed limitless, and I was becoming very fast. I read the Toronto newspapers daily and kept track of the top sprinters, most notably Ben Johnson. I had visions of beating him someday. Quite often I thought of joining either the Scarborough Optimists or the track team at York University. I was considering switching from competitive bodybuilding to sprinting. I was getting turned off of bodybuilding because of the use of steroids, which were drugs in the same category as street drugs as far as I was concerned. Drug abuse is drug abuse, whether you are building or destroying your body. I was into fitness for the health of it. As far as running was concerned, I knew I had what it took to become one of the world's best.

My body type was designed more for running anyhow, unless I took steroids. I considered myself the ultimate running machine. Although I didn't belong to a track club, when I ran or worked out I only had one vision, and that was to be the best. My second interest was business, and I was reading as many books on business as I was on fitness. Donald at work was helping me whenever I asked. I watched the salespeople and knew I could do their jobs as well or better than they did. I could see they lacked discipline.

I had received permission to buy video, audio cassettes and stereo equipment at the wholesale price. So I was selling things on the side to people at the gym and whomever I knew. I always carried a catalogue and price list of all the company's products wherever I went. I loved the idea of being a businessman. I mean, since childhood I had always been selling things. The paper routes, lemonade stands, stolen goods and drugs had already given me sales and business background. I knew now my future would centre around fitness, sales, and business. All I had to do was keep learning.

As spring arrived all my spare time was centred around my training for the two contests I would be entering. April, May, and June were the months of the most intense training and eating schedules. My eating habits were becoming even more strict as my knowledge of nutrition grew. Although I was small for bodybuilding I made up for it in muscularity and could attribute that directly to my diet. My strict dietary habits were second to none. Even as far as strength was concerned, pound for pound I was the strongest in the gym. When I was running, no one could beat me. All this was because of nutrition. Proper nutrition can have the most desirable effects on a person spiritually, mentally and physically. The enjoyment available in a day, no matter what the day may bring, can be tremendous if our bodies and minds are tuned for it. The feeling of well-being that comes with energy, alertness, clear thinking and confidence is so rewarding that if you know how to produce it, you will probably make the necessary effort. The essence of life itself is derived from the food we take in. From the food on the table to the intellectual and spiritual food, we need it all. So you can see that nutrition is a three-way proposition. Unfortunately I didn't know it at the time, but I'm sure you know which category I had a deficiency in. With any kind of deficiency one cannot attain one's optimum level of performance. With all that I was doing wrong, I was however doing the best that I knew how.

I had arranged at work to take a week's holiday, starting the week before the contests. I would have nothing on my mind but my training and preparation for the contest. That week I was 100 percent an athlete, in a class of my own. The Friday before the contest J.D.

and I departed for Sudbury and stayed at her parents' house. Everything was ready for my third appearance at this annual affair. Had my time come to be the best?

# Chapter 19

This year the contest was being held in Fraser Auditorium at Laurentian University. Ron, my friend who had inspired me to be a competitive bodybuilder, was again the promoter and MC of the event. As in the past two years I went through the prejudging and then had to wait until the evening for the show itself. There was only one overall weight class for the Mr. Sudbury contest. In the Mr. Northern Ontario contest I was in the middleweight division. I was really entering the latter in order to gain experience competing at a higher level, and I didn't expect to do well. There would be no most muscular or best poser trophy, which disappointed me as I knew I could win the most muscular again in the Sudbury contest. I was more defined than the previous year.

The daytime prejudging passed, and I nervously waited for the evening show. J.D. attended with me and was my best cheerleader. When all was said and done, I had placed second overall in the Mr. Sudbury contest, which was again an improvement over the previous year. Now there was only one level left. In the middleweight division of the Mr. Northern Ontario competition, which was open to anyone anywhere, I placed third. I was ecstatic with my placing. I had beat some of Ontario's top bodybuilders, including "steroid boys." Now after three and a half years of reorganizing my life I had proven beyond a doubt that I was one of Ontario's top athletes in my sport. I was disappointed though at the noticeable increase in steroids. I could sense that this was probably my last year in competition. I knew I couldn't go any higher in this sport, as everyone was becoming unnaturally large because of drug use.

Back in Toronto with a break from training I got back into work. My superior and I had never really got along, but things were getting worse. I had outgrown my position and was sort of taking over. I was reorganizing the warehouse, improving the Cardex system and almost single-handedly filling the orders. Efficiency had improved over 30 percent. Whereas we were processing thirty orders a day before we were now doing up to fifty. I also was suspicious of my manager's honesty. J.D. and I were still coming into work on Saturdays on occasion to do extra work. We had also started looking for a new apartment and had settled on the area of Don Mills and Sheppard. We were lucky to be in the right place at the right time and were offered a two-bedroom apartment on Parkway Forest Drive at Don Mills and Sheppard. We would be moving in on August 1st. We were excited, as it would be much more convenient for us to get to work and for me to go to the gym.

The apartment was of average size, on the seventh floor, and overlooked a small park. We had all modern-day conveniences of apartment living, including appliances and laundry facilities on the premises. A recreational centre off-premises in the park included a small weight room, a basketball court, handball courts, indoor swimming pool, saunas, ping-pong tables, video games and party rooms. Outside we had access to two swimming pools. In the park was a football field where I could do my sprint training, three baseball diamonds, three tennis courts, and swings and such for the kids. Fairview Mall, a block away, is a major Toronto mall. On our own street we had a small plaza containing a grocery store, convenience store, drugstore, bank, restaurants, dentists, hairstylists, and so on. We couldn't have asked for anything more. The only problem had been getting a loan for $2,000 to buy some basic furniture. J.D.'s dad did co-sign our loan. On August 1 we moved in.

We had bought living room and dining room sets, some carpeting and a basic box spring and mattress. There were other miscellaneous items. We couldn't afford a TV so we rented one from Granada. J.D. and I had already bought a top of the line stereo from my workplace, where we paid wholesale prices. Whatever else we would need or want would have to wait until we saved some money. The second bedroom we set up as a small in-home gym. Our rent was just over $400 per month and our loan payment was about $150. Once we had gotten settled, J.D.'s parents visited one weekend and brought J.D.'s black and white fixed tomcat, which they had been taking care of, down to us.

During our first month at our new address we got settled into our neighbourhood. I sure felt good having a real place to call our own. J.D. even started pumping iron at the recreation centre with me. I usually worked out at Super Fitness during the week. On Sundays, as that gym was closed, I worked out at the rec centre. Work was becoming a problem because of my supervisor. I knew he should be doing a better job. I could sense that he knew I could do a better job than he was. Even so, I knew I was cut out for more in life than being a shipper-receiver.

My problem was my lack of education and work experience. Employers don't always take enthusiasm as a reason for hiring someone. Still, increasingly I was becoming interested in business and was setting my sights on a sales career.

About the second week of September, things came to a head between my supervisor and me. My supervisor was about five foot two or so, and I outweighed him by about forty pounds. In comparison, I was Goliath and he was David. Well, we were having a squabble one day. I was fed up with him somewhat. I picked him up, sat him on his desk and told him to start doing his job properly. He went running to the big boss's office, and then I was called in. Well, I was fired, and I didn't care too much, as there were many jobs listed in the papers.

Within two weeks I was again working as a shipper-receiver for a merchandising company. The company was only fifteen minutes from home, which was great. Again I was only earning $5 an hour. This company dealt mainly with car companies, doing specialty advertising and premiums and incentives. They sold things like caps and jackets with crests and such applied, all those things you see in souvenir shops, like pens, cups, and shirts, with names on them.

Over the next couple of months I learned a great deal about sales and marketing, and my visions of running a small business grew even more. I was still selling products from Paco Electronics to people I knew. This meant I was still in contact with Donald, who was by now making inroads in his field. By this point in my life I knew the only way to get what I wanted out of life was to be determined and to persevere through thick or thin.

October 31, 1981, holds a special memory in my heart. I have always felt a special caring for the less fortunate and was in the habit of giving money to the human wrecks who walked the streets. I knew they would buy booze, so I would usually buy some food and give it to them. My other concerns were fatherless boys and crippled kids. Well, it was Halloween night, and J.D. and I planned something special for the kids at The Hospital for Sick Children.

We had arranged to bring candy to the hospital and give out to the kids. J.D. was made up as a clown and I was bodypainted from head to toe in green. I was the Incredible Hulk's little brother. I wore a pair of jean shorts and a ripped shirt. Believe it or not, the weather allowed me to be out in this near nakedness. We arrived at the hospital with our arms full of candy. We had been under the impression we could visit these suffering children on each floor. Then we were told we could tour only the one floor as the children on the other floors were too ill to receive candy.

As we went from room to room I was brought to the point of fighting back tears. I thought that if these children were the healthiest in the hospital I would not have been able to stomach seeing the others. J.D. and I tried to make the kids laugh; some did, but others couldn't. I could see that my suffering had been a party in comparison to these kids. They were suffering both physically and emotionally. I knew how much pain I had felt and could sense their interior suffering. I thanked God that I had my health and could walk, run, play or anything else I desired. This was quite revealing to me, as I'm sure it was to J.D. When we left we just sat outside awhile in tears. We then went to the Eaton Centre to watch all the weirdos out on the streets of Toronto. J.D. took a picture of me as I held up traffic at the Yonge and Dundas intersection. The memories of that visit to the hospital still can bring tears to my eyes.

Again Christmas came and J.D. and I stayed at her parents for a couple of days. Again I had no contact with any of my family. Again I shed tears for my sister. This Christmas was the worst for me emotionally. New Year's came and went, and I got drunk. This was one of maybe three times I drank during the year. I would turn twenty-three on the 15th of the month. What fortunes would 1982 bring?

# Chapter 20

For some strange unknown reasons I had migraine headaches on a regular basis and was worried that it had to do with being beat up as a kid. My temper flared up also at this time, and I thought that there might be a connection.

As usual my daily routine was very regimented. A typical day would consist of my daily 6:30 a.m. running schedule followed by a hearty breakfast, which never varied, of bananas, milk, juice and never less than a half-dozen eggs, either boiled or poached. On Sundays I would allow myself a fried omelette. Monday to Friday I was then off to work with a grocery bag full of nutritious food for snacks and lunch. After work I worked out either at Super Fitness or with J.D. at the rec centre that was part of our apartment complex. Daily I read the business sections of the *Globe and Mail* and the *Toronto Star*, along with business books. On the weekends I worked out for hours on end. In an average month I would pump two million pounds of weights and run and sprint many miles. I was a very disciplined individual—I had to be in order to achieve my goals.

In the back of my mind I still had visions of running as a sprinter in the 1984 Olympics or running across Canada in aid of treatment for drug and alcohol abuse. Terry Fox had attempted to run across Canada two years before but unfortunately succumbed to cancer, which he was raising money for. God rest his soul. Terry's run only fuelled my own dream of a cross-country run, which had begun when I first became fit, before his run. I also wanted to finally be Mr. Sudbury, and this year, 1982, would be my year.

My headaches persisted through January and were getting worse. On occasion they were accompanied by an ear infection. I reasoned that my ills were either because my head been bashed around so much growing up or because my cholesterol level might be too high. I mean, I had eaten no less than half a dozen eggs a day for the previous four years. This calculated out to at least 8,760 eggs, and you could probably have nearly doubled that. I knew that each egg contained about 240 mg of cholesterol. This meant I was ingesting no less than 1,440 mg a day just from eggs, let alone the cholesterol from other foods. Since I had never had my cholesterol level checked, it was possible that cholesterol was the cause of my problems. And I had always held within a fear that I might have brain damage from the many head bashings.

It had gotten to the point that I had become neurotic, and I booked an appointment at Lockwood Clinic, an outpatient clinic on Bloor Street, to be thoroughly checked out over a three day period. I was apprehensive about keeping my initial appointment. After the three-day period of several appointments, some of which were located elsewhere, I waited for the results. I was told there was no brain damage and my cholesterol level was below average. What a relief it was to find out that after all the years of having my head bashed there was no physical damage! Quite remarkable, if you ask me. But the cause of my migraine headaches and ear infections continued to be a mystery.

At work I was bored. Being a shipper-receiver was not very stimulating. As at Paco Electronics, I noticed that the salespeople were making quite a bit of money and were doing so with little effort. The merchandising company I was working for sold a lot of jackets with team company crests or logos on them. I could see that the company was just a middleman of sorts, going to companies and taking orders. The orders were then placed with the appropriate manufacturers. I figured that if I started my own business I could do the same, and I wouldn't need any capital. More and more I thought about being self-employed, as no company would hire me as a salesperson without experience. I also spoke with Donald at Paco Electronics about my plans.

One day in early March I left work early and went to Yonge and Wellesley and registered a business, JRT Marketing. With the first step taken towards my dream, I dreamed some more. The *J* was the initial for J.D.'s first name, and *R* and *T* were representative of my name. I was listed as the marketing manager and J.D. as my associate. We had business cards made up and bought order forms, receipts, etc. J.D. set up a simple set of books so as to keep adequate records. I had decided to set my sights on selling team jackets, uniforms, caps or anything that involved specialty advertising. My market would be schools, colleges and universities. I set about during my lunch hours phoning manufacturers and inquiring about selling their products. Within a couple of weeks I had a line of jackets, uniforms, wearing apparel and caps. Now I was ready to go out and get some orders.

At this time my friend Donald from Paco Electronics came to me with an offer I couldn't refuse. He had in his travels to a trade show received the Canadian rights to market a new specialty advertising item, which he thought would be a rage. The product was a scarf with pockets, called a fanbanna. It was about 66 inches long and double knit. Two pockets were formed in the seams of the scarf at about arm's length. The scarf would come in team, school or company colours. A slogan would be woven into the underside of the fanbanna. While wearing it as a scarf you could put your hands in the pockets to keep them warm or to raise the fanbanna above your head, displaying the slogan.

What a great idea for sporting events and such! Can you imagine screaming fans waving this emblazoned scarf as a banner to cheer on their favourite teams? If the fanbanna was, say, for the Toronto Maple Leafs, it would be blue and white and when displayed could read "Go Leafs Go." We thought we could make a "killing" selling this item. Donald said I could have the rights to sell to schools, colleges and universities and once sales had begun we would work out the royalty percentage for him based on the revenues above costs. First at hand was to find a manufacturer able to produce the fanbanna at a reasonable price and minimum quantity.

Both of us worked full-time, and it was difficult to make the time for this project. I was considering quitting work and collecting unemployment insurance until things got started. First I would take a week's holidays and test-market the fanbanna.

Donald and I found a manufacturer capable of making the scarf, but the minimum quantity was quite high. We figured that if I could get a sufficient number of initial orders the manufacturer would lower the minimum quantity per order. The problem with this type of unique scarf was that a special machine that cost upwards of $100,000 was needed, and only three existed in Canada, only one of which was in Toronto. We had no alternative but to hope they would work with us. I arranged for a week's holidays. J.D. and I went to work one weekend at my company, typing and photocopying to put together a sales booklet pertaining to the fanbanna.

I went to my bank for a line of credit. The bank gave me a Visa card with a $500 limit. I would take cash advances as needed to pay for incurring expenses. I also opened up a business account. I was now officially in business, and another dream was being realized.

My strategy was to do product feasibility testing. If things were successful with the fanbanna, other doors would open. Once the schools, colleges and universities were buying the fanbanna exclusively from me, I could then manage to take away jacket, uniform and other specialty advertising business from the already established companies. The fanbanna would be my ace in the hole.

I had decided to go to Sudbury for the week of testing product acceptance as I knew the area and knew people at each school. I stayed with J.D.'s parents, believe it or not. I also ran into my dad and one of my brothers, and a few words were spoken. By the time the week was over, everything was as expected. The product was a hit, but the minimum quantities were too high. I had verbal orders for thousands of dollars, providing the minimum quantities were dropped to about twelve dozen per order. Unfortunately the manufacturer rejected our pleas on the basis that if the quantity was lowered there would be too many orders for them to manufacture, and they wouldn't be able to fulfill their obligation to us.

I had now had a taste of business and loved it despite the barriers. There were challenges, and I thrived on challenges. As Theodore Roosevelt once said, "Far better it is to dare mighty things, to win glorious triumphs even though checkered by failure, than to rank with those poor spirits who neither enjoy nor suffer much because they live in the gray twilight that knows neither victory nor defeat."

Now I figured I would try my hand at being self-employed on a full-time basis and ended up quitting my job. I had decided to collect unemployment insurance while trying to establishing clientele for my marketing business. With J.D. working we would still have enough money coming in to pay the bills.

The fanbanna idea was on the back burners for now. I was out every weekday drumming up business at schools, businesses, etc. I was visiting manufacturers in order to find more possible things to sell. This was actually a bad time to be trying to sell to schools as they did their purchasing in the fall. Any money I was making I put back into the business. It would take a couple of years of hard work before one could earn any substantial income.

My headaches were still bothering me. My fitness level and muscle quality were still improving. I was sure I would be Mr. Sudbury that year. This would also be my last year of competitive bodybuilding because of the steroid issue. If I didn't win this year, oh well. At least I would have given it my best shot. Running was now more of a priority than trying to put on more muscle. I had achieved more from fitness than I ever had thought possible, and I was satisfied. I would just maintain my body frame after this year's contest. I would make what I had stronger and faster.

I was thinking of joining the Scarborough Optimists if possible if the fall because I was now at the level of running that I needed competition so I could improve more. My dreams of running in the 1984 Olympics could become reality. I know I had the potential and the drive. I kept tabs on Ben Johnson, who was fast becoming the world's best. I wanted to be faster than he was in the 100-metre sprint and trained accordingly.

The football field in front of the apartment building was used well. There was also a 400-metre track a block away. I had a mile measured out around the park on our street. I would shock them all when I joined the club, an apparent overnight success. Fitness was a way of life for me. After being a cross-addict and knocking on death's door so many times, I knew what it was to be almost physically dead. Now I knew what it was to be alive.

I was living proof that one could change one's life around and achieve the goals set for oneself. From a burnt-out drug and alcohol addict to one of Ontario's top bodybuilders and runner—what a sales pitch that would make. People would be able to identify with me the changes that people could make in their lives. If I could win an Olympic medal, I could then really go out and help people. I could then run across Canada preaching about drug and alcohol abuse.

When June came I was ready for my final appearance as a competitive bodybuilder. The week before the contest I went to Sudbury. I was collecting unemployment insurance and trying to make my business a going concern. It was great having the freedom to work when I wanted to. I had the self-discipline to be self-employed. I didn't stay at J.D.'s parents in Sudbury but at my stepbrother Doug's place. After two years I finally had got in contact with him. J.D. stayed in Toronto, as she was working.

The day of the contest arrived, and I was up at Fraser Auditorium. Well, things had changed since the previous year, and several of the competitors in the Mr. Sudbury contest were blown up from using steroids. I was adamant in my thinking about steroids, so I didn't compete. To me, being all drugged up to win a city title was stupid. I was disappointed, because I had worked as hard, if not harder, to become a winner naturally. Now I am glad I decided not to get involved with steroids. Since that day in 1982 some of my past training partners and friends have had operations because of steroid abuse.

Well I guess you think things are only going to keep improving in my life. I wish it was to be so, but now ahead of me was the unknown downhill psychological spiral. I don't even want to write about it. By now you know I'm not a quitter!

Back in Toronto, schools were out for the summer, and I decided to wait until fall to start up things again as far as my business was concerned. If things didn't work out by Christmas, I would get a job somewhere, as my unemployment benefits would run out by March 1983. I could enjoy the summer until the middle of August, which was about six weeks away. I trained with weights and ran seven days a week and spent time swimming and suntanning. I even started flirting with other girls.

J.D. was soon out of work, as her company filed for bankruptcy. So now we both would be collecting unemployment benefits. We had enough between us to pay our bills, so we both were enjoying the summer together. The more time we spent together, the more we argued. Our relationship was starting to dissolve quickly. The subject of bisexuality was again brought up on occasion. As things got worse, I started to think I would never have a normal relationship with a girl. Psychologically I was again becoming distressed about my sexual identity. With all the free time I had, I was becoming bored and depressed. My headaches bothered me more than ever.

Things that had been suppressed because of my busy schedule were getting the better of me. J.D. and I spoke of having "affairs" with partners of our own sex, maybe even doing some swinging. We contemplated putting ads in the classified section of the *Toronto Star* but dismissed that idea for the time being. Increasingly

I was becoming messed up in the head, and I was disgusted with the thoughts I had. Feelings of guilt and hate were driving me crazy. I even started buying wine on the premise that I wanted to be somewhat of a connoisseur. I figured that buying and sampling good wine was all right. Being a recovered alcoholic gave me a sense of strength over my ex-friend alcohol. If I had had any real sense I would have known that buying wine was a danger signal indicating the troubles arising within.

With the wine sampling came deeper bouts with depression. J.D. and I argued, more sometimes, ending in pushing and shoving. I was against physical abuse, so I took out my guilt-filled anger on our personal belongings. One day I pitched J.D.'s black-and-white twelve-inch TV out our seventh floor bedroom window. Another time I destroyed pictures and dishes and damaged some furniture. Yes, the anger and guilt towards myself and Mother were again coming to the surface.

J.D. soon got another job as a receptionist. We decided she would still keep receiving UIC benefits for a few weeks in order to make up for some of our lost income. By the middle of August I was getting ready to start up my business for the start of school year. I had answered a help wanted ad in the newspaper. Regal Gifts and Greeting Cards was looking for independent salespeople to promote some fundraising scheme in schools. The salespeople had to already be selling their own products to schools. This seemed like an opportunity for me, and I made an appointment to be interviewed.

At the interview I—not by accident—had my sample of a fanbanna with me and showed it to the gentleman interviewing me. We talked about the fan-banna, and by the time the interview was over I had a new business associate. We would try to get the fan-banna or a close facsimile manufactured. Over the next few days we met, went around to manufacturers and had lunches with other salespeople. It ended up that we ran into the same problems as Donald and I had run into.

Never say never. Again the fanbanna was put away. Well, as schools and such started in the fall I found out that getting into this business of specialty advertising wasn't as easy as hoped and was made up of tightly knit groups of businesses. I would have to get a job until I learned more about business.

In October I got a job in Scarborough as a shipper-receiver at yet another merchandising company. At least I would learn more about this type of business. I kept receiving UIC benefits. Now J.D. and I had quite the income coming in for the next couple of months until we stopped collecting UIC cheques. J.D. had collected about $2,000 in extra benefits while working, while I made about $1,000.

My headaches were still bothering me, and I scheduled appointments through the Lockwood Clinic again. This time they would have me checked more thoroughly. One test included injecting me with a dye and then having my head examined by some huge strange machine. All the results came back negative again. They would try one more thing. They arranged for me to have my sinuses drained as I mentioned that sometimes my nasal passages seemed clogged. I won't talk about the nose job, as it was the most painful thing a doctor had ever done to me. Again nothing was wrong. The people at Lockwood Clinic suggested it was psychological and said I should see a psychiatrist.

Over the next few weeks I saw a lady psychiatrist a few times after work in search of the elusive cure. Never did I mention my sexual hang-ups and only talked about my childhood abuse. So you can see, as much as I wanted help I couldn't admit to the true problems. I would just have to deal with them myself.

Over the past few months of boredom my fantasies about homosexuality had been increasing. I hated the thoughts in one way but was aroused in another. If I thought of myself as a woman making out with a man, it was fine. When I was myself it was disgusting some-what. I was just so confused.

J.D. and I decided to answer some companion ads in the newspaper. We were both going to try and meet someone of our own sex. Talk about being screwed up. We had pictures printed of ourselves and sent them out to prospective people along with a short note. Since we were both attractive we figured we would get imme-diate responses. Soon the phone was ringing. The thing was that no one was calling for J.D. Anyway, I decided to meet one of the guys. We were to meet at a gym for a workout in his neighbourhood.

One Saturday morning in November I met this guy at the gym. He was reasonably attractive and we seemed to get along fine. We worked out together, and of course he was impressed with my physique and strength. I was nervous but had made up my mind to go through with this scenario. I had to find some answers. Who the hell was I? I surely didn't realize how messed up my mind had become over the years since childhood.

After our workout we stopped off at his place and I watched my first porno flick. This guy had over a couple hundred X-rated videos. Well, one thing let to another and then I was driven home. I introduced him to J.D. God only knows what she thought of this, but J.D. was more open to homosexuality than I was and she was more experienced and enjoyed the company of a female.

This had also been the first time since I had moved to Toronto that I had done anything with a guy such as working out. It was also my first sexual relationship with a male since I was sixteen.

J.D. had still not received a reply from her inquiries. I saw my new friend a couple of times before I asked him to take me to some gay bars. My curiosity had been piqued. I was drinking more often and every time I was with my friend. One Saturday I was escorted around the gay section of Toronto and dropped by a few bars. I expected to see only a few guys. Well, I was surprised; I couldn't believe the hundreds of guys I saw. This was quite an attitude-changing experience. These were also the only bars of any kind I had been in since moving to Toronto.

Now I didn't think homosexuality was some kind of freakish abnormal behaviour. I saw that I wasn't just one of a very few who felt the same. I was told that the lesbian bars were similar. There were also bars for swingers where a couple could go and meet another couple. So now I was thinking bisexuality was quite normal, which lessened my guilt somewhat. I told J.D.

about this experience and told her we could start bar-hopping together and pick up our own companions. So started our trip into abnormal behaviour of the sexual kind. J.D. and I were quite attractive and never had problems picking people up.

As the weeks went by I found out I was bisexual, psychologically anyway. I had to think of myself as a female in order to achieve sexual gratification. The guilt returned worse than ever, the headaches, the hate. Those weeks leading up to Christmas were all centred around gay bar-hopping with J.D. and pornography, which further demented my already deteriorating personality, and drinking. Unknowingly I was again losing control of what I had been working so hard to achieve.

I was still thinking ahead and had planned to start taking business at Seneca College, which was only ten minutes away. J.D. and I spent this Christmas in Toronto. Her parents came to visit and stayed at a hotel. As usual Christmas was an extremely depressing time of year. I longed to see my beautiful sister Vickey. I would only have been able to see her if I went to her mother's house. This I vowed never to do. For the rest of my life I didn't want to face Vickey's mother.

Since 1980 I had neither received nor given presents to anyone but J.D. and her parents. Inside I was the loneliest person on earth, or so I thought. New Year's Eve I got pissed drunk. So long, 1982. The last two years in Toronto had been the most stable in my life. Now the next six months were going to be some of the most unstable of my life. I wish I could skip writing about them, but they are the heart of the rest of this account. So much did or didn't happen in such a short time period that putting things down on paper is difficult. In fact, I could write a whole novel about those months. For purpose of expressing the psychological aspects, I will try to be as brief as possible. Because so much happened, it is hard to remember dates. I will do the best to keep it flowing as chronologically as possible. All I can say is, things were completely chaotic.

# Chapter 21

In January 1983 J.D. and I were working and our financial troubles were nil. We were bar-hopping from gay bar to gay bar on weekends. Some weeknights we were out as well, and not always together. I was earning extra money selling sports equipment to guys at the gym on a small scale. I was drinking two or three times a week. I wasn't as dedicated to my running and weight training as before, and I knew that I wouldn't be joining a track club to train for the Olympics, only eighteen months away. I was still reading business books and had just enrolled at Seneca College to take two courses that were part of a diploma program, an introduction to business on Wednesday nights and Accounting 101 on Saturday mornings. I would attend the gym Tuesday and Thursday nights and Saturday afternoon after my class. Mondays through Fridays were for work. I might run only three mornings a week now.

My nutritional habits were still important aside from the use of alcohol. I was still 100 percent against the use of drugs of any sort. J.D. and I were fighting constantly. I still had headaches, and my temper was becoming volcanic again. I was filled with guilt and hate of myself and was isolating myself from the rest of the world. My homosexual behaviour was driving me crazy, and the bars weren't exactly a turn-on, because I noticed that there was nothing but drug and alcohol abuse amongst most guys. It seemed everyone had to be under an influence to have sex.

February was pretty much the same as January except I was slipping into a deep depression. I was extremely lonely. I pretty well stopped seeing men. J.D. had a steady girlfriend. The confusion and attitudes towards love, sex, and fidelity were driving me up the wall. The world was just fraught with sexual immorality. I needed something to hold on to before I fell into the dark abyss of unwanted despair.

When I was a youngster dogs were the only true friends I had, and I had always wanted a purebred golden retriever. I decided that we would buy one, and we went shopping for our new family addition. As luck would have it, the first shop we went to had a female retriever for about $500. We bought her, and I named her Sandy after a yellow lab we had around the house when I was an infant to about ten years of age. Now we had two cats, two rabbits, two doves and our new puppy. The good thing about Sandy was that I had to take her outside frequently, which got me back into running every morning at 6:30. I knew when Sandy was older I would have a faithful friend and running companion.

In March I was still attending my school courses and enjoying them, although I was distant in an emotional sense. I loved spending time with Sandy, who was growing quickly. This dog helped alleviate the stress I was under. The two of us were always outside in spite of the cold. I wasn't seeing any men, while J.D. still had her butchy girlfriend. My drinking was only moderate as I was back into fitness. I hated my job and by the end of the month was fired after I got mouthy once with my supervisor. Now I was in the position of not being able to collect UIC benefits as they would find out I had cheated them the previous year. I would have to get a job ASAP.

By April I still hadn't got a job, and J.D. and I needed money. I was getting cash advances on my Visa to use for groceries. I was becoming very distressed, to say the least. J.D. and I were driving each other crazy. To make matters worse I came home from school one evening to find J.D. in bed with her female lover. Actually seeing what was happening to us drove me wild, and I threw them both out after a screaming battle. J.D. spent the night at her lover's. It was one thing to know what she was doing, but I couldn't stand seeing it in the flesh. Had this woman not been a masculine butchy broad, things might have been different.

J.D. within days quit her job. Now we both had no income coming in and would soon be on the street again if we didn't get some work. I was going crazy. I was going to my classes and was having trouble concentrating. My fitness training lessened again and so did my drinking, because I couldn't afford it. J.D. and I were living off my Visa cash advances. I was now over my credit limit.

I was looking for a job daily and was concentrating on commission sales in department stores, such as the

Bay, Simpson's and Sears Canada. I had applied at them all, and only the Bay had been interested. They had set up three appointments at different stores. The sales managers all liked my attitude, but I had no experience as far as they were concerned. I tried telling them that if given the chance I could be one of the best. It was of no use.

J.D. and I were becoming desperate, and we thought of selling Sandy, but I couldn't bring myself to do that. By the end of the month we were broke, with only enough money to pay the rent for May. We decided that we would use our good looks to make money. Up to now we had allowed ourselves to have affairs with people of our own sex. Now we would have sex with people of the opposite sex, providing it was for business purposes only. We would start up an escort business and hire others once we had established a client list.

I registered the business as "Sincerely Yours." Once we got started we would have a business phone put in. We each placed an ad, with our phone number, in the companion section of the *Toronto Star*. I used my middle name, Richard, while J.D. used the name of one of her past lovers, Terri. From day one the phone rang from morning until night, at which time we had to unplug it. Most people didn't expect the ads to be a front for a business. Ninety percent of the calls were men calling for J.D. We would agree to meet with prospective clients first for coffee. At this time business would be discussed, and J.D. and I would decide if we would start seeing them.

Well, J.D.'s business was booming as April ran into May. For me things were different. Whenever I mentioned on the phone that this was a business proposition, the woman would hang up. I changed my strategy somewhat. I wouldn't mention business until I met with them. I would meet only older married ladies who weren't looking for anything but sex. Ninety percent of J.D.'s clients were married men. So much for my ideals about marriage.

Men were more than eager to pay for sex. Women were harder to approach about such matters. I met a couple of ladies whom I did not charge any fee for my services, because they were truly attractive, desirable women who fulfilled my need for a mother figure.

There was one lady whom I never even had sex with and with whom I enjoyed some of the most memorable times of my life. We would go to lunches together, on shopping sprees, and had good conversations. This lady was fifteen years my senior and extremely attractive. We had a mutual agreement that she would be my godmother. She introduced me to philosophy, mysticism and Buddhism. Our relationship continued through the next few months until she moved out of the city with her husband and children. For as long as I live I shall remember those few months of a mother-and-son relationship. I always felt incredibly happy being with her. Words can't explain how I felt for the first time in my life.

Well, with the others it was pure sex and money. I was a sex object and hated it. J.D. and I had a tough time booking the bedroom of our apartment. Occasionally the sex was elsewhere, such as in hotels. J.D. was making three times as much as I was. I wasn't all that busy, and my school courses were finishing up. I would take a couple more in the fall.

I had a lot of spare time and decided I could make a few hundred dollars a week being a private stripper for gay men. In the past I had stood on stage in posing trunks flexing my muscles before hundreds of both males and females. I figured this was a market for an award-winning bodybuilder to tap. I placed an ad in the companion section of the *Toronto Star* for a male companion. The phone was now ringing constantly for both J.D. and me. As I took my calls I told the callers about my physical attributes and that this was a business proposition only. Well, men in all their degeneracy, whether gay or straight, would pay for anything sexual. I had struck a gold mine. For $60 I would at the apartment strip down to nothing, then work out with weights to pump up my muscles while they watched, and then go through a posing routine. All this was done to heart-throbbing rock and roll. I also had to be mildly intoxicated to do this. This meant I had to drink off and on all day. I didn't even have to go to the gym with all this working out at home.

Now our lives centred around sex or sex-related business. After several weeks of this business of selling ourselves, we both had lots of money and were always on spending sprees. Clothes, art, furniture, anything we desired. Our relationship was worsening, and one day in May she took off to her lesbian lover's place. She took her belongings, some furniture, her cats, and Sandy, my golden retriever. She said she wasn't coming back.

I hated women, I hated men, I hated myself. The whole world was full of degenerates. The men who watched me strip were almost all married men with families, as were the women. J.D.'s clients were the same. I was now in total chaos mentally and drinking again. The phone still was ringing non-stop. I had to stop this business but couldn't, or else I'd lose everything.

I was now on my own. Now I had to hustle my ass off to keep up my newly acquired lifestyle. I wanted everything. So what did I do? You need not guess; I will tell you. I doubled my prices and started having sex with all of those messed-up married men. I'd even go out for dinner and such with my gay clients. I could charge more then. The guys were only too happy to be seen out with me.

I was busy from morning to night. Eventually one of my clients introduced me to some film and magazine people of the pornographic kind. I was offered a chance to be in magazines and porno flicks. Of course the majority of them would be gay entities. The money offered was okay, and I liked the idea of travelling to and from New York City. I told them to let me think about it and to call the next time they were in Toronto. I'm sure if there was no homosexuality involved I would have taken up the offer then and there. To think I could have become a porn star. How disgusting!

I was spending money as fast as I could make it. I suppose that buying things helped me feel better about myself. I was psychologically screwed up more than ever. I was even starting to enjoy the company of men. I hated to think of being gay. I couldn't live with the thought of being completely homosexual for the rest of my life. I was sinking into despair, so I spent money to alleviate the problems. I was being taken to the best restaurants. I shopped in the best shops. I was making $1,000 a week easily. Occasionally I saw J.D. and we went out or she stayed overnight. She had given our dog away, which broke my heart.

So much happened in such a short period of time that I was getting burnt out. Just writing about things is confusing. One day in May the phone rang, and to my surprise a nice lady propositioned me. So what, you ask? The lady introduced herself as the personnel manager of Sears' Markham place. I was asked if I was still interested in a position at their company. I said, "Yes." She said it would only be a part-time position in the sporting goods department. I told her that was all right. An interview and some prehiring aptitude testing were arranged. Well, I was hired for $5 and change an hour. I didn't care, as I could then get a full-time commissioned sales position.

Well, things could be looking up, and I could soon discontinue being a male slut. I decided I could cut back on my prostitution and get a roommate to help pay the rent. I hated the idea, but it was either that or continue prostituting myself on more occasions than I cared for. After placing an ad for a roommate I ended up getting a guy younger than myself, a typical street-type kid, "sex drugs and rock and roll." He was employed and had been for some time, so I decided to let him share my apartment. He moved in on June 1. It would still be about three weeks before I would be called into work. In the interim I was hooking up with men and seeing a couple of special ladies in my life on a non-business basis, including my godmother. I was enjoying her company immensely.

My roommate must have found things strange, as the phone was always ringing. The majority of time people were asking for either Richard or Terri. I had informed him to tell whomever called for Terri that she had moved to parts unknown. Richard, I told him, was a friend I had once taken messages for. I didn't need any new clients, and I had told the old ones my first name, so when they called they asked for Randy.

I couldn't wait to start working at Sears. Sears was located at Don Mills and Steeles Ave, which was only two major streets north of my home at Don Mills and Sheppard. Super Fitness and Seneca College were located between home and where I would be working. So you can see, everything was perfectly situated for my needs. To live in Toronto and have everything to suit yourself on one street is extremely rare.

My first night at Sears I worked in the sporting goods department from 5:40 to 9:40. Now I've had bad luck before, but that night took the cake. About 7:30 I was visited by two plainclothes detectives. I thought maybe they came to arrest me for prostitution. They said they had come from my place after my roomie told them where I was. They mentioned they could have busted him because the apartment had reeked of marijuana when he had answered the door. They said they wanted to talk to me. I pleaded with them to wait until I got off work at 9:40. I thought for sure I would lose my job because of this visitation.

I sure was nervous as I finished up for the night. The plainclothes cops met me, and I got into the back of the unmarked cruiser. I asked them what all this was about. They said they'd tell me at the cop shop. Guess who else was there, although I didn't see her? Yes, J.D.

I was being questioned for the fraudulent use of J.D.'s Toronto Dominion Bank Green Machine card.

J.D. had used her card to withdraw money from our joint account after making a fake machine deposit. The amount was $300. We each had access to our joint account through the use of our own cards. We each had our own personal identification number. It had been her card that had been used, but she was saying that I had used her card. To make a long story short, we both were charged with fraud and eventually went to court. The money had been paid back—$150 each. We were then let off. I now had another criminal charge on my record.

I worked at Sears as often as possible and as an escort as little as possible. I liked working at Sears and was usually in the camera department. I was hoping to be hired full-time so as to leave my other life behind. I wanted desperately to have a normal life. I was still being hounded to pose for skin magazines and to do porno flicks. I kept turning down the offers but thought if I wasn't soon full-time at Sears I might take them up on the offer.

I was told in July that *Playgirl Magazine* would be holding a photo session for Canadian prospects. This was the only magazine I would pose for, as it catered to women and I thought of it as respectable. It was looking for twelve models for a spread on Canadian men. I decided I could use the money and the exposure. It could lead to more opportunities. On the day of the interview I donned my $600 three-piece grey pinstripe hand-tailored suit and went down to the Harbour Castle Hilton Hotel on the waterfront at the foot of Yonge Street. Numerous men were in attendance—in all over 300 guys showed up during the day. I figured my chances were slim but stayed anyhow. We filled out some forms and had photos taken with just our upper bodies exposed. I was informed that I would be called if chosen.

I didn't get chosen, but an acquaintance involved in the porno business told me I had been 23rd on the short list. I'm now glad that I wasn't picked, although at the time I wished I was so if things didn't work out at Sears I could have commanded double or more for my services as an escort. I could have become the highest paid stud in the city.

At the end of July I kicked out my roommate and was again on my own. I now had to turn a couple of extra tricks to make up for the lost income. Within a couple of weeks, J.D. and I were back together and were trying to live together as friends. Occasionally we did sleep together. We seemed to be getting along okay, but as I reflect back now I realize how truly screwed up we both were.

I was filled with so much guilt and hate. As usual, when I felt bad I either drank or went on a spending spree. Being with men was really screwing up my mind. Psychologically I was straddling the fence separating heterosexuality and homosexuality. My design for reality was a great fantasy. Would I ever achieve normalcy? My adopted godmother had recently moved, and I was in tears the last time I saw her. She had been the closest I had ever come to being a son loved by his mother.

I had worked the past two months as often as possible at my part-time position at Sears. I had shown my enthusiasm and desire to work. At the end of August an opening for a full-time commissioned salesperson in the electronics department became available. I applied for the position and was interviewed by the sales manager and the head of personnel. I was deliriously happy when I was hired. I could now earn enough money to support myself comfortably. I was told the earning potential was only limited by my own limitations as a salesperson.

I went home and told J.D. I was hired full-time and we were to stop hustling. Although we were living together supposedly platonically, I told her I would support her until she found a job herself. I was so happy that I broke down and cried. I swore never to be with men again. Thank God, all the hustling was over. When the head of personnel had offered me the position I wanted to reach over and hug and kiss her. Little did she know she had just saved two people from the dark life.

Like in the past when I had initially joined a gym and vowed to be the strongest and the best at the club, I now said to myself that in one year I would be the best salesperson Sears ever had. Within a couple of weeks J.D. started working part-time in the catalogue department. I knew that she would soon get a full-time position as well. Again I could have kissed the head of personnel. I will always be grateful to her for giving us the chance to live our lives as we had dreamt. It had been a lifelong struggle but one that would now pay back dividends.

I was now making hundreds of dollars a week legitimately and was satisfied with my job. I had always been interested in electronics and since working at

Paco Electronics had kept that interest alive. I knew the more I sold the more I would earn, so I learned as much about the products as possible. I treated customers as royalty, as this was also the store policy.

At home I had stopped drinking and had resumed my fitness and running training to previous levels. My weekly schedule was again regimented. Monday: 6:30 a.m., running, then breakfast; 9:10 a.m. to 5:40 p.m., work; 6:00 p.m., home for supper, watch news, read and watch TV. Bed by 11:00. Tuesday, day off from work: 7:30 a.m., run, breakfast; 10:00 a.m. to 1:00 p.m., Super Fitness, then lunch; 1 to 6, at work to work on customer problems, sometimes going to their residences; 6 p.m., home, read or watch TV. Wednesday: 6:30 or 7:30 a.m. run, depending whether I worked from 9:10 to 5:40 or 1:10 to 9:40. In bed by 11:00. Thursday: 7:30 a.m., run, breakfast; 10 to 12, work out at Super Fitness, lunch at the gym; 1:10 to 9:40 p.m., work; 10:00 p.m., home. In bed by 11:00. Friday: same as Wednesday. Saturday: 6:30 a.m., breakfast; 9:10 to 5:40, work. 6:30 p.m., home. I never went out as I had to get up first thing Sunday morning to work out. Sunday: 8 a.m., breakfast; 9 to noon or 1 p.m., work out at the rec centre that was part of the apartment complex. After working out, I usually swam in the pool, then did a ten-kilometre run and sprinting. All of my running was timed and recorded. Sunday after working out I would have a huge lunch and then do some outside activities. I read the *Toronto Star* daily, as well as business or other educational books. My weeks were full, with as little time wasted as possible. This routine would be the same, with little change, for the next year and a half.

J.D. and I were getting along better, although we still argued. I was so involved with my training and work that all my previous problems seemed to be cured. In October J.D. was offered a full-time position as assistant manager of the ladies' wear department and accepted the offer. I worked on the second floor, while J.D. worked on the first. We had again decided to see other people. Once J.D. saved some money she would go her own way and we would remain friends.

During the month of October I was so involved with my job that I had no time to date. I was all wrapped up in making as much money as possible. I was finally getting into business, although I worked for someone else. I was independent in a lot of ways and could plan my business volume, according to upcoming sales and availability of product. I loved figuring out ways to outsell the two gentlemen I worked with. Both had ten or more years of experience as professional salespeople.

One night in November, as I was getting ready to leave at 5:40, I caught sight of a new girl working the cash terminal at a sales centre. She was a goddess, the essence of loveliness, tall, slim, and exceptionally beautiful. Her hair, long and thick, cascaded over her shoulders like a waterfall. This young lady exuded femininity like no one I had seen before. It was love (lust) at first sight. I made sure she saw me as I strode past to have a closer look. There was something about her that I hadn't sensed in others. I wanted her.

I bought a lamp and had her ring up the sale. Someone was helping her, as this was her first night. From her nametag I read "Diana," and I bashfully introduced myself. Her radiant beauty entranced me as I stood before her. Never before had I been so struck by the presence of a female, and I didn't understand why I was so taken by her. I left for home and couldn't get Diana out of my mind.

At home I ate my supper without Diana leaving my thoughts. As Sears was open until 9:30 weeknights, I decided to drop back there later if for nothing more than a look. I showered and changed into one of my best outfits in order to make a visual impression upon this beautiful young lady. I must have been crazy to trek back outside, as the snow was blowing about in blinding madness.

At the store, Diana was ringing up customer purchases. I went by and flirted with her while another employee teased me about bothering her staff. Yes, I knew that I wanted to know this young lady named Diana better.

J.D. was working that night also. I went downstairs to her department to chat with her. When I saw J.D., I knew then and there we would soon be apart forever. J.D. in her own right is a very beautiful person, both in looks and personality. Just too many things had come between us while on our search for happiness.

I waited at the store until closing in order to take J.D. home. As on most nights, we slept together, as we only had one bed. On occasion we still had sex. Tonight I had no such thoughts and was very confused. I envisioned Diana in all her loveliness and couldn't wait to see her at work again.

Over the next week or so, I saw Diana at work on occasion as she only worked part-time, nights and weekends. Diana, I found out, was six years my junior at eighteen and a college student. I spoke with her as often as possible and flirted constantly. After a couple of weeks we were spending all the time she had for coffee breaks together, and I finally asked her for a date after explaining my live-in relationship with J.D. Diana told me she couldn't date me because she had a boyfriend. She went on to tell me that things were shaky between them.

We continued spending time together at work. We seemed to be becoming quite fond of each other. I knew I thought she was the greatest and had only one irritating quality. This was the nauseating habit of cigarette smoking. I was as much against cigarette smoking as I was against drug and alcohol addiction. I disliked seeing anyone smoking, let alone someone I knew and liked.

Now J.D. was jealous of my carrying on with Diana, in spite of the fact that our own relationship was more platonic than anything else. In fact, J.D. was as taken with Diana as I was. I told J.D. that the years together had taken their toll on my mind. The lies, the illicit sex, the homosexuality—I couldn't stand any more. From the day J.D. had come back into my life, everything had been abnormal between us. I told her I needed a new relationship, one based on love and trust, and that I couldn't trust her.

This was just as hard on me as it was on her. We had grown up in the same town, went to the same schools, lived only houses from each other for years, dated each other, then lived together for three strange years. We knew each other as no one else ever would, but yet we knew nothing of each other because we knew not ourselves.

Things were changing for the better, and I wanted to keep it so. My physical health was back up to par, excellent. Work was going great, and I loved my job. By the end of November, J.D. had moved back to her lesbian friend's place and I was on my own.

Finally Diana accepted a luncheon date, and I picked her up after her classes at the college one day. We spent a couple of hours at my favourite health restaurant, Sunshine's at Bayview and Sheppard. The restaurant was a health addict's paradise, and I had been frequenting it a couple of times a week. Their salad bar presented a feast for a king and his queen.

Now we were officially dating and I was falling in love. Outside of her nicotine habit, Diana was what dreams are made of. I, however, felt a great loss and was upset at knowing J.D. and I were no more. I still felt responsible for her well-being.

It was now December, and Christmas was only weeks away. As usual I got very depressed. I longed to see my sister, Vickey. It had now been three and a half years since I last saw her. I wanted to send her presents and such but didn't, because of Mother. I was sure by now that her mother had filled Vickey's head with ghastly stories about me. Always at Christmas I longed to belong to a normal family. The loneliness of the Christmas season was always the deepest. Since moving to Toronto, I had not even put up a Christmas tree. Lights and such were put on the balcony, only for the benefit of the kids around.

Working in a retail store only made things worse. All day long I had to put up with all the aspects associated with Christmas. Christmas music played throughout the store. I worked in the stereo, TV, and video department and could only play Christmas music. Shoppers were always asking me for suggestions of what they could buy for their brothers, sisters, mother, father, etc. If it weren't for Diana and the fact that I was so busy at the gym and at work, making up to $1,000 a week during this time of the year, I would have cracked. That was all I had in my life now.

I finally took Diana out for an evening date. I was also to meet her family that day and had bought her mother and grandmother, who lived with them, each some chocolates. But I wouldn't get to meet her family that day. Diana picked me up in her mother's car and gave me a little gift. I couldn't believe how lovely she truly was. I was now in love. Diana was a vision of great radiant beauty, dressed in a body-clinging knit dress and a fox fur jacket. With her high heels on she was as tall as my own six-foot height. She looked like she had just jumped off the cover of Vogue.

I was dressed in an expensive hand-tailored suit, with all the proper accents, including a London Fog trench coat. We sure made a glamorous couple. We were going to dine at my favourite Italian restaurant, the intimate Pastificio, located across from the Eaton Centre on Yonge Street. As we walked from the parking garage and made our way through the Eaton Centre, we were showstoppers.

The evening passed much too quickly as Diana had a midnight curfew. As I lay in bed after being dropped off from the dreamy evening, I dreamt some more. I had visions of grandeur. Diana, I wanted forever. My life was now taking on a whole new perspective, one of happiness and normality. My life's dreams were becoming reality. I was off the streets. I had a great job within the structures of a prosperous and growing company. Above all, it seemed I had found the love of my life. All the years of struggling and fighting to be someone going somewhere with someone were now in the palm of my closing fist, and I didn't want any of it to get away. I would have to work harder to be number one so as to show Diana I was worth being with. One thing hindered my optimism constantly. What would Diana think of my past, when and if it came to the point in our relationship for her to know?

# Chapter 22

When I met Diana's family, they seemed to like me. Her parents seemed nice, as were her two brothers, one of whom was Diana's twin. Diana's live-in grandmother had a pleasant disposition. I was dropping by the house now a few times a week and was invited for meals. Diana's family's home was only one street away from our workplace, and I would walk her home from work when we both worked nights.

Christmas Day arrived, and I spent the day at home alone. I opened my one present, from Diana. She had bought me a pair of brass swans I had shown her once in the store. I had been invited to spend the day visiting some of her relatives with her and her family. I chose not to, as I still hardly knew her family. I wept for my beautiful sister, Vickey. Throughout the year I tried not to think of her as the pain was too much to bear.

As December came to an end, I couldn't believe the money I had earned during the month—about $3,000 before taxes. Diana and I spent some time together on New Year's Eve. This was the best New Year's Eve on record.

Diana and I were in love with each other, and I was the happiest I had ever been in my whole life. Yet at the same time I lived in constant worry of losing her eventually when she found out my past. My resolutions this year were to be married to this angel from heaven, keep my health up, take a couple more college courses, and to be the best salesperson at Sears, Markham Place.

On January 15th I turned twenty-five. About this time I was nominated to be on the social club at work, and I accepted. I was then elected to be treasurer because of my college credit in accounting. Commissioned salespeople were usually not permitted to be members of the social club because of their need to be constantly on the sales floor. We were the backbone of the company. It was one thing to have merchandise to sell and another thing to get it sold. An exception was made because of my enthusiasm and willingness to put in the extra time to both jobs. Outside of Tuesday and Thursday mornings when I worked out, I was always at work during opening hours, Monday to Friday 9:30 a.m. to 9:30 p.m., Saturdays 9 a.m. to 6 p.m. Tuesday was my regular day off and was the day I worked on customer problems and catching up on my obligations to the social club.

I was giving myself to my job 100 percent and was reaping the monetary rewards. My employers did not know why I was always so willing to attempt so much. I just didn't ever want to be back on the streets and without money. Now it was also for Diana; I wanted to marry her and give her everything a woman would want. Our relationship was blossoming like the flowers of spring. Diana saw in me what every girl dreams of—

an attractive, muscular male holding down a good job, living in a well-appointed apartment and always willing to please her. She was proud of me and my accomplishments. She saw that I could do anything I set out to do, and this pleased her.

We had talked of our future dreams, and I had told her about my ultimate goal of running across Canada to speak out against drug and alcohol abuse. Diana was in love, as was I. Yes, this was who I truly was, but I was being hindered by the guilt. I had respect from Diana, the people at work and my buddies at the gym. There was, however, one person who gave me no respect, and that was me.

It was now February, and Diana and I decided to get married after her school year ended. Her parents had been to my place for dinner once, and I thought they liked me. One evening we told them about our plans to marry, and I could tell they were not impressed. Within a day or so I was forbidden to come to the house or to phone Diana, as her parents had found out I had previously lived with J.D. I knew this was just an excuse against me. Diana was told that if she married me she would be disowned. All of this was extremely disturbing to me. I had always wanted to be part of a family, and now I saw that if I married Diana I would still have no family. The worst was, Diana wouldn't either.

Diana was eighteen and very mature, more so than J.D., who was a few years older. She said she still wished to be my wife and that we would show her parents how wrong they were. Now that Diana had accepted my proposal of marriage, I had to face the hardest task of my life before things were officially announced. I would have to tell her about the man she was going to marry. I didn't want to tell anyone, let alone the lady who was to become my wife. I loved Diana with all my heart and accepted the fact that once she heard about everything she might have a change of heart. Only someone very special could accept my past and take me as who I was now.

Diana and I were at my place one evening and lying together in each other's loving embraces. Tonight I had planned on telling her of my past. All she knew was that I hated Vickey's mother. "Diana," I said, "I have something to tell you about me that might change your decision to marry me."

"What is it, my love?" she asked.

By now tears were streaming down my face and I was having a hard time trying to compose myself. I then started telling her about my abusive childhood, the hate, drugs, booze, crime, jail, and eventually the prostitution and the homosexual experiences. We talked for what seemed like ages. We talked about not having children, as I didn't think I deserved to be a father and didn't want any children of mine knowing about their dad. However, I love children dearly.

Diana said she would need a couple days to think things over, which was understandable. I'm sure she must have been quite shocked to hear what I had told her. She knew me as one so special and different from my past. As Diana left for home that evening, I held her in my arms as if it might be my last chance to do so. I told her I loved her as none other, which was the God-honest truth.

It was some time before I found sleep that night—

my mind was in total confusion. To no one before had I been so brutally honest. It was deemed necessary, as marriage is not something to play games with.

The next time Diana and I met at work, she told me she would marry me and love me forever in spite of all limitations. What a blessing! This lady of angelic presence was a dream come true. Tragically, though, I would never have Diana know my feelings or thoughts again.

One day in March we drove to Sudbury. On the way we were in an accident after driving into a whiteout on the 400. That is a story in itself. In Sudbury I introduced Diana to Doug and his family. Someday I would have her meet my sister, Vickey. Diana knew of my suffering and wanted to meet my sister.

In April I bought Diana's engagement ring and formally proposed to her over a candlelit dinner at a local seafood restaurant. As I slipped the engagement ring on her finger I was overcome with a great feeling of joy, as never felt before. We kissed and professed eternal love for one another. I was the happiest man in the world. Or was I?

I was still fighting daily within myself. To make things worse, the Unemployment Insurance office had caught up with me about the overpayment of over a year before. One day I was called into the personnel manager's office and informed that my wages were being garnished, to the tune of 30 percent, until about $1,000 was repaid. I told the personnel manager that I would straighten things out. In the end, after dropping by the UIC office, things were worked out so that the money would be paid back through payroll deductions over the rest of the year. This worked out to about $40 a week, which was manageable. At least that was off my conscience.

At work everything was fine. I was outselling my two coworkers and was right on target for the year's earnings. As a member of the social club I helped plan fundraising affairs. The objective that year was to give the employees who were members of the social club a free Christmas dinner and dance. In the past they had to buy tickets. As treasurer I tried to keep the social club workers enthusiastically involved in raising money to meet our objective.

We were planning a dance, and I persuaded them to hold the affair on Saturday, May 11, because Diana's nineteenth birthday was on May 12. No one knew why I wanted May 11 so much. I planned on giving Diana the biggest birthday party she ever had. I also knew Diana and I would not be having a wedding reception after our wedding, which was now slated officially for June 9. This dance would be the chance to do something very special for the lady I loved. A private hall was booked for Saturday May 11.

The night arrived. I had bought a birthday cake, champagne and flowers. Her presents I would give to her on Sunday. As one of the organizers of the dance I was kept quite busy making sure things were kept running smoothly. As midnight arrived I quietly disappeared to await the magic moment. By now most people knew of my plans. As the clock struck midnight I emerged with some cohorts carrying lit candles, champagne glasses, champagne and cake. Everyone stopped dancing, and the disc jockey played "Happy Birthday" while everyone sang along. Diana was surprised, to say the least. She was aglow with the radiating beauty of a queen. I poured champagne for us, and we toasted her birthday. If ever she had doubts about being in love with me, they had now disappeared.

A waltz was played, and we danced together to the applause of the people we worked with and some of their friends. Diana and I were in heaven. This had been the nicest thing I had ever done for anyone. Diana was a princess with her prince. In less than a month she would be a queen. She was now just a starry-eyed young lady in love.

Even I couldn't believe how things had changed. Only a year before I was unemployed, a prostitute living a life of sin. Now a year later I was engaged to be married, holding down a good job, booze free, fit and in love. Now I wanted to be the best husband, and it seemed I would succeed. If this evening was any indication as to how happy I would be married to this wonderful princess, how could I lose?

Our wedding had by now been arranged. We would be married in the wedding chapel of the North York Civic Centre, on Yonge Street, on Saturday, June 9, 1984, at 2 p.m. The service was to be performed by Reverend J. D. Moore, whom I knew from Super Fitness. Reverend Moore had counselled Diana and I on a couple of occasions in order to make sure we wanted to be married.

We would be off work for two weeks. The first few days would be spent in Niagara Falls, followed by a couple of days in Toronto at home and then off for a week of fun in the sun in a cabin at West Arm Lodge on

Lake Nipissing. Only a few of Diana's relatives and friends would be attending the wedding. Her best friend from college would be her bridesmaid. The bridesmaid's boyfriend, whom I had met, would be the best man. I would have no family or friends attending. I had not made any friends in Toronto, as I was a loner. I had lots of acquaintances at the gym and such, but because of personality conflicts I never made a permanent friend. Diana's immediate family would not be attending either, as they didn't want her to marry me. Not a good start for a marriage, I must admit.

Now, with only a week before our wedding, I was slipping into a guilt- and hate-induced depression. I was having second thoughts because of my true love of Diana. I hated the fact that I was taking her from her family without their consent. Diana had been told that if she married me they would disown her. I didn't understand their dislike of me, especially since only Diana knew about my past. As I was now, who wouldn't want their daughter to marry me? Without going into my psyche, I would appear to anyone to be the all-Canadian male.

Neither Diana nor I really wanted to be married under such circumstances. Although Diana stated otherwise, I am sure she felt quite bad herself. She was close to her family, and here they were ostracizing her. I hadn't seen her family since being told I couldn't come by the house or phone. I didn't know how to deal with such things as family matters. Although I didn't tell Diana, I could relate to her soon being away from her family, and I knew that it would eventually take its toll psychologically on her. I myself knew what it was like, wanting to belong to a family. I knew I still wouldn't belong to a family and never would if I married Diana, and this bothered me. I knew that eventually we would become a very lonely couple, more so because we would be having no children. I didn't have the guts to do what was right and postpone the wedding until family squabbles had been patched up. I was just so confused. I could put on quite the facade of happiness, and no one knew of my inner turmoil. Those last few days, money was getting scarce and Diana helped me out.

On Friday, June 8th, 1984, I picked up a burgundy Lincoln Town Car from Budget Rent A Car. Lincoln Town Cars are my favourite, and I wanted to have one for my wedding day. I would have preferred Diana's parents' '59 Cadillac Sedan De Ville with its huge fins and all. This was to be my last day as a bachelor, and I was having second thoughts about marrying Diana, certainly not because I didn't love her. I loved Diana unendingly. I was so guilt-ridden about myself and who I was. I was taking Diana away from her family, and I had no family for her to be part of. I was still unsure of my own identity. I was just so messed up.

I spent most of the morning just cruising around and thinking. I had taken the day off, although my two-week vacation didn't start until the next day. Everything was prepared for the next day's celebration, as small as it was to be. All that had to be done today was to move Diana's belongings from her parents' house to what was now our apartment.

During the afternoon Diana borrowed her father's pickup truck and brought her things to our place. Once done I drove up to her parents' house behind her so that she could return the truck and I could drive her back to our place. Diana then was going to spend the rest of the day and evening at her bridesmaid's.

Diana dropped off the truck, and I waited in the Lincoln across the street as I wasn't allowed to be at her house. She emerged from the house with her twin brother, and they stood for a few minutes conversing. I was being tormented by guilt. They gave each other a hug and a kiss, and I could see they were crying. They had spent every day of their lives growing up together, going to school together, and now I was breaking them up because their parents despised me. He was going to be my brother-in-law, and we weren't even talking to one another. I was hurting inside as I knew how hard it must be on Diana being disowned.

All I ever did was destroy people's lives. I knew how close Diana was to her brothers, parents and grandmother. I felt disgusted with myself for doing this to the woman I loved, but we were past the point of no return.

Diana bravely left the arms of her caring brother and strode purposely to the Lincoln. I could sense she was hurting emotionally. I knew that she wanted her family to attend our wedding. Tomorrow was supposed to be the day all girls dream of. I knew how lonely it was to not have a family. I asked her if she was okay, and she said she was fine. If she could be as happy as never before, so should I.

We were silent as we drove the ten minutes to our home. She spent a couple of hours arranging her belongings. We both were cheerful and seemingly very happy.

I drove Diana the few blocks to her girlfriend's place. I now had the rest of the day and evening to myself. I spent a short while at work straightening up my affairs. As the time passed, I became increasingly agitated and upset. I was slipping into the depths of repressed emotions. At a time when I should be very joyous, I was extremely lonely. Tomorrow was the day I had always dreamt of, but things just weren't right. More than anything I wanted my sister to be present at my wedding, as well as the rest of my stepsiblings and stepfather and Vickey's mother, for no other reason than to show off my accomplishments and my beautiful, loving and compassionate wife.

Back at home alone I sat sipping wine and crying. I knew that if I was hurting this much and wasn't close to my family, Diana must be in even greater turmoil, as she loved her family very much. How the hell could I do this to her? How? Yes, we would be married but would have no families to visit and such. I knew that wasn't what I wanted. I wanted to belong, to be accepted, to be loved, not only by Diana but also her family.

I drank a bit more that afternoon and checked on last-minute details. I very seldom drank and only when out to dinner or when company was over. As night was falling I decided to get dressed up and go cruising the streets of downtown Toronto in the Lincoln. I got dressed to the nines and was soon cruising the downtown strip under the cover of night. Aside from the two times I had come downtown with Diana for dinners, I had not been downtown in nine months. I hated the memories. I was slightly intoxicated and extremely depressed. Hookers propositioned me as I drove slowly along the main drag in this big Lincoln. The radio was blaring away and the sounds escaped through the open car windows.

In the area of Yonge and Wellesley, I cruised by the gay bars and decided to take one last look inside. I parked the car and went inside one of them to check out the action. God only knows why on my wedding eve night I would be cruising gay bars. All I knew was that I hated myself for being in there and that I wasn't the man to be Diana's husband although I loved her as best I knew how. I was just too screwed-up in the head to be involved with anyone.

I left the bar immediately after buying a couple of bottles of brew. I sat in the Lincoln chugging back the brew. I was falling deeper into despair and was crying uncontrollably. Would I ever be normal? I wanted to save Diana from marrying me, but it was too late. I loved her so much and wished I was man enough to be honest with her. I might never again have the chance to marry the lady of my dreams.

I was again mildly intoxicated, and I started the car, drove out to Yonge Street and cruised the area. Eventually I spotted a couple of girls who worked part-time at Sears. I knew that both of them liked me. I honked the horn and pulled up alongside of them and beckoned to them. They must have thought I was a john looking for some quick action, and they kept walking until I called out their names. They both hopped in the front seat and they told me they were surprised to see me driving around in a Lincoln. We drove around and talked about me getting married the next day. I eventually drove them to where they were going. I then stopped off at a straight bar for a couple of drinks, and then again I was off to cruise the city.

Soon the bars were closed and the streets were more my own as the night life went home. The only ones up now were the hookers, johns, druggies, alcoholics, cops and lonely people like myself, just killing time. I should have been home sleeping as I had a busy day ahead of me. I didn't want to sleep and I didn't want to be married, because of my screwed-up head.

I drove to Lakeshore Blvd., parked the car and walked to the boardwalk. I sat, kicking at the beach sand and watched the waves die as they hit the shore. Shadows swept across the beach but not a speck of sand rose up in their paths. I looked into the starry sky, closed my tear-filled eyes and contemplated why during our walk in life we are more like a mighty wind. I returned my gaze to the water. I was now having vivid revelations of suicide in order to save Diana's future. What better way to leave this world than maybe racing down the Don Valley Parkway in a brand new Lincoln and then totalling both of us into pylons or a street lamp? Or maybe testing the air brakes at the Scarborough bluffs. Thoughts of terminating my life filled my tormented mind. At least I would die while having someone loving me. As usual I was a chicken.

I finally arrived home around 4 in the morning. I drank a bit and then fell asleep on the couch fully clothed. In less than twelve hours I would be married to the most wonderful young lady in the world. I still wonder what went through Diana's mind that night.

I awoke on my wedding day, Saturday, June 9, 1984, at about 8 o'clock. Looking outside I could see a picture-perfect day. The beautiful sunshine shone gloriously across the park in front of the apartment complex. A near cloudless sky was overhead. If only I could get my head together. I was scared as hell.

Soon Diana was over with her girlfriend. Diana was going to have her hair done this morning, while I had to pick up her wedding ring. If only I was man enough to call off this so-called wedding. I wasn't good enough for Diana was all I thought.

I picked up a rented tux at Fairview Mall, only a block from our apartment. I then went to Birk's Jewellers in the same mall to pick up Diana's ring. When I had purchased the engagement ring I had been quoted the price of the matching wedding band. When I had gone back and placed the order for the wedding ring, I did not ask the price. Now here I was on my wedding day expecting to pay X amount of dollars. What a shock it was for me to find the price almost doubled. I spoke with the salespeople and then the store manager. I was pissed off, to say the least. I had no choice but to pay the price.

I didn't have enough cash on me, so I was going to give the cash I had and the balance by cheque. At first the store manager wasn't going to accept my cheque. Then he phoned around to check on my cheque. Here I was, a Birk's account holder, being questioned over a cheque. None of that would have happened at Sears. Well, he got the cheque cleared.

I gave him a piece of my mind about doubting my honesty, grabbed the cheque and my money, and told him I'd pick up a ring elsewhere.

I was pissed off as I walked through the mall and out to the car. I drove home and told Diana, who was still home, what had happened. I told her I'd go shopping for another ring, although it wouldn't be a match. She was upset. I told her I wasn't going back to Birk's. She said she would pick up the ring then. I agreed, and we drove to the mall. I gave her the money and the cheque, and she went in and picked up her ring. She brought it to me and then went to have her hair done. I would pick her up when she phoned.

By noon everything was in order, and now only two hours remained until that supposedly glorious moment when two people are joined in holy matrimony. All I thought about was who wasn't going to attend. I didn't have so much as a friend coming.

By 1:30 we were ready to leave for the chapel in the North York Civic Centre. Diana was a vision of great radiant beauty in all her all-white skirt-and-jacket suit, topped off with a matching summer hat and complementing accessories such as purse, stockings and shoes. She wasn't wearing a traditional gown because of the circumstances of our screwed-up wedding. Any man in his right mind would have given his right hand to marry such a loving young lady and beautiful to add. So would any man not in his right mind, as I was. I was a mental case.

Diana's bridesmaid and her boyfriend were leaving with us, and we were now outside the apartment building and having our pictures taken alongside the gleaming burgundy Lincoln Town Car. Diana and I sat in the back seat and were chauffeured to the chapel by her friends. I was feeling much better now but still distant.

Everything was in order when we arrived. There had been a service before us and one was scheduled for after us. Reverend Moore was waiting, along with a few people, relatives and friends of Diana. I knew one lady, who had known Diana for quite some time, as she worked part-time at Sears. In all there were maybe a dozen in attendance. Diana's favourite uncle, a radio personality, would stand in for her father. I was introduced to everyone, and at precisely 2 p.m. it was our turn.

The small gathering took its place in the small chapel. The ceremony then began. I broke out in a nervous sweat and was trembling. It wasn't until we were pronounced man and wife and were placing rings on each other's fingers that the most amazing rush of happiness overcame me. I was in tears. At that moment I felt like never before, truly loved and happy. I kissed my beautiful wife and held her close to my heart. My strong arms never wanted to break this embrace. All my suffering through the years, self-perpetuated or otherwise, had seemingly ended in that one moment. I was now to embark on a new life with this most beautiful and loving lady. Everyone was congratulating us. Diana and I signed the register as Mr. and Mrs. Randy R. Tunney.

All of a sudden I was saddened. How I wished my family had been here, especially my beautiful sister. I'm sure Diana must have felt likewise about her family. We all then went outside for pictures. I paid the gratuity to Reverend Moore, and then everyone was invited to our place for a small get-together.

Diana—my wife—and I were chauffeured back home to our place. Since we lived on the seventh floor, I waited until we left the elevator before gathering Diana into my arms and carrying her the length of the hallway and then into our apartment. My lips never left hers all the while. We had our small gathering, which lasted most of an hour. Now Diana and I were alone to start our lives together.

Our bags were packed, so we cleaned up and made love before we left for Niagara Falls. Just before we were to leave Diana and I had our first argument on my account. With all the formalities over, I had become very depressed because our families had not attended our wedding. I told Diana I had never wanted to get married the way we had just done. Diana and I were both in tears. She consoled me, and soon I was smiling again.

Soon we were on our way happily to Niagara Falls and spent four days of wedded bliss together. Back in Toronto the following Wednesday night we spent the next two days making my apartment our home. I had returned the Lincoln. On Friday I picked up another car for the week of our northern holiday. Prior to leaving I had to make sure my rabbits and bird had plenty of food and water. Now we were off to cottage country.

We would spend the week of June 16 to 23 at West Arm Lodge in a rented cabin. I loved this area of Canada as we had had our cottage not far away. The owners of the lodge had known me since I was a babe in arms. I had spent most of the few happy moments in my life at our cottage.

Friday night we camped out in a trailer park in Sudbury. Diana and I went to the drive-in. My wife also spent her first night in a tent. Needless to say, I kept her safe. Saturday morning before driving to the lodge, we drove to Copper Cliff, where I showed her where I grew up, the home, school, the superstack, etc. Then it was off to the lake. How I wanted her to meet Vickey, but we had no contact with anyone. To this date, I don't know why we didn't even drop by Doug's.

During our week at West Arm Lodge, we had the time of our lives. We sunbathed nude on deserted islands, went canoeing, had midnight swims and bonfires. We drove to Sudbury, an hour away, twice for dinners, workouts at a gym and shopping. I finally found the Care Bears Diana had wanted. One day we went to the country fair. A couple of nights we went bear watching but saw no bears. Another day we took the short drive to where my family's cottage had been. The old place still looked the same and brought back memories, both happy and sad. Although I was suffering silently. I had the best week of my life.

Before we knew it our week at the resort had ended. Prior to departing on the morning of June 23 I told the proprietors not to mention to any of my family that I had been there. I had been told my Dad and his girlfriend spent some time each summer in the trailer park. My sister, Vickey, sometimes came as well. Diana and I still had a busy day ahead of us and wanted to be home by noon. The annual Sears employee picnic, which I had helped organize, was being held the next day, and I had some things to do at the store before closing hours. I shall cherish the memories of those two weeks forever. Now it was back to the proverbial old grind, which I didn't mind.

# Chapter 23

The first thing I did Monday was check the sales figures for the past two weeks to make sure I was still number one in the department. At the rate I was selling I was sure to be the top earner, just as I had projected for myself. As the summer went by I seemed to be a different and happier person. I was becoming so involved at work that I forgot all my problems, it seemed. Diana was offered a full-time position in the portrait studio, a concession of Sears, which she took.

I was back on my regimented schedule of fitness training and working. If Diana and I had not been working together, we wouldn't have seen much of each other. We usually ate our lunches or suppers together at work. If I wasn't at the gym I was at work six days a week. Sunday was my marathon working out day. Diana usually joined me to work out on Sundays. She had started running and had quit smoking, which pleased me very much. I surely didn't want to see the lady I loved dearly harming herself.

I watched as much of the Olympic games as possible on TV, most notably the sprinting. How I wished I had followed through on my aspirations! Oh well, there was always 1988, as I would only be twenty-nine. Now I always tried to promote fitness and in September got in touch with an owner of Super Fitness whom I had met a couple of times. I asked for a free one-year membership so that I could organize a fitness promotion at work. Mr. Eddie Aziz donated the membership as per my request. I set up a one-month run, walk, and bike program where employees kept track of the miles they completed. The chart was put where the employees entered the store. Whoever participated would have their name drawn at the end of the month. Also in September Diana and I decided to each run ten kilometres on Terry Fox day. We would raise the money from the employees at work and run on behalf of Sears, Markham Place. We ran each Sunday anyhow, so there really wasn't any extra effort put out on our part. We managed to raise $200 for cancer research.

Diana was being a wonderful wife and was doing her utmost to make our apartment our home. I thought I was being a perfect husband by working so hard in order to provide the finer things in life for us. Although I was buying a lot of luxury items, we would still be debt free by the end of the year. With our combined incomes we were financially secure, so much so that in the new year we could maintain our lifestyle on my income alone.

I was thinking of starting a part-time sales company and with a friend from work registered Halton and Associates. We were going to try and market the fanbanna again. We would also try to pick up other items to sell. Also at work I had talked over with the store manager my dream of running across Canada in order to raise money for drug and alcohol programs and research. I told him if it was at all feasible I would start my run in May 1985. I was, I thought, prepared now to do something special for the less fortunate. I wanted to be an example of how one could change one's life around. No one knew what was really driving me to show others what a healthier lifestyle could do for you. I went from being an emotionally tormented drug addict and alcoholic to an award-winning athlete and top professional salesperson. I was married, had a nice apartment, and the list goes on. I figured people could identify with me, and maybe, just maybe, I could affect one person's life in such a way that he or she might too find hope and the courage to strive for the seemingly impossible dream of happiness and love.

The store manager said that he would offer his help and the company's if at all possible. With that I was full of confidence that I could give back to the others some of my knowledge from experience in a special way. I knew that for every one like me who made it off the streets there were thousands who never would. These thoughts had always bothered me. The run would be as much for myself as it was for others. I loved running and pushing myself to new limits. Diana was behind me in my decision to do this. She didn't like that I didn't want her to come along if I was able to put this run together.

In October, Thanksgiving Day arrived. We spent the day by ourselves. We had been invited to have dinner at a lady friend's family's home. To me Thanksgiving was a family affair, and I didn't feel like intruding on someone else's home just because Diana and I had nowhere to go. Diana was close to this family, but I had persuaded her to stay at our place for the day. She went along with anything I said. Although we had a nice day I was slipping into the darkness of depression. This would be how all our holidays and special occasions would be—alone!

I now worked even harder as I slipped farther into the dark. I again was feeling guilty and not good enough for Diana. So I spent more money and bought us more things. As usual when things weren't right emotionally, I thought it was because I was really turning off from women. The thoughts were tormenting me again. Of course, not a word was said to Diana. I just crawled into my shell. I didn't know what Diana might be thinking as I never asked her. Not once since being married did we carry on a personal conversation. Everything was fitness, business and spending money. The subject of our families never arose. I just didn't want to deal with it. I was used to being unwanted, so why should things change?

On October 31st, we went out for Halloween with a girlfriend of Diana's. This was the second time that we had gone out since our honeymoon. The first was a Sears' dance I had helped organize. I had no time to go out. We usually worked Friday nights and always on Saturdays until 6 p.m. I had to be in bed by midnight because I had to work out for hours at the gym Sunday mornings. Our only time out together was maybe Sunday afternoons. We did however about once a month throw a party on Saturday night for people at work. The people who came were between Diana's and my age. This was also my now once-monthly drinking session. And I did always get drunk.

Well, this Halloween night I was dressed as a pimp, Diana had made a crayon costume and her friend was a bunny of the animal variety. We were attending a semi-private party in a rented hall of a hotel at Yonge and Eglinton. I didn't care too much for bars, and as the evening went by I told Diana something or other and then stepped outside for a bit. I had been drinking and was extremely depressed.

Toronto is quite the place to be on Halloween, especially downtown along the strip. Thousands of people go downtown to watch the made-up people. I walked the two blocks to the subway station and then went south on the train the few stops to Yonge and Bloor. The streets were alive with strange beings. Dressed as a pimp, I fit right in. I walked south on Yonge a couple blocks, into the heart of the gay scene. Guess where I ended up for some deeply rooted reason? Yes, a gay bar. I was just as messed up as the married men I had as customers during my days of being a prostitute.

For five minutes I stood around with men's eyes sexually transfixed on me as usual. I could have made a fortune. Hundreds of questions were going through my mind. I hated myself for being there and knew I was definitely a mental case. Soon I was back with Diana. In all I had been gone only about forty-five minutes. From that night on I knew that I wasn't the man for Diana even though I loved her more than anyone in this world.

It was now November and I was working harder. I was becoming hostile and my temper was returning.

One day I almost got fired after losing my temper in front of another employee. I was just losing control. Diana and I hardly spent time together at work. I had told her we had to be more professional since we were married and worked together. Her manager arranged Diana's schedule so she would have the same day off as me. That didn't matter, as I was always at the gym and then at work. I was closing her out of my life as I sunk deeper.

Now for the clincher. For the first time in five years I started cross-dressing at home when Diana wasn't there. I was again drinking more. Let's just say I was losing my mind. Every day I was fighting with myself mentally. To make up for my guilt I bought more furniture, clothes and such. The retail Christmas season had already started, and everything at work was Christmas oriented. This was only adding fuel to the psychological fire burning within. Every day I heard Christmas music. The customers were always asking about Christmas presents for friends and family. I hated Christmas.

I was now in charge of the social club, as the employee who had been president was now working elsewhere. I just took over. I was busier than ever at work as the Christmas party was near. There was also a Handicap Night approaching. The store would be open after hours on a Saturday night so that people in wheelchairs and such could do their Christmas shopping. Sears threw a party for them as well. People from senior citizens homes would be bused in. Boy Cubs and Scouts would be on hand to help out. This was an annual affair, and Diana and I would be helping out.

We had also bought some gift certificates to be given away as prizes.

I had never been so busy in my whole life, or so depressed. If I had not been so busy I would have cracked up. As far as my job was concerned I was working on what could turn out to be a major sale for Sears to a corporate customer, Dupont Canada. I had set up a sales meeting at their office in order to sell some of the employees a computer monitor, TV, and video combination to use at home along with an employee payroll-deduction-purchased computer. I put together a sales booklet and received permission from the management to take from the store a TV, video, computer monitor, video cassette recorder and a movie cassette, *Rocky*. I was determined to show this monitor to its best. The *Rocky* movie would be an icebreaker.

At the meeting were the staff and three or four monitors of competitors. Everything was so well received by the company that there was talk of a major sale on a national basis. Initially I sold about ten units on an individual basis, which netted me $250 in commission. Being the business man I was trying to be, I also asked their opinion of my fanbanna. I knew that Dupont was a very diversified company. A lady gave me names of several companies in Canada that might be able to manufacture the scarf. Unfortunately, nothing could be worked out. The monitor sale had been my largest sale, and I was proud of myself. I kept in contact with Dupont, working out the possibility of a large one-time sale. I had now proven my sales ability.

The night arrived for our employee Christmas party. We on the social club had achieved our financial objectives. It was a Saturday night in late November. I had rented a Lincoln Town car for the weekend. I worked only half a day that Saturday as I had many last minute details to take care of. As treasurer, I had the use of the social club's Sears credit card. That afternoon I went on a spending spree, buying all the prizes for draws and such. I had worked all year for this night and hoped everything would go as we had planned. As there was no formal president of the committee, I had more or less taken over. I would be busy all evening, and Diana was going to help me.

That evening Diana and I arrived in the Lincoln and were dressed to the nines. Diana had made her own gown of red fabric and was wearing her fur coat. She was the loveliest lady there. She looked stunning, and I couldn't believe she had such dressmaking talent. I was dressed in a brand new, navy-blue wool double-breasted pinstriped suit that had set me back $600. We both were wearing complementing accessories. I had dropped by the rented hall early and then went home to pick up Diana after the partygoers started arriving. I have to admit I was a snob and had things timed for our entrance.

The formal dinner went as hoped. Some prizes were handed out, and then the dancing was to begin. As I was somewhat the host, Diana and I after dinner initiated the dancing. I sure was proud to be up there in my wife's presence. I know now things were wrong, but I did love her as best as I knew how.

After the party ended and I had taken care of things Diana and two other girls and I went cruising the streets of Toronto. We had decided to have a little fun.

As we were all dressed to the nines and driving around in a Lincoln, we would have some fun with pedestrians. We pretended I was a pimp and the three girls, all seated in the back, were hookers. As we drove around, they called to pedestrians. The best part was when the four of us at about 4 in the morning walked into a busy all-night restaurant for breakfast. You could sense that the customers and staff thought I was a pimp out with his girls. It was a scene right out of a movie.

December was upon us now, and Diana had talked me into buying an artificial Christmas tree. I hadn't bothered putting up a Christmas tree while living in Toronto with J.D. Seeing a tree would have just depressed me more. I was also talked into helping Diana make handmade decorations. Here was Diana trying to make things special for us while I didn't give a care. So now I had a decorated and lit tree to upset me. As if I didn't have to put up with enough of the Christmas season at Sears. All this Christmas bull was just driving me up the wall. Oh well, at least at the moment I was making $1,000 a week or more. The last two weeks prior to Christmas I made $2,600 in commission. Diana and I were now debt free as planned.

Diana and I spent Christmas alone, and it was upsetting to me to think this was the way it was always going to be. I'm sure Diana felt the same, although neither of us spoke of these worries to each other. New Year's Eve came. We got off work at 6 p.m.

Diana and I went home and I got into the booze while Diana watched. As usual, which was fortunately seldom, I got drunk and pissed off. I hated myself and wished my life would end. Diana sat in silence. She had no idea what was going on in my mind. I was going mad! I drank and drank and soon felt like I was going to die. I was yelling and screaming as my mind was overloading with guilt and loneliness. I longed to see my sister. How I missed her! Finally I had gone over the edge and deep into misery. Diana must have been scared. I begged her to phone for an ambulance as I thought I would go berserk. Finally she phoned.

In minutes attendants were at the door, as an ambulance station was a block away. I was almost passed out, in as much emotional pain as ever yet. The attendants just talked for a few minutes and then left. I later got sick as a dog and passed out. Poor Diana, that poor girl. Happy New Year.

# Chapter 24

January 1, 1985, I awoke with a hangover. I apologized to Diana, and I was forgiven. She asked if she could help me and I told her nothing was wrong. This was a new year, and maybe things would change. I was finally debt free, and we had money in the bank. I had finished 1984 as the top sales person in my department. My objective this year was a 20 percent increase. I had decided not to run across Canada, as there was too much to organize. Anyhow, Steve Fonyo would be running across Canada in the shadow of Terry Fox. Steve was also a one-legged cancer victim.

Diana is of Yugoslavian descent, and in her home country they celebrate Christmas two weeks after we do in Canada. Although her family celebrated Christmas on December 25th, they also had a special day two weeks later. Diana had told me this, and I told her I didn't care. I said Christmas is December 25th and that's it. On January 8th, which was her country's Christmas, I did nothing for her. I certainly wasn't going to start celebrating Christmas twice. Things were bad enough as it was.

Diana was upset because I hadn't even given her a card out of respect. A week later, on the fifteenth, was my birthday. She gave me a present and baked a cake for me. I didn't give a care about birthdays and gave Diana trouble for making me a cake. She knew that I didn't eat cake because of my training. So, being the nice guy I am, I didn't even eat a piece.

I guess Diana by now had noticed that her twenty-six-year-old husband was not the man she had thought she married. She once said we needed to talk, and I said there was nothing to talk about. Sexually, we would have sex and then I'd turn over and go to sleep.

Since birthdays were always depressing times for me I had gotten into the habit of buying something expensive for myself to cheer myself up. Christmas was the same. Well, this year I wanted to go all out—I wanted to buy a Lincoln Town Car and had picked one out. It was a 1981 model, white with burgundy interior. I had more or less told Diana that was what we would buy. What girl wouldn't want to drive around in a Lincoln? Diana was more practical and wanted a Honda or the like. As usual I had my way and went out and put 10 percent down on the price. The balance would be financed. Unfortunately I needed a co-signer, and since neither of us could ask our families, I was out of luck. I had even offered to put down another $1,000. We could have bought a less expensive car, but my mind was made up. I would wait. I got my deposit back and then invested it in silver.

At work I was busy and still working on the possibility of a large order from Dupont Canada. I was on the social club again, but not in an officiating position as I wanted to spend more time working on the sales floor. By the end of January I had closed the largest sale of this store's history. Dupont had agreed to purchase $30,000-plus worth of a monitor T.V. combination and some VCRs. That meant $1,500 in commission for me. I had shocked all the salespeople and staff in the store. I was numero uno undisputedly. To top things off, some months later a memo was sent from head office to the electronics departments nationwide. The memo stated that sales of that particular TV and monitor were up and gave the number. I looked at the totals and realized that on a national basis I had sold 30 percent of them. I had selling that monitor to customers down to a science. Again I had reached for the impossible and succeeded. Nothing could stop me now. Now I would have to outdo myself some more. I would be the top electronics salesman in Canada within the next two years.

Money was the name of the game. I was learning about the stock market and soon would embark in that area. I was applying for sales positions at major electronic distributors, because even if I did become number one at Sears I could still earn more elsewhere. I was becoming hostile at work, and Diana was also looking for a higher paid job. At one point the personnel manager said I should talk to a shrink as she suspected some deep problems.

I was now a confirmed workaholic. By the end of February Diana had switched jobs and was now earning 50 percent more. Now we were in the $35,000 to $40,000 a year bracket, depending on my commissions.

All I thought about now was that we would next year be able to buy a sailboat. We had already decided on the name. In Roman mythology, Diana was the goddess of the hunt, so that's what our new boat's name would be. As we were going to be a childless career couple, we wouldn't need a house. Our plan was to have a thirty-six-foot yacht-type sailboat.

Out of the blue we received a phone call from Doug, the first ever. He and my young nephew were to be going to Niagara Falls during the school March break to attend a juvenile hockey tournament. He asked if they could spend a night at our place. Of course I said, "Sure." I was delighted, as I could show off all the trappings of the good life. Diana made a comment to the likes of "What are we to do, look like we are happy?" I didn't respond to the remark as I always tried to avoid conflict. Had I not been so screwed up I would have picked up on what she was insinuating.

Doug and his son, Jeffrey, arrived one day in March. I had taken the day off work but had a couple of customer problems to take care. As I expected, Doug was shocked to see all the luxurious things Diana and I owned. He was most impressed with the art collection, antiques, stereo, TV and stereo equipment. He knew I had come to Toronto penniless, and now he saw me with everything a man could want. I showed him my paycheque stubs as I kept a bookkeeping system for everything I earned so I could improve the following year. We went up to Sears, and I showed him and my nephew around. We then went to a customer's house as I had a problem to take care of. Diana, after coming home from work, made a wonderful supper, after which Doug, Jeff and I went to visit Doug's biological brother and relatives. Diana stayed behind as she had to get up at 5 the following morning. I chauffeured them around, and it was strange when Doug introduced me to his brother as his brother. After visiting I toured them around downtown Toronto. The following morning they departed for Niagara Falls. Doug said he was glad that I was happy and doing well.

Now since Diana had changed jobs we saw nothing of each other. I went to work or the gym and then came home and went to sleep. Diana's job as a shift worker at a factory had us on opposite schedules. When I came home at night she was either at work or in bed sleeping as she would have to be up at 5 a.m. I didn't like that she was coming home in the middle of the night. I decided to forgo buying a Lincoln in order to buy Diana a small car. I made arrangements to buy a VW Rabbit from a friend. I told Diana I would sell my silver certificates to pay for it. She told me to wait a few weeks. As usual I went ahead with my plans to buy her the car. I certainly didn't want the lady I loved to be out in the middle of the night alone.

This was the second week in March. I remember one night when I was trying to sleep I heard Diana talking to herself. Whether she was awake or asleep I don't know. The words I heard were "You'll miss me when I'm gone." I thought nothing of it and was soon asleep. I know now that the subtle hints I had been hearing were Diana's cries for attention from her husband. I also knew at this time that Diana was again in contact with her family quite often. I ignored this also, as I was upset because I wanted to belong as well.

Saturday, March 16, 1985, I awoke at 6:30 so I would have enough time to go for a five-kilometre run, shower, eat and change before leaving for work. I was a while getting ready for work after my run, telling Diana what I had forecast for the day's sales. She had the day off today and was up and making me breakfast. It wasn't unusual for me to make $300 on a Saturday, the busiest day of the week. Once I had made $350. As it was March I might make $200 today. Diana told me she would grocery shop and clean. She asked what would I like for supper. I told her to surprise me. She asked if she could phone me later. I said "no" as today was the busiest day of the week.

We both left the apartment together at 8:30. I was going to work, and Diana was going grocery shopping up the street. We kissed each other goodbye and professed our love for each other. Unknown to me, this was the last time I would ever kiss the lips of this wonderful young lady, my wife.

When I happily came in the door after a long day's work, there was no aroma of supper permeating the air. I dropped my briefcase and let out a painful scream. No! No! No! Diana, no! Yes, some of the furniture was gone. Pieces were missing out of each room. Tears were streaming down my face as emotional pain struck me like never before. I was screaming at the top of my lungs and fell onto the couch. Part of me was in the throes of death. I knew Diana had left me, and I was cracking up. I immediately phoned her best friend (the bridesmaid) and told her what had happened. She had not heard from Diana. God, I was in so much pain! I phoned Diana's parents' house and spoke to her twin brother. I was told she hadn't been in contact with them. I didn't believe him and would have to go up there myself.

I was still crying hysterically. I composed myself as I took the ten minute ride to Diana's parents' house. I begged and pleaded with them to let me talk to her. They insisted that she wasn't there. I knew they were lying. I had no choice but to go home. The pain from all the beatings I had ever endured as a child together couldn't match the pain I was feeling now.

At home I phoned a lady who lived five floors up with her son. She invited me up for a talk. She was somewhat aware of my family background and knew of my hatred for my mother. I poured out my heart to her and after some time went downstairs to my place, where I proceeded to get drunk. I cranked up the stereo. Diana had taken the other one. I yelled and screamed as I drank like a fish. The music was so no one would hear my suffering.

I wanted to die. I hated myself and knew I deserved this even though I loved my wife. My wife, yes, I loved her so. I swore I would have nothing to do with women again. I knew for sure I wasn't cut out to be with women. Women were just out to hurt men. All night I cursed women and especially Vickey's mother, who had messed up my mind royally, right to the point that I couldn't have any personal relationships. I loved Diana, yet I knew she was better off without me. It was about 4 in the morning by the time I passed out.

I awoke suddenly, alone. Who would want to do their training on a morning like this? There was no beautiful, loving wife beside me. I was hung over and broke out in tears. I was yelling for Diana to come home. I had fallen asleep on the couch as I didn't want to go to sleep alone in an empty king-size bed. I got off the couch and rummaged through a cupboard looking for pictures of her and of us. They were all gone, just as was everything she had bought or we had bought together. All that was left were my own belongings, which still filled the apartment, a pair of brass swans, which were the first present Diana had given me, and a band of gold around my finger. Every other trace of her was gone.

I went to the fridge for a brew and said, "Forget women." They were the cause of all my problems. I spent the morning dialling Diana's family's phone number, only to hear a busy signal. They had taken the phone off the hook. By noon I was cracking up just from the loneliness of being alone and with no one to call. My thoughts when depressed usually centred around homosexuality and hatred towards women. I contemplated going downtown to a gay bar to get picked up. I was not good enough for women. I knew why Diana had left me. She didn't want to be married to some bisexually-inclined faggot. Diana knew of my past experiences and some of my present thoughts. I hated myself that day, and it's a wonder I just didn't end my life.

I drank some more and made up my mind to go gay bar-hopping. Sunday is the day gays go to "tea parties." Maybe I just had to accept the fact that I was gay and that's the way I was meant to be. So here I was now. My wife had only left me the day before, and within twenty-four hours I was getting ready to go out and get picked up in some gay bar. Now you tell me that is not abnormal. I was a mental case.

Believe it or not, at about 1:30, just as I was putting my coat on, the phone rang. It was Diana checking on me to see if I was still alive. I tried to get her to meet with me so we could talk. She refused, stating, "You don't know how to talk." She said she was at her parents' and that we were finished, and then she hung up.

"Forget women," I said, "forget all women," and I left for downtown. I didn't care much for Toronto's gay bars as they had no class. Ninety percent were run down and filthy. The one on Yonge Street where I ended up stopping for some lunch was no exception. In fact, the hot roast beef sandwich I ate was the worst I've tasted. It wouldn't have passed Ralston Purina's quality control line in their pet food division.

I usually had milk with lunch but today I was drinking brew. I noticed my wedding band and took it off and slipped it into my coat pocket. By now I was moderately drunk and was cruising the place. I fought back tears every second and tried to look cheerful. I hated myself. As in the past I could pick up anyone I chose. I decided to let some younger stud have me. We struck up a conversation and threw back some brew together and soon were both quite drunk. We ended up at my place, where I now was having second thoughts but was under an obligation of sorts to let him have me sexually. It was quick, and I'm sure too quick for him. I'm sure he expected to stick around for the evening. It was only about 6 p.m. I made up some excuse that I had plans for the night, and he left.

I then cracked up. I hated myself, Vickey's mother, and how I loved Diana. I knew she was better off without her screwed-up husband, and now I didn't deserve her back. I got drunk and was in such psychological madness that I wanted to die. I didn't want to be gay. I wanted to live normally; that's all I ever wanted. I wanted once and for all to be free of this mental madness, which had been perpetuated from the days of my youth. I was losing my sanity. I was totally lost and alone, totally void of any sense of reality. How I hated being alone! All my life I had been alone and had dreamt of things changing someday. When they did, I blew it. In my heart I was a kind, compassionate person who had a deep sympathetic love of human souls except for two—myself and Vickey's mother.

In my mind World War III was now taking place. It seemed all the cells in my mind were full of prisoners of war who wanted to be free. Freedom, freedom, freedom. When would I be free? If you have read thus far, you can imagine how I must have felt lying around drunk and alone this evening, battling this psychological war with my personality. The emotional pain cut like Satan's razor-edged blade. I was in total chaos. Visions of Diana were as vivid as real life. How I was hurting! I was up all night.

Monday, March 18: I phoned in sick at work. I spent the day drinking after making a trip to the liquor store. I didn't leave the apartment in case Diana dropped by. I knew she wouldn't be at work on the day shift until Wednesday. I slept a few hours that night. I was going right crazy. I would just stare out the window for hours.

Tuesday, March 19: The same as Monday. I was going, or had gone, insane.

Wednesday, March 20: I awoke after maybe three hours of sleep. Since Saturday I had maybe twelve hours sleep and had not eaten since Sunday afternoon at the gay bar on Yonge Street. I knew Diana would be at work today and phoned, but she didn't want to talk to me, I was told. I had to see her. I phoned Budget Rent A Car and reserved a car for later that day.

The time dragged by, and I didn't drink as I didn't want to show up drunk at Diana's workplace. Man, I was full of anxiety. About 2 p.m. I picked up the rental car, a 1985 Pontiac Bonneville with only a few hundred kilometres on the odometer. The clerk gave me a special rate as I had been a regular customer over the past couple of years. There would also be no deductible on the insurance in the event of an accident. I didn't think much of it at the time as I didn't plan on getting into an accident or damaging the car.

I drove down Lawrence to Birchmount in Scarborough and parked adjacent to Diana's place of work. Her mother, whom I hadn't seen in over a year, showed up to pick up her daughter. I knew I wouldn't be talking to Diana that day. I waited anyhow just to get a glimpse of my beautiful and loving wife. My mind was fraught with hate, anger and resentment for pretty much everything and everyone. Finally Diana in all her loveliness emerged and got into the passenger seat of her mother's Honda Civic. They were now on their way and turned north onto Birchmount. I was behind and turned south on Birchmount. Within seconds I decided to pull a U-turn and was now going north as well.

Before getting to Ellesmere I pulled alongside and was now face-to-face with Diana. Diana glanced over, and when she saw me she took a cigarette from her purse and spitefully lit up. She knew how much I hated smoking, which was why she had stopped. Now here she was making this gesture to infuriate me. I flipped out and sped up in order to get ahead of them. I planned on stopping her mother's car, hauling Diana out and taking her home. Once ahead of them, I pulled a 180-degree turn while speeding. I believe the front axle components broke. I was now facing them head on.

I got out of the car. The smell of burnt rubber permeated the air. In an insane state of mind I ran over to Diana and tried pulling open the locked door. I was oblivious to my surroundings and was yelling and screaming to Diana how much I loved her.

Realizing that this course of insane action was of no use, I ran blindly back to the rental car screaming, "I'm going to kill myself! I'm going to kill myself!" I threw myself into the driver's seat and slammed the door closed. I put one foot on the brake and one on the gas and raced the engine. The revs went up to an engine-killing high. My foot came off the brake as I put the car in gear. The wheels were now screeching and trying to grip the road as the car spun around to face north. Like a bat out of hell I raced forward. I was aiming the car into the rear-end of a parked car. The car increased in speed until I heard the sound of crunching metal. I was mentally blacked out and was thrown about.

I wasn't dead as I had hoped. I wasn't even hardly injured. I was now at the intersection of Ellesmere and Birchmount. A fire hall happened to be across the street. My back was sore, but I decided to fake a more serious injury and stayed in the car. Firemen rushed to my rescue, and I was told not to move. Finally an ambulance arrived. I was still in a trance-like state of mental confusion. I was taken to Scarborough General Hospital.

I asked them to phone a friend at work and then took a vow of silence and just stared madly at the ceiling. The police had been informed that I had tried to kill myself, and the decision was made to keep me overnight on the psychiatric ward. My friend and his girlfriend visited me, and we spoke a bit about Diana leaving me. I was then left alone. The nurses took x-rays and such of my back. The room I was in had wire-screened window coverings so that a patient couldn't jump.

I spent the night in total turmoil. The past was coming back to haunt me as never before. I didn't know at the time that the battle between myself and my personality, which had been perpetuated since childhood, was going into the final rounds. This fight for mental freedom was a fight even Rocky would hesitate to step into the psychological ring to fight. There I was on the mental ward of a hospital in total anguish. This place was for lunatics and the like. I didn't belong there. I did succumb to sleep that night.

The next morning I told the doctor I was fine and wouldn't do anything so stupid again. He wrote up a prescription and later released me to go home. Home, yes, my empty home, alone.

I took the bus home and just stared silently and hatefully at the outside world. I poured myself a drink and broke out in tears. I proceeded to break dishes and throw things about. I smashed my body building trophies and threw them off the balcony. I turned up the stereo to ear-splitting madness to drown out the thoughts crossing my mind. I had nothing and no one to live for, and who the hell was I? All I knew was who I wanted to be. Would I ever be free to be me?

I got in touch with work and told them I would be in the following day. I also phoned Reverend Moore, who had married Diana and I. I informed him of my circumstances, and he said he'd try to help and invited me to go to church with him and his wife on Sunday. I don't know why but I accepted.

Back at work I struggled with my hurt and decided to see a doctor. I knew that if I couldn't keep a wife whom I loved dearly, I needed help. There was a medical centre in the mall where I worked, and I made an appointment for the following week. Only a few people at work knew about Diana leaving me. I wanted no one to know as they all knew both of us.

Friday, March 22: I rented a car for the weekend from a different Budget office than the one I usually dealt with because of the accident. I struggled through work that day and the following day, Saturday. I was in great turmoil and drove by Diana's parents' house frequently.

Sunday, March 24: I awoke early as usual but not to work out. I had promised Reverend Moore I would attend his church service. I hadn't been in church since 1980 and I felt strange going today. Life Tabernacle was located in Scarborough and was actually held in the gym of a school. Just the same, a church atmosphere permeated the room. I was introduced to some of the parishioners, and then Reverend Moore proceeded with the service and worship. The service was different than any church I had ever been to. During praise singing there was hand clapping, and everyone seemed too happy. I was reminded of cultism and the like. As Reverend Moore spoke the Word of God, I broke down and left the room. How I loved Diana! Why hadn't I ever gone to church? Like a lost lamb I just walked the halls and tried to keep my composure.

When the service was over I spoke with Reverend Moore briefly and then left. At home I again broke down and was filled with guilt and hate of myself for my thoughts. I tried phoning Diana, and all I got to listen to was a busy signal. I changed from my suit to casual apparel and then went for a drive. I ended up stopping at the home of a young lady from work. I was met at the door by her mother. I spoke with my friend about Diana and me. We made a casual date for the evening to go to a show so I wouldn't be alone. The rest of the day I drove about and cruised by Diana's parents' house a few times, hoping for just a glimpse of her. I was so terribly alone and confused. I went to the show that evening with my friend, after which I thanked her for being a friend. It was the first time in my life I had reached out to a friend for help.

On Monday I returned the rented car prior to going to work. This week several things happened. I was served with a summons to appear in court. I had been charged with criminal negligence in the operation of a motor vehicle. I didn't think much of it as I had a spotless driving record. I decided to attend court without a lawyer, and when the date arrived (April 17) I pleaded guilty, and a pre-sentence report was requested before sentencing. I was to return to court on May 16.

In the interim I was in touch with the probation office, and a lady there took the necessary information from me. Two examples show how I felt at the time of questioning as per the pre-sentence report: "When questioned on his mother's name, the subject replied he did not have a mother. It was only after repeated questioning on the topic that he gave his background history, omitting his mother's name." "When asked if he was suicidal, he replied he was and then stated if he was going to kill himself he would kill his mother first."

At the medical centre I met a Dr. G. Lutz, a general practitioner. I told him my circumstances, and since I mentioned drug and alcohol abuse in the past, he became interested in my case, as these topics were of interest to him. I broke down in his office, and he could sense my troubles went deeper than just having Diana gone. In retrospect, even I knew that Diana's leaving was not the most serious of my problems. The doctor agreed to see me, although he was not a psychothera-pist. He prescribed some mood elevators and such to keep me from falling deeper into the hole of despair. I would however in the course of seeing Dr. Lutz not once mention my personality hang-ups.

Reverend Moore had gone to Diana's workplace, but Diana didn't say much except that she and I were finished. I knew so already, but I had to hold on to something. Diana was the thread that kept me together, and I had to hold on to the hope she would have a change of heart.

My earnest angel from the heavens above
I miss the glow of your smiling face
And the warmth of your tender loving
Now and forever you will be close to my heart
Always you are here, always on my mind.

# Chapter 25

The month of April arrived. Every second of every day was emotional torture. I hated being at work as Diana was living only a block away with her parents. I knew she had to pass by the store daily. I was sending her gifts, letters and tapes of me pleading with her. Her parents had their phone number changed, and it was now unlisted. I was missing work and had started calling clients of the past from my "red book" and was again in the escort business. I had also placed an ad in the companion section of the *Toronto Star* for a female companion. Depending on the females I met, I would either charge them or see them as a friend. I was sleeping with someone, either male or female, almost daily. I wasted the money to maintain my lifestyle. I also wasn't as selective as before, but who cared? I was usually half drunk or high on prescription drugs that I was getting from a few doctors. I was making $1,000 a week between my two jobs and was spending more than that. My zero-balance credit cards were being rung up over their limits.

I cashed in my silver certificates as well. I replaced everything that Diana had taken and more. I was filling up the apartment with luxuries. More art, antiques, brass placemats, Royal Doulton vases and candlesticks, gold-plated dishes, a $200 chess set, a sectional sofa, and the list went on. A whole new wardrobe hung in my closet. I was just going spend-crazy. I now had not a cent in the bank. Who cared; I would just have sex for more.

I was now seeing Dr. Lutz a couple of times a week, and I was still being prescribed drugs. How I wished I could be honest with him and tell him of the real struggles going on inside. I was going to church on Sundays and reading the Bible Reverend Moore had given me. Diana had taken the one he had given us as a wedding present. I wasn't working out or running; who the Hell cared. I was buying women's lingerie and wearing them under my clothes at work and sleeping in them. All of this was tormenting me more. It was hard trying to hold onto my sanity—or had I already lost it?

On some of my business dates I was smoking marijuana, which I hadn't done since I was twenty (six years before). What was happening to me? I was regressing back to my teenage years. When I was at work I wasn't doing my job well. How I needed Diana to keep me sane! Not a day went by that I didn't shed tears for her. Why couldn't I be normal like most everyone else? Why?

I had sent Diana a present for Easter, and it was returned to the store. On Sunday, May 12, I didn't go to church and was extremely depressed. It was Diana's twentieth birthday. Only one year ago I had given her the best birthday party ever. I prayed for her sincerely. I was drinking and popping prescription drugs all day. I also made a couple hundred dollars. I couldn't stand living this dual life, and I was going even more crazy. "Insanity," the misunderstanding of extenuating circumstances.

On May 16 I awoke to face the not-so-pleasurable experience of criminal court again. Instead of breakfast I popped some prescription drugs. By the time I arrived in court I was quite high. In court I saw Diana sitting with the probation officer who had completed my presentence report. How I wanted to talk to her! I took a seat across the room. I sat nervously and stole glances at Diana. Reverend Moore was seated alone a couple of aisles over.

The judge was going through the morning cases. I took a few more pills as I sat waiting for my name to be called. I was going crazy inside, to say the least, with Diana across the room. It had been two months since I had spoken with her. I had no attorney as I thought I would just get fined and have my license suspended.

My name was called, and I strode to the front of the courtroom. I was dressed to the nines in a tailored three-piece $500 suit. I looked every bit respectable and composed as Judge Tinker read the charges and asked how I was going to plead. I said guilty, as I had on my first appearance.

Now my mind being so confused had of late been misinterpreting things. Something to the effect of me stepping into custody was said, and at that word *custody* all fear and anger erupted inside. I had years ago vowed to never be taken into custody alive. All my future flashed before my eyes, and I was resolved to keep that promise. I took a handful of mixed pills from my suit coat pocket and swallowed the contents.

I was jumped by two guards. I'm sure they didn't expect what was to happen next. With all my trained power I tore them off me and suckered them both. I was then tossing them around like baseballs. I was now so full of fury I didn't notice the courtroom being cleared and cops rushing in. I was taking on five or six of them. It wasn't until I was put in a chokehold and succumbed to semi-consciousness that I was subdued, cuffed and dragged away. My suit was torn, and I was tossed like a bag of garbage down a flight of stairs. I don't remember too much of what happened next as I was stoned out of my tree. One thing led to another, and I ended up at the Queen Street Mental Health Centre, which meant I had been certified by court order. I was virtually a prisoner as this floor was locked up. I was to be there for ten days or so for assessment.

During the time there I put on the facade of my life. I was cheerful, polite and got along with everyone. If I would have been as I truly felt I might not ever have gotten out of there. I had phoned Sears and spoke with the personnel manager and store superintendent. I arranged that these days hospitalized would be my summer vacation. What a holiday.

Lo and behold, a friend from Sudbury was on staff there as an orderly. He had been a training partner of mine on occasion. As if I didn't have enough problems to deal with! I was quite ashamed to be around him now and tried to avoid him at times. He was my keeper, and I was just another mental case on the ward. Was I glad to leave there after ten days! I was returned to court by police cruiser. Just like the good old days.

Sitting cuffed in the back of the car brought back some very unmemorable memories.

At the courthouse a lawyer was waiting for me. Reverend Moore had retained him for me at my request. I was also served papers for two assault charges. I saw my freedom slowly being taken from me. I would lose my job, which I was sure was already on the line. I told the lawyer just to get me out of there ASAP or I'd go completely nuts.

By suppertime I was released. For each assault charge I had to pay a $250 fine or spend fourteen days in jail. I was given sixty days to pay the fines. As far as my criminal negligence charge was concerned, I had to return on June 26 for sentencing after the medical assessment had been reviewed.

In a month I would be back in court. During the interim I worked steadily at my day job at Sears and my night job as an escort. I was also dating a young lady, a nurse, believe it or not. I was working out at the gym quite regularly and had quit running. I was drinking and abusing prescription drugs daily. I was still attending church and had taken to reading the Bible a bit daily. I had also received my legal bill for that last day in court. The bill was less than $2 short of $1,000. After phoning Reverend Moore I realized he had hired a $120-an-hour lawyer. So in fact that day in court, including my fines, had cost me $1,500. So much for a lawyer! I would go into court in June without a lawyer.

I was still seeing Dr. Lutz regularly, but I still wasn't being honest with him. I was deteriorating mentally daily. The more I slipped, the more I tried to keep up the facade to others that I was a man of steel and could handle anything. As soon as I was alone at home I would flip out.

Every night I cried for hours before falling asleep. One day I did go running and attempted a ten kilometre run. I succumbed to chest pains that tore at my insides. I managed to get home and phoned Dr. Lutz. A female friend I phoned came, picked me up and drove me to the medical centre. The doctor told me not to run for a while as I was under too much stress. The next time things might be worse. So now I was on the way to giving myself a heart attack. I was master of the greatest facade of all. From all physical appearances I exuded health, vitality and total masculinity. I knew, however, that I was as ill as anyone.

June 26, 1985: Well, today was the day of sentencing, and I was worried about being sentenced to a jail term. I would be in court without legal counsel. I didn't give a care. I'd rather be in jail. Diana would at least have second thoughts and come back to me.

Reverend Moore was in court to witness the outcome. Diana wasn't to be seen, although I was sure I had seen her mother's car in the parking lot. I was high on drugs and was waiting for my name to be called. Well, I was soon standing before the judge ready to be sentenced. When the judge asked if I had anything to say before sentence was passed, I stood silent. I knew he was going to only give me a period of probation, so I shut up. He gave me thirty seconds to say something or I'd go to jail. I didn't give a care. I could see people watching their watches. Fifteen seconds, ten, five, four, three, two, one—I said nothing. I knew now I was gone. The judge spoke and sentenced me to thirty days in jail, plus two years probation.

I had played out this hand and lost. I had just punished myself as much as I ever could have. I knew I would lose my job now. I had nothing to live for now except to go back on the streets, a sexually, mentally screwed-up individual. I was led down to the basement of the courthouse, cuffed, and soon was tossed into a police van for a ride to the East Detention Centre.

Inside the van, I cracked as I thought of everything I had worked for slipping away. I was now yelling and banging my head against the van's steel walls. Man, I wished I could escape from this mental prison of mine. I was driven the few blocks to the jail where I was to do my time. I had by now crossed the line of sanity and was falling deeper into my misery by the second. The sounds of locking doors behind me as I passed through were taking their toll on me. I felt with every step like I was walking deeper into the bowels of a living hell. The worst was yet to come.

Flashbacks of the days, nights and months spent in jail as a seventeen-year-old crossed my tormented mind. I was becoming increasingly tense and angry. I had worked so hard to have what I had, and now it was slipping away as I again found myself incarcerated. Years had passed since then, but now those times just seemed like yesterday. I felt no different now as then. I was still mixed up and fighting a losing battle. I was still angry at Vickey's mother and wished she'd go to hell. Most of all I was more angry and full of hate towards myself. Both of us were the worst beings to walk this earth. I even felt deserving of this jail sentence, as punishment for all things I had done in my past. Just the same, I hated being in jail.

I was taken to an area where I was to be checked in. The handcuffs were taken off. By now I was fully enraged, and I was being asked stupid stinkin' questions. I was photographed and fingerprinted and then ordered to strip. The police officers had told the guards I was higher than a kite, and I was. They had also been informed that I wasn't one to be messed around with as I could tear a couple of them apart.

A couple of other guards were called down to assist in booking me into this fortress of human tragedy. I could tell that I unnerved them as I undressed, my bulging muscles now exposed to their gaze. In tailored clothes I didn't look so massive, but undressed I told no lies. I knew I could intimidate them, so in a maddened rage I tensed my upper body into a most muscular pose. All my veins were popping out, and I looked like a road map. I was told to settle down.

I finished undressing until all I wore was a band of gold. I was told to hand it over. I always stated that when the ring was put on my finger it was not meant to be taken off. I must admit I did take it off when I went on dates. I now told them they would have to kill me before they'd get it off my finger. "Hand it over, Tunney," I was ordered.

I screamed to about six of them, "This is all I have left of my marriage and life, and it stays on my finger." By now I was in fighting position and ready to take on the bunch of them. I must have looked strange, as I was naked. I was sucking in great quantities of air and pumping up my muscles in order to psyche myself up mentally to do battle. I knew of the power of the mind and had trained mindfully in order to achieve the great strength I possessed. "Mind over Metal" was my motto at the gym, and I had proven it by bench-pressing a free weight of 225 pounds for thirty continuous repetitions, bench-pressing a single repetition of 380 pounds and squatting 390 pounds, all at a body weight of 180 pounds. I had achieved other feats of endurance, all because I trained my mind along with my body. Also, all the years of being physically abused had built up a tolerance to pain to the point that I was impervious to physical pain. So here I was, ready to do battle.

I was cursing and voicing my objections to removing my wedding band while maintaining a psychological advantage over these guys. I did feel kind of stupid carrying on like this in my birthday suit, but I didn't give a care. Finally I took off my band of gold and threw the ring across the room. I told them to pick it up. Well, I ended up picking the ring up.

They had by now decided to put me in solitary confinement after I threatened to kill myself. Like nine years previously, I was given one of those tear-proof baby-doll gowns to put on. I told them I wasn't going to wear that thing. I was then taken naked to some part of this jail and tossed into a segregation cell. I'd sworn I'd never end up here alive, and here I was. A blanket and gown were thrown in, and then the door was slammed shut and locked. I was now yelling insanely just like old times. Before when I was imprisoned I had nothing. Now I had a good job, a beautiful and well-appointed apartment, and I suppose somewhat of a future. This was just as had been foretold in the past, when I wanted to sell my soul in return for freedom from jail. I was to be freed and achieve everything, then lose it and go to hell.

I wanted to die. Right then and there, just like nine years before, I vowed to starve myself to death in this hell hole. How life can come back to haunt you! I would die in a jail cell. It was as if nine years had never passed. I had overcome almost every obstacle to finally have a good job. I was going crazy. In my cell was a mattress, a blanket, a baby-doll gown and a toilet that had to be flushed from outside the cell. They didn't want anyone to overflow the john. This was my death cell.

Every time a guard came by I told him to get lost. Because I was thought to be suicidal I was checked on much too frequently. Soon I was like a freak in a circus. Everyone stopped in passing to see a real live psycho. I was sure putting on quite the performance. I was at war within myself like never before. I refused to eat my meal when it was brought to me.

That night I didn't sleep, and over the next couple of days I kept up my psychotic madness, hardly slept and never ate. How I missed Diana. How I wanted to be free of this fence-hopping sexual madness. The thoughts of my homosexual tendencies were eating me alive. I couldn't live if I was to be gay. I couldn't speak to anyone about my problems, so I had to always battle it out within my mind.

I think it was on the third day that I got an idea how to kill myself in this solitary cell. I figured with my strength and ingenuity I could tear up the supposedly untearable mattress and braid a rope. I could then strangle myself. There was no way I could tear the blanket or the gown, which I still wasn't wearing.

In actuality, it wasn't very difficult to find a weak section of the fabric covering the mattress. Once I had started the tear, the rest was easy. I made three strips about one and a half inches in width and the length of the mattress. I then braided them together, and soon I had a rope about five feet long. The torn side of the mattress was now face down, and no one would know I now had a rope. I was hungry from the days without food or drink and knew I could only live about seven days without these essentials of life.

I had been given a New Testament to read and was reading it quite a bit, but nothing was sinking in. As the time came and went, I decided it was time to attempt to kill myself. I figured that if I psyched myself up I'd be able to virtually break my neck in the process of self-strangulation. I sat Indian style on the cold concrete floor. My bare ass was chilled, to say the least. I went into a deep self-induced hypnotic state of mind to summon up the strength to strangle myself. I don't know how long I was sitting there, but soon a guard was banging on the few-inch-square window to break my concentration. I heard and let on I didn't.

After a few minutes there were a few guards taking turns peering at me like a freak in a sideshow. All the while I was going deeper into a state of mental madness. I was silent and had brought my heart rate down as low as possible. My body was totally relaxed while my mind was alive and infuriated. I heard them talking about me knowing martial arts, because of the incident when I was being checked in. I had every one of them terrified of me. In a trance-like state, I stood up and went through my martial arts type movements. I did this to psyche myself up more. If they wanted a show, they'd get one.

I was now psyched up, and my adrenaline was pumping. Now was the time. I let out a cry of deep emotional torment and asked them if they wanted to see me snap my own neck. I stood naked before them and retrieved my handmade rope from under the mattress. I held it in front of myself for their eyes to see. I threatened them with it and told them that if anyone tried to come in and take it from me I'd kill them with my own bare hands. I'm sure they believed me, as they made no attempt to come in. All the while I was psyching myself up in case they tried. I yelled at them, "Have you ever seen anyone kill himself with his own strength?" I told them I could break a neck with one blow if I put all my psychic powers into one arm. They watched in amazement, one at a time, through the tiny window.

I now stood with my feet shoulder width apart and held an end of the rope in each hand. I knew that if I succeeded in my death wish, they would have lots of questions to answer as to how someone in segregation could make a rope in order to use it as a weapon or against himself or others. After all, I was put in there because I was suicidal.

I wrapped the rope around my neck. With all the power I could physically and psychologically muster, I proceeded to tighten the rope. I was totally psyched out now and had no realization as to where I was. I let out one last blood-curdling scream and then pulled the rope tighter and tighter. I swear I could feel my neck ready to crack when I collapsed into a pile on the concrete floor...unconscious.

When I came to, some of the goofs were around me. "Watch out! Watch out for this psycho," someone said. I was then left alone to drown some more in my self-perpetuated misery, which I blamed on Vickey's mother. My mattress and rope had been taken, and now I would have to sleep on the cold concrete.

Someone was peering at me through the small window. I told him to get me out of there and let me go home or else I'd go crazy—as if I hadn't already gone over the edge. I'm telling you, the battle inside of me had never been so violent as now. "Get me out of here! Get me out of here!" I screamed repeatedly. Man, I was hungry, thirsty and tired from next-to-no sleep. I wasn't going to give in this time. I was determined to die.

That night I hardly slept, as the concrete was not the greatest comforter. Nor was the Bible I was reading off and on. I wished I was at home, even if I had to be alone.

It was now the fourth day of complete mental madness of the first degree. I decided that I should write about myself a bit, so that when I died, which would be in a few days if I kept up this self-starvation, someone would at least have an idea of what drove me over the edge. So I asked for a pencil and some paper and began to write a short synopsis of my life. Although I wrote a bit, I left out the most serious of my problems. My sexual hang-ups, the root of my identity crisis, would be omitted.

What is to follow is that piece of writing, rewritten from the original on August 13, 1987. I am completely silent as I write out this synopsis. Ironically as I write this I am in a segregation cell, but with a 100 percent plus improved attitude. Two years have passed. I was in total mental confusion and great suffering as I wrote those original pages, so things aren't all chronologically correct. This is the day the title of this book came to mind.

---

Diana and I were in love. I have never been so in love. By December 1983, it was wonderful. We had a wonderful Christmas. Life was amazing, my job was going great, I was in the money. I felt I was part of her family; everything was changing so fast. We were in love, but I was still guilt-ridden because of my past. Diana didn't know about it, just vaguely. She saw me as I was then—hard working, a non-drinker and non-smoker, health addict, super positive, over-confident, etc.

After six months of dating, we decided to get married. We told her parents, and that's when trouble began. I couldn't phone her or visit her place, etc. We still wanted to get married, even without her parents' consent.

Next came what I dreaded most of all. Telling my fiancée, the person I dreamed of having, whom I loved the most, about my past. It was hard, because I knew she might change her mind, and I loved her. I would understand if she did, but she didn't. I was so happy but so scared of getting hurt, but when we had dinner and I gave her an engagement ring, it was wonderful. We were getting married on June 9, 1984.

Diana was turning nineteen, and we had a surprise planned for her at a dance. It was great. I was trying to be everything to her, a nice person, and was feeling loved for the first time in my life. I was always on a natural high.

Diana finished school in May. We were getting ready for our wedding. We knew her immediate family wasn't going to be there. It wasn't easy on her; she was young and leaving home was a big step. We were getting married in a civil ceremony. Both of us never wanted to get married like that, but we loved each other.

On June 8 we moved everything of hers to our place. Her family was upset. I understood, I thought, even though I was never loved. She stayed at a friend's house that night.

June 9 was a beautiful day. I rented a Lincoln Continental and a tuxedo. Diana was the most beautiful bride anyone would want. We were getting married by Reverend J.D. Moore, whom I had met at the gym. He had counselled us on marriage. He is a wonderful person. When we got married, a strange feeling came over me as we were joined as man and wife. I was the happiest I had ever been in my entire life. Our honeymoon was great. As I write this letter, we were to be on our second one. It hurts to know how things can change.

We were married nine months before she left. She was a perfect wife; none could be better. I, on the other hand, was not living up to my promises. I started to get selfish; I spent too much time at work. I became the best salesperson in our department. I was working on the social club at work. We both worked there full-time. We saw each other twenty-four hours a day. I worked on commission, and I saw my paycheques getting bigger, $400 to $1,300 a week. I wanted more. We paid off our debts by January 1985.

I wasn't giving my wife the attention she needed. I loved her, but I didn't really know how to love. Diana made our house a home, while I kept buying us material things. In February 1985 I closed a $30,000 sale. Thirty TVs and thirty VCRs. One sale, $1,500 in commission. I worked even harder. Even though we worked together, I hardly saw her. I didn't make the time. I wanted too much, too fast. Because I only thought I knew about love, I destroyed our marriage.

In the middle of March, I came home from work to find out she had left. I was devastated. I haven't talked to her since. I didn't sleep for days. I went to her work—she had changed jobs three weeks before she left. I saw her leave work with her mother. I was angry. I followed them. It was then that I went crazy and tried to die by destroying the car in an accident. It didn't work. I got charged with criminal negligence.

Now three months later I am in jail again. I promised I would die if I ever went to jail again. But I am too smart to give up my life.

---

"But?"

It was back to the mental madness in this solitary confinement cell. I had definitely gone over the edge. It was now the fifth or sixth day of this anguish. I was now drinking some water and begging them to send me to a hospital where I could get some much-needed help. I don't know how they swung it, but I was told I would finish the rest of my thirty days at Whitby Psychiatric Hospital and I would leave in the morning. The thirty-day sentence was really only twenty days, as they take one-third off for good behaviour, which you can lose. My release date was either July 16 or 17. I ate my first meal afterwards and told them if they were lying, I'd resume starving myself.

Sure enough, the next morning, I was dressed, cuffed and shackled, hand and foot, and taken by van to the Whitby facility. I figured anything would be better than jail.

# Chapter 26

In less than one hour we drove up to the admitting office. From the onset of driving onto the hospital grounds, I thought I had arrived at a lakeside resort. It was on the shores of Lake Ontario. The well-manicured lawns ran to the edge of the bluffs overlooking the expansive waters. This place was built architecturally, in my opinion, as an upscale tourist resort. Instead of one main hospital, there were a series of numbered two-storey buildings.

I was taken into the administrative building and was told to wait in the waiting area. I was offered milk and accepted. At this point I was still cuffed and shackled. It wasn't until I was booked in that the correctional officers took off the restraints and left. I was taken by a security guard to the building where I would be staying. I was further processed and told of the rules and regulations. Although I wasn't in jail, all the exit doors were locked and we could only go outside if we had ground privileges. If I remained well mannered and behaved, I could have outside privileges in a few days. Also, this place was co-ed, although none of the females were very attractive. I was shown where my bed was in the men's dorm. There was a lounge area where we could sit and watch TV. Well, all this sure as hell beat jail.

I noticed that some of the people were very disturbed, and I felt sorry for them. I could handle being here for a couple of weeks. My death wish that had been induced by the jail setting was gone from my mind. Over the first few days I was tested and counselled by staff. Reverend Moore had brought me some clothes from home as he was taking care of my place. I had given him a key, and he was feeding my rabbits and doves.

By now I had befriended every one of the patients there and was being as nice as possible to these unfortunate people. I ordered in pizza and pop for us sometimes. I was given ground privileges, and we would go for walks to the beach that adjoined the property. In all, I was learning a great deal about the suffering people go through emotionally. Some of these people were lonely and tormented, each fighting some battle within himself or herself, as was I.

I wasn't being honest with the doctors and staff as I never mentioned anything about my personality disorder associated with my sexual identity. I just blamed everything on my rotten childhood. I would just work out my problems by myself. I was reading the New Testament daily and praying constantly that someday I would be free to be me.

There was one person there who was having great personal difficulties. C.H. was a young girl about Diana's age. She had been dumped by her boyfriend and had gone a little over the emotional edge. She seemed quite unstable, more so than me. As we got to know each other, I learned that she had nowhere to go after being released from there. In fact, she couldn't be released unless she had an address to go to. I figured she just needed someone to show a little concern for her. I decided that now was as good a time as any to help the less fortunate. After thinking about it for a couple of days and weighing the pros and cons, I told C.H. she was welcome to share my apartment with me until she got straightened out.

Now in making this offer, I knew that if Diana ever found out about this she wouldn't understand. If there was any chance of her coming back, that might change as well. My feelings of compassion towards the people I had met there were very strong, and I would take the chance.

C.H. accepted after we discussed the terms and such. She would pay half the rent, and I would give up my bedroom and sleep in the den on the sectional sofa, which was plenty large enough. I didn't know if I was doing the right thing and might end up regretting my decision. At least I wouldn't have to sell my body for the extra spending money I didn't truly need.

At this point I didn't know if I had my job or not. When I had phoned work and spoke with the new store superintendent, I had just been told to come into work when released to discuss the matter. The lady who had hired me was now working down at the Jarvis Street head office. So I was left hanging in limbo about my job for the time being. I was sure I would be fired.

Well, the day finally came that I was released. C.H. was leaving as well. We took the local transit to the GO bus station, the GO bus to the GO train station in Pickering, the train into Toronto, and a TTC bus to my place. I was now having second thoughts about my philanthropic gesture as I wouldn't have my privacy. Oh well, I would just have to make do with this change. I rented a car, and C.H. and I went to her mother's place to pick up her belongings.

The following day I finally got up enough nerve to go into work and find out about my job. I went up to the store superintendent's office and waited until he was free. I made small talk with the secretary in the meantime. I was called into the office and took a seat across from the manager. We spoke for a few minutes and then I was told I was being let go. We talked some more until I convinced him to give me another chance. Now he had to talk it over with head office.

I was called back in and I was told that head office had already terminated me and the decision was final. Tears welled up from within and I rose, left the office and then the store. Outside and on the edge of the mall property, I sat on the grass and bawled my eyes out. My job was everything to me. I loved going to work each day. I didn't want to keep being an escort. Sure, my UIC benefits would pay the bills, but I had a lifestyle to keep up. It goes to show, no matter how good you might be at your job, you are always replaceable. I knew in my heart I had been the best salesperson in the store although I was hindered at times because of my personal crisis.

Back at home, C.H. was out, and I just cried the afternoon away, drowning my sorrows in alcohol. No one in this world knew the struggles I faced every day within. I now had only two choices. One, to get another sales job ASAP, or two, to run an escort business full-time, which I didn't want to do. I was determined to get a job. I was losing everything, including my mind, which in some respects I had already lost. How I missed Diana; she was always there on my mind.

Over the next few days I went through the want ads, applied for UIC benefits, went out with some clients or acquaintances, and lay around in the sun bronzing my deteriorating sculptured physique. One night I had stepped off the elevator on my way out on a business date and almost ran into a very sexy young lady. We smiled at each other casually in passing. I left the building, hoping she lived here and I might see her again.

The week after I had been let go from Sears, an ad appeared in the *Toronto Star* in the employment section for a salesperson in the electronics department of The Bay at Fairview Mall. I thought, *What luck*, as the mall was just across the way and I could see it from my balcony. I knew I would get the job easily as I was confident in my sales ability and had a proven track record to show them. I went and applied and within a couple of days was interviewed. At the time of the interview, I was also told the same position was available at The Bay in Oshawa. I mentioned to the interviewer that I might be more interested in the position in Oshawa as I could use a change from this neighbourhood. This was even better now; I would have two chances at employment. I figured from what I was told that I could earn more money working at The Bay than at Sears.

Well, at least my spirits were raised, and I couldn't believe my luck. The following day I rented a car and drove to Oshawa and applied for the position. Unfortunately no one was available to interview me at that time. I drove around Oshawa, checking out the city to see if I might like living there. It seemed like a nice place, and I figured it would be okay. I sure needed a change, and I figured a complete change was in order.

At home I was having problems with C.H. She really was a messed-up young lady, and I wanted her to leave. I finally told her to pack her things and get out. She told me she wasn't going, and we ended up arguing. I didn't need this junk, and I physically threw her out. I told her to have someone pick up her things ASAP.

Believe it or not, she returned shortly with the cops. I told the police that she had to leave as I couldn't handle this mixed-up broad living here. They all left, and C.H. returned with a police escort some time later and removed her belongings. I didn't want her to be on the streets, but having two screwed-up people under the same roof was not for me. I had enough problems of my own to deal with. So much for trying to help someone out.

A few days went by, and I was interviewed in Oshawa by The Bay. I would have to come back again for an interview with the sales manager. In the meantime, I looked around for other jobs just in case. I was also escorting much too often and couldn't stand it any more.

One afternoon I saw that pretty young lady whom I had practically run into that day when getting off the elevator. She was out back of the apartment building suntanning in a bikini with another young lady. I was suntanning myself, and as I watched her, I knew I wanted to meet her. She was a small girl in stature and very sexy.

Well now I was suntanning daily, and one day we ended up talking. Her name was Julie, and the girl she was with was her sister. I met her sister's boyfriend as well. The three of them lived together on the fifth floor. That was about it until a couple of days later when again we talked outside while suntanning. This day Julie was with a friend named Susie. We got to talking about this and that, and I ended up finding out that Julie and Susie were looking for an apartment to share together. Julie's sister and boyfriend were going to be moving to, of all places, Oshawa on the first of September. Julie had the nicest French accent as she had just moved from Quebec about a year earlier.

I had been thinking that if I worked in Oshawa I would sublet my apartment fully furnished for one year and I would share an apartment with someone. This way I could live and work in Oshawa for a year and then decide if I wanted to move permanently out there. I mentioned to the girls that I might be subletting my apartment if I got the job in Oshawa. The girls came up to the apartment and agreed immediately to sublet it if I was to move. When the girls found out the place would be furnished they were really surprised as they had no furniture of their own.

That afternoon I asked Julie for a date, and she accepted. That evening we went out with Susie and some of their friends, dining and dancing. Well, things might be turning out okay after all. Whenever I was out on non-business dates, however, I was full of guilt and wished I was with Diana. Yes, I missed Diana immensely, and I hoped I would get the job in Oshawa so that I could embark on a new start. Away from the fast pace of Toronto, away from the gay bars, the memories.

Julie and I kept dating, and I stopped hooking, as I had some scruples. One day during the first week of August, Julie and I spent the day in Niagara Falls and had a wonderful time. At this point Julie didn't know I was married, as I was in the habit of taking off my wedding band when I went out and putting my ring back on when I came home. One day I forgot, and Julie asked about my wife, and I explained that Diana had left me. She said it was okay, and as long as it was really over we could still see each other. I assured Julie the marriage was over. In my heart I longed for my wife, and every minute I spent with Julie I was wishing it was with Diana.

I had another interview in Oshawa and was quite sure I would get the job. I didn't know what was taking them so long to make a decision as two weeks had passed since I first applied. I was looking for a place to live in Oshawa but was having difficulty finding suitable accommodations. I was now thinking of buying a car and was checking out the car lots. I had decided to buy a small four-cylinder car because I would be driving a lot and would have only one income. I really wanted a Lincoln Town Car but knew the maintenance costs would be high.

During the second week of August I received notice that I had the job and would start Saturday August 10, only three days away. Great! I had only been unemployed for three weeks. Now I had to get a car as I would have to drive back and forth to Oshawa until the first of September, when the girls would be taking over the apartment. I picked out a car, and what a machine it was, a brand new 1985 Turbo Shelby Charger by Chrysler. Standard equipment included a sunroof, rear window louvres, ground effects package, special paint job, upgraded stereo and much more. The saleslady took me for a test drive as I didn't know how to drive a stick shift. A female friend of mine helped me arrange financing as I needed a co-signer.

On Friday I picked up my car and managed to bunny-hop the car across North York to the Seneca College parking lot at Finch and Don Mills Road. I practised driving a five-speed for a couple of hours, and once I got the hang of it I was having the time of my life. I took the sunroof off, cranked the stereo up, and went cruising in this new sports coupe. Well, I now had a new toy to play with. Let me tell you, when the turbo charger kicks in you take off like a bat out of hell. I couldn't believe the power this four-cylinder engine was capable of producing. I was cruising the Don Valley Parkway that night at over 120 mph. I loved this car already. I had also just had the best day since Diana left.

Saturday August 10: My first day at work went okay. I was doing the same job at The Bay as I had done at Sears, only the people were different. All I would have to do is get used to selling a different line of electronic equipment and learn a different company's policies.

My first couple of weeks went by okay, but as I got to know how things ran—or didn't run, I realized there was no way I could sell as well here as at Sears. The main problem was that I couldn't satisfy my customers the way I could at Sears. I wasn't allowed to make home deliveries, the ordering system sucked, and I couldn't assure the customers when they would receive their purchases if I had to order a product. Management of the company on the whole was mickey mouse as opposed to Sears, from my view anyway.

As August drew to a close, I didn't want to live out there as I now had a car and the twenty-minute drive wasn't so bad. Why, people in Toronto took an hour or more getting to and from work just driving in Toronto. I was driving against the traffic, and getting to Oshawa and vice versa was a breeze in more ways than one. I raced back and forth daily trying to set speed records. I now had a stopwatch hanging from the rear-view mirror and a notepad on the dashboard to keep track of my runs. On some trips I averaged about 100 mph on the highway part of the drive.

Since starting to work again, I had stopped doing pills and getting drunk. I was again working out regularly, and I was feeling much better psychologically. I now considered myself to be Julie's boyfriend. I did, however, have one major problem. I had two girls moving in September 1, and they had already paid first and last months' rent.

I told Julie and Susie that I was having a hard time finding a place in Oshawa, although I had already given up looking. I asked them if I would be able to stay until I found a place and that sleeping on the couch would be no problem. As we were all friends now, they said yes. So by September 1 they were moved in. I had to get rid of some of the furniture in the den as it had to be converted back into a second bedroom. I didn't want to do it, but I had made a commitment to these young ladies.

I also had to get rid of my two rabbits that lived in their pen on the balcony. This was very upsetting to say the least. I drove through the park by Edwards Gardens in Don Mills, found an out of the way spot, and tearfully bid goodbye. They had lived on the balcony year round and were as acclimatized as wild rabbits.

Saturday, August 31: After work I spent the night with Julie at her sister's new house in Oshawa. I had been attending church regularly and missed this Sunday because of not being at home. Julie missed attending her church as well. Both Julie and Susie professed to be Christians and always went to church and read their Bibles daily.

After another week or so, the girls figured out that I didn't really want to move, and we talked about it. They were pissed off at me and accused me of setting up this whole scam so that I would have the rent paid. We argued, and Julie really got pissed off at me. I told them I'd sleep in the car or on the balcony where the rabbits had lived. So for the next week or so I slept some nights in my car and some on the balcony.

One night after work there was a dance in the cafeteria of the store. I got a little intoxicated and spent the night asleep in my car in the mall parking lot. Needless to say I was not late for work the next morning.

All of this frustration was again driving me deeper into my own misery. It was pretty bad. I couldn't even live in my own place, which wasn't really mine according to my arrangements. Legally I had every right to the apartment, but morally not as I had promised the girls a furnished place for a term of one year.

By the end of September Julie and I had made up and the three of us were now living together. I was not only sleeping in the apartment but with Julie. We seemed to be getting along better than ever. We were doing the things I had promised to do with Diana. I made as much time for Julie as possible. Emotionally I had levelled out somewhat.

At work I was disappointed and was now in negotiations with Super Fitness pertaining to a sales manager position. An agreement had been reached that I would work part-time in sales until the end of January 1986. This was to see if I would like working for them. Also I didn't want to miss the mega bucks I'd make during the Christmas season at The Bay. The management at Super Fitness were talking about me earning upwards of $50,000-plus per annum as a manager. Those numbers were perfect. It seemed natural that as a fitness- and sales-oriented person that I would do well.

So now I was working seven days a week. On Tuesdays, my day off at The Bay, I was going through the training process of Super Fitness Inc. On Sundays I was working 9 to 5 at a club learning their ways of business. On top of both jobs I had to do my fitness training. I was very busy, to say the least, and now couldn't attend church. Julie was pleased with me working so hard to try and better myself financially.

Throughout October things were seemingly okay, although I was still in constant mental turmoil. By the end of the month, things were catching up to me, the seven-day work week, etc. I would still have to keep this schedule up for three months more. During the last week of October Julie was off from her job and went to visit a brother in Montreal, which left me alone with Susie, the other roommate. Julie would return late Halloween night.

Thursday October 31, 1985: It was Halloween, the last day of October. At The Bay we were told we could work in costume. I was to work from 1 until 9:30 p.m. I spent the morning at Super Fitness working out, then dressed into my costume and went to work. I was dressed as a "Chippendale" nightclub waiter-dancer. I wore a pair of grey leather shoes, matching socks, and a pair of grey parachute pants. I wore no shirt but a pair of cuffs cut from a white shirt and a collar cut from the same. I had on a pair of gold cufflinks, and the matching tie pin was pierced into the left side of the shirt collar. A grey bowtie set off my neckline. In both my left ear and left side of the bowtie were diamond earrings. On my head was my trend-setting Panama hat, and shading my eyes was a pair of Ray Ban sunglasses. Since I couldn't be in the store barechested, I wore a white bomber style jacket, which was zipped up to my navel. In all I looked like something out of a fashion magazine. The women working in the store were in awe of my physique, and I posed for several pictures.

Now this outfit was perfect for me in more ways than one. I had worn similar outfits before during some of my business dealings (sex for sale). In fact, this getup was tuned down somewhat, but it fit in with my work. Since I worked in the electronics department, I spent

411

the day playing the part of a male dancer to a tee as the stereos played in the background. As customers went by I would do a little dance routine. I was even told I should dance for a living. Ha ha—if they only knew I had done this for money.

Julie was due back from Quebec that evening on the train, and I should have gone to pick her up. Instead I had decided to have some fun. After the store closed at 9:30, I sped from Oshawa to downtown Toronto and the Yonge Street strip. Halloween in Toronto is awesome—anything goes, and you see it all. I cruised up and down Yonge Street with the sun roof off. I passed by Julie's place of work at a car rental company just north of Bloor on Yonge. I was glad she wasn't working that night or she would have sure been mad.

At every red light or whenever I was stopped (the traffic was at a crawl), I would pop through the roof and climb on top of my car and do a strip routine of sorts. The girls around were going crazy at the sight of this muscular stud dancing atop his sports car. They were begging to have their pictures taken with me, as most everyone brings cameras downtown on Halloween. I was holding up traffic as girls climbed atop my car with me to pose for pictures. I felt as if I were a movie star and loved the attention.

I had offers of a one night stand from several women throughout the night but declined because of my relationship with Julie. I cruised the strip and at times drove by the gay bars. A couple of times I stopped in at one of them to check the place out. As usual I had numerous offers of companionship and could have made a few hundred dollars had I wanted. I still didn't know why I kept coming into these places though. What the hell was I searching for?

Later as I cruised the strip, holding up traffic and posing for pictures, a cop got the notion to give me a ticket for driving without a seatbelt. I had just left a twenty-foot patch of rubber on the pavement. I received a $53 ticket. Oh well, I was having a great time.

Around 2 a.m. I drove home and then crawled into bed beside Julie. She was upset that I wasn't home when she arrived. I told her I had gone out with some friends from work after the store closed.

Saturday, November 2, 1985: Julie and I awoke. I had to work today, while Julie had the day off and was going to visit her sister in Oshawa. I drove her to her sister's and then went to work, which was only ten minutes away. After work I went back to Julie's sister and boyfriend's place for supper. Later we decided that the four of us would go to a bar called Stairways in Whitby. We drove our own cars to Whitby, waited in line, and finally got in around 11. I was tired and had to get up at 8 the following morning to go to work at Super Fitness. I ran into some friends and flirted with a gorgeous young lady who worked at the gym also. I snuck away from Julie on occasion to talk with her.

As the time went by, I noticed Julie smoking, and that upset me. Prior to her going to Quebec she had stopped. Cigarette smoking disgusted me to no end. Well, I was slightly intoxicated and angry. I broke a couple of glasses, which almost got me into a fight with a stranger. The four of us then left, and Julie and I headed for Toronto at over 100 mph. Julie hated it when I drove fast as much as I hated it when she smoked. She sat silent for the duration of the drive. At home we slept apart, and still not a word was said to each other.

Sunday, November 3: I went to work at Super Fitness from 9 to 5. Back at home Julie and I argued, and it was decided that she and Susie would move out. I had paid the rent for November, as Julie and Susie had paid September and October. I was pissed off and got drunk.

The next day Julie was living at her sister's in Oshawa. Susie would stay, as she had nowhere to go at the moment. I was fed up with women for sure now. When Julie came a couple of days later to pick up her things, I was drunk, and I ended up throwing my $200 Italian chess set and a beer bottle through the balcony windows, shattering two of them.

Between that first week of November and the 15th, my drinking and popping 222s with codeine was increasing. I wasn't on prescription drugs, so I was using the 222s to get high. Susie had moved out, and I was now on my own. I was high at work on both jobs the whole week of the 11th to the 15th. Man, I could handle working seven days a week. I was also escorting some clients and had stopped working out.

On Friday the 15th I had been popping 222s all day and was stoned. I had decided to enter a dance-strip contest at a gay bar just to win an easy $50. I had always won any contests I entered. I got off work at 9:30, and the contest was to start at 10:30. This was just enough time for me to speed from Oshawa to Toronto, change at home, and then drive downtown.

As I sped home I was stopped for speeding. Luckily

I had just slowed down a bit as I knew where the radar traps were. I received a $21 speeding ticket, the second ever. The first had been for over $100, the day after I bought this speed machine. Anyway, now half my earnings would be spent.

I sped home, changed into the outfit I had worn on Halloween, and headed downtown. As I had figured, I won the $50 in the strip contest, and then I earned another $100 for a private session at some fag's house. I was quite drunk by then, to say the least. Man, I was disgusted with myself. As I fell asleep at home that night, I didn't know that the next day would be the beginning of a new chapter in my life. I hated myself for what I did and thought.

Saturday, November 16, 1985: Dawn of a new and living hell.

I woke up with a hangover and late. I had to be at work at 9 and it was already 8. I looked outside and it was snowing, the first real snowfall of the year. There was no way I would make it to Oshawa on time. I hurriedly ate and dressed. Outside in the frigid air I cleaned the snow off my sleek sports coupe. I let the engine warm up before I started off. I wouldn't be making an attempt at a speed record today.

I drove out to the on-ramp of the Don Valley Parkway, a block away. The traffic was backed up, and I had to get off the Parkway at the first exit to get on the 401 eastbound. I decided to drive along the shoulder of the road. The snow was blowing, and the visibility was impaired. I could see up ahead the tail lights of a parked car on the shoulder. I would have to get back into the stopped traffic.

The tail lights were those of an OPP cruiser. Never had I seen the cops parked here before. I was stopped, and a female cop came to my window and said I was going to be ticketed $53 for driving on the shoulder of the road. She also stated I could be ticketed for not having a front license plate on the car. I was mad, two tickets in less than twelve hours. So much for half my earnings last night.

I finally got onto the 401 eastbound and was quite enraged as it was now 9 o'clock. I said, "Forget this, I'm not going to work," and took the next exit and made my way home. At home I popped about ten 222s so I could get high off the codeine and drank some wine. At about 10 o'clock I drove to Fairview Mall, a street away. I went to the wine store and bought three magnums of cheap wine. At the drugstore I picked up a bottle of 222s containing 100 tablets. I popped some of the 222s. I drove back home and by 11 a.m. I was pissed drunk and stoned. I was wallowing in my misery. I didn't care if I lived; I just didn't give a care. I was just a messed-up mental case going nowhere. What did I have to live for?

Saturday, November 16, to Friday, November 22: I did nothing at all except drink and pop 222s. I didn't work at either The Bay or Super Fitness, nor did I even call in sick. I was totally wiped out physically and mentally and deteriorating rapidly. I only left the apartment to buy a minimum of food and purchase wine, beer and more 222s. I didn't answer the phone or door. I parked my car away from the building so no one would think I was home. I listened to music or the TV through a pair of headphones. I was usually dressed in female lingerie and was fantasizing about being someone other than me.

By Tuesday my hearing was becoming impaired because of the abuse of the 222s. I was taking at least fifty per day. Every second of every day was torment at the maximum. Wednesday to Thursday, things just got worse. I was losing, or had already lost, touch with reality.

Friday, November 22: I awoke and feebly attempted to pull myself together and didn't drink or take pills. Sounds were barely audible, and I couldn't hear the phone ring unless I was within five feet. I decided to go to work and see if I still had a job. Man, I was totally screwed-up. I tried to gather myself together and in the afternoon somehow drove to Oshawa. Man, the sounds of the world seemed strange; every sound was abstract. At The Bay I spoke with the store manager, and he could tell I was still high although I had taken nothing that day. I was told to go home and to come into work tomorrow. I managed to drive home, but man, was I in another world.

At home I had to have a drink and then it was some more 222s. Within an hour I was wiped out again. I never did make it to work on Saturday and said, "Forget it. I'm going to die. Forget the whole world."

I spent Sunday, Monday, Tuesday, and Wednesday in this continuous downhill spiral and knew the end was near. My stomach was in constant pain from the several hundred 222s I had ingested over the past two weeks. My hearing was almost gone, but I could hear my thoughts as clear as a bell.

During those days I started thinking about one last great vacation. I knew I would have no job now and everything would be gone soon. All I wanted was to die and put an end to this life of non-stop tragedies. I knew I could sell all my belongings and scrape together several thousand dollars in order to take that one last vacation. I had always wanted to go to Florida to lie on the beaches, swim in the ocean, see the space centre and everything else Florida has to offer. I would just sell everything, pack up and drive to Florida. After all my money was gone, I would buy some good drugs and OD somewhere on a beautiful beach.

Thursday, November 28: With my decision made to die in Florida, I now had to liquidate all my assets. Some things were too valuable or sentimental to me to get rid of. I decided to give some of my things to Diana and Julie. I wrote up a will, stating what would go to whom. Of course my sister, Vickey, was included. I got in touch with Julie and told her she could have the majority of my furniture, since she had no furniture in her and Susie's new apartment, wherever that was. Julie said she and Susie would come by Saturday.

Saturday, November 30: I awoke and started popping 222s and drinking. By noon Julie and Susie arrived in a rented van to truck off their inheritance. Julie knew of my plans but didn't seem to care. They made two trips and trucked off my living room set, dining room set, part of my art collection, antiques, drapes, custom blinds, gold-plated telephone, plants, and an assortment of other choice valuables. In all they totalled several thousand dollars. I made her vow to never sell the art and antique writing desk, as they were to be family heirlooms. In fact she had a copy of my will and was to, upon my death, make sure my sister received some of my art and other valuables.

Julie spent the night with me in my near-empty apartment. We were both drunk and stoned. I guess it was her way of saying "Thanks, sucker." So much for Christian girls.

Sunday, December 1: I spent the day drunk and high on 222s. I was figuring out how to get as much money as possible for my final vacation. It had now been over two weeks that I had been on this permastone. This was just like ten years before, and I wasn't myself any more. I had regressed back into my teens. I was full of hate, anger, guilt, and the list goes on. I was still sinking deeper into infinite depths of despair. I just had to leave this damn world. Everything I had worked for was going or gone.

Monday, December 2: Drunk and stoned, although I was cutting back on the 222s so my almost-lost hearing would return. I went to Oshawa to get money owed me and returned some merchandise I had bought and received the cash back. In Toronto I returned my $1,000-stereo TV to Sears and had my account credited. I then took gift certificates, bought merchandise at one Sears store and returned it to another for cash. I drove to Diana's place and dropped off a letter and an eighteenth century reproduction of a Chinese decorative screen. Inlaid were ivory, jade and soapstone carvings, and it had cost several hundred dollars. I just left it by the garage door.

Tuesday, December 3rd: I stayed sober, although I had enough alcohol and drugs in me to keep me totally screwed-up. My mind was so screwed up that my speech was all scrambled. At Sears where I had worked I wrote some rubber checks, but who cared, I was going to die. By nightfall all my credit cards were over their limits and I had several thousand dollars. By 10 p.m. I was ready to leave on my great Florida getaway and stayaway.

At home I still had some belongings, stereo equipment, art and miscellaneous items. I left a will stating who was to get what, with my sister receiving most everything. I figured I'd drive all night and be in New York City the following morning. My car was loaded with clothes and such, including the pair of brass swans, the first present Diana had given to me. I was in tears as I turned the key in the apartment door for the last time. It hurt to leave, but I just had to do this. I had nothing and no one to live for.

# Chapter 27

The weather was cold, but the roads were clear as I sped away from my misery. I hadn't drank or popped pills that day so I wasn't in danger of causing a car accident. My hearing was still impaired though, and as I drove and listened to the music, everything seemed unreal.

I took the QEW to Niagara Falls. As I neared Niagara I ran into a dense fog as thick as pea soup. Rain was falling lightly. I picked up a hitchhiker, a resident of Niagara, who helped me along the highway. I dropped him off on Lundy's Lane and drove to the Canadian-American border.

Now on the American side, I tanked up with inexpensive gas and bought a road map. I had earlier in the day converted some Canadian money to American. I would exchange the rest in Florida.

I received directions to I-395, the state-owned highway that went into New York City. I-395 was what it stated, 395 miles long. The fog was very thick, and what I was hoping to be a five- or six-hour drive was going to take much longer. Already it was after 1 a.m. I drove throughout in the near blinding fog. Traffic was next to nil, and most of the time I drove behind truckers and let them be my guide. I tried to put the past on a mental hold as I wanted to enjoy my last days of life.

As dawn arrived, the fog was clearing up and I stopped at a truck stop, had a bite to eat, gassed up and grabbed a couple of hours' sleep in the front seat of my car. I set out again and didn't reach New York City until about noon. I drove through Harlem and received culture shock. As I drove downtown I passed by the Empire State Building, which was what I had wanted to see. I thought Toronto was a busy city, but it has nothing on New York except some semblance of sanity. New York was as off the wall as I was. "Total pandemonium." A drive by Central Park came next, and it looked peaceful enough.

Since it was now about 2 p.m. I decided I should get the hell out of the city before rush hour. I found my way back to the highway and passed Yankee Stadium. I now had to get to the New Jersey turnpike, then I-95 and the trip into Florida. Well, I found out that life here is always a rush hour, and as I drove the NJTP I realized that the DVP in Toronto was an expressway even during rush hour as a comparison.

For a few hours the pace was that of a snail, and my temper was flaring. At times I drove along the paved shoulder. Finally, past New Jersey, the highway opened up, and it was clear sailing in the 100-mile-an-hour range.

I drove most of the night and grabbed a few hours' sleep at a rest stop. I ate whenever I stopped for gas. On Thursday, December 5, I drove all day and was soon leaving the cold weather behind. The stereo was constantly playing my favourite tunes. My hearing was almost normal now, and I hadn't drank or popped 222s for three days. Psychologically I was feeling better because of the spring-like temperatures. The Christmas season wasn't on my mind as there was no snow. This was great as it felt like I had just skipped winter. I was cruising with the sunroof off and was racing cars as I sped along.

A tape got jammed in my stereo, so I had no music to listen to as even the radio wouldn't play with the tape jammed in. I had a ghetto blaster but no batteries. It was raining a bit that evening and I was still racing at 100 miles an hour, most notably against a Porsche 944. I slept that evening at a rest stop in Georgia. The Porsche had stopped there also.

Friday December 6: I awoke in the front seat of my car. The weather was sunny and warm. I spoke with the guy in the 944, who was a salesperson. He set out before me. It was about 8 a.m. and I was now in summer shorts. I couldn't believe I was here in summer attire in December. I felt like a new person in a new world, and I couldn't wait to be on the Florida beaches. Sometime later I crossed the Georgia-Florida border, and I couldn't believe the sights, the birds, swamps, palm trees, etc. The temperatures were in the seventies, and clear blue skies were overhead.

Now I had to decide where to go. As I drove across the state and along the endless ribbon of highway, I wished Diana was there with me. Other than that, I had put my problems into the recesses of my mind as I was too engrossed with the beauty of this place. This was better than I had seen on TV, and I loved it. Not a hint of Christmas was about.

I made it to Daytona around suppertime and didn't make it to the speedway. I was a little disappointed with this side of the state and decided to drive across to the Gulf side to St. Petersburg, via Tampa. By the time I made it to Tampa it was about midnight and I was tired, as I had been driving for the past sixteen hours except for pit stops. I got lost somewhere between Tampa and St. Pete's and I gave up on driving around after having a run-in with the cops. I was lost and getting pissed off. I had gotten on some toll road and off again and then somehow back on again. I told the female booth operator that I wasn't going to pay again because I was just going to turn around and get off the highway. She must have pushed a button, because a cop pulled up behind me. I ended up paying after some words about all the toll roads set up in the United States. I stated that any money I had saved on gas went to the toll roads. I paid and exited at the next ramp, and as it was late I decided to sleep in the car again.

Saturday, December 7: Finally I found my way into St. Petersburg, and the place was a picture of paradise come alive. *Yes, what a place to die in*, I thought. How I wished I wasn't there alone. The beach ran as far as the eye could see. As it was off-season, the beaches seemed quite empty. That was okay as I couldn't stand crowds anyhow.

I checked out rates at various motels and hotels and found suitable accommodation on the main strip. I paid a week's rent and unloaded the car. I placed the brass swans beside the bed. I was right on the beach, and my room was nice, like a bachelorette. The room had a small kitchen, bedroom-living area, bathroom, colour TV and air conditioning. An art-deco-style mall was almost directly across the street. The owners of the motel were retired Torontonians. I walked the beach and then went across to the mall to buy groceries, booze and 222s. I was surprised that I could buy beer right in the grocery store, and the price was right, so I stocked up.

At an adjoining drug store I was to find out that I couldn't buy 222s, as anything with codeine, a cocaine derivative, was not sold over the counter as in Canada. Now what would I do? I had only brought one bottle with me. I figured I would have to buy some street drugs when it came time for me to end my life in this tropical paradise. I also bought from another store ladies' stockings, garters and panties.

Back at the motel I drank some beer, popped 222s and dressed up in the women's garments. I lay on the bed flipping through some pornographic magazines and wishing I was a woman. The feelings of hate for myself were now again in the forefront of my mind. Although I was on the beach, I spent the rest of Saturday and all of Sunday drunk and stoned. I left the room only once or twice to take a short walk on the beach. I just wanted to drown my soul full of sorrow. I wished Diana or Julie was there with me for company. Then my thoughts would turn to homosexual deviations and I would be glad they hated me.

Again I was slipping into this madness of mental anguish and hereditary hatred. I had now run 1,500 miles away from home and was in another world. I was finding out there was no running away and the only way to cure my misery was to rip my mind right out of my screwed-up head! Yes, just cut away the part of my screwed-up brain that held the memories of the past.

Monday, December 9: Converted Canadian currency. Went to Chrysler dealership about busted stereo. No go without leaving car for several days. I bought a DC car adapter for my ghetto blaster so I could have music. I bought a new $60 panama hat. I checked out a Gold's Gym and met a cute girl, a resident of St. Pete's. Washed the car, swam in the ocean (Gulf of Mexico) and drank beer. Monday night I drove to Clearwater along Gulf Port Road. I drag raced parallel to the beach, just like I had seen in movies. Back at the motel before going to bed I sat on the empty beach and cried for an hour or so.

Tuesday, December 10: I phoned Julie, wired her flowers and a vase and mailed Diana a Christmas card. I was becoming more depressed, and death was always on my mind, maybe even driving my car off the road. I was drunk and high. I also ran out of 222s.

Wednesday, December 11: Went to Gold's Gym and met up with the attractive girl I had met. She asked me out as it was her birthday. I stayed sober all day. That evening we went out and about St. Petersburg to celebrate this young lady's birthday. In all I had a very pleasant evening and struggled to keep up the facade of happiness.

Thursday, December 12: Decided to check out Fort Lauderdale via Alligator Alley, which meant I had to cross the state of Florida. I woke up to another beautiful day. I was looking forward to driving the famed

Alligator Alley highway, which would take me through the Florida Everglades. After about an hour of driving and not yet along Alligator Alley I passed a BMW. The lady driver was older and very attractive. We flirted with each other as we drove side by side. The highway was quite our own, and we ended up drag racing. Man, this lady liked to drive fast, and we cruised at over 100 miles an hour. Since I had a few hours of driving ahead, this flirting and racing took away some of the boredom.

The lady's license plate read Georgia. We ended up pulling over and talked a bit. We were both dressed in summer attire, and as she stood beside me I was staring at a very beautiful lady. I always had a weakness for older women. She was going to Fort Lauderdale. We made a luncheon date to stop somewhere off the main highway. After lunch we stopped somewhere along Alligator Alley for a casual sexual encounter of the most erotic kind. The wildlife had nothing on this woman. On the highway again, we proceeded to race along the now two-lane highway. When we reached the end of the toll road at the end of Alligator Alley, we kissed each other goodbye.

I then started to drive into Fort Lauderdale but got lost as the main thoroughfare was under construction and I had to detour. I decided just to head back to St. Pete's and enjoy the scenery on the way back as I had been pleasantly distracted on my way across the state. Along the way back I stopped here and there to look for alligators to wrestle. Fortunately for the critters, none were seen, or they would have had to meet me, Alligator Randy. I did, however, see countless hundreds of birds of various species. I had noticed panther-crossing signs but saw no signs of the elusive Florida panther. Some areas around were sandy, like a small desert, so I drove my car around as if it was a dune buggy

At one point I drove along a trail that led into the forest. I had a small tent with me and contemplated camping out for a night here in the midst of the Everglades. If I wasn't so scared of the couple of snakes I had seen I would have.

Not a minute after I got back onto the highway I received a speeding ticket from a state trooper. Oh well, I wouldn't be around to pay it anyway. That day's trip into the interior of Florida is one I'll never forget. The sights were beautiful, the wildlife plentiful and the women as wild as all outdoors.

Friday the 13th: I was drunk all day, lay on the beach for a few hours and became more depressed. Thought of driving my car into something at maybe 100 mph or so. I couldn't have picked a better date, Friday the 13th. Friday night I drag raced in and about Clearwater and almost lost control a couple of times. Was told by a state trooper not to speed through the beach-front parking lot. Oh, Diana.

Saturday December 14: I woke up hung over in my female attire. I cruised a beach close by the motel and was warned again by a state trooper not to drag race. After noon, I was parked along a beach, and some guys were coming on to me. I met Joe and Scott and was invited to dinner in Tampa. *What the hell*, I thought, and Scott and I drove to my motel while Joe followed. I packed up some clothes and then was on my way. I followed Joe, who was driving a Nissan 330 ZX. Scott accompanied me. We raced from St. Pete's to Tampa in record time, I was told. We averaged almost 100 miles an hour, and at times I was no more than five feet away from Joe's car bumper. Talk about a death wish. I felt just like a NASCAR driver and loved the exhilarating rush as the adrenaline pumped through me.

At their home (they were lovers) we showered and changed for supper. I knew what I was getting into but didn't give a care. We took my car to the gay section of town. This was the main reason I accepted their invitation—I wanted to check out the gay community of a U.S. city. I would find to my disappointment that it was the same as Toronto's. After dinner we checked out a gay bar. We danced and drank the night away. I was dressed to the nines and was a hit as usual. I ended up spending the night in Tampa. Oh, Diana.

Sunday, December 15: I spent the day with Joe and Scott and the night again at the bar. I had now decided to fly back to Toronto to get more cash together as I wanted to enjoy this climate as long as possible.

Monday, December 16, 5 a.m.: I drove from Joe and Scott's to St. Pete's and cleared out of the motel. I left the money owing on the kitchen table as the place was closed. I drove back to Tampa to Joe and Scott's as I would be leaving my car at their place. By 9 a.m. they had gone to work and I was on my own. Since I was locked out, I had to pass the day away as my flight wasn't until about 7 p.m. I was nervous about flying. The only other time I had flown was back in 1976 when I was escorted by police in a Cessna after being released from jail at Monteith and flown back to Sudbury.

I passed the day driving around and in the early afternoon drove back to Joe and Scott's. I had already given my hosts a second set of keys, and I left my car in the drive. Since I still had hours to pass, I decided to walk to Tampa International, which was only ten or fifteen miles away. I was carrying one small suitcase and a flight bag. It was too hot to walk, and a few miles along I hailed a cab for the rest of the distance. At the huge airport, I bought my ticket and since it was about 3 p.m. or so I found a patch of grass and had a nap. At about 5, I watched the flights come and go and waited to see the Wardair 747, the plane I would be flying on, arrive from Toronto. I was totally alone and mentally lost but quite calm. At 6:30 I was ready to board after buying a 40-ounce duty free bottle of Beefeater Gin. Upon boarding I ran into the parents of a friend whom I had worked with at Sears.

At 7:00 p.m. or so I was nervous but ready for lift off. Once in the air all apprehension was gone and I relaxed. It was about 70 degrees when leaving Tampa. When we arrived in Toronto it was raining and just above freezing. I took a limo home to my apartment, which I had thought I would never return to. I was worried about an eviction notice as I hadn't paid the rent for December.

I walked sadly into my near-empty suite, which at one time was pretentious. There was a late-rent notice that had been slipped under the door. I drank some beer and popped some 222s and was soon flying and crying. The stereo, which was almost all I had left, was playing quite loud. I pulled my mattress from the bedroom to the near-empty living and dining area. I sat and wondered how to get together a few more thousand dollars so that I could fly back to Florida and finish this death wish scenario. I fell asleep in a drunken stupor and awoke to the reality of this living hell. Diana.

Tuesday, December 17: After being in Florida, waking up to this wintry and Christmas-type weather sure didn't do anything for me. I wanted to be back on the beaches of Florida once again and to never return. Now I had a problem! I figured the police might be looking for me because of the bad cheques at Sears.

That morning someone knocked on the door. I didn't answer and looked out the balcony window and waited to see who it was. Leaving the building was Bob, the security manager at Sears where I had worked. Well, I knew he hadn't got the police involved yet.

I later phoned my probation officer from a pay phone as I had no phone hooked up. I hadn't been in touch with him for a while and just wanted to keep him off my back. To my dismay I was informed that the police were looking for me to serve me with a summons to appear in court, pertaining to my probation order and Diana. Apparently she had informed the police that I was driving by her house and had left presents and such at the doorstep. I told him to arrange a court appearance. Later when I phoned him I was told that the date of December 23 was set up. It was to be before Christmas because Diana was worried that I'd show up at her family's place for Christmas.

I also phoned Julie at her work place. She was surprised that I was back in TO and alive, I'm sure. I spent the rest of the day drunk on wine and high on 222s and was slipping even farther into total despair. Now it looked like I could end up in jail for breach of probation.

Wednesday, December 18: Stayed in apartment—drunk and stoned. Diana.

Thursday, December 19: Stayed high and drunk all day. That night I saw Julie at Fairview Mall under the pretense of giving her a Christmas present. I had bought her a pair of diamond earrings with a rubber cheque. I told her I had to go to court on Monday the 23rd and asked her if she would celebrate Christmas with me on Sunday the 22nd as I might be in jail for Christmas once the police got their hands on me.

Friday, December 20 to Saturday, December 21: I stayed drunk and high on 222s, my hearing and speech becoming impaired. I left the apartment only to make phone calls from a pay phone and to buy some groceries for my Christmas celebration. I was totally screwed-up! Insane?

Sunday, December 22: Today I was to celebrate Christmas with Julie. I figured it would be my last Christmas alive so I wanted it to be special. Julie would be coming over about suppertime. I drank nothing during the day, but my body was still on overload. I decorated the near-empty apartment as nice as possible with the decorations and lights I had from the previous year. I was going to cook a full-course chicken dinner. Our dining room table would be the carpeted floor as I had given Julie my dining room set as an inheritance after my death.

Julie arrived, and we drank some wine. We had supper and then continued our little party. By midnight we were both drunk, and Julie opened the small gifts I had bought her. We continued to drink wine and ran out at about 2 a.m. As I had to go to court in the morning, I wanted this party to last all night long. I was totally depressed and thinking of death. I knew also I would never be in Julie's arms again. Two beautiful girls gone from my life in a year. About 3 a.m. I started into the 222s and also the forty ouncer of gin I had bought at Tampa International. By 6 a.m. I had taken over fifty 222s, drank a litre and a half of wine and at least ten ounces of gin straight up or slightly diluted, all of this in the past twelve hours. Now I knew that even if I made it to court, I would hardly be able to stand and surely be put in the slammer. I could hardly stand now.

At 7:30 or so, Julie had to help me start getting dressed and ready to go to court. I figured Diana would be there and she would see me in this screwed-up state. I didn't care; everything was gone now. *Just let me die*, that's all I thought. *Please!* I was still drinking gin and water and popping 222s like candy as Julie and I left the apartment. I had what was left of the gin mixed with water in the inside pocket of my winter trench coat. Julie was carrying an antique mantel clock I had given her to keep for me while I was in jail. I had left a note about what to do with the rest of my belongings. Julie already had the majority of my furniture.

We staggered to the bus stop and talked for a few moments. Julie promised to write me if I went to jail. I apologized for all the trouble I may have caused her and then we said our goodbyes. Julie was taking a bus north while I would go south. I staggered across the street to await a bus. I don't know how I was still standing. I was tired from the lack of sleep, and with all the alcohol and drugs in my system this was a miracle.

The bus arrived, and I took a back seat and tried my best to look sober. I waved feebly to Julie as I passed. Man, it was hard to act sober in my condition. The bus went south on Don Mills Road, and I got off at Eglinton Avenue and waited for an eastbound bus. While waiting I took a few swigs of the watered down gin and popped more 222s. By now I must have taken at least seventy of the hundred-tablet bottle. I was starting to fade out and was wishing I'd just drop dead.

The bus came, and I boarded and again took a back seat. As we drove along Eglinton I started to nod off but forced myself to stay awake. *When the judge sees me, he'll surely throw away the key*, I thought. Not only that, this would be the same judge who sentenced me in June and the same one who watched me tear apart the court-room prior to that.

I pulled the buzzer when my stop approached and was let off almost directly in front of the courthouse. I went to the side of the building and drank some more and popped more 222s. I then stashed the bottle of booze in a nearby snowbank and went inside the court-house. First at hand I had to take a piss, and then I checked into the DA's office to officially be summoned prior to my court appearance. I now had to wait for my name to be called. I continued to pop 222s and stepped outside for a drink now and again. Now I was starting to really trip out.

I looked for Diana, but she didn't seem to be there. My probation officer was to meet me, but he also wasn't around, so I phoned his office and spoke with him. I told him I was drunk and stoned out of my tree and didn't think I'd make it through the morning. He said he'd be there soon. I then phoned Sears to speak with Robert, the security manager, about my bad cheques in order to find out if he had gone to the police yet. Robert said no. We talked and I told him I was tripping out and also where I was. I would soon find out that this was a mistake. I didn't expect him to double-cross me.

My probation officer showed up shortly afterwards, and he wasn't too impressed with my condition. Soon two cops came to speak with me about something. I was told I was to be locked up until my court appearance at the judge's request. I waited calmly. Soon I was taken to the courtroom after being shackled, hand and foot. Again the judge's order. I guessed he was going to throw the book at me. My life was over.

Sitting in the prisoner's box, I looked around for Diana. No beautiful Diana. As I waited, I started to pass out and a couple of times fell off my seat and onto the floor while everyone, including my friend the judge, looked on.

When my name was called, I stood with the help of a police officer. The proceedings went on as if no one noticed I was drunk, which puzzled me. It was also against the law. I guessed that they just wanted to get this hearing over with and be rid of me. All that happened was that an addition was added to my two-year probation order I had received in June. The addendum was that I was not to go within 300 metres of either Diana's home or place of work. I agreed to the terms and then was escorted again to the jail cell and told I had to wait until the new probation order was typed up. I thought this was strange.

By now I had been double-crossed by my friend Robert at Sears. I was furious and told them to let me go. I took the bottle of 222s from my pocket and swallowed the rest of them and threw the empty bottle at a cop. They should have searched me before throwing me in the cell. I was still cuffed and shackled, and soon they had me sign my probation order.

Two cops from York Regional escorted me to an awaiting cop car, and I was now going to be taken up to Richmond Hill, just north of the Toronto city limits. I was going to be booked on three counts of fraud pertaining to the bad cheques at Sears. Man, I was out of it now and had to fight passing out and maybe into a coma. In about half an hour we arrived at York Regional Police HQ. I was finally uncuffed and deshackled, questioned, and then thrown in a cell to spend the night. Tomorrow I would be arraigned in front of a judge.

I lay on the metal bed tripping in and out of reality. My stomach was in great pain from the ASA in the 222s. I was going to spend Christmas 1985 in a jail. I was always in a mental prison at Christmastime anyway. So what if the bars were now real. The only difference before was that in my imprisonment at least I walked the land. I had been imprisoned as a child through to adulthood. My mind was a prison with countless little cells. Most held a tiny prisoner to whom the thought of freedom dwelt.

Now life inside any prison can be a riotous affair. All this human tragedy, most in total disrepair. Yes, sometimes all those tiny prisoners in the cells of my mind went mad from the solitary and endless years of confinement and wreaked havoc on anyone about. Today all the prisoners were simultaneously screaming to be set free. I just lay on the cold metal bed and stared at the concrete ceiling, listening to the terrifying screams.

Man, I was out of the picture. During the past eighteen hours I had drank at least a litre and a half of wine and twenty-five ounces of ninety-proof gin and swallowed 100 222s with codeine. It was a wonder I was still alive.

Around 3 p.m. the sergeant in charge told me I was being let go because they didn't have the facilities for me. In other words, they were worried I'd drop dead in the cell, and they didn't want to have anything to do with such a happening. I signed a paper stating I'd show up in court on Tuesday, January 7, 1986, and was then released. I knew I'd not be showing up for court as I'd be in Florida.

I felt as if I wouldn't make it home in one piece as I was on the edge of falling into a coma. Like a zombie I walked to Yonge Street, north of the city limits. I caught a GO bus to Steeles Avenue and then a bus east to Don Mills Road. I was becoming sicker with every moment. At Don Mills and Steeles I stared across the road to the Markham Place mall where I had worked at Sears. The Don Mills bus came and I boarded. Man I was getting sick. All this bouncing around was upsetting my stomach, and hot flashes were making me sweat as if under the summer sun. I hoped that I would make it home before becoming ill. It was futile, and as we passed Finch Avenue I ran to the front of the bus and told the driver to let me off as I was sick. The bus came to a stop, the door opened and no sooner had I stepped off the bus than I painted the snowbank with my projectile vomiting. Everything was going in circles, and I wished I was at home. After recovering somewhat, I staggered to the closest bus stop to await another bus. I finally made it home, and no sooner had I closed the door than I just fell onto my mattress that was in the middle of the near-empty living room floor and passed out.

I awoke about three hours later, feeling no better. I was totally messed, as was my body against all the poisons within. For well over a month there had been only three days that I had not ingested either 222s or alcohol. Even the three days of abstinence when I had driven to Florida I still had the poisons in my body. I'm sure that if I hadn't been a healthy person before all of the abuse I'd been putting my body through the last while, I would have been dead by now. Oh well, I was sure trying hard enough, and it would only be time before I finally kicked off. At the rate I was going my days were numbered to a very few. I fought with my mind and my stomach pains until some hours later I fell asleep.

Tuesday, December 24: When I awoke I felt no better and was still a space cadet. As far as being physically sick, this was the worse day yet since Diana left. I had no appetite, my stomach was fraught with cramps, my hearing and speech were impaired, my mind—what mind! I drank some water and would have to walk to the grocery store and pick up some ginger ale. I had defied death again. This kid must have 100 lives.

About 9 a.m. I walked the block to the store and back again. Just walking was almost impossible. I spent the day like a zombie, just lying around, sleeping and sipping room-temperature ginger ale. I was still so screwed up that I had no inclination to drink.

It was now Christmas Eve, and this was the worst ever. I hated Christmas but never so much as on this day. I lay alone, sick, the Christmas lights twinkling in the living room. Music was playing in the background. I wept the night away. During the last nine months I had lost everything—Diana, my job at Sears, my health, my furnishings, my apartment soon—and now insanity was becoming evermore present. I had degenerated from a mature adult to the lost teenager of ten years ago. All I had left was my stereo equipment, three works of art and other insignificant items. I would soon be selling them as well to continue my last vacation, part two.

Christmas Day, 1985: I did manage to fall asleep, and when I awoke at early dawn it was once again Christmas Day. Some Christmas this was going to be. It was going to be worse than the Christmas almost two decades before when Mother in all her hell-bent madness whipped me relentlessly over a mix-up over a Superman colouring book. I had then spent the day in bed without opening my presents. That day was also one of the first days that I wished Mother was dead as a skunk in the middle of the road. Yeah, she deserved to be road pizza! Today was another day of the same— alone, no presents, no one to share moments with. *Oh, Diana, I love you, my princess. Mother, I hope you drop dead*, I thought. *Oh Vickey, my sister, how I miss you.* I was alone, oh, so lonely. This life of mine was bringing me again to confront insanity.

I wept for a couple of hours. The world around me was slipping away. I would soon be universal. I had to die soon. For hours in the afternoon I stared out a bedroom window into oblivion. It hurt so much to think of what I didn't have after struggling so hard, the years of struggling to achieve my goals. I had fought the greatest of battles and had been victorious. Now I had nothing again.

It wasn't the nothing I cared about any more; it was not having someone in my life. It was always the times I was loneliest that I slipped deep into my mental misery. Now I was the deepest I'd ever been. The only thing deeper was death itself. All I wanted was a family, a sense of belonging, security, just something to hold on to. Love from people unconditionally, a mother who would love me, a father who'd do likewise. Today I wasn't beaten as in the past, but let me tell you the pain hurt more than any whipping I had ever received. My head was just throbbing from emotional torture inflicted by the memories.

The day dragged by, and at one point I saw Julie, her sister and her sister's boyfriend drive by. I thought they might be coming to visit, but no, they just drove right by. My eyes met Julie's gaze as she looked up at the apartment. That girl had everything of mine and wouldn't even stop to wish me a merry Christmas. Julie professed to be a Christian; then who the hell wanted to be part of Christianity. *To hell with God, to hell with everything. You can't trust anybody but yourself and even then when you are a mental case like me, you can't even trust yourself. One minute you could be sane and the next you'd be delving into your deep psychologically deranged mind.* What a sick person I was, and all out of innocence. It was a unalterable hereditary disease that had been bred into my subconscious. At times I had no control of my thoughts and actions. The proverbial Dr. Jekyll, Mr. Hyde syndrome so to speak. One minute a loving, compassionate pacifist, the next a raging lunatic hell-bent on self-destruction. I couldn't wait to get back to Florida to spend my last days in some semblance of peace and tranquility.

The next few days I was in an emotional fog. I prepared to go to Florida and the world beyond. A car was rented and I purchased a plane ticket for New Year's day. I really can't remember too much.

I celebrated New Year's Eve by falling asleep by 10 p.m. as I had to get up about 6 a.m. in order to catch my morning flight. What an end to a *hellish year.*

Happy New Year!

# Chapter 28

Wednesday, January 1, 1986: I awoke about 6 from a dreadful sleep and the last night in my home. I went to the fridge and grabbed a Labatt's Blue and twisted off the top. I brought the bottle to my parched lips and gulped down the contents. I did the same with the second while showering and shaving. By 7-ish I was ready to leave. I put about a half a dozen Blue in my flight bag. I figured I'd let Scott and Joe sample some Canadian brew, smuggled across the border. I wrote a note saying to phone the Salvation Army and let them pick up the rest of my personal belongings, things such as clothes, bed, mattresses, stereo cabinet, coffee table and an assortment of other household effects. I took one last look and tearfully left.

Outside it was cold and sunny; soon I'd be on a beach. I got in the rental car, started the engine and let it warm up. I opened another beer and then started out. I drove down the DVP to the Gardiner Expressway. I was drinking beer and tossing out the empties so I could see them smash on the pavement through the rear-view mirror. Yeah, what a party this was going to be. I pretty well had the expressway to myself so I sped up to about 100 mph. I was feeling the effects of the alcohol but didn't care. If I died, I died.

I made it to the airport, checked the car in with Budget and waited for my flight to board. Finally I was on board and winging it to Florida.

During the flight we were served breakfast and complimentary champagne as it was New Year's Day. I drank champagne the rest of the trip, and when we landed at St. Petersburg airport I staggered off the plane. Scott had driven my car to the airport, and he and Joe met me and we walked to our cars.. They were off to a house party, and I was invited but declined. They said I would have to pass the day on my own then and they'd meet me at their home later that evening. We drank the brew I had brought along from Canada, which they liked. Joe and Scott then went on their way.

I changed into a pair of shorts as it was over 70 degrees and sunny. I took the sunroof off the car for the open air feeling and got behind the wheel of my sports coupe. I sure felt good being in my car as it was all I had left. I raced into St. Pete's, bought some American beer and then passed a few hours drinking on the beach. At suppertime I drove into Tampa, cruised around the gay bars for a while and then drove to Joe and Scott's to spend the night. I felt better just being away from the cold. I parked in their drive and awaited their return. I drank and listened to the car radio as Joe had got the jammed tape out of the tape deck. I still couldn't listen to tapes though. I soon passed out from drinking all day.

I was awakened when my acquaintances arrived home. We went in to their home and started a party of our own. I couldn't stand it any more, and while they were making love to me I let out a scream. "No! No!" I asked if I could sleep in the spare room. They said yes, and I fell asleep with a great deal on my mind. I wanted nothing to do sexually with men any more. The guilt was eating me alive from the inside out. I just wanted to die.

Thursday, January 2: I awoke at 9 a.m. to find that Joe had left for work. Scott was up and was getting ready for work. I told him I had decided to check out Cape Canaveral as the shuttle Challenger was to blast off on the 6th or 7th. It was one of my dreams to see a lift off. As a space news follower since childhood, I had seen every shuttle launch. Now I could see one live on the grounds of the space centre.

At 10 a.m. I followed Scott to his bank, where he helped me exchange some Canadian currency into U.S. funds. We then said our goodbyes. Today I would again cross the state of Florida and be on the shores of the Atlantic Ocean by nightfall.

I loved driving, so the day was okay, and later that evening I checked into a motel some miles away from the space centre. Tomorrow I would tour the facilities. I unpacked the car and within minutes was lying in bed with the drapes drawn closed. On the night table I put the pair of brass swans. My wearing apparel was panties, garter belt and sheer black stockings. How I wished I was someone else, preferably female and attractive. I lay there drinking beer and flipping through a porn magazine of the homosexual kind and thinking. To people I was a figure that exemplified male vitality. I was tall, attractive and had an exceptional physique. What an

445

illusion, if there ever was one. When I cross-dressed all feelings of manlihood went out the window, as did my problems. I liked myself when I felt feminine. I guess it justified my homosexual thoughts. To me it wasn't homosexuality; it was a real female-male sexual relationship. When I thought of it as male to male is when I hated the thoughts that entered my mind. Most times if I thought of myself as a woman I'd be a lesbian, because women treated each other as equals, showing more tenderness and concern for each other. My greatest fantasy was to have a sex change and then be a lesbian.

Talk about being messed up! Yes, I was a nutbar for sure, totally off the wall and suffering from "lapse of the brain." Now to think that all this mental misery started when I was a young child. Are you as a reader not surprised that I'm still alive? I'm sure most would have succumbed to suicide by now or have ended up institutionalized for life as a mental case. And to think it started all out of innocence and the human need to be loved maternally and paternally, the love that never came. I was always desperately seeking love and attention any way I could. The suicide attempts, crime, sex, the drive to be someone, as in my fitness and work. Even now all this running away was actually a dream of running to someone, something, a happy life beyond the physical. Love, love is all I wanted. What I do now know is that no one can love us enough to fulfill us if we do not love ourselves. When in our emptiness we go looking for love, we can only find more emptiness. Look what happened to J.D. and me, Diana and me! I loved them more than anything or anyone!

I lay there now in tears, wishing I could change things. I longed to see my sister, Vickey. I guessed I would die without seeing her, knowing her. Vickey wouldn't want to know me anyhow. Just the same, I wanted to see her just once. How she must have grown over the past several years! I saw her last when she was nine. She would now be fourteen, fifteen in April. I sure hoped her mother hadn't driven her crazy too. All this perpetuating madness. Would it ever end? Would it?

I needed another drink, so I got up and grabbed a room-temperature beer and some 222s. I was somewhat hungry, so I donned clothes over my female attire and then drove to an all-night grocery. I bought bread, cheese, ham and a six-pack of canned brew. I checked out a couple of bars, but things were dead. Back in the motel room I undressed down to my lingerie, ate, and then drank myself into a fitful sleep. I couldn't wait to die.

Friday, January 3: I woke up to another sun-filled day. I threw back a brew and a couple of ham and cheese sandwiches. After slipping out of my female attire, I showered, shaved, and dressed into boring male clothes. I then went for a drive along the coast. This side of the state was quite boring, and the only thing that would keep me here was the shuttle Challenger's liftoff slated for next week. It was a glorious sunny day, and I decided to wash the car and found a U-Wash-It along the main drag. The proprietor was quite a sexually attractive young lady, who was also selling real estate, as I found out. Too bad she wasn't selling her island of flesh, because I would have bought. I washed my car and we talked a bit. She hinted at a date and mentioned that some of her friends and she were going to a particular bar that night and if I so wished I should drop by. I told her that should I be around. I would certainly do just that.

I then went back to the motel and checked out, as I didn't know if I would be staying another night after visiting the Kennedy Space Center. I stopped at the world's largest surfing store and bought some summer clothes. I cruised the main drag for a while and then headed out for the drive to the not-so-distant Space Center.

I had a shocking experience as I drove along a two-lane highway. I was racing an older model Datsun 260Z at about 120 mph. The guy couldn't keep up to me, so I kept slowing down to let him catch up to me. One time I let him pass me, and as he pulled alongside me he pulled out his badge. Oh no, a cop! My license would be taken on the spot, and I'd go to jail. I had heard about these ghostriders and how they teased you in your sports car, initiating a race and then throwing the book at you.

I hesitantly pulled over, and he strode up to the car as cops do and asked what the hell I had under the hood. I rambled off the tip of my tongue the specs, 2.2 litre, turbocharged, fuel injected, overhead cam and one horsepower more than a Porsche 944. He said he couldn't believe the power of this little car. I was in a sweat and my adrenaline was pumping. He then went on to say he wasn't a cop but a space centre worker and the badge was for clearance. The guy had just wanted to check out the car. I couldn't believe my luck.

I then drove on to the Space Center while still racing the guy in the Datsun. As I approached the facility I couldn't believe my eyes. Rockets of yesteryear were on display right out in the open. I parked the car and went for a stroll through the complex. I walked by a large digitalized clock ticking away the seconds to next week's launch. I was simply in awe of the rockets on display and then signed up for an afternoon bus tour, which would include a drive by the shuttle Challenger on the launch pad. Little did I know that the launch a few days from that day would be scrubbed and on the subsequent date, January 28, the Challenger would explode after launch, killing all on board. I'm glad I wasn't there to witness such a tragedy as I had never seen anyone killed before, let alone people who were always striving to reach their highest potential as humans. Astronauts were the people I most venerated.

On the tour I saw a lunar lander, the rover (the odd moon mobile, which should have had on its rims "Goodyear Gatorbacks") and heard a simulation of a takeoff. The highlight was yet to come. I saw not only one launch pad but two. On each stood majestically a shuttle ready for launch. What a symbol of human capabilities! To think the Challenger only later that month would be blown out of the sky moments after takeoff.

On the bus I met a couple of attractive young ladies who like myself were on vacation, although mine was my last. They were from Pennsylvania and staying in Orlando, by Disneyland. Since I had no ties, I took up the offer of going to Orlando for the night. Believe it or not out of the hundreds of cars they had parked their car right in front of mine in the Space Center parking lot. I found it too much of a coincidence to think that my meeting them was not planned beforehand. And I thought I had been the aggressor. They must have seen me pull into the parking spot and decided that they would pick up this Canadian stud.

Well, I followed them along the long drive to Orlando, which was halfway across the state. I could always come back to the Space Center in a few days to see the launch. By the time I followed the girls into Orlando I was having second thoughts about partying tonight as an extreme feeling of guilt came over me. How I longed to be with Diana and no one else. I was tired of all this sex anyhow. So what if I could spend the night with two attractive females. It would be meaningless anyhow. I was tired of it all.

We stopped at a diner. Night had already blanketed the earth. We lunched at my expense and then I told them I'd be on my way. They seemed disappointed, and I'm sure they didn't spend the night alone. Sitting in my car I waved goodbye, and again I was on my own.

It would be days before the shuttle would be launched, and I didn't feel like driving back to where I had just come from. Where would I go? Well, I had seen most of Florida. I took out a road map and picked out a highway around the Gulf of Mexico that went into Texas. Yes, that's where I would go for a spell, what the hell. I always had wanted to drive over a desert, and I was sure my car and I would have a great time.

I charted my course and started out. I drove through Orlando and stopped at a corner store for beer along what seemed like the main sex strip. It also seemed like I was the only white person about. I bought the beer and sat in the car and drank one as I hadn't drank anything since the morning. When I finished I opened another and was on my way, but not before I smoked the tires as I entered the thoroughfare.

Darn it, if the state troopers weren't across the intersection. I was stopped and questioned, the beer was found, and my license was run through the computer. Well, it came up clean. I could have been arrested on the spot but was let go with a warning. I was lucky. Again I was on my way to somewhere and I would drive throughout the night. My thoughts, however, started to wander, and all I could see were visions of my sister. How I wished I could see her before I died. Just once to hug her and tell her that I loved her dearly. Vickey had not seen me for five years, nor heard or received a letter or gift from me. I didn't even know if she thought of me any more. I was sure Mother had by now brainwashed her as to why I had left Sudbury anyhow. At one point I had to pull to the side of the highway in order to wipe the tears from my eyes. I just sat and stared tearfully into the night. I then drove on for who knows how long but finally succumbed to my thoughts.

I stopped the car somewhere in the middle of God only knows where and pulled out my map. I scoured it, looking for the quickest way to get to I-75, the main expressway that went right up to the Canadian border. I drove the rest of the night, only stopping for gas and to piss. Vickey was always on my mind. Like a magnet, I was being drawn home some 1,500 and more miles away. By morning I was driving through the countryside of Alabama and still not on the highway I was looking for. Sometime later I was on I-75, and by late afternoon I had driven through Tennessee and decided to stop in a rural Kentucky town off the expressway, as

I was totally exhausted, mentally and physically.

The scenery was panoramic; the mountains and roads around looked like ideal places to put this car through its paces. I decided to spend the next two nights there in that quaint town. I would spend the next day searching out the best mountain roads to play on. One thing I noticed was that I had left summer behind along the Florida Gulf coast. Although it wasn't winter as I knew it to be, it was quite cool, probably just above freezing. Thank God there was no snow.

I checked into a motel adjacent to a stand of fast-food outlets. I sure hated the change of weather and knew that as I headed north it would only get worse. If it wasn't for my longing to see my sister, I'd never be going back to Canada. As it was, I just had to see her, providing I didn't crack up the car or myself in an accident first. In my shabby room I flicked on the TV and opened a beer and popped some 222s. I was hungry, so I then went next door to a Kentucky Fried Chicken outlet. To think I'd be buying it right in Kentucky. I found that amusing.

I was tired and quite agitated, and no sooner had I entered the establishment than a young Kentucky chicken slinger asked for my order. My response was "Damnit, I just got in the door, just wait." A lady came out and I placed my order and waited, my thoughts running amok within. I had never spoken to people like that before, outside of family squabbles. I was usually so polite. They probably thought I was some psycho or something. The lady and girl looked terrified while they served me. I paid and with my order in hand I left and went back to my room.

I washed down the chicken, fries and 222s with

some brew. I then went out for a drive in the night around this small town. Back at the motel, I donned my female attire, popped some 222s, drank some more, and fell asleep while listening to the country and western music on the radio of my ghetto blaster. I was a totally messed up man. I dreamt of the mountain roads I hoped to conquer all day tomorrow.

Sunday, January 5: I awoke to another day. The weather was cold and dry. I noticed that frost was on my car. I had a breakfast of beer and chicken. I showered and shaved while listening to C and W music on my ghetto blaster. I was soon ready to go road hunting; the more dangerous, the better. I found a U-Wash-It and washed my Chrysler sports coupe. I then set out to conquer, hopefully, some awesome roads.

It was Sunday, and barely any traffic was around this Kentucky country town. Once out of the town there was next to no traffic along the back roads. The radio was blaring away all the while. I raced all day through the countryside. My Dodge Turbo Shelby Charger was put through some gruelling work. I found some good roads, but not truly what I was looking for. I sure as hell had fun testing my driving skills though, and the scenery was simply splendid.

I cruised until late afternoon and then made my way back to the little town before nightfall. The thrill of tempting death while road racing had livened me up, and I spent an enjoyable evening watching TV, eating, popping 222s and drinking. Tomorrow I'd head out on my way to Canada, still looking for my ultimate ride to the edge or maybe over. I felt I could handle my car through any test.

Monday, January 6: Awoke to another cool morning, ate munchies, had a couple of beer, showered, shaved, etc. I was reluctantly ready to head out for Canada. I stopped at the combination fire hall and cop shop to ask what roads ran parallel to I-75 that would give me better scenery. It was pointed out on my map that Highway 125 ran somewhat parallel to I-75 but criss-crossed back and forth through the countryside. I decided that would be my best choice, as at anytime I could get back onto the expressway. I thanked the firemen and cops and left. I tanked up on gas and set out.

Right from the onset, I was driving some of the best roads ever and was having the time of my life. All of my problems had to be put on a mental hold so I could concentrate on driving. I also wasn't worried about the troopers as I was off the main highway. As I drove through Kentucky, the mountains seemed to be getting taller with each mile. I guessed they were the Tennessee Blue Ridge range. I drove back onto the main expressway. My adrenaline was flowing, and I had an insatiable craving to find a wild road. I stopped here and there to admire the magnificent views this state was bestowed with.

Sometime during the hours around noon while on the main expressway, I-75, I passed a state park right in the middle of this mountain range. I decided to double back and check it out. The park was right on a mountain, and the road wound its way towards the top. What a great road! Higher and higher I went. What excitement, but nothing in comparison to what was to come. The air was getting colder as I drove up the mountain road. Disappointment came as I noticed some snow. As I drove on, more snow. Now this was different for me. Down at the bottom of the mountain there was no snow, although it was cool. Up here it was like winter. Well, so much for mountaintops.

I pulled a U-turn and descended until I reached a fork in the road. I started driving down the mountainside in a different direction. I came upon another road that had a sign saying "Primitive road; use at your own risk." Could this be it, the road and ride of my dreams? I figured the road for a fire route as it was paved but only the width of one vehicle. What a challenge this would be!

I was becoming more excited as I drove this winding road. I wasn't racing, as I wanted to figure out the road first. The view was nothing short of spectacular. I looked down the treed slopes to my left—wow, what a drop! If I wiped out I'd be finished. I didn't care; this would be the ultimate death ride if I failed to negotiate this road. The road in places was falling apart, and I bottomed out once. I would have to remember that spot on my way back. Finally the road was so bad that I didn't want to go further. I parked the machine after managing carefully to turn around.

Out of the car, I stood admiring the panoramic surroundings. The tree-lined mountains around looked like giant monuments to Earth's creation. I truly felt I was on top of the world. I then checked the car for scratches that might have been sustained on this treacherous road. Sitting back in my blue-and-silver speed machine, I decided I would do the commentary for this trip back down this mountaintop road. I had not gone high enough, so there was no snow. I took my ghetto blaster that was plugged into the lighter and inserted a blank tape that I had bought for just such an occasion. It would be like a flight recorder in case of an accident. I then placed it under the dash so it would pick up the engine noise as well as my voice. I spoke into the microphone and stated that I was at the top of a mountain on the road of my dreams and was ready to test my driving skills to the max. My adrenaline was pumping.

"I'm ready to go now. Gentlemen, start your engines." I brought the car to life, revving up to an imagined red line, the recorder picking up everything. The engine was screaming to be let loose. "Get on your mark, get set, go!" I popped the clutch and smoked the tires. The smell of burnt rubber permeated the air. "I'm in first gear, second gear, approaching a corner, back to first, second, now third, back to second, I have to slow down for that pothole, down to first, up to second, now third. I'm flying, approaching another corner, Oh no, I won't make the corner!"

I pumped the brakes and came to a screeching halt. I spoke into the recorder as my adrenaline was pumping. "I didn't make it and stopped with the front end pushing dirt into the mountainside." I had a nose bra on the front of the machine so I knew no harm was done. I squealed the tires in reverse and backed up. I then raced down the rest of the road, commentating all my actions. At the bottom I rewound the tape and played it over a couple of times. Each time brought excitement to me. I then raced up again and back down. As it was off-season here, there were no other cars about. I will never forget that mountaintop ride ever. I even had it on tape for posterity's sake.

What a thrill, and I would do it again, and some day I will, and in a much better car with better gearing. Maybe I'll go over the edge and maybe I won't. The challenge is to beat death at its own game. So far in my life I would say I have fared very well. I should be dead by now, so any day is a bonus.

I drove back to the highway and again was heading north, the thoughts of that mountain road still doing reruns in my head. I could even listen to it on tape. I raced along the endless ribbon of highway. I had again tanked up on gas and was now racing anything in sight. Within a short while I was racing a Pontiac Fiero on I-75, the direct route to Canada. My car was much faster, but we still had fun. We were both cruising over 100 mph at times for about two hours non-stop until we came to the outskirts of Ohio, where I had to turn off and fill up with gas. The two guys in the Fiero must have thought I had a radar detector, because at least five times we had passed state troopers and by a stroke of luck had just slowed for a few minutes to give our car engines a break. As I was the leader, they just stayed behind me in their gutless Fiero. That race was probably the best open-road ride I'll ever have in my lifetime. The fact that we had raced across nearly two states averaging 100 mph on the busiest highway and didn't get ticketed was just pure luck. All this driving was done with the radio playing rock and roll at full volume. Totally awesome.

I bypassed Cincinnati by suppertime and, while still in Ohio, after nightfall I was pulled over for speeding.

Fortunately I was only going seven or eight mph above the double-nickel speed limit, as I had seen the copper ahead, although not in time enough to slow right down to the limit. Now here in Ohio you pay on the spot. The trooper asked for my Visa or MasterCard, which I couldn't believe. I told him I had neither. He then said I had to pay cash or else go to jail. I tried to talk my way out of it by saying I only had enough money to get me back to Canada, which was a lie. I had a pocketful of Canadian C-notes. I would have paid, but I had no American cash. We talked and finally he told me to follow him to the station.

At the cop shop I asked the lady copper at the desk what the exchange was, and she said 30 percent. Well, I pulled out a C-note and handed it over. This C-note was worth only $70 U.S., and my ticket was $50 or so U.S. This meant that this seven or eight mph infraction almost cost me my whole C-note. The lady copper made the calculations and then started counting out my change, which I already figured to be some around $20. Instead, I was given around $70. This dumb lady had credited me 30 percent on my C-note, which meant I had $130 minus the ticket. With the money in hand I was ready to leave, but I didn't need the troopers on my case later on. I explained to the copper about the exchange rate, and she recalculated everything. The cop who had stopped me said to follow him back to the highway. I told him I'd find my own way. To think I could have ripped off the state troopers then and there!

Soon I noticed traces of snow here and there. How I hated the thought of snow. Nearing the Canadian border I was driving through light snow flurries. I stopped in Michigan to tank up in order to save money on gas. The price was $1.19, which was a bargain.

Snow was everywhere, and it was freezing out. I thought again of just turning around and heading back south to a more favourable climate. I couldn't, as seeing my sister was of utmost importance. At the Canada-U.S. border, I regretfully crossed the bridge into Canada and right into a major snowstorm, which was typical of Canada in January. I was going east on the 401 in near whiteout conditions. My only company was my car radio and tormented thoughts.

I was to show up in court in the morning as tomorrow was the seventh. I had already decided I wouldn't be going. I had to see Vickey before I died or got locked up. I preferred the idea of death. I was going now to what had been my home on Parkway Forest Drive in Toronto. I just hoped they hadn't changed the locks yet so that I could get a few hours' sleep, as I had been driving since about 10 o'clock that morning. Cars were off the highway everywhere, and I drove with caution. By the time I reached the city limits, the weather had cleared some, although the roads were still hazardous.

About 2 a.m. I arrived at the apartment complex. Fortunately the locks hadn't been changed, although an eviction notice was on the door. The apartment was as I had left it. At least I could grab a few hours' sleep and then be off to Sudbury. I was exhausted and fell asleep immediately on the mattress on the living room floor. I set the alarm for 6 a.m. My court case was for 10, and I wanted to be out of the city before a warrant went out for my arrest.

Tuesday, January 7: At 6 a.m. I awoke groggily from a deep sleep. I showered, shaved and had a beer, as I hadn't drank while driving the previous day. I then left the apartment for definitely the last time about 7 a.m. The note I had left on New Year's Day for the Salvation Army to have my belongings picked up was as I had left it. I was now on my way to Sudbury to finally see my sister.

The trip to Sudbury was slow going because of the previous night's storm. The four and a half hour drive took about seven, and I arrived in Sudbury about 2 p.m. I drove to my old stomping grounds, the City Centre Mall, and parked the car in the parking garage. All the past memories of this place were haunting my mind. I sat there a bit and drank a couple of beers. I then took a walk through the mall. Everything seemed the same as ever; even some of the faces were the same, although I didn't walk up to anyone I knew. I stopped at a drugstore and bought a bottle of 222s. I took about 20 of the 100 tablets to start. Next was a wine store, where I purchased a couple of bottles of cheap wine.

What to do? I knew if I wanted, I could stay with Doug's and his family or at a motel, as I still had sufficient funds to do as I pleased. I was now a wanted criminal and had at least one warrant out for my arrest. The first would be by York Region and the second from Metro Toronto, pertaining to the cheques I wrote for Julie's earrings and the VCR I pawned.

I phoned Doug's place and spoke with my sister-in-law. She invited me to their place in Val Caron. I took up the offer and then went up to the parking garage where in my youth I had made plenty of drug deals, smoked drugs, drank and met the fag with whom I had my first sexual encounter. In my car I opened a bottle of wine and drank some more to wash down some more 222s. Now ten years later I was up here doing as before and much in the same mixed-up frame of mind but worse. *Some things never change*, I thought to myself.

I drove out to Val Caron and was soon at Doug's house. It was near suppertime when I half-drunkenly buzzed their doorbell. The family was home, and we exchanged greetings and caught up on personal current events. I had only visited maybe four times in five years. They knew Diana had left as I had phoned back in March and had visited one day in September when I had also talked to my stepfather for the first time in five years. They could tell I was drunk and on a downward spiral to nowhere but self-destruction. I explained that I only came to Sudbury to see Vickey.

We spent the night drinking and talking. I went to sleep that night thinking of facing Vickey's mother tomorrow and hopefully seeing Vickey. My sister was the only thing on my mind. How tall was she? What did she look like? How was she doing in school? Countless questions ran through my deranged mind. Also, Vickey's mother! I would have to finally talk to that woman. I hoped she had changed. I tossed and turned all night and couldn't wait until morning.

Wednesday, January 8: I awoke in the middle of the morning. Doug had left for work, the two kids for school. I had breakfast and chatted with my sister-in-law. By noon I was on my way to Vickey's mother's. I popped several 222s in order to mellow me out for my meeting with the evil harridan. I hadn't spoken with her for ten years. For all I knew she wouldn't even talk to me.

461

I drove up to Murray Mine, which is in the middle of nowhere, just minutes from Copper Cliff, where I was born and raised. There was only one street lined with company houses and an office building of sorts. The mine itself was closed. I couldn't think of raising kids up there. They would be deprived of a proper social setting. *What a drag it must be for Vickey*, I thought as I drove the private road to their place. I saw the row of houses in the distance and stopped. I just stared down the lone street to the house I knew was Vickey's. I was nervous, angry and a multiple of other confused emotions. I had to do this or I wouldn't see Vickey.

I put the car in gear and proceeded to turn around and get the hell out of there. I had no guts. I just couldn't bring myself to face Vickey's mother and all she didn't stand for in my life.

I drove to Copper Cliff and stopped at the liquor store, bought some beer and went parking. I downed a couple of beers and then headed back to Murray Mine. I again parked in sight of the house, and again, after deliberation with myself, I left and went back to Val Caron. I again spent the night there and vowed to have enough courage tomorrow. Doug and family hadn't seen Vickey for I don't know how long, so they didn't know where she went to school. I suppose I could have phoned Dad and asked him where Vickey went to school, but I didn't want him to know I was in town. The only way I could spend time with Vickey was to face mother. Again I slept in confusion, only thinking of Vickey.

Thursday, January 9: The day went much like the

day before except the second time I drove up to Vickey's mother's I was higher and more drunk. I was still quite in control of myself though. It was early to mid afternoon when I parked the car in front of Vickey's house. I hoped her common-law husband wasn't home, as I despised him because of his influence over Vickey. I nervously got out of my machine, walked to one of the side doors, opened it, and knocked. I was doing what I had vowed never to do.

The sound of barking dogs met my ears. It figured, Mother always loved her dogs, I guess because they seemed to love her back. I knocked harder and soon I heard the voice of doom and destruction. "Down, down, you stupid dogs." Vickey's mother in all her ugliness opened the other side door and poked out her aged face and said, "Yes?"

I just looked at it and was lost for words. She must have thought I was a salesman. She was right in one respect. I said hi and mentioned my name. "I'm Randy."

She looked at me and then asked, "Randy who?"

I said, "Tunney."

"Randy Tunney, oh, just a minute." She closed the door she was at and again I heard her yelling, as was her nature, at her dogs. I didn't expect her to even come to the door I was at. I just stood there nervously. Finally she opened the door and let me in. The house reeked of dog. She apologized for the mess and the dogs. She said there were eight of them, all purebred bassett hounds except Peppy the mutt. I remembered that mutt, Vickey's dog. I was surprised he was still alive.

Vickey's mother then said, "We should let whatever happened between us be forgotten," and then reached outstretched arms to hug me. I backed away. I didn't want her to touch me. I was here for only one reason.

We spoke of Vickey while I sat across from her. Being polite, I looked at her while we spoke. I produced pictures of Diana and I and spoke of my separation. I said that I had taken some time off work to get away from things. I couldn't tell her what really happened. We talked about my brothers, but my concerns were for my sister. James was in Toronto, while Bob was still around Copper Cliff and unemployed.

I asked if I could see Vickey, and she said yes and was actually glad and stated that Vickey would like nothing better. Vickey was attending Sudbury Secondary School and was in grade nine. After school today she was having her picture taken with Dad at Eaton's. I said I'd try to meet them there.

You can't believe how I felt at the thought of seeing Vickey in a couple of hours. How could I have stayed away so long, I'll never know. I hadn't sent a letter or anything. The years had just tearfully gone by.

Her and I spoke a while longer, but I could tell that she was still the same. From what I sensed, she ran Vickey's life with an iron hand although not physically. I knew though that emotional deprivation was worse than physical abuse, and how I hated her for that.

I soon left and was happily but nervously driving downtown to the City Centre Mall where Eaton's was located. I parked on top of the mall and took a flight of stairs that went right into Eaton's. I hurriedly walked to the portrait studio and asked if a Mr. Harold Tunney had his appointment set up. I was told they had their pictures taken early and had just left. *Oh no*, I thought.

I walked through the mall looking in almost every store, hoping they might still be in the mall. I finally made my way to the fast food concourse. I scanned the tables, and my heart began to palpitate at the sight of Dad sitting with a young blonde girl who had her back to me. My sister, yes, I was finally going to see her, although I wished it wasn't at this point of my deteriorating life. I walked up behind Vickey, bent down behind her, wrapped my arms around her and gave her a kiss on the side of her face.

Vickey just looked at me strangely, as did Dad. Dad didn't say a thing as I sat down at the table. I just looked at Vickey, drinking in her loveliness, while she looked at me inquisitively, not recognizing me.

A minute passed before anything was said. It wasn't until I said, "Hi, Sis," that Vickey realized it was her big brother across from her. I had a hard time holding back the tears of happiness.

Vickey didn't know what to say. Dad said he hadn't recognized me either. He had only seen me once in the past five years. Vickey and I just stared at each other, tears seemingly ready to burst from within. I was so happy I couldn't hold back the flood any longer. I said I had to go for a walk and I'd be back. I stood, the tears now streaming down my face. I walked from the food concourse to a hallway overlooking the street. I just stared tearfully out a window and tried to compose myself. Not until then did I realize how much my sister meant to me and how dearly I loved her. I wiped the tears from my face with the sleeve of my coat.

I walked back to the table and sat down. I asked Dad if it was okay to spend some time with Vickey if she wished. I wanted to take her shopping and to talk to her. Vickey wanted to but first had to check with her mother. With everything okayed, I told Dad we'd drop by his place later.

I couldn't believe I was with my sister. The only thing better would be to be with Diana also. Vickey and I walked, talked and went shopping, and I bought her a new winter coat. She was to have a ringette practice but missed it.

We drove to Dad's and his girlfriend's, where we spent some time. I then wanted to drive to Doug's and show off Vickey. Words came easy between us, and we were soon comfortable with each other. When we arrived at Doug's, I rang the door bell and then said, "Guess who came to visit?" The only time I was happier was when Diana and I were joined in marriage. How I had wished then that Vickey was there.

We all sat around and talked, and then I asked if Vickey and I could go downstairs to talk. I wanted to explain why I hadn't been around. I figured that since Vickey was almost fifteen it was time someone told her about the truth about our family. I didn't know if it was right or wrong, but I figured it was better now than years from now.

As we talked I realized how brainwashed Vickey was because of Mother's lies about me and Dad. I showed her the short story I had written in jail six months earlier. I'm sure she was shocked to find out things. I told her that I was adopted by Dad, which also shocked her. It was all very emotional, and I was sure this could change her perception of things permanently. I still wasn't sure whether I was right or wrong to have explained the truth. We ended up crying in each other's arms. I had spoken of my own situation honestly and right to the point of being totally messed up. I told her the only reason I came to Sudbury was to see her before the law caught up with me.

Vickey told me she was doing well in school, was into running and playing ringette. I was proud of her, to say the least. Back upstairs we talked with Doug and his family, and then it was time to drive Vickey home.

Back at Vickey's I was invited in. I told Vickey I didn't want to have to look at Mother. Vickey said she just wanted to show me her trophies and pet ferret. I now gave Vickey another present, one that meant so much to me. The gift was the pair of brass swans that Diana had given me for Christmas 1983. I had been lugging them around since December. Vickey had also seen the pictures of Diana and I. Well, I went inside and saw Vickey's trophies and pet. It seemed Vickey was becoming an excellent athlete and student, which made me more proud of her. I soon gave her a hug and then left and went back to Doug's.

Back at Doug's we talked about Vickey and her situation, living in that house in the middle of nowhere and being deprived of a normal social life because of it. Those dogs and the stench of the house. Vickey's mother and the brainwashing lies. It was just deplorable, and I was in no position to do anything as I couldn't even take care of my own life properly any more. All this perpetuating tragedy, just like a contagious disease.

Friday, January 10: I spent the day in Val Caron talking with my sister-in-law. Doug was at work, the two kids at school. By early afternoon I was in downtown Sudbury and was going to surprise Vickey by picking her up after school. At 3 p.m. I was at Sudbury Secondary School and had left a message in the office to have Vickey paged when classes were dismissed. They would tell her I was waiting for her.

Vickey was glad to see me, and we cruised around before I drove her home. She had a ringette game that night, and I said that I'd watch her. In fact I picked her up later and drove her to her game. I happily watched her skate circles around her opponents. She really was quite an athlete.

I drove her back home, where I tried to be polite to Mother. Later Vickey and I were to pick up James and his girlfriend at the bus depot. They were coming up for the weekend from Toronto. I would now get to see James after five years. Nothing like a family reunion! James and I were never close, and he is about three years younger than me. Our meeting wasn't so emotional as that of Vickey's and mine. James and I shook hands and few words were said. His girlfriend seemed very nice and was quite attractive. James had put on a spare tire around his waist.

We drove to his girlfriend's family's to drop her off and then it was back to Vickey's. I didn't stay long, and as I drove home I realized that my hatred towards Mother was ever on the rise. The more I saw of her, the more I despised her.

Back at Doug's we talked a bit, and then I was off to bed. So many things were driving me crazier. This day I had not drank or popped any 222s.

Saturday, January 11: In the morning, I watched Vickey play in a ringette tournament. Doug and the kids came also. Mother was there, and Doug's kids, her step-grandchildren, saw for the first time their step-grandmother, whom they only had ever known in conversation as "the witch." Doug spoke with her for a few minutes, to his dreadful luck. He hated the witch as well and hadn't spoken to her since his wedding, and that had only been out of politeness. The witch's common-law husband was also at the arena, and I spoke with him.

Vickey invited me to have supper at her house. I said no because I didn't ever want to look at her mother again. Vickey pleaded with me, stating she wanted to have dinner with three of her brothers, James, Bob and I. Out of my love for her I said I would come.

I spent the afternoon tobogganing with my young niece and nephew and then got ready to go for supper. I really didn't want to go as I had seen enough of Vickey's mother to last the rest of my life.

Well at Vickey's I saw brother Bob after all these years. I never did trust him, especially since one weekend at J.D.'s in 1981 when Bob phoned and threatened to kill me if I didn't leave town. I now wasn't sure if he thought I sabotaged brother Tom's car, in which Tom was killed. I met Bob's girlfriend as well. In all, there was Mother, James, Bob, Vickey, myself, both James' and Bob's girlfriends, and Mother's common-law husband. Oh yeah, and all the foul-smelling dogs.

We sat around until supper was called. Mother had made a fine full course turkey dinner. Believe it or not, I was the only adult not drinking as I had to keep up the health nut facade. I was seated beside my sister. At least Vickey was happy to be with as much of her family as possible. I knew this would be the last time. Dinner went okay. I didn't say much and couldn't wait to get this farce over with.

When dessert was served, I was shocked. Vickey had left the table and went upstairs. After a minute or so Mother went to the kitchen to get dessert. If she didn't come in with a birthday cake for me, as my birthday was the following Wednesday. A surprise birthday party! The witch put the cake in front of me and wished me a happy birthday. I held back the profanity.

Vickey came downstairs with an armful of presents. They were all now singing "Happy Birthday." If they only knew how much I hated celebrations such as Christmas and birthdays. Vickey told me to blow out the candles.

Halfway through their singing rendition I spoke up loudly. "I came here to have dinner with Vickey and not for some party." I knew Vickey was hurt, but I couldn't put up with this facade any longer.

Everyone was shocked and speechless. The witch's husband ended up blowing out the candles and cutting the cake. I didn't eat any; nor did I open my presents. I just had to leave.

Bob, Vickey and I went tobogganing somewhere. I then went back to Doug's. I was to have no more to do with the super witch.

On Sunday I didn't see Vickey and started drinking and popping 222s. Monday and Tuesday I saw Vickey a couple of times during her lunch hour at school. I stayed moderately high at all times. The end was near.

On Tuesday the 14th, I decided to spend my birthday in Toronto so I could be with someone, hopefully.

Wednesday, January 15: Happy birthday. I was twenty-seven years old.

I was going to go to Toronto for a couple of days. I knew a warrant or two was out for me, and I didn't want to get picked up. I had decided to leave my car in Sudbury because so few of my model existed and it stood out like a sore thumb. I would take the Grey Coach. Doug drove me to the depot for the 8 a.m. bus. By 1 p.m. I was in downtown Toronto. First I phoned Julie's place of work on Yonge north of Bloor. She wouldn't be in until 3 p.m. Well, it was my birthday, and I was so desperately lonely that I phoned up some ladies, but no one seemed to be home. Just my luck. I checked out some bars and started drinking. I had bought a bottle of 222s and popped several. Between the bus and wandering about, I killed a few hours.

I walked up to Yonge and Bloor to surprise Julie. I surprised her all right, and an argument ensued. I left pissed off and walked south a couple of blocks and checked out some gay bars. What a way to spend a birthday. I just wanted to die. I was popping 222s and drinking and later decided to go back to Julie's work-place, only minutes away. Again we argued, and then I got mad and said I might as well turn myself over to the cops as I had nowhere else to go. I don't know what time it was, but it was well after dark. I used their phone and phoned the Richmond Hill cops, stating that I'd turn myself in providing they'd pick me up at the city limits. I didn't want to get picked up by the

Metro cops, as they might also have a warrant out for my arrest. I certainly didn't want to end up at the Don Jail. I said I'd take the subway up to Finch and then bus it to Steeles, where they could pick me up. Julie wasn't too impressed, nor was the lady working with her. I wasn't really going to go through with it though.

About this time I saw a cop car with its lights flashing. I guess Julie had phoned the cops or the cops had traced my call. They weren't going to catch me. I started running. The cop car screeched to a halt. I was carrying the flight bag, which contained clothes, my only pictures and negatives of Diana, and the original outline of this book, which I had written in that solitary jail cell. I never would get them back.

The cops were out of their cruiser and chasing me. I was running through the Canadian Tire parking lot on Yonge Street north of Bloor. My heart was pounding. Thank God I had been an athlete and a runner. I heard a cop yelling at me to stop or he'd shoot. I didn't give a care.

I had an eight-foot fence to hurdle, which was a barrier from the subway line. This was just like a scene from television. I climbed the fence easily but tore my pants and winter overcoat. I didn't care. As you'll soon find out I was dressed for a run-in with the cops.

I jumped down onto the subway tracks and knew the cops wouldn't risk it. I heard a cop scream to get reinforcements. A subway train was coming right at me, and I jumped out of the way. What a birthday party! I crossed the second set of tracks, making sure not to touch the electricity-filled third rail. Then it was over the fence onto the other side.

I heard sirens all around. They'd have to kill me before they caught me. My heart was going crazy, and so was I. I crossed a road and then a field and made my way to a ravine, from where I could see cop cars everywhere. This was going to be tough, and I'd have to outsmart them. I snuck through some yards, down the ravine and up the opposite side.

The cops were slowly cruising the streets. I would have to be extra careful. By now they'd have a description of me. Tall, six foot, 180 pounds, Caucasian, male, dirty blond hair, wearing a brown winter trench coat and brown corduroy pants. Well, up the other side of the ravine in the back of someone's yard I tossed the torn winter coat under a porch. I was now wearing a white chintz bomber jacket. Yes, I had another coat underneath. I was prepared. I then snuck across the street to another yard and took off the torn cords. Underneath I had on a pair of jeans. Talk about brains.

I was also in Rosedale, a neighbourhood I was familiar with. The cops were still around, but I had one final change to make after going through a few more backyards. *Man, this is exciting*, I thought as I trudged through the snow. In someone's garage I slipped out of my jeans and then track pants. I put the jeans on and then the track pants. I had completed my transformation from a wanted criminal to a neighbourhood jogger. I just stepped out onto the street and jogged along on my way. I passed a couple of cruisers, but the cops took no heed. I was half hoping they'd ask if I had seen myself.

Well, I had been prepared, and it had paid off. The

problem now was that I had nowhere to go and all those 222s were taking effect, all 100 of them. I knew that I'd soon be in intense pain physically. As I jogged along, I figured I'd check out the house of a woman I knew who lived in the neighbourhood. I jogged to her place, and fortunately she was home, although I awakened her. I was invited in and given a birthday hug and kiss. This had been all I wanted all day. I told her of my predicament and she said I could stay the night. I spent the night awake and in pain, but not alone at least. I was stoned and in emotional distress. My friend, a nurse, held me in her arms all night as if I were a lost child. She knew what I had been through in the past year. I'm glad I had a friend like that on that particular evening. This was not the first time this lady had helped me out. Thank you, my friend, Nancy K. Well, happy birthday— one I'll never forget.

Now during that emotionally and physically painful night I started to conceive a plan. I knew now I had both the Metro and York Regional cops on my tail. I knew that death or jail was inevitable. Well, if I was going to live and go to jail I was going to make my time behind bars worth the agony. I knew I'd crack in jail and maybe come out in a pine box. I still had a total fear of imprisonment of any sort.

I thought over and refined my plan until I came to a final decision. I would abduct Mother and drive her to Toronto and then turn myself over to a TV station and the cops. I would let every child abuser know to what extent child abuse affects someone and to what extent someone may go to put a stop to it. I was against physical abuse, so no harm would physically be done to her. On the other hand, I would emotionally torment her all the way to Toronto. She would think I was going to kill her every mile of the way.

Now I was definitely certifiable. I just wasn't going to jail for next to no reason. My life was finished, and she just had to answer for the chance I never had, a chance to live as I wanted. I was now twenty-seven and never had a day of total peace of mind. There was always something I was fighting, and I hated it. No one knew the battles that were always being waged within. I had lived thus far never knowing my real identity or if I even had one. Who was I? What was I? Why was I?

All I knew was that I couldn't fight the war any more. I had seen too much during my life, everything no one should see or live through. I knew, though, that I was only one of countless thousands who suffered needlessly from childhood. Some suffered more, God help them, some less, and some of them had life snuffed from them before they knew what pain was.

I had always done things in a big way, whether good or bad. I had always excelled at whatever I did. This would be my final contribution to this society. **I would give up my freedom to make my point clear.** If I spent all the days of my life behind bars, it would be worth it if just one parent out there took note of my actions and changed from an abusive parent. Oh God, just one kid and it would be all worthwhile. One child's life is oh, so precious, and they have the God-given right to develop to the maximum of their potential and not be deprived of doing so. All that night I thought over and over my plan.

After some days, I returned to Sudbury. I left Val

Caron, saying I was going back to Toronto, but I had other plans. Downtown I went to Canadian Tire and bought two five-gallon gas cans, locks, chains, ropes, tape and a hunting knife for visual effects. All the things were bought for the mothernapping. The gas cans I filled with gasoline. I wanted enough gas so I wouldn't have to stop at a gas station on the way to Toronto after tying the witch down in the car. I would spend tonight partying by myself in a motel. I was still on a perpetual high from the 222s and booze. I checked into a Regent Street motel by nightfall.

I figured I'd find out from Vickey when Mother would be alone and then I'd pay her a not-so-friendly visit. The witch's lover worked shifts, so she had a lot of time alone. Since they lived on that lone street at Murray Mine, it would be easy to abduct her. I would pick up some girl for sex. It ended up I came back to the room alone, drunk and confused. I slipped into female lingerie and drank until I passed out. I was totally messed up, to say the least.

The next day, I saw Vickey but couldn't go through with the mothernapping. I stayed high and drunk and ended up back at Doug's. Again I lived. It had now been ten weeks since I last was free of booze or codeine. Ten weeks of this downhill death trip. Why was I still alive?

I came to the realization that I couldn't even hurt the person I hated the most. As much as I wanted to go through with my plan, I just couldn't do it. I picked up Vickey after school and drove her home. I saw the witch and could sense she was becoming agitated that I hadn't gone back to Toronto. All my senses told me she was getting tired of Vickey seeing me.

I still hadn't recovered from yesterday's overdose and spent the night at Doug's, just laying back and recuperating. Doug gave me trouble for being high around the kids. The scent of death was becoming nauseating.

One day I was phoning Vickey, and we spoke about the weekend ahead. Doug and his family would be away, which meant I'd have the house for the weekend. I wanted Vickey to spend the weekend with me, but Mother in all her love had said no because she had grounded Vickey. I would have to talk to her in person.

Vickey and I over the phone decided that as an excuse for me to drop by I would come over to pick up her Atari game and cartridges so that I would have something to occupy myself with while I was alone for the weekend. Well, if I was going to face her I'd have to drink a bit and pop some 222s so that I'd have courage enough to speak up for myself in her presence. I expected an argument, maybe, but hopefully nothing more.

Not knowing what would happen upon this encounter with her, I prepared for the worst. I thought that there might be a chance I'd get so pissed off at her that I might just decide to mothernap her. I drank some more and popped more 222s. If Mother would refuse me permission to see my own sister alone for a couple of days after all the years apart, she deserved to be used as an example to others. I didn't want it to come to that, but I had nothing to lose anyway. I went down to the basement and from my suede briefcase took out a notepad and pen and hastily wrote two of the most desperate letters ever, one to my estranged wife Diana and one for the law. They read as follows:

Dearest Diana,

How's the most beautiful lady in the world? I know I am not supposed to write you, but it doesn't matter now. Diana, I love you very much. I've got pictures of our wedding. You left the negatives. I found them when I was moving.

Diana, I've seen my sister this week. She is very pretty and smart too. Also, I saw my mother! She messed up my head for life with those thousands of beatings. Diana, they messed me up sexually, and I'm sorry. I sincerely love you. Don't be scared of me. If I wanted to hurt you I would have by now. Diana, I can't even physically hurt my mother because of my sister. I am in Sudbury to kidnap my mother and mentally torture her for a few hours then let her go. I think a few hours of mental torture is a small price to pay for the years I put in. I want to make a point to other parents who beat their kids, and since I've managed to destroy my life this past year, **I will give up my freedom to maybe save someone else's life.**

You don't know half the things that happened to me growing up. Diana, remember I love you forever as I promised. I made a sacred promise to God on June 9, 1984.

Loving you always,
Randy

To whom it may concern:

"The Devil's Blade Is Dull"

I am the judge and jury in this case, and the verdict had been handed down. It reads as follows: The accused and convicted child beater, Sonja, on all 1,000 approximate counts of child abuse, also twenty-seven years of mental and sexual anguish, is to serve approximately six hours of solitary confinement in the hands of the plaintiff. There is to be no "physical damage" done to the accused. But, on the other hand, the mental trauma that she can go through has no limits. After six hours, she will be freed and I will turn myself in. It is a small price to pay for what she did to me!

I want other parents to realize the effects of child abuse. They are permanent. Beat your kids today, get beaten by your kids tomorrow. She messed me up permanently. **I will give up my freedom to save someone else's life from the hands of a child beater.**

Please don't chase me. I want to live to help people but if pushed I will give up my life. I have two containers of gas in the car. One is behind the front seat, and the fumes are bad. All it takes is one flick of my Bic and you will have a barbecue to attend.

She will think I am going to kill her every minute with me. I used to think she would eventually kill me, and she is still slowly killing me. My mind is tormented.

I will phone later.

With these letters written, I finished off another beer and was now ready to leave. I put Diana's letter in an envelope, addressed it, and put a stamp on it. I hoped I wouldn't have to mail it though nor leave the second behind after I mothernapped the witch. I popped more 222s, bid goodbye to my sister-in-law and went out to my sports coupe. After letting the car warm up, I drove off on my way to Vickey's.

Night had fallen, and the roads were snow covered. I didn't know what to expect with this confrontation with the witch. I had never spoken up for myself to her except but once when she had called me a son of a bitch once too often during one of my beatings. I had made the comeback that she would then be the bitch, after which I was beaten to a pulp.

Thousands of memories ran through my mind as I drove. At Vickey's, I chatted with my sister for an hour or so and was given the Atari game and accessories. Expecting the worst, I took the Atari game to the car and returned with my briefcase. Inside was my knife, chains, ropes, locks, and the letter. I sure hoped Mother was going to be human for a change. I still didn't think I'd have the guts to do anything if she told me no. I asked Vickey to go upstairs, so that I'd have an excuse to talk to Mother. I walked to the kitchen where mother was ironing and casually started small talk, all the while trying to get up enough nerve to ask her to please let Vickey spend the weekend with me. I was always such a coward.

Finally I asked, and she said no. For the first time in my life, I spoke up for myself and Vickey and questioned her authority. I asked her if she would ever change. All the while she kept ironing. I was now getting mad and the past was becoming present.

"Mom, there's something I've been meaning to tell you."

"Yes?"

I screamed and swore at her.

"Get out of my house right now," she screamed. I told her I wasn't a little kid to be pushed around any more. We were arguing now. I yelled upstairs and told Vickey to pack her things for the weekend. This set Mother off, and she came at me with the iron.

As a kid I had always been scared that Mother would one day attack me with the iron. Well, it was happening. I yelled, "You are finally taking the iron to me!" Now it was open warfare. "I'm not a little kid any more," I yelled as I grabbed her arm and pulled the hot iron from her grasp. I held it in a threatening manner and then tossed it into the sink. It was now like old times, except that I was the Superman I had always wanted to be when it came to Mother. I grabbed her and punched her four times. Once for Doug, once for Dad, and twice for me. I asked her what it felt like.

Mother and I were now two of a kind. Two raging lunatics let loose upon each other. I was now so mad that I decided to go through with the mothernapping. I told her she was coming for a ride, but she in all her own insanity was putting up a good fight. I reached into my briefcase, which was close by, and took out the hunting knife. I threatened her menacingly.

All hell had broken loose. I had lost complete control. I had reached the bottom of the pit of despair. We called each other every name in the book while we fought.

Vickey was watching and screaming. Mother told her to get a neighbour. Soon some stranger was at the door. I was calming down but still screaming. I told her to tell Vickey about all the abuse she had inflicted upon her father and myself. "Tell her, tell her," I yelled.

She blurted out some statements and yelled at me that I was crazy. I replied, "Yes, I am, and it's all your fault."

Now I knew it would be hopeless to abduct Mother and ran out the door, passing Vickey, saying, "I love you, Sis." I couldn't believe what had happened.

I was in my machine. I threw my briefcase in the back, started the engine and was off, the scenes of the last several minutes playing reruns over and over. I was just as crazy as Mother. My poor sister had just witnessed the worst scene that she could have seen.

I drove, in total mental shock. What had I done? I had just brought myself down to Mother's level of existence. I was the lowest form of inhabitant on this earth. I realized it wasn't Mother I hated these past years. It was me I despised. Yes, me.

I hated Mother for what she had done to me physically and psychologically. But I had known she was a sick lady, and now I was a very sick young man. Mother's problems were probably as deeply rooted as my own. I knew what had led me to beat her up tonight, and she in the past had probably similar encounters, who knows? It was a contagious disease that we had. Mother probably had it bred into her somehow. The hatred was passed on to me, and I in turn had spread it among the people I loved the most. It was as plain as day.

I just kept driving about. I knew how much I loved everyone, Diana, J.D., other past girlfriends, yet I had somehow messed up their lives, all out of innocence and abstruse feelings about myself and the world around. I loved them more than anything, yet to them it would seem I was destroying them. God, how all this misery kept perpetuating!

Time was passing nightmarishly as I drove around in a state of psychological shock. I wasn't sure what to do. Part of me cared about myself, yet part didn't. Part of me felt like dying, but I never could take my own life, as I had no guts. Someone would have to take it for me. I figured now the cops would be out for me in full force. Again I'd be one of Sudbury's most wanted.

I decided to "go for it" and again drove up to Mother's. *I'll give the cops a good run for their money.* Since where Vickey and Mother lived was isolated, any car in the area would be noticed. I kept my eyes open for cop cars and the like. I knew once they saw my car the chase would be on. I would go out with a bang, so to speak. I didn't care. I deserved to be shot anyhow. What I had done was savagely brutal in most respects.

I was driving up the lone road to Mother's expecting to see cops around, but none appeared. As I parked up the street, I noticed no cops. An hour or more had passed, and either Mother had not called the police or they had come and gone.

I drove off again and found myself driving around in endless misery. What should I do? I had nowhere to go! Next to no money! I couldn't go to Toronto, because I was wanted. I couldn't stay in Sudbury, because I would be wanted. Hey, what do you know, after all these years of searching I was finally wanted by everybody! I could go to the States but would have to support myself by crime and prostitution. My options were limited, and I wanted this to end, but I didn't have guts enough to kill myself. I now had only two choices: Keep perpetuating this misery, which at the rate I was going wouldn't last much longer, or get help!

I was as deep into my misery as ever I could be. I really didn't have much choice. I chose the latter and drove up to the hospital. As I drove I wept. If I kept going without help, I would just keep destroying everything and everyone I encountered. I just had to admit my sexual hang-ups or I'd never survive. If I was to live, I couldn't live as a human straddling the psychological fence between heterosexuality and homosexuality. I had to learn to cope with my problems.

I pulled into the hospital parking lot. I sat, cried and thought. I had to go in, it was then or never. I either had to go to my grave or battle my way back out of the gutter of life, for God only knows how many times. I'm sure that if I had not known that anything was possible if one was willing to put in the effort, I surely wouldn't have driven to the hospital. I knew the difference between victory and defeat.

I stepped out of my car and into the winter night. I locked up the car and walked hesitantly to the front of the hospital and stopped. Gathering some inner strength, I walked in and up to the admitting desk. I told the nurse I needed help. I was on the verge of tears as I tried to speak. "I need help to get off drugs and booze."

She asked me to take a seat, and I did. While sitting there I felt like leaving but just knew that this was my chance. When my name was called, I went and sat and answered the questions on some form. I then had to wait to see the doctor on call.

It was about 1 a.m. on or about January 23. The nurse said I could see the doctor. I sat on a hospital bed in the emergency room. I was not very high or drunk by now.

The doctor came in and asked me what was wrong. I told him I was addicted to drugs and booze and that I had just beat up my mother and needed help. He could plainly see that I was in a frenzied state of psychological turmoil. After more questions he said I could spend the night on the psychiatric ward. After a couple more questions, he asked me the ultimate question, "Have you ever had any homosexual encounters?" and stated that with the AIDS scare he had to ask. I hesitated for what seemed like hours. Inside of me I was going crazy. *Now or never, now or never*, I thought to myself.

Then all the walls came tumbling down. "Yes, yes," I blurted out, "that's why I'm here. I don't know who I am any more. I don't know if I'm straight or gay!" I was now crying hysterically. This was the first time that I had ever admitted my true problem to a professional. I knew now I could get help, and it was such a relief.

I was admitted, and the next day I was taken to the Sudbury Algoma Hospital, which dealt with psychiatric problems. I would be hospitalized for almost one month. In the interim I was charged with assault, for which seven months later I would receive a two-year sentence and at the same time an additional total of nine months for fraud and breach of probation.

While hospitalized, I learned about myself, but it wasn't easy and I got extremely upset twice because I couldn't yet face some facts. I read the Bible daily and was promising myself to attend church upon my release. I spent the last ten days hospitalized at Penetang, a maximum security hospital for the criminally insane. The reality of Penetang shocked the hell out of me as I was locked in a cell almost twenty-four hours a day. Someone, I don't know who, was trying to have me locked away indefinitely.

The doctors realized I was not insane, and I was going to be released to the street on February 19, 1986. I was told I was only one of maybe two people who ever had been released from the institution directly to the street. I had also had the shortest stay of anyone in the history of this prison hospital. During those ten days in the solitary confinement of the cell, I read the Bible from cover to cover as I had done in a similar cell ten years earlier. I also prayed hours on end for the strength to do God's will. I promised to go to church every Sunday, to help the less fortunate, and to regain my health. I came to the realization that there was more to health than looking good. I now had to learn about spiritual and mental health in order to keep a balanced mind, body and soul. I promised God I would write the best book I possibly could to witness to others.

The morning of February 19, 1986, my last morning in the maximum security hospital, was the most revealing in my life. I was worried about being released. I had less than $10, and the hospital was buying me a bus ticket to go from Penetang to Sudbury.

I had nowhere to stay as Doug and family wanted nothing to do with me. Arrangements had been made for me to stay at the Salvation Army on Larch Street. Quite ironic was the fact that my last address in Sudbury in 1980 prior to going to TO with J.D. was the Salvation Army. Now my first address upon coming back would be the same. Talk about a complete sixty-six-month circle. From penniless, to having everything in man's world, to penniless.

I was to be driven to the bus stop sometime after lunch. During the morning our range was let out to watch a movie in the TV room. About a dozen of us, some of whom were murderers, sat silently in the room, as we were never allowed to talk to one another or we'd get charged. A few guards sat in the back of the room. I had heard that the movie was the story of St. Francis of Assisi. Somewhere during life I had heard of such a person.

The movie, *The Richest Man in Assisi: Brother Sun, Sister Moon*, played on, and I became entranced by the story of this soon-to-be saint. I was oblivious to everyone around. It was as if the movie was a message directed to me. As the story unfolded, I saw so many of my own beliefs and search for the truth. I saw a man who had everything but gave it all up for the glory of God, to help the less fortunate and suffering people.

I didn't know what was happening to me. I was silent and in tears, but I was happy, oh, so happy. A great feeling of cleansing love washed me, and I felt new. I was full of great love as never before.

The movie played, and I kept on being transformed. I knew nothing of being born again. All I knew was that I was a new person. I was sitting there in the pits of hell, the worst possible place in the world, amongst some of the worst suffering people on earth, and I was happy. I was ready to go out in the world and try to give it my best. Then and there I dedicated my life to the glory of God.

Lunch was called before the movie ended. In my cell for my last meal I was overjoyed. St. Francis of Assisi had saved another soul in God's name. He had died centuries ago but had been alive today and reached out to grasp my reaching hand.

A couple hours later I left that hellish prison hospital that held the worst of the worst with a new attitude, a new hope and new loves. I was a new man. Love of God, love of myself, love of everyone, and the best love a human can have, love of his mother. Without them we would not be here.

Yes, Mom, I love you very much.

Your son,
Randy.

# Dear Reader,

March 2008

Grace and peace to you.

Do you realize that you have just read a biography that no one person should have had to write? However, countless thousands endure parallel lives.

I myself just finished reading and editing the publisher's proof. I had not so much as read one page of my hand-printed six hundred page manuscript since I finished it in January of 1988 while in the penitentiary.

As you have just read, I forgave my mother.

*Beloved, forgiveness is the most powerful force you will ever come in contact with.*

I left that hospital and went back out into the world to face life and the criminal charges. I committed the assault on or about January 23, 1986 and was sentenced August 22, 1986 to two years for assault and nine months for fraud. My full sentence expired May 21, 1989. Between the hospital and sentencing I attended church and studied the Bible. I was beginning to have a new heart and spirit. I promised to write the best book I could in spite of its cruel and harsh realities.

By the time I was sentenced for the assault not one word had been said by me against my mother in the court of law.

*Beloved remember, forgiveness really is forgiveness and please do not ever forget this very fact.*

You are well aware of by now that confinement would be hard on me, and it was.

However, by God's grace, mercy and generosity I was able to endure. I studied God's Word and memorized Scripture and some New Testament letters. I wrote *The Devil's Blade is Dull* and promised to have it published in order to help the worst of the worst. It had to be real and honest and I do sincerely apologize for some of the stories told. I designed artwork, one piece of which you have seen, titled John 3:16-17. I spent hours writing messages. Two of my letters conclude this book.

Since 1990 I have helped people live healthy lives. Since 1991 I have been married to my wife, Nancy, the most forgiving person I have ever met. Nancy is a footcare specialist called a chiropodist. From 1996 to 2005 together we owned and operated Life-Styles Fitness Center. Nancy still worked at the hospital saving soles.

We now live in Athens, Ontario, Canada in a church we bought and converted to our home and ministry offices.

Yes, I, Randy, the least of you all, live in a church. Also may I state that I am by no means a saint in spite of all the Scripture I know. I am just a sinner saved by grace and trying my best to improve.

*Beloved, there is absolutely no doubt that each and every one of you can accomplish much more than you think.*

When I first became a Christian, I thought that I would become perfect before I did this project.

*Beloved, like Paul I have a thorn in the flesh to keep me from forgetting what lies behind in order to reach forward to what lies ahead.*

I will press on. Please pray that I, Randy, will not falter along my path too much and too often.

My prayer for you is that you will always live a forgiving life and become more like Him who wants you in His image as best you can, in spite of personal limitations.

*Beloved, I want to do nothing against the Truth, but only for the Truth.*

I will rejoice when I myself am weak and you are strong.

This I also pray for, that you be made complete.

2 Corinthians 13:8-9, paraphrase

Finally, remember,

*God has chosen the foolish things of the world to shame the wise, and God has chosen the weak things of the world to shame the things which are strong, and the base things of the world and the despised, God has chosen, the things that are not, that he might nullify the things that are.*

1 Corinthians 1:27-28 NASB

I say to you all also, press on toward that goal.

From the house in a church in Athens,
*Randy*

# Prison Letter #1

Saturday, March 26, 1988—1:30 a.m. to 4 a.m.

I, Randy, a prisoner of Christ Jesus by the will of God, also a prisoner of man, to you my beloved brethren who have been saved through faith and who by an earnest endeavour are striving to become more like Him in your daily conduct, also to you who have not yet made a decision for Christ: to you all, who as myself have transgressed the laws of man, more so the laws of God, grace to you and peace from God our Father and the Lord Jesus Christ.

At this time, in time, with pen in hand, I write to you, my fellow brethren in time, from the bowels of this fortress of human tragedy, where were it not for the saving knowledge of our Lord Jesus Christ I, as well as many of you, would be suffering much from our enforced association with some of our uncongenial companions. However, because of the nourishing of our souls with His sacred body and precious blood, we can love them as lost sheep and pray that some day they may be brought home to live as God our Father would have it be.

Not only do we pray for our brethren in time but also for all the lost souls who dwell upon the earth.

Verily I say to you emphatically: More people are imprisoned by their hearts and souls than by all these fortresses of human tragedy combined.

At present, we are in this womb of hell, where the prison sentence for those who are still dark is the gestation period, whereupon highly superior social outcasts are born who will remain imprisoned within the confines of their mind and body until, and only until, they find peace and tranquility in the saving knowledge of our Lord Jesus Christ.

He Himself gives us peace for today and purpose for tomorrow that transcends all understanding.

As it is willed by God our Father my deep concern is for you all, the saved and the unsaved. Made known to mine heart by both the Holy Spirit and mine own life's lessons learned by the grace of God is that all the bars of your own fleshy imprisonment have yet to melt away, as a lit candle. The flame does flicker, but not with the intensity with which to accomplish His predetermined plan for your life.

You, my beloved brethren, must take what light of faith is in you and search more diligently for Him as never before, as it was written of old: *"Then you will call upon Me and come and pray to Me, and I will listen to you. You will seek Me and find Me when you search for Me with all your heart"* (Jeremiah 29:12-13). Brethren, although He may seem far away He is only half a mind away. I beseech you to fill all your mind with Him at all times, and supreme happiness shall be yours.

*"Trust in the LORD with all your heart And do not lean on your own understanding. In all your ways acknowledge Him, And He will make your paths straight"*

(Proverbs 3:5-6, NIV). Now this by no means is an easy task, as we are all too human by nature. However, we are obligated as followers of Christ to strive at all times towards this goal.

All this is brought about by faith, and *"faith is the assurance of things hoped for, the conviction of things not seen"* (Hebrews 11:1).

Facetiously, I ask you my fellow brethren in time, do you know about convictions?

As you continue to grow in faith you will come to a certain realization, that the knowledge of Truth through Christ is wonderful and is immeasurably capable of acting as a personal guide, so much so that it justifies the aspiration toward that very knowledge of Truth.

All this, my beloved, takes the strictest amount of discipline in the Lord. Now this word *discipline* is the very stuff which disciples are made of, so I beg you on behalf of Christ to learn discipline as you might never have before.

You must learn His Word, love His Word, and, most important of all, live His Word; and if you thought tasks before were difficult while living your life while indulging in the desires of the flesh and mind, my friends, be sure to now put on the full armour of God in preparation for what lies ahead (Ephesians 6:10-18).

Now these difficulties ahead are not as behind and are not fraught with the sorrow that once was. Again, I say *once was* and, for many of you, still is. I ask you now to recall the past, as I tell you of a revelation that came to me one evening while alone in solitary confinement.

Not a pen, pencil or piece of paper was at my hand,

but by the grace of God I recalled it and wrote out what was revealed the following morning.

I am quite certain that many of you can relate to this poetic message.

Imagine being imprisoned as a child through to adulthood
Never understanding and no one understood
Your mind, it was a prison with countless little cells
Most held a tiny prisoner to whom the thought of freedom dwells
Now life inside any prison can be a calamitous affair
All this human tragedy, most in total disrepair
As at Jericho the walls came tumbling down
As time would have it be
You walked anew in this world of ours, thinking,
Finally I am free
Now the bars are real
I feel their coldness in my hands
Before in my imprisonment at least I walked the lands
Sitting down alone quite tearfully
My face buried deep in my palms
Humming hymns of holiness, reciting verse from Psalms
Wiping away tears of happiness
Each tear a memory of the past
I look up, smile, and thank the Lord
I know I am free at last
Now the philosophy of this poet as you can plainly see
"There are no greater prisons than trapped in conflict with your personality"

Yes, my brethren, the prisons of the flesh are infinitely more confining than these fortresses of human tragedy. However, by coming to know our Lord Jesus Christ as your personal saviour, you too can have newfound personal freedom in spite of your present circumstances. *"I tell the truth in Christ, I am not lying, my conscience also bearing me witness in the Holy Spirit"* (Romans 9:1, NKJV).

Yes! There will still be sadness and moments of weakness, but it is then you will pray; for when you are praying the joy will return and you will know why you are living this life in this world. It is in the Name of Jesus for the benefit of humanity in order that the grand scheme of heaven might be fulfilled and all things apart will be together.

In the name of Jesus at the pounding of mine own grievous heart I entreat you who are not yet partakers of the promise through Christ to let another bar or more melt away from your fleshly confinement and step closer to Him who died for our sins, *"once for all"* (Hebrews 10:10, KJV), *"the just for the unjust, that he might bring us to God"* (1 Peter 3:18, KJV).

I know some of you are thinking to yourselves, *This guy is delusional and believes in fantasy.* Verily I say to you, this is a fantasy that will affect your design for reality, a fantasy that changes minds, hearts and souls; for you the bars are not to melt today as you are weak of mind.

However, to you who today take a step in faith towards the foot of the cross, I say, as once I read and put to mind: The greatness of a man's power is the measure of his surrender. It is not a question of who you are or of what you are but whether *God* controls you. Come to the foot of the cross, which is in the hand of God, and let Him have control of your life.

You have tried everything, and all has failed; now respond to the compassion *of* the Lord, and He will turn your sorrow into joy (John 16:20). Break free from the entanglement of the web of the past, and step by faith fearlessly into the web of the future and become enmeshed lovingly in the silken web of Christ's love.

Your flame will flicker brighter, and another bar will go the way of the wax. As it was written: *"'AT THE ACCEPTABLE TIME I LISTENED TO YOU, AND ON THE DAY OF SALVATION I HELPED YOU.' Behold, now is "THE ACCEPTABLE TIME," behold, now is 'THE DAY OF SALVATION'"* (2 Corinthians 6:2).

As Jesus was born in Bethlehem, let Him be born again by faith in your heart. *"If you confess with your mouth Jesus as Lord, and believe in your heart that God raised Him from the dead, you will be saved"* (Romans 10:9).

*"May the grace of the Lord Jesus Christ, and the love of God, and the fellowship of the Holy Spirit be with you all"* (2 Corinthians 13:14, NIV).

In His love,
Randy

# Prison Letter #2

*Easter Weekend 1988*

Christ has died
Christ has risen
Christ will come again

I, Randy, a prisoner of Christ Jesus by the will of God, also a prisoner of man, to you the saved and the unsaved: Grace to you and peace from God our Father and the Lord Jesus Christ. May Their richest blessings be yours.

On this day, as when I last wrote to you, my beloved, I am writing to you from the bowels of this fortress of human tragedy, this womb of hell—for those who are not light in the Lord. Not as before, when I wrote concerning my brethren in time; this day I write to all.

At present, I am not able to see the world as you see the earth on which we live. On this day, as on the seemingly many countless past, I am alone with the Spirit of Christ in the windowless tomb of a cell; I see no forests, no sky, no sunrises; nor do I see the setting of the glorious sun beyond what seems beyond.

I ask you not to lose heart at my tribulations. I pray they are for your glory.

Moreover, as for me, I am not alone as many of you are alone. This is what urges me to write to you.

For this you can give praise to Him who is in me.

Today I look to you all, who are in the so-called free world, with spiritual eyes, eyes that shed streams of water because they see a not-so-free world. Gazing among you who are reflections in the mirror of my mind; I see a sea of faces, many of which are not powdered with happiness. I ask myself, Is this because they cannot face the sea they see within?

I peer spiritually through the beaten hull of your fleshly vessel, you who are without happy countenance. Your body is a breakwater to the sea within. You have been rising and falling on the waves of life, as a ship without sail.

The pounding of your sorrow-fraught heart is as the sea to the surf.

All hope seems lost as you have been washed ashore on the desert island of life in the midst of uncharted waters.

You are a derelict; a human ship washed ashore and abandoned; a human wreck whose sails might never carry you again regally across Earth's seas.

Viewing you all now is like looking at a mirrored reflection of myself as I am not now but once was, alone without love and having no direction to life, you who as myself were given everything to live life with but nothing to live life for.

"I can sense in you a want of strength, a lack of will and a desperate shortage of hope." Yes, what a tragic reality it is that so many are so few in spirit in the midst of many. You lie ashore on the sands of time; you are parched and have great thirst; the water you desire will only satisfy your needs for the moment.

In no time you will again feel as if the sun on high is drying you out, a blade of grass withering away.

I, Randy, write to you, hoping to help you put a breeze into your sails, in order that you may again set out to conquer Earth's oceans.

> *For my part, I am eager to preach the gospel to you...For I am not ashamed of the gospel, for it is the power of God for salvation to everyone who believes...For in it the righteousness of God is revealed from faith to faith; as it is written, 'BUT THE RIGHTEOUS man SHALL LIVE BY FAITH'''* (Romans 1:15-17).

This is our God, who does rule the swelling of the sea; when its waves rise, He does still them. The Son on high that I will tell you about will give you living water, and it will become in you a well of water springing up to eternal life (John 4:14).

Jesus Christ our Lord is the Son on High, and He is our advocate with God our Father (1 John 2:1). From Him, and none other, will you receive this living water and spiritual breeze that will keep you sailing the sea of life. You may not be able to adjust the wind, but you can adjust your sails.

There will be breezeless days when you ponder, Will I ever get anywhere in life?

There will also be days when a zephyr will instantaneously arise into hurricane hell. I tell you, adjust your sails accordingly and you shall overcome all before you.

The pages of His Holy Book are the sails of your earthen vessel. Just as you try to read the prevailing winds of change, read the pages—your sails—as if your life depended on it.

Your life does depend on it; so climb to the crow's nest of life and be certain you are headed true to course. I do not speak to you of life here in the temporal, for here we are for but an instant. I am infinitely more concerned with the purity of your soul.

As surely as God lives, *"I tell the truth in Christ, I am not lying, my conscience also bearing me witness in the Holy Spirit"* (Romans 9:1, NKJV).

I, *"the least of all the saints"* (Ephesians 3:8, NKJV)— *"O wretched man that I am!"* (Romans 7:21, NKJV)—am an ambassador for Christ as though God were entreating you through me. I beg you on behalf of Christ, be reconciled to God (2 Corinthians 5:20).

I may go the way of Hell, and so be it. But for you all, I do not wish for you to follow in my steps. From the depths of my sinful heart I pray unto our Lord for you, that you will follow in His steps in order that you will see the glories of heaven.

I can bring you to Christ in prayer, but only you can bring yourself to Him by faith.

As it is written, *"For by grace you have been saved through faith; and that not of yourselves, it is the gift of God"* (Ephesians 2:8).

Do not live in your sinful ways any longer, for as written, *"The wages of sin is death, but the free gift of God is eternal life in Christ Jesus our Lord"* (Romans 6:23).

This is not only a gift but a free gift—that is yours by faith. I say to you, what gift ever given to you in the past has freed you from the locked holds of your earthen vessel? Assuredly and without reservation I say emphatically, "None, and none ever will!"

So why not accept this gift, which will in you become a treasure in your earthen vessel?

You are still lying awash on the desert island of life.

You have been there so long now that your thirst is seemingly unquenchable.

You have even tasted the salty water of life again; however, that has only worsened your predicament. You have heard the word *treasure,* and it conjures up visions of treasure, maybe buried beneath the very sands of time you are stranded on.

I tell you, that both the water and the treasure you seek are neither of the earth nor below the earth. Do not claw fruitlessly at the sands of time any longer, but raise your hands unto the Lord.

Right now, reach up to the heavens, to touch death, so that you be born again a new vessel in Christ. "*If you confess with your mouth Jesus as Lord, and believe in your heart that God raised Him from the dead, you will be saved*" (Romans 10:9).

This is the christening of your new vessel that is above all, because our God and Father is above all and through all and in all.

Open the holds of your soul unto Him, and He will inundate it to overflowing with the Holy Spirit.

Your thirst will be quenched, and you will be ready to start anew in your new vessel.

Now be thankful and grateful that Jesus Christ your

Lord was given up to death on a cross in order that you could have living water. Humble yourselves before Him and praise His mercy and generosity toward you, a poor sinner. Show your gratitude to Him in the sacrament of His love by obedience to your duties, by kindness to your neighbour and by an earnest endeavour to become more like Him in your daily conduct.

*"Be anxious for nothing, but in everything by prayer and supplication with thanksgiving let your requests be made known to God"* (Philippians 4:6).

A prayer attributed to Saint Francis of Assisi

Lord
Make me an instrument of your peace
Where there is hatred let me sow love
Where there is injury let me sow pardon
Where there is doubt let me sow faith
Where there is despair let me give hope
Where there is darkness let me give light
Where there is sadness let me give joy

Oh Divine Master, Grant I that may not try to be comforted but to comfort
Not try to be understood but to understand
Not to be loved but to love

Because
It is in giving that we receive
It is in forgiving that we are forgiven
And it is in dying that we are
Born to eternal life

Now set sail with hope and faith in your spiritual wind; you are no longer alone as you leave the desert island of life.

Christ is with you.

Your companions of the past, the timeless days, one of which was Friday, will stay behind. Bid Friday so long, for, God-willing, Sunday is on the horizon. You can see it rising; the glorious Son does rise.

As surely as God and Christ reign in heaven, I say unto you: Darken the doorways of a church.

"Now—when you're passing through the waters of deep sorrow and despair, and you get no help from others, remember, Christ is there."

"Looking to Jesus, my spirit is blessed. The world is in turmoil; in Him I have rest. The sea of my life around me may roar. When I look to Jesus I hear it no more."

*"Peace be to the brethren, and love with faith, from God the Father and the Lord Jesus Christ. Grace be with all those who love our Lord Jesus Christ with incorruptible love"* (Ephesians 6:23-24).

In His love,
Prisoner #773747A

Dearly beloved, I, Randy, cannot end this book without leaving you with Scripture to read.

Bless you all.

*The Epistle of Philippians*
Chapter 2:1-18 (NKJV)

## Be Like Christ

*1 Therefore if there is any consolation in Christ, if any comfort of love, if any fellowship of the Spirit, if any affection and mercy, 2 fulfill my joy by being like-minded, having the same love, being of one accord, of one mind. 3 Let nothing be done through selfish ambition or conceit, but in lowliness of mind let each esteem others better than himself. 4 Let each of you look out not only for his own interests, but also for the interests of others.*
*5 Let this mind be in you which was also in Christ Jesus, 6 who, being in the form of God, did not consider it robbery to be equal with God, 7 but made Himself of no reputation, taking the form of a bondservant, and coming in the likeness of men. 8 And being found in appearance as a man, He humbled Himself and became obedient to the point of death, even the death of the cross. 9 Therefore God also has highly exalted Him and given Him the name which is above every name, 10 that at the name of Jesus every knee should bow, of those in heaven, and of those on earth, and of those under the earth, 11 and that every tongue should confess that Jesus Christ is Lord, to the glory of God the Father.*

*12 Therefore, my beloved, as you have always obeyed, not as in my presence only, but now much more in my absence, work out your own salvation with fear and trembling; 13 for it is God who works in you both to will and to do for His good pleasure.*

*14 Do all things without complaining and disputing, 15 that you may become blameless and harmless, children of God without fault in the midst of a crooked and perverse generation, among whom you shine as lights in the world, 16 holding fast the word of life, so that I may rejoice in the day of Christ that I have not run in vain or labored in vain.*

*17 Yes, and if I am being poured out as a drink offering on the sacrifice and service of your faith, I am glad and rejoice with you all. 18 For the same reason you also be glad and rejoice with me.*

# Donations

*Athens Gospel Mission*
non-profit, non-registered
Christian Mission
Info: www.free2live.org


**Total amount enclosed:**          $_____


Name: _____

Address: _____

City: _____ State/Prov: _____

Zip/Postal Code: _____ Telephone: _____


Send to:

Athens Gospel Mission
P.O. Box 321
Athens, ON
KoE 1B0


*Ministry through the spoken word*